English File

Upper-intermediate
Teacher's Guide

WITH TEACHER'S RESOURCE CENTRE

Christina Latham-Koenig
Clive Oxenden
Kate Chomacki

with Anna Lowy
Krysia Mabbott

fourth edition

Great Clarendon Street, Oxford, OX2 6DP, United Kingdom

Oxford University Press is a department of the University of Oxford.
It furthers the University's objective of excellence in research, scholarship,
and education by publishing worldwide. Oxford is a registered trade
mark of Oxford University Press in the UK and in certain other countries

© Oxford University Press 2020

The moral rights of the author have been asserted

First published in 2020

2024 2023 2022 2021 2020
10 9 8 7 6 5 4 3 2 1

All rights reserved. No part of this publication may be reproduced, stored
in a retrieval system, or transmitted, in any form or by any means, without
the prior permission in writing of Oxford University Press, or as expressly
permitted by law, by licence or under terms agreed with the appropriate
reprographics rights organization. Enquiries concerning reproduction outside
the scope of the above should be sent to the ELT Rights Department, Oxford
University Press, at the address above

You must not circulate this work in any other form and you must impose
this same condition on any acquirer

Links to third party websites are provided by Oxford in good faith and for
information only. Oxford disclaims any responsibility for the materials
contained in any third party website referenced in this work

Photocopying

The Publisher grants permission for the photocopying of those pages marked
'photocopiable' according to the following conditions. Individual purchasers
may make copies for their own use or for use by classes that they teach.
School purchasers may make copies for use by staff and students, but this
permission does not extend to additional schools or branches

Under no circumstances may any part of this book be photocopied for resale

ISBN: 978 0 19 403981 9

Printed in China

This book is printed on paper from certified and well-managed sources

ACKNOWLEDGEMENTS

Back cover photograph: Oxford University Press building/David Fisher

The authors would like to thank all the teachers and students round the world whose feedback has helped us to shape *English File*.

The authors would also like to thank: all those at Oxford University Press (both in Oxford and around the world) and the design team who have contributed their skills and ideas to producing this course.

Finally very special thanks from Clive to Maria Angeles, Lucia, and Eric, and from Christina to Cristina, for all their support and encouragement. Christina would also like to thank her children Joaquin, Marco, and Krysia for their constant inspiration.

We would also like to thank the following for permission to reproduce the following photographs: Alamy pp.163 (Kiwi bird/Alamy Stock Photo), 172 (couple smiling/PhotoAlto), 176 (police officer/Cultura Creative), 181 (Mont Blanc, Damiano Lavati), 195 (stethoscope/Michael Willis), 200 (black bear/FLPA), (rioting on the streets, Belfast/Michel Phillipot), (great white shark/Fuse), 206 (frightened couple/Aleksandr Davydov), 207 (fruit and vegetables/Image Source Plus), 212 (Lake Como/Ingold Pompe 93), Astronaut Buzz Aldrin/NASA Archive), 221 (woman eating chocolates/Blend Images); 227 (stack of newspapers/Johnny Greig, Frasers Autographs p.193 (Leo Tolstoy, Shulz, Charles Dickens, Elijah Wood, Damien Hirst); Getty pp.161 (mother and daughter/Image Source), 163 (man in suit/Goodluz); Shutterstock 163 (man in suit/Goodluz), 172 (smiling woman/dibrova, man), 180 (children in science lab), 181 (Moscow church), 193 (Wireimage/Britney Spears, Lindsay Lohan, PCA/Paris Hilton), (Barack Obama, Startraks Photo/Paris Hilton, Sipa Press/Usain Bolt, Peter Brooker/Paul McCartney, Ken McKay/Sean Connery), 200 (quicksand/Daniel Lee Nutley), (fire/Julia Senkevich), 206 (upset family/Iakov Filimonov), (sad boy/wavebreakmedia), (man and woman with laptop), 207 (muzzled dog/lightpoet), 208 (microphone/beau lark), Shutterstock pp.207 (man driving car/Minerva Studio, Swedish town), 218 (blood pressure monitor/romiri, pills/Mega Pixel, plaster/Copter Pixel), 222 (tropical storm/Marc Serota); Oxford University Press pp.163 (penguin/Photodisc) 200 (Brazillian snake/Photodisc).

Illustrations by: Meiklejohn/Gavin Reece p.179; Roger Penwill pp.162, 166–168, 182, 196–198; John Haslam pp.164, 171, 174–175; Bess Harding p.170.

Contents

p.4	**Syllabus checklist**

p.8	**Course overview**

- **Introduction**
- **What do Upper-intermediate students need?**
- **For students**

Student's Book
Online Practice
Workbook

- **For teachers**

Teacher's Guide
Teacher's Resource Centre
Classroom Presentation Tool
Class audio
Video

p.12	**Lesson plans**

p.12	File 1 A–B	Colloquial English Episode 1
p.28	File 2 A–B	1&2 Revise and Check
p.43	File 3 A–B	Colloquial English Episode 2
p.60	File 4 A–B	3&4 Revise and Check
p.72	File 5 A–B	Colloquial English Episode 3
p.88	File 6 A–B	5&6 Revise and Check
p.101	File 7 A–B	Colloquial English Episode 4
p.117	File 8 A–B	7&8 Revise and Check
p.129	File 9 A–B	Colloquial English Episode 5
p.145	File 10 A–B	9&10 Revise and Check

p.158	**Photocopiable activities**

p.158	Introduction
p.159	Grammar activity answers
p.161	Grammar activity masters
p.183	Communicative activity instructions
p.190	Communicative activity masters
p.214	Vocabulary activity instructions
p.218	Vocabulary activity masters

Syllabus checklist

		GRAMMAR	VOCABULARY	PRONUNCIATION
1				
6	**A** Questions and answers	question formation	working out meaning from context	intonation: showing interest
10	**B** It's a mystery	auxiliary verbs, *the…, the…* + comparatives	compound adjectives, modifiers	intonation and sentence rhythm
14	**Colloquial English** Episode 1	talking about…getting a job		
2				
16	**A** Doctor, doctor!	present perfect simple and continuous	illnesses and injuries	/ʃ/, /dʒ/, /tʃ/, and /k/
20	**B** Act your age	using adjectives as nouns, adjective order	clothes and fashion	vowel sounds
24	**Revise and Check 1&2**			
3				
26	**A** Fasten your seat belts	narrative tenses, past perfect continuous, *so / such…that*	air travel	irregular past forms, sentence rhythm
30	**B** A really good ending?	the position of adverbs and adverbial phrases	adverbs and adverbial phrases	word stress and intonation
34	**Colloquial English** Episode 2	talking about…books		
4				
36	**A** Stormy weather	future perfect and future continuous	the environment, weather	vowel sounds
40	**B** A risky business	zero and first conditionals, future time clauses	expressions with *take*	linked phrases
44	**Revise and Check 3&4**			
5				
46	**A** I'm a survivor	unreal conditionals	feelings	word stress in three- or four-syllable adjectives
50	**B** Wish you were here	*wish* for present / future, *wish* for past regrets	expressing feelings with verbs or *-ed / -ing* adjectives	sentence rhythm and intonation
54	**Colloquial English** Episode 3	talking about…waste		

SPEAKING	LISTENING	READING
politely refusing to answer a question, reacting to what someone says, tough questions	understanding the stages of a short interview	understanding questions, working out meaning from context
reacting to a story about something strange, *You're psychic, aren't you?*	following instructions	understanding facts vs theories
Doctor, doctor, health	understanding an anecdote	reading and summarizing
The joy of the age-gap friendship, managing discussions, politely disagreeing	understanding a discussion – opinions, explanations, examples	scanning several texts
Flight stories, telling an anecdote	understanding formal language in announcements	using a diagram to understand a text
reading habits		reading for pleasure
the environment, climate change	understanding examples	scanning for examples
risk-taking	focusing on the main points	summarizing an argument
emergency situations	understanding mood and feelings	recognizing positive and negative experiences
ways of talking about how we feel, wishes	understanding a poem	checking hypotheses

		GRAMMAR	VOCABULARY	PRONUNCIATION
6				
56	**A** Night night	*used to, be used to, get used to*	sleep	/s/ and /z/
60	**B** Music to my ears	gerunds and infinitives	music	words from other languages
64	**Revise and Check 5&6**			
7				
66	**A** Let's not argue	past modals: *must have,* etc., *would rather*	verbs often confused	weak form of *have*
70	**B** It's all an act	verbs of the senses	the body	silent consonants
74	**Colloquial English Episode 6&7** talking about...performances			
8				
76	**A** Cutting crime	the passive (all forms); *have something done; it is said that…, he is thought to…,* etc.	crime and punishment	the letter *u*
80	**B** Fake news	reporting verbs	the media	word stress
84	**Revise and Check 7&8**			
9				
86	**A** Good business?	clauses of contrast and purpose	advertising, business	changing stress on nouns and verbs
90	**B** Super cities	uncountable and plural nouns	word building: prefixes and suffixes	word stress with prefixes and suffixes
94	**Colloquial English Episode 8&9** talking about...advertising			
10				
96	**A** Science fact, science-fiction	quantifiers: *all, every, both,* etc.	science	stress in word families
100	**B** Free speech	articles	collocation: word pairs	pausing and sentence stress
104	**Revise and Check 9&10**			

106	**Communication**	115	**Writing**	122	**Listening**	132	**Grammar Bank**

SPEAKING	LISTENING	READING
sleep	understanding reasons	using contextual clues
music	understanding a talk	scanning across several texts
role-playing an argument	understanding advice	identifying solutions to problems
Guess what it is, describing photos	understanding instructions	understanding the principle of an experiment
Beat the burglar, crime	using your knowledge of the world to help you understand formal advice	understanding truth and lies
Strange but true, the media	identifying the main events in news stories	using heading to understand the main point of a paragraph
Misleading ads, advertising, business	understanding explanations	dealing with an authentic text
cities	understanding place names	identifying advantages and disadvantages
science, talking about future possibilities	understanding specific explanations	understanding the language of speculation
public speaking	identifying dos and don'ts	understanding context

152 **Vocabulary Bank**   164 **Appendix**   165 **Irregular verbs**   166 **Sound Bank**

Course overview

Introduction

Our aim with *English File fourth edition* has been to make every lesson better and to make the package more student- and teacher-friendly. As well as the main A and B Student's Book lessons, there is a range of material that you can use according to your students' needs, and the time and resources you have available. Don't forget:

- videos that can be used in class in every File: Colloquial English, Video Listening, and Can you understand these people?
- Quick Tests and File tests for every File, as well as Progress Tests, an End-of-course Test, and an Entry Test, which you can use at the beginning of the course
- photocopiable Grammar and Communicative activities for every A and B lesson, and a Vocabulary activity for every Vocabulary Bank

Online Practice and the **Workbook** provide review, support, and practice for students outside the class.

The **Teacher's Guide** suggests different ways of exploiting the Student's Book depending on the level of your class. We very much hope you enjoy using *English File fourth edition*.

What do Upper-intermediate students need?

Upper-intermediate students rightly feel that they are now quite high-level learners of English, and are ready to 'push on' to become very proficient users of the language. To achieve this they need motivating materials and challenging tasks. They need clear objectives to focus on taking their skills to a higher level, as well as dealing with more complex language input. Finally, they need classes to be as fun and dynamic as they were at lower levels: there is no reason why higher-level lessons should become dry and over-serious. Students still want to enjoy their English classes – role-plays, language games, challenges, and quizzes are still as valuable pedagogically as ever, and can often be exploited more effectively at this level.

Grammar

- Improve their control of main structures
- Learn more complex grammar structures
- Opportunities to use and test their language instinct

English File fourth edition Upper-intermediate puts an emphasis on consolidating and putting into practice known grammar as well as learning new structures. It provides contexts for new language that will engage students, using real-life stories and situations, humour, and suspense. The **Grammar Banks** give students a single, easy-to-access grammar reference section, with example sentences on audio, clear rules, and common errors to avoid. There are at least two practice exercises for each grammar point. Students can look again at the grammar presented in the lesson on **Online Practice**. The **Workbook** provides a variety of practice exercises and the opportunity for students to use the new grammar to express their own ideas.

Vocabulary

- Systematic expansion of topic-based lexical areas
- Increase the range and variety of their vocabulary
- Opportunities to put new vocabulary into practice

At this level, expanding students' vocabulary is the most visible and motivating measure of their progress. Many lessons are linked to the **Vocabulary Banks** which help present and practise the vocabulary in class, give an audio model of each word, and provide a clear reference so students can revise and test themselves in their own time. Students can review the meaning and the pronunciation of new vocabulary on **Online Practice**, and find further practice in the **Workbook**.

Pronunciation

- 'Fine-tuning' of pronunciation of difficult sounds
- Continue to develop their instinct for rules and patterns
- The ability to use appropriate rhythm and intonation

Clear, *intelligible* pronunciation (not perfection) should be the goal of students at this level. There is a pronunciation focus in every lesson, which integrates clear pronunciation into grammar and vocabulary practice. There is an emphasis on the sounds most useful for communication, on word stress, and on sentence rhythm. **Online Practice** contains the Sound Bank videos which show students the mouth positions to make English vowels and consonants. They can also review the pronunciation from the lesson at their own speed. There is more practice of pronunciation in the **Workbook**, with audio, which can be found on **Online Practice**.

Speaking

- Up-to-date, stimulating topics to get them talking and exchanging opinions
- The key words and phrases necessary to discuss a topic
- Practice in more extended speaking
- Improvement in accuracy as well as further development of their fluency

We believe that a good topic or text is very important in motivating students to speak in class. Every lesson in *English File Upper-intermediate* has a speaking activity which enables students to contribute their own knowledge, opinions, or experience.

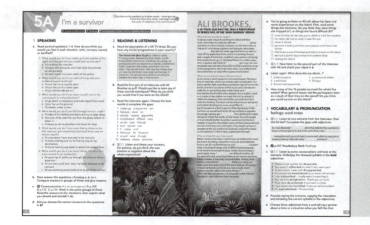

Listening

- Motivating, integrated listening material
- Achievable tasks but with an increasing level of challenge
- Exposure to longer listenings and a wide variety of accents
- Exposure to authentic and colloquial spoken language

For most students, listening is still the hardest skill and it is vital that listening material is both interesting and provides the right level of challenge. *English File Upper-intermediate* introduces some unscripted authentic listening alongside more controlled material in the main lessons to provide challenge and support appropriate to the level. These expose students to a wider variety of language, accent and speed of speech with achievable but challenging tasks. The Colloquial English lessons give students practice in listening to unscripted authentic speech. On **Online Practice**, for each File students can find further listening practice related to the topic. They can also access the listening activities from every lesson, to practise in their own time, and to read the script to check anything that they have found difficult.

Reading

- Engaging topics and stimulating material
- Exposure to a wide variety of authentic text types
- Challenging tasks which help them read more skillfully

Many students need to read in English for their work or studies, and reading is also important in helping to build vocabulary and to consolidate grammar. The key to encouraging students to read is to provide material where they feel there is a reason to read and tasks which help them to get the most out of a text. This level contains a variety of readings from real sources (the British press, magazines, websites, forums, infographics) and have been chosen for their intrinsic interest and potential to generate a reaction. The opinions expressed in these texts do not necessarily reflect the view of the *English File* authors or of Oxford University Press.

Writing

- Practice in planning, organizing, writing, and checking
- An awareness of register, structure, and fixed phrases
- A focus on 'micro' writing skills

It is often difficult to motivate students to write at this level. In *English File Upper-intermediate* each guided writing activity flows out of a main lesson to ensure that students have plenty of ideas to start with and focuses on key areas of language, style, and organization to help break the writing process down into a series of achievable tasks.

Students can use **Online Practice** to develop their writing skills further. The Discussion board also provides opportunities for informal written interaction.

Colloquial English

- Get used to listening to authentic colloquial speech
- The ability to deal with different speeds and accents
- Exposure to high-frequency colloquial phrases and idioms
- Techniques and strategies for participating in a conversation

The five *Colloquial English* lessons focus on an unscripted interview with a person who is an expert in his / her field and a spontaneous conversation between three people answering a question related to the lesson topic. There is also a 'Looking at Language' focus, which looks at a particular aspect of functional language as used by the speaker. On **Online Practice**, students can use the interactive video to record themselves and hear their own voice as part of the conversation. The **Workbook** provides practice of all the language from the Colloquial English lessons.

Revision

- Regular review
- Motivating reference and practice material
- A sense of progress

Students will usually only assimilate and remember new language if they have the chance to see it and use it several times. Grammar, Vocabulary, and Pronunciation are recycled throughout the course. After every two Files there is a two-page Revise & Check section. The left-hand page revises the grammar, vocabulary, and pronunciation of each File. The right-hand page provides a series of skills-based challenges, including street interviews, and helps students to measure their progress in terms of competence. These pages are designed to be used flexibly according to the needs of your students. On **Online Practice**, for each File, there are three **Check your progress** activities. The first is a multiple choice activity for students to test themselves on the Grammar and Vocabulary from the File. The second is a dictation related to the topic and the language of the File for students to practise the new language in context. Finally, there is a **Challenge** activity, which involves a mini-research project based on a topic from the File. After every two Files, the **Workbook** contains a *Can you remember...?* page, which provides a cumulative review of language students have covered in the **Student's Book**.

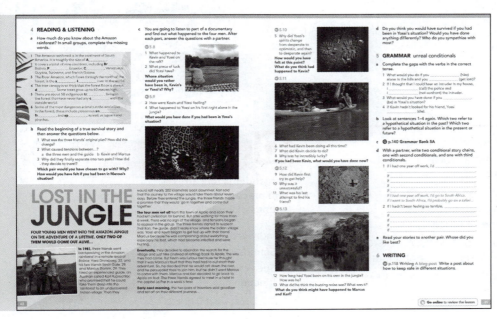

Course overview

For students

Student's Book

The Student's Book has 10 Files. Each File is organized like this:

A and B lessons

Each File contains two four-page lessons which present and practise **Grammar**, **Vocabulary**, and **Pronunciation** with a balance of reading and listening activities, and lots of opportunities for speaking. Every two Files (starting from File 2), the B lesson ends with a **Video Listening** section. All lessons have clear references to the **Grammar Bank**, **Vocabulary Bank**, and where relevant, to the **Sound Bank** at the back of the book.

Colloquial English

Every two Files (starting from File 1) there is a two-page lesson where students develop their ability to listen to authentic English and look at elements of natural language. Integrated into every *Colloquial English* lesson is an interview with an expert in his / her field, and a conversation.

Revise & Check

Every two Files (starting from File 2) there is a two-page section revising the **Grammar**, **Vocabulary**, and **Pronunciation** of each File and providing **Reading**, **Listening**, and **Speaking**. The *'Can you…?'* section challenges students with engaging reading texts and street interview videos, which give students exposure to real-life English.

The back of the Student's Book

The lessons contain references to these sections: Communication, Writing, Listening, Grammar Bank, Vocabulary Bank, and Sound Bank.

The Student's Book is also available as an eBook.

Online Practice

For students to practise and develop their language and skills or catch up on a class they have missed.

- **Look again:** students can review the language from every lesson.
- **Practice:** students can develop their skills with extra Reading, Writing, Listening, and Speaking practice.
- **Check your progress:** students can test themselves on the main language from the lesson and get instant feedback, and try an extra challenge.
- **Interactive video** to practise the language from the Colloquial English lessons.
- **Sound Bank videos** to learn and practise pronunciation of English sounds.
- **Resources:** All Student's Book audio, video, scripts, wordlists, dyslexia-friendly texts, and CEFR Language Portfolio.

Workbook

For language practice after class.

- All the Grammar, Vocabulary, and Colloquial English
- Pronunciation exercises with audio. The audio can be accessed on **Online Practice**
    - *Can you remember…?* exercises for students to check their progress
- Available with or without key

Say It: English pronunciation app

For students to learn and practise the sounds of English

- Individual sounds
- Sounds in key words
- Speak and record functionality

10

For teachers

Teacher's Guide

Step-by-step procedural notes for all the lessons including:

- an optional 'books-closed' lead-in for every lesson.
- **Extra challenge** suggestions for ways of exploiting the Student's Book material in a more challenging way if you have a stronger class.
- **Extra support** suggestions for ways of adapting activities or exercises to make them work with weaker students.
- **Extra ideas** for optional activities.

All lesson plans include answer keys and audio scripts.
Over 50 pages of photocopiable activities.

Grammar
see pp. 159–182

- An activity for every Grammar Bank, which can be used in class or for self-study extra practice

Communicative
see pp.183–213

- Extra speaking practice for every A and B lesson

Vocabulary
see pp. 214–230

- An activity for every Vocabulary Bank, which can be used in class or for self-study extra practice

There is more information on page 158 of this Teacher's Guide about the photocopiable worksheets and tips on how best to use them.

Teacher's Resource Centre

- All the Student's Book audio/video files and scripts
- Detailed lesson plans from the Teacher's Guide
- Answer keys
- All the photocopiable activities from the Teacher's Guide, including customisable versions
- All the Workbook audio files and scripts
- Tests and assessment material, including: an Entry Test; Progress Tests; an End-of-course Test; a Quick Test for every File; and complete test for every File. There are A and B versions of all the main tests and audio files for all the Listening tests
- CEFR documents

Classroom Presentation Tool

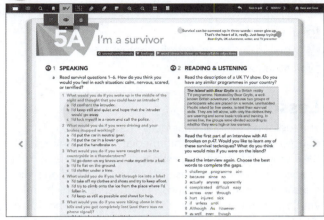

- The complete Student's Book
- Photocopiable activities from the Teacher's Guide
- All class audio and video, with interactive scripts
- Answer keys for exercises in the Student's Book and photocopiable activities
- Dyslexia-friendly texts
- The Workbook is also available as a Classroom Presentation Tool.

Class audio

All the listening materials for the Student's Book can be found on the **Teacher's Resource Centre**, **Classroom Presentation Tool**, **Online Practice**, **Student's eBook**, and the **Class Audio CDs**.

Video

Video listening

- Short documentaries for students at the end of even-numbered B lessons (2B, 4B, 6B, etc.)

Colloquial English

- Interviews and conversations that go with the Colloquial English lessons in the Student's Book

Revise & Check video

- Street interviews filmed in London, New York, and Oxford to accompany the Revise & Check section

All the video materials for the Student's Book can be found on the **Teacher's Resource Centre**, **Classroom Presentation Tool**, **Online Practice**, **Student's eBook**, and the **Class DVD**.

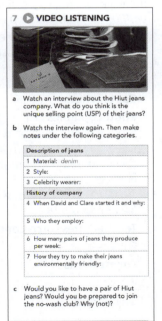

1A Questions and answers

G question formation
V working out meaning from context
P intonation: showing interest

Lesson plan

The topic and the grammar focus of this first lesson is questions. Even at Upper-intermediate level, many Sts still have problems forming questions correctly. This lesson aims to revise all aspects of question formation, including indirect questions, negative questions, and questions which end with a preposition. By the end of the lesson, Sts should be forming questions more accurately and more confidently, and we suggest that from then onwards you insist on questions always being formed correctly.

The lesson has two distinct halves. In the first half, Sts read two interviews from *Q&A*, a regular feature in *The Guardian* newspaper, with the singer Florence Welch and the actor Dan Stevens. They then focus on the grammar of question formation and this is followed by Pronunciation, which revises how to use intonation in questions to show interest.

In the second half, the topic is job interviews and Sts read an article about the kind of 'extreme' questions which some companies now use. The vocabulary focus is on working out the meaning of new words in a text from context. This is followed by a listening where Sts hear four speakers talk about strange questions they have been asked in interviews. The lesson ends with Speaking, where Sts role-play extreme interviews and write a question of their own.

If you would like to begin the first lesson without the book, there are two photocopiable 'first day' activities on *p.161* and *pp.190–191* (instructions *p.183*).

There is an Entry Test on the *Teacher's Resource Centre*, which you can give Sts before starting the course.

More materials
For teachers
Photocopiables
Grammar introduction *p.161*
question formation *p.162*
Communicative Tell me about it *pp.190–191*
(instructions *p.183*)
Ask me a question *p.192*
(instructions *p.183*)
Teacher's Resource Centre
Entry test
For students
Workbook 1A
Online Practice 1A

OPTIONAL LEAD-IN – THE QUOTE
Write the quote at the top of *p.6* on the board and the name of the person who said it, or get Sts to open their books and read it.
You could point out / elicit that Oscar Wilde (1854–1900), a playwright and poet, is famous in particular for his novel *The Picture of Dorian Gray* and play *The Importance of Being Earnest*. Elicit / Explain what *indiscreet* means.
Get Sts to discuss what they think it means. Do they agree with the quote?

1 READING & SPEAKING understanding questions

a Focus on the photos and ask Sts if they know anything about the two people. Elicit as much information as you can. If they don't know them at all, tell Sts that they are both very well known in the UK, and that after reading about them, they may want to listen to Florence's music and / or watch some of Dan's TV series or films.
Give Sts time to read about who they are.
Elicit answers to the two questions and tell Sts if you know them and what you think of them.

b Focus on the two interviews and ask Sts what the title *Q&A* means (= *Questions and Answers*).
Then give Sts time to read the interviews and complete the questions. Point out the **Glossary**. You may also want to elicit / explain *wallpaper* (= the background pattern or picture you choose to have on the screen of your phone, computer, etc.) and the expression *a guilty pleasure* (= sth you enjoy, but think you shouldn't) in Dan's questions.
Get Sts to compare with a partner, and then check answers. You may want to point out that although *Who* would also fit Dan's question 4, it would not be a natural question to ask someone in an interview, as it would presuppose that the answer was a person, whereas the answer could be anything, e.g. a neighbour's dog, worrying about something, etc.

EXTRA SUPPORT Before Sts read the interviews the first time, check whether you need to pre-teach any vocabulary.

Florence Welch
1 What 2 did 3 don't 4 was 5 who 6 would
7 Where 8 Have 9 What / Which

Dan Stevens
1 When 2 do 3 What 4 What 5 Who 6 would
7 How 8 does 9 Do

c Focus on questions 1–8 and go through them quickly, making sure Sts understand all the lexis. Highlight that the questions begin *Who do you think…?* not *Who…?*, as the answers are implied rather than directly stated.
Now tell Sts to read the interviews again and to answer the questions with the celebrities' initials.
Get Sts to compare with a partner, and then check answers.

12 1A

1 D – question 9
2 F – question 5
3 D – question 7
4 F – question 4
5 D – questions 1 and 8
6 D – questions 1, 2, 3, and 4
7 F – question 9
8 F – question 3

EXTRA CHALLENGE You could get Sts to close their books, and then call out some of the answers (or part of the answers) from the two *Q&A* questionnaires, to see if Sts can remember the questions, e.g.

T *I go for walks in Griffith Park, in LA.*
Sts *How do you relax?*
T *What's the wi-fi password?*
Sts *What word or phrase do you most overuse?*

Deal with any other new vocabulary. Elicit or model the pronunciation of any tricky words.

d Put Sts in pairs to decide which question is the most and least interesting, or too personal to ask a person whom you don't know well. You might want to tell Sts that they don't have to agree with each other.

Get feedback from various pairs.

e Focus on the task and put Sts in pairs. Give them time to choose their six questions.

Now focus on the **Politely refusing to answer a question** box and go through it with the class. Elicit / Explain that these answers should be said very politely, as normally, whoever asked you the question didn't mean to be rude or intrusive.

Get Sts to ask and answer their questions. Encourage 'questioners' to ask for more information where possible.

Get feedback by asking Sts for any interesting / funny answers, and deal with any vocabulary problems that arose.

EXTRA SUPPORT Demonstrate the activity by getting Sts to choose questions to ask you. Give reasonably full answers and encourage Sts to ask follow-up questions.

2 GRAMMAR question formation

a 🔊 **1.2** Focus on the instructions and make sure Sts understand the situation.

Play the audio once the whole way through for Sts just to listen.

Now play the audio again for Sts to write the four questions. If necessary, give Sts the first word of each question: *What, How, Don't, Can.*

Get Sts to compare with a partner, and then play the audio again if necessary.

Check answers, eliciting each question onto the board.

1 What brings you to London?
2 How long are you going to be in London for?
3 Don't you like London?
4 Can you tell us if there's any truth in that?

🔊 **1.2**
(script in Student's Book on *p.122*)
J = journalist, C = Cindy
All four journalists Excuse me…, Excuse me…, Cindy…, Cindy….
J1 Just a few questions…
C OK, OK, but you have just one minute.
J1 What brings you to London?
C I'm here to accept an award and do some interviews.
J2 How long are you going to be in London for?
C Just forty-eight hours, then I'm flying back to the States.
J3 That's a very short stay. Don't you like London?
C I love London, but unfortunately my new movie starts shooting on Monday.
J4 There've been rumours that you and your husband are having relationship problems. Can you tell us if there's any truth in that?
C No, no, no, no. No comment. No, no more questions.

b Focus on the task and go through the questions. Make sure Sts remember what, for example, an auxiliary verb is (*do, have,* etc.).

Do it as a whole-class activity, or put Sts in pairs and then check answers.

a question which ends with a preposition = 2
a subject question, where there is no auxiliary verb = 1
a question which uses a negative auxiliary verb = 3
an indirect question = 4

c Tell Sts to go to **Grammar Bank 1A** on *p.132*. If your Sts have not used the *English File* series before, explain that all the grammar rules and exercises are in this part of the book.

Grammar notes

The **Grammar notes** in this Teacher's Guide aim to add more information to the notes and rules on the **Grammar Bank** pages in the Student's Book. There is a direct link between the number of each rule in the Teacher's Guide and the Student's Book. If there is no extra information about a rule in the Teacher's Guide, this is either because we assume that Sts at this level should already know it, or because all the information needed is on the Student's Book page.

Question formation

- **Rule 1: basic word order in questions**

  Sts at this level should be familiar with basic rules regarding question formation, though they may still be making mistakes, especially when they speak.

- **Rule 2: word order in negative questions**

  The word order is the same as in normal questions, i.e. just add *n't* to the auxiliary verb, e.g. *Aren't you going to come? Why didn't you tell me?*

  You may want to point out that when full forms are used, you have to put the *not* between the subject and verb, e.g. *Are you not going to come? Why did you not tell me?*

  You should point out to Sts that it is much more common to use the contracted negative, especially in spoken English.

Indirect questions

You may want to highlight that in this kind of question, the question is formed in the first part (*Can you tell me…?* etc.) and the main question becomes a normal clause.

1A 13

Other expressions followed by the word order of indirect questions

Highlight that we only use a question mark when the introductory phrase is a question, e.g. *Could you tell me…? Do you have any idea…?* Where the introductory phrase is <u>not</u> a question, e.g. *I'm not sure…, I wonder…*, then the sentence ends with a full stop.

Focus on the example sentences for **question formation** and play audio 🔊 **1.3** for Sts to listen and repeat. Encourage them to copy the rhythm. Then go through the rules with the class.

Repeat for **indirect questions** 🔊 **1.4**.

Then go through the **Other expressions followed by the word order of indirect questions** box with the class.

Now focus on the exercises and get Sts to do them individually or in pairs.

If they do them individually, get them to compare with a partner. Check answers, getting Sts to read the full questions.

a
1 Should I tell her how I feel?
2 How long have you known your best friend?
3 Could you tell me when the next train leaves?
4 What are you thinking about?
5 What do you like doing at the weekend?
6 What kind of music does Jane like listening to?
7 Do you know what time the film finishes?
8 How many students came to class yesterday?
9 Do you remember where the restaurant is?
10 Who does the housework in your family?

b
1 How often **do you usually do** exercise?
2 Who **wrote** *Oliver Twist*?
3 Could you tell me how much **this book costs**?
4 I can't remember where **I parked** my car this morning.
5 **Did you enjoy** your trip to Paris last weekend?
6 What kind of work **does your sister do**?
7 Who **ate / has eaten** the last biscuit?
8 Do you know what time **the swimming pool opens** on Saturdays?
9 Why **didn't / doesn't your sister like** the present you gave her?
10 **Do you have to** play your music so loud?

Tell Sts to go back to the main lesson **1A**.

EXTRA SUPPORT If you think Sts need more practice, you may want to give them the **Grammar** photocopiable activity at this point.

d Put Sts in pairs, **A** and **B**, preferably face-to-face. Tell them to go to **Communication** Indirect questions, **A** on *p.106*, **B** on *p.110*.

Go through the instructions and make sure Sts know what they have to do.

Monitor and help where necessary.

Check answers by getting some Sts to ask their questions.

Finally, deal with any new vocabulary, and elicit or model the pronunciation.

Tell Sts to go back to the main lesson **1A**.

3 PRONUNCIATION intonation: showing interest

Pronunciation notes

Non-native speakers can unintentionally sound uninterested or even unfriendly if they use very flat intonation. The first two exercises focus on encouraging Sts to use a wide voice range when asking questions, and on stressing words.

These exercises do not focus specifically on distinguishing between the different intonation patterns for *yes / no* questions and question-word questions (*yes / no* questions usually have a rising intonation and question-word questions a falling intonation). In practice we think it is very hard for Sts to notice this distinction, and what is more, native speaker intonation, especially among young people, is constantly changing.

In exercises **c**, **d**, and **e**, Sts focus on using interested intonation to respond to what someone says. This is another context in which using flat intonation (e.g. when responding *Really?*) can unintentionally convey a lack of interest.

a 🔊 **1.5** Focus on the task. Tell Sts they are going to hear someone asking each question twice – once with interested intonation and once not – and they must decide which one has the more interested intonation.

Play the audio once the whole way through for Sts just to listen.

Now play the audio again, pausing if necessary after each question has been asked twice.

Check answers. Elicit what difference Sts notice between the interested and uninterested intonation.

1 a **2** b **3** b **4** a **5** b

🔊 **1.5**
See questions in Student's Book on *p.7*

b 🔊 **1.6** Tell Sts they will hear the five questions again with interested intonation. They must listen and then repeat the question, copying the intonation.

Play the audio, pausing after each question for Sts to listen and repeat.

🔊 **1.6**
See questions in **a** in Student's Book on *p.7*

Now repeat the activity, getting individual Sts to repeat each question.

c 🔊 **1.7** Focus on the **Reacting to what someone says** box and go through it with the class.

Tell Sts they are going to hear five conversations, each starting with the questions in **a** in the same order, and they must complete the four gapped reactions. Point out that the first one (*Wow*) has been done for them, and make sure Sts remember what a *vegan* is.

Play the audio once the whole way through for Sts just to listen.

Then play the audio again, pausing after each conversation for Sts to complete the expressions and questions.

Get Sts to compare with a partner, and then play the audio again as necessary.

14 **1A**

Check answers.

> **2** Why not **3** Me too **4** How interesting **5** Oh really

---

🔊 **1.7**

W = woman, M = man

1
W Do you have a big family?
M Yes, actually, I'm one of seven. I've got five sisters and a brother.
W Wow! That's a huge family.

2
M What don't you like about the place where you live?
W Well, for one thing, I don't like my neighbours very much.
M Why not? What's wrong with them?

3
W What sports or games are you good at?
M Well, I'm not really very sporty, but I'm quite good at chess.
W Me too! We could have a game one day.

4
W Do you think you have a healthy diet?
M Yes, very. In fact, I'm a vegan, so I only eat fruit and vegetables, and grains, and no meat or fish.
W How interesting! How long have you been a vegan?

5
M What makes you feel happy?
W Lots of things. Er…like buying new shoes.
M Oh really? I can't think of anything worse!

---

d 🔊 **1.8** Tell Sts that this time they are just going to hear the responses and they must repeat them. Highlight that with these responses, it is also very important to use interested intonation. Encourage them to use a wide voice range and to get the correct rhythm.

Play the audio, pausing after each response for Sts to listen and repeat.

🔊 **1.8**

1 Wow! That's a huge family.
2 Why not? What's wrong with them?
3 Me too! We could have a game one day.
4 How interesting! How long have you been a vegan?
5 Oh really? I can't think of anything worse!

Now repeat the activity, eliciting responses from individual Sts.

e Put Sts in pairs and get them to ask and answer the questions in **a**. Encourage them to use interested intonation and to react to their partner's answers.

You could get some pairs to practise in front of the class.

4 READING & VOCABULARY working out meaning from context

a Focus on the cartoon and do the questions as a whole-class activity, or put Sts in pairs and then get some feedback.

b Focus on the task and give Sts time to read the title and first paragraph.

Now focus on questions A–G and make sure Sts understand all the lexis, especially a *CV* (= a written record of your education and the jobs you have done).

Put Sts in pairs and get them to answer the questions.

Get some feedback and elicit which question Sts would least like to answer. You could tell Sts which question you would least like to be asked.

EXTRA SUPPORT Read out the title and first paragraph, and do the task as a whole class, asking the questions to individual Sts.

c Focus on the article and give Sts time to read it and complete it with questions A–G, and find out how the questions should be answered.

Get Sts to compare with a partner, and then check answers.

EXTRA IDEA You may want to tell Sts what kind of companies the ones mentioned in the article are:

The Phoenix Partnership, Palantir Technologies, and Clearwater Analytics are software companies.

Condé Nast is a mass media company which publishes magazines.

Page Group and Switch Consulting are recruitment companies.

Badoo is a dating-focused social network.

EXTRA SUPPORT Before Sts read the article the first time, check whether you need to pre-teach any vocabulary, but not the highlighted words and phrases.

> **1** G **2** C **3** E **4** B **5** D **6** A **7** F

Finally, ask Sts if they would now feel more confident answering the questions.

d Focus on the **Guessing the meaning of new words and phrases** box and go through it with the class. Many of the texts in *English File* Upper-intermediate have glossaries, but obviously there will sometimes be other words whose meaning Sts can't guess and will want to check with a dictionary. Nowadays, many Sts will use online dictionaries via their phones. While these can be very useful, it's worth pointing out to Sts that there are circumstances, e.g. in exams, when they need to try to guess the meaning of words, and that if they always rely on their phones, they won't develop this skill. It is also sometimes not easy to find phrases or idioms in dictionaries, which is another reason for developing the skill of guessing from context.

Now tell Sts to read the article again, trying to guess what the highlighted words and phrases mean.

In pairs, Sts compare guesses.

e Now get Sts to match the highlighted words and phrases to definitions 1–8.

Check answers. Elicit or model pronunciation.

> **1** gut feeling **2** foolproof **3** light-hearted response **4** geek **5** work–life balance **6** the point of **7** good-natured rivalry **8** job-seekers

Find out how many of the words Sts guessed correctly and deal with any other vocabulary problems.

f Focus on the task and make sure Sts understand *genuine* /ˈdʒenjuɪn/ (= real). Elicit or model its pronunciation.

Quickly go through the questions, making sure Sts understand all the lexis. If Sts ask about the companies mentioned in brackets, you could tell them that Airbnb allows people to let accommodation, Banana Republic and Next are clothing companies, Redbox software is a computing company, TES Global helps teachers and schools worldwide, and General Electrics is a multinational company dealing in transport, renewable energy, healthcare, etc.

1A 15

Put Sts in pairs or small groups to discuss what the questions tell the interviewers about the candidate, and whether this type of question really helps to choose the best candidate.

Get some feedback from various pairs or groups. You could tell Sts what you think or if you have been asked any similar questions at interviews.

g Put Sts in pairs and get them to choose two questions in **f** to ask their partner.

Get some feedback for each question if possible, or ask Sts for the most interesting answers they heard.

5 LISTENING understanding the stages of a short interview

a Focus on the questions and elicit answers from the class. If you have a class of older adults, all of whom are likely to have had some kind of job interview, you could put Sts in pairs and then get some class feedback. Find out if any Sts have been asked tough interview questions as in the article in **4**.

b 🔊 **1.9** Focus on the task and the chart. Give Sts time to look at the four gapped questions, and elicit / teach the meaning of *reincarnated* in 4.

Play Speaker 1 all the way through and then pause the audio. Get Sts to complete the question.

Check the answer.

Now repeat the process for the other three speakers.

EXTRA SUPPORT Read through the script and decide if you need to pre-teach any new lexis before Sts listen.

1 have dinner, three people
2 have, boyfriend, get pregnant
3 practise philosophy
4 What animal

🔊 **1.9**
(script in Student's Book on *p.122*)
I = interviewer, D = Dominic, H = Heidi, S = Sean, A = Alice
1 Dominic
I Have you ever been asked a strange question in an interview?
D Yes, it was my interview for a place at Sarah Lawrence University in New York – where I'm studying now.
I What was the question?
D The question was, 'If you could have dinner with three people from the past, who would you choose and why?'
I And what did you answer?
I It was one of the first questions I was asked, and I said, 'I can't answer this right now. Can I answer at the end?' because I couldn't think of anyone. So they said OK, and then they asked me the question again later, and I said something ridiculous like John Lennon, um, Picasso, and…er…I can't even remember who the third person was, it was another sort of artist or musician I think.
I Do you think it was a good question?
D Yes, because it made me think – I mean, it wasn't something I was expecting at all, and all the other ones were more yes / no, direct questions, so this one made me think a bit more.
I And you got the place?
D Yes, I did.
2 Heidi
I Have you ever been asked a strange question in an interview?
H Yes, I have. That was many years ago, it was one of my first job interviews, in London, actually, after I moved to London from Germany. It was for a financial department, and the manager who interviewed me, I can't remember, but I believe he, he must have been German – he asked me, 'Do you have a boyfriend?' and 'Are you planning to get pregnant?'

I That's illegal now, isn't it?
H Yes, I know, I believe that was illegal then.
I And what did you answer?
H I said no, I didn't have a boyfriend, and I had no plans to get pregnant any time soon, but at that point, it was pretty clear to me that I did not want to work for that company.
3 Sean
I Have you ever been asked a strange question in an interview?
S Yes. I was being interviewed for a job with an advertising agency and the interviewer kept checking information on my CV and then asking me about it, and he saw that I'd studied philosophy at university, and he said, 'Oh, I see that you studied philosophy at university. Do you still practise philosophy?'
I What did you answer?
S I said the first thing that came into my head – I said, 'Well, I still think a lot'.
I Was the interviewer impressed?
S Well, he obviously liked the answer, because I got the job.
4 Alice
I Have you ever been asked a strange question in an interview?
A There's one I can think of, which was when I was being interviewed for a job with a company in Switzerland.
I What was it?
A Well, the interviewer asked me, 'What animal would you like to be reincarnated as?'
I Weird question!
A Totally.
I What did you say?
A So I said a cat because it was the first thing I thought of and because cats have a good life – well, at least in Britain they do. And then the interviewer immediately looked embarrassed and said that he'd been told to ask me that question to see how I'd react, but that he thought it was a stupid question.
I What happened in the end?
A I didn't get the job, so maybe the interviewer wasn't very fond of cats!

c Now tell Sts they will hear the audio again and this time they must make notes on how the people answered the questions and what happened in the end. Give Sts time to see if they can remember any of the answers.

Play the audio, pausing after each speaker to give Sts time to make notes. Play again if necessary.

Get Sts to compare with a partner, and then check answers.

EXTRA SUPPORT Check the answers to the first question (*How did they answer?*), then play the audio again and check the answers to the final question.

	How did they answer?	What happened in the end?
1	I can't answer this right now. Can I answer this at the end? John Lennon, Picasso, and another artist or musician (he can't remember).	He got the place at university.
2	No, I don't have a boyfriend, and I have no plans to get pregnant.	She decided immediately that she didn't want to work for that company.
3	Well, I still think a lot.	He got the job.
4	A cat	She didn't get the job.

16 **1A**

EXTRA SUPPORT If there's time, you could get Sts to listen again with the script on *p.122*, so they can see exactly what they understood / didn't understand. Translate / Explain any new words or phrases.

d Do this as a whole-class activity and elicit opinions.

6 SPEAKING

a Put Sts in pairs, **A** and **B**, preferably face-to-face. Tell them to go to **Communication Tough questions**, **A** on *p.106*, **B** on *p.110*.

Go through the instructions and make sure Sts know what they have to do. Make sure too that Sts understand the questions they're going to ask. You may need to explain, for example, *aspect* and *desert island* in **A**'s questions and *treat*, *superhero*, and *lead role* in **B**'s questions.

Get Sts to decide what kind of company they are interviewing for and then tell each other.

Tell Sts **A** to start by asking their partner the eight interview questions.

Monitor and help Sts, correcting any errors with question formation.

When they have finished, Sts **A** should tell their partner if they have got the job and why, or why not if they didn't succeed.

Then they swap roles.

Get feedback to find out if there were any particularly interesting answers. With a show of hands, you could also find out how many Sts got the jobs.

Finally, deal with any new vocabulary, and elicit or model the pronunciation.

Tell Sts to go back to the main lesson **1A**.

b Focus on the task and give Sts time to write their question. You might want to remind Sts that the aim of the question is for potential future employers to get information about the candidate's personality and / or abilities.

EXTRA SUPPORT You could tell Sts to look back at all the previous questions in the lesson, to help them with ideas, or elicit a few possible questions from the class so that Sts know what they have to do. Then get Sts to write their question in pairs. For **c**, divide the class in half (with one student from each pair in each group) for the mingle.

Monitor and correct any mistakes in question formation.

EXTRA CHALLENGE Get Sts to write two or three questions.

c If possible, get Sts to stand up and move around the class, asking as many other Sts as possible their question.

Deal with any general vocabulary problems that arose.

d Do this as a whole-class activity and elicit opinions.

1A 17

1B It's a mystery

G auxiliary verbs, *the…*, *the…* + comparatives
V compound adjectives, modifiers
P intonation and sentence rhythm

Lesson plan

The topic of the lesson is understanding and explaining mysterious and unusual events.

The first half of the lesson starts with a reading based on a true story of the disappearance of three lighthouse keepers in Scotland. Sts then listen to the end of the story, in which a detective tries to solve the mysterious disappearance of the men. This is followed by the grammar focus on auxiliary verbs, which includes both revision of question tags and *So do I / Neither do I*, and the use of auxiliaries for emphasis and in reply questions. Sts then work on intonation and sentence rhythm in questions and sentences using auxiliaries. Finally, the first half of the lesson ends with Sts pretending to be psychics and completing sentences about a partner.

In the second half of the lesson, the focus shifts to an unusual personality test. Sts listen to a mysterious voice guiding them on a walk through a forest. They listen to some instructions, make notes, and then analyse their answers. Sts then discuss other non-mainstream ways of analysing personality. Grammar in Context focuses on how to use the structure *the…*, *the…* + comparatives, e.g. *the sooner, the better*. This is followed by Vocabulary, where Sts expand their vocabulary of compound adjectives to describe personality, and use modifiers and compound adjectives to talk about people they know.

More materials
For teachers
Photocopiables
Grammar auxiliary verbs *p.163*
Communicative What's in a signature? *p.193*
(instructions *p.183*)
For students
Workbook 1B
Online Practice 1B

OPTIONAL LEAD-IN – THE QUOTE

Write the quote at the top of *p.10* on the board and the name of the person who said it, or get Sts to open their books and read it.

Elicit who Sherlock Holmes and Arthur Conan Doyle (1859–1930) are.

Get Sts to say what they think the quote means and whether they agree with it. You may want to tell them that this sentence, or slight variants of it, is something that Holmes says in many different stories and is one of his main strategies for detecting.

1 READING & LISTENING understanding facts vs theories

a Do the questions as a whole-class activity. If Sts don't recognize any of the names, tell them not to worry, as they are going to find out.

EXTRA SUPPORT If Sts have heard about some of these mysteries, write their ideas on the board to help with the listening in **b**.

b 🔊 1.10 Play the audio, pausing after each story to elicit as much information as possible about each mystery.

Now ask Sts what the three stories have in common.

> They are all unsolved mysteries.

🔊 1.10
(script in Student's Book on *p.122*)
On the fourth of December eighteen seventy-two, a ship called the *Mary Celeste* was found floating in the Atlantic. There was no one on board. The ship wasn't damaged, and everything was in order, although the lifeboat was missing. None of the crew or passengers were ever seen again.

On the fourth of March nineteen eighteen, a huge ship called the *USS Cyclops* left Barbados with three hundred people on board, and sailed into what we now call the Bermuda Triangle. Then it disappeared without a trace. No distress call was made, and no bad weather was reported in the region. A huge search for the *Cyclops* was launched – boats and planes scoured the area for wreckage or survivors – but nothing of the enormous ship was ever seen again.

On July second, nineteen thirty-seven, Amelia Earhart, the famous American aviator, took off with her navigator from New Guinea, in a small plane, on the last stage of their around-the-world flight. It was the last time they were seen alive. Four million dollars was spent on the search, but no trace of Amelia or the navigator was ever found.

Finally, ask Sts if they think we will ever find out what happened. You might want to tell Sts the following:

– After looking at all the facts, the most likely conclusion is that the captain and crew of the *Mary Celeste* panicked, thinking their ship was going to sink because the pump was making a strange sound, and took the lifeboat along with the navigational instruments. There was a terrible storm, and their lifeboat probably sank.

– The U.S. Navy says in its official statement about the *Cyclops*, 'The disappearance of this ship has been one of the most baffling mysteries in the annals of the Navy, all attempts to locate her having proved unsuccessful.'

– Some remains were found in 2018 on Nikumaroro island, in the western Pacific Ocean, which might be Amelia Earhart's.

c 🔊 1.11 Focus on the article and the photos to make sure Sts know what a *lighthouse* is (= a tower or other building that contains a strong light to warn and guide ships near the coast) and *lighthouse keepers*. Highlight that this is a true story, and the photo of the men is one that appeared in newspapers at the time.

Now focus on the task. Play the audio for Sts to read and listen at the same time. You might want to tell them that 75 ft (feet) = 23 m.

18 1B

EXTRA IDEA You may want to tell Sts that a film about this mystery, called *The Vanishing*, was released in 2019.

EXTRA SUPPORT Read through the article and decide if you need to pre-teach any new lexis before Sts listen, but not the words in **d**.

🔊 **1.11**
See article in Student's Book on *p.10*

Now tell Sts to cover the article. Focus on the two sections and questions 1–5, making sure Sts know the meaning of *facts* and *theories*.

Put Sts in pairs and get them to answer the questions.

Focus on *The facts* and check answers to questions 1 and 2. Then focus on *The theories*, eliciting the ones mentioned in the article, and getting Sts to respond to them in questions 4 and 5.

1 There was nobody at the lighthouse. This was discovered by the three new lighthouse keepers who arrived at the island to relieve the men who had been working there for three months.
2 the lighthouse door was unlocked
  a chair was knocked over
  one rain jacket was hanging on its hook, but the other two had disappeared
  the clocks had stopped
  the last entry in the log book was 9 a.m. on 15th December
3 The men had argued about a woman; they had been kidnapped by German agents; they had been carried away by a sea serpent, a giant bird, or a boat full of ghosts.

d Tell Sts to uncover the article and complete the definitions.
Get Sts to compare with a partner, and then check answers. Elicit or model the pronunciation, and highlight that the first *a* in *extraordinary* is silent.

1 puzzle　2 baffle　3 remote　4 extraordinary　5 trace
6 solve

e 🔊 **1.12** Tell Sts that they are going to listen to the rest of the story. Focus on the task and elicit who Muirhead /ˈmjʊəhed/ is (an Edinburgh policeman). Point out the **Glossary** and go through it with the class.

Play the audio once the whole way through for Sts just to listen and get the gist of the story. You might also want to tell them that 100 ft (feet) = 30 m.

If necessary, play the audio again, pausing at intervals to give Sts time to answer the questions.
Check answers.

EXTRA SUPPORT Read through the script and decide if you need to pre-teach any new lexis before Sts listen.

Muirhead thought that the men had been washed away by an enormous wave.
People rejected his idea at the time.
Now people think that small waves can combine to create a huge wave, which swept the men away.

🔊 **1.12**
(script in Student's Book on *p.122*)
An Edinburgh policeman, Robert Muirhead, was sent to the island to solve the mystery. Muirhead was a hard-working, practical investigator, and not at all superstitious. Among other clues, he

found equipment lying all over the island, and also a huge rock, much too heavy for any men to carry, lying on the steps leading up to the lighthouse. In the end, the only explanation he could think of was that the men had been carried off by an enormous wave. Muirhead's explanation was immediately rejected. But more than one hundred years later, in nineteen ninety-five, the ship *Queen Elizabeth II* was hit by a one-hundred-foot wave which, according to her captain, 'came out of the darkness' and 'looked like the White Cliffs of Dover'.
Then a paper published in a scientific journal recently proved that the 'monster wave', which for centuries had been considered a sailors' myth, is a mathematical reality: many smaller waves can suddenly combine in mid-ocean and create a huge wave of devastating force. Most marine scientists now agree that it is a naturally occurring – though rare – event.
So finally, the only explanation that fits the facts is that the three lighthouse men had rushed out to attend to some emergency and had then been swept away by an enormous wave. Inspector Muirhead, it now appears, was almost certainly right. He solved the case back in nineteen oh one, but he had to wait another century for the proof.
However, science still cannot answer all the questions surrounding the Flannan Islands mystery. Why did one man leave his rain jacket behind? Why were the bodies of the men never found? Maybe these are things we will never know.

f Focus on the task and give Sts time to read items 1–5.
Play the audio again, pausing after each item has been mentioned to give Sts time to make notes.
Get Sts to compare with a partner, and then check answers.

1 A huge rock was lying on the steps leading up to the lighthouse, but it would have been too heavy for anyone to carry, so it adds evidence to the idea of the huge wave.
2 The ship *Queen Elizabeth II* was hit by a 100-ft wave in 1995, a modern example of Muirhead's theory.
3 A paper in a scientific journal has recently been published saying that monster waves really exist.
4 1901 was the date when Muirhead actually solved the mystery, but then there was no proof.
5 There are some things we will never know the answers to.

EXTRA SUPPORT If there's time, you could get Sts to listen again with the scripts on *p.122*, so they can see exactly what they understood / didn't understand. Translate / Explain any new words or phrases.

2 GRAMMAR auxiliary verbs

a Tell Sts they are now going to tell each other about some more mysteries or unusual events that are difficult to explain, sharing any experiences they have had or stories they have heard. You could teach the term *paranormal* (= that cannot be explained by science or reason and that seems to involve mysterious forces).

Focus on the **Reacting to a story about something strange** box and go through it with the class.

Now focus on the task and make sure Sts understand all the lexis, especially a *UFO* (= an unidentified flying object), a *psychic* (= a person who claims to be able to predict the future or communicate with dead people), and a *faith healer* (= a person who treats sick people through the power of belief or prayer). Elicit or model pronunciation, especially *psychic* /ˈsaɪkɪk/.

Give Sts a few minutes to think about a story they want to tell.

1B 19

Put Sts in small groups of four or five and get them to tell their stories. The Sts who are speaking should give as many details as possible, and those listening should try to react to the stories.

Monitor and help, if necessary, whilst Sts are talking.

Deal with any general vocabulary problems that arose.

Get some feedback from the class. You could also tell the class how you feel about the paranormal and relate any experiences you have had or stories you have heard.

b Focus on the task and give Sts time to complete the gaps with the correct auxiliary verbs. Conversations 1, 2, and 3 should be revision, but Sts may not be familiar with the emphatic use of the auxiliary in conversation 4.

Get them to compare with a partner.

c ◀)) **1.13** Play the audio for Sts to listen and check.

Check answers.

> **1** Did **2** do **3** have **4** have **5** did

◀)) **1.13**
1 A I heard a noise in the middle of the night.
   B Did you? What kind of noise?
2 A You don't believe in ghosts, do you?
   B No, I don't.
3 A I've never been to a fortune-teller.
   B Neither have I.
   C I have. It was really interesting.
4 A I don't believe you really saw a UFO.
   B I did see one. It couldn't have been anything else.

Now put Sts in pairs and get them to match auxiliaries 1–5 in **b** to A–E.

Check answers.

> **A** 5 **B** 4 **C** 2 **D** 1 **E** 3

d Tell Sts to go to **Grammar Bank 1B** on *p.133*.

Grammar notes
Auxiliary verbs
Auxiliary verbs (*are, is, do, did, will*, etc.) and modal verbs (*can, must*, etc.) have a variety of uses in English, and a good command of these will help Sts become more proficient speakers. Sts will be familiar with the basic uses, i.e. in question formation and short answers.

- **Rule 2: to say that someone / something is the same**
  Highlight that *neither* can be pronounced /ˈnaɪðə/ or /ˈniːðə/.

- **Rule 3: to say that someone / something is different**
  Highlight that in these kind of responses, you must stress the pronoun as well as the auxiliary, e.g.
  A *I loved the film.* **B** *Really? I didn't.*

- **Rule 4: reply questions**
  Highlight that these have a rising intonation (the voice goes up).

- **Rule 5: using auxiliaries to show emphasis**
  This will probably be new for many Sts, who may find it strange to see an auxiliary verb used in a positive sentence. This use of auxiliaries is common when we contradict or deny what someone has said, or when we want to give extra emphasis, e.g.

A *Are you a vegetarian?* **B** *No, I <u>do</u> eat meat, but I prefer fish.*

A *You can't swim, can you?* **B** *I <u>can</u> swim, but not very well.*

Highlight that:
- if the auxiliary verb is part of the tense, e.g. *is, will*, or a modal, the main verb can be left out, i.e. in the second example above you could also say *I can, but not very well*.
- Sts must stress the auxiliary verb in these sentences.

- **Rule 6: question tags**
  These probably won't be new to most Sts, but they are not easy to use with fluency because they require quick manipulation of auxiliaries. In many languages, this kind of question is covered by the simpler '..., no?' You may want to demonstrate the two different types and their intonation to Sts.

Focus on the example sentences and play audio ◀)) **1.14** for Sts to listen and repeat. Encourage them to copy the rhythm. Then go through the rules with the class.

Now focus on the exercises and get Sts to do them individually or in pairs.

If they do them individually, get them to compare with a partner. Check answers, getting Sts to read the full sentences.

> **a**
> 1 He's booked the flights, **hasn't** he?
> 2 It's hot today, **isn't** it?
> 3 I **do** like it, but it isn't my favourite.
> 4 Neither **would** I.
> 5 **Is** he? I thought he was arriving today.
> 6 Tom liked it, but I **didn't**. I thought it was awful.
> 7 She **does** like you. She just doesn't want to go out with you.
> 8 Yes, I am, and so **is** my boyfriend.
> 9 You'll remember to call me, **won't** you?
> 10 I really want to go to Egypt, but my boyfriend **doesn't**.
> **b**
> 1 It's a great club, **isn't** it?
> 2 **Don't** you?
> 3 Neither **have** I.
> 4 Oh, **don't** you?
> 5 I **do**.
> 6 **Do** you?
> 7 Why **didn't** you go?
> 8 I **did** go, but I arrived really late because my car broke down.
> 9 So **am** I.

Tell Sts to go back to the main lesson **1B**.

EXTRA SUPPORT If you think Sts need more practice, you may want to give them the **Grammar** photocopiable activity at this point.

3 PRONUNCIATION & SPEAKING intonation and sentence rhythm

Pronunciation notes

Reply questions

The auxiliary is stressed and the intonation rises as in a normal question, e.g.

A *I'm a vegetarian.* **B** <u>*Are you?*</u>

The important thing is to encourage Sts to use a friendly, interested intonation.

To say that someone / something is different, both the subject and the auxiliary are stressed, e.g.

A *I've never been to a fortune teller.* **B** *<u>I have</u>.*

So (do) I / Neither (do) I: In these responses, the auxiliary is normally unstressed, with the strong stress falling on the other two words, e.g.

A *I believe in ghosts.* **B** <u>*So*</u> *do* <u>*I*</u>.

Question tags

Here, equal stress falls on both the auxiliary and the subject. The intonation native speakers give to a question tag depends on whether we are asking a real question or not. If we genuinely don't know the answer, we tend to use the rising intonation of a question, e.g. *You haven't seen my car keys, have you?* (= I don't know if you have seen my car keys). However, if we are not asking a real question, but are just making conversation or asking for confirmation of something we already know to be true, our intonation falls and the question tag sounds like a statement, not a question, e.g. *It's a beautiful day, isn't it?* (= I know you will agree with me).

Using auxiliaries to show emphasis

In these sentences the auxiliary is stressed strongly.

As there are several issues of stress, rhythm, and intonation with auxiliary verbs, the pronunciation practice has been broken into parts. In **a–b**, Sts practise reply questions and auxiliaries for emphasis. In **d**, they practise *So / Neither do I*. In **e**, they then practise question tags.

a 🔊 **1.15** Focus on the task and the three conversations. Play the audio once the whole way through for Sts just to listen.

🔊 **1.15**
See conversations in Student's Book on *p.11*

Now play the audio again for Sts to listen and underline the highlighted auxiliaries that are stressed.

Check answers.

1 <u>Did</u> you?
2 I <u>don't</u> believe…, I <u>do</u>.
3 You <u>don't</u> like…?, I <u>do</u> like them.

b Give Sts a few minutes, in pairs, to practise the conversations, swapping roles when they get to the end. Monitor and help them with their rhythm and intonation.

You could get some pairs to practise in front of the class.

EXTRA SUPPORT Play the audio again, pausing after each line, for Sts to listen and repeat, copying the rhythm and intonation.

c Focus on the task and give Sts time to complete the eight sentences about themselves. Make sure Sts understand what a *verb phrase* is in sentence 2 (= verb + noun).

d Focus on the task, making sure Sts are clear that they should first respond with a reply question and then say if they are the same (*Neither am I*) or different (*I am*).

Focus on the examples, or demonstrate the activity first by completing the first two sentences for yourself and getting Sts to respond.

Then put Sts in pairs, **A** and **B**, and get them to respond to each other.

EXTRA SUPPORT If you think your Sts are going to find the responses difficult, elicit what the 'same' or 'different' alternatives are for the sentences and write them on the board, i.e.

AREN'T YOU?	NEITHER AM I. / I AM.
ARE YOU?	SO AM I. / I'M NOT.
DO YOU?	SO DO I. / I DON'T.
DON'T YOU?	NEITHER DO I. / I DO.
HAVEN'T YOU?	NEITHER HAVE I. / I HAVE.
WOULD YOU?	NEITHER WOULD I. / I WOULD.
WERE YOU?	SO WAS I. / I WASN'T.
DIDN'T YOU?	NEITHER DID I. / I DID.

e Put Sts in pairs, **A** and **B**, preferably face-to-face. Tell them to go to **Communication You're psychic, aren't you?**, **A** on *p.106*, **B** on *p.111*.

Focus on the title and the instructions for **a**. Elicit / Explain that the word *psychic* is both an adjective and a noun. Remind Sts of its meaning and pronunciation.

Go through the instructions and make sure Sts know what they have to do. Elicit that when they check their guesses, they should be using rising intonation on the question tags unless they are 100% sure of the information.

Get feedback to find out who was the better psychic in each pair.

Finally, deal with any new vocabulary, and elicit or model the pronunciation.

Tell Sts to go back to the main lesson **1B**.

4 LISTENING & SPEAKING following instructions

a Do the question as a whole-class activity. You could also tell Sts how you would feel.

b 🔊 **1.16** Focus on 1–6 and elicit what the icons represent. Focus on the task and tell Sts they must imagine themselves in the forest and follow the instructions they hear on the audio. Tell them that you won't pause the audio, so they must write the first answer they think of. There are some natural pauses in the audio (indicated by *** in the script) after each question. You could also tell Sts that you will play the audio a second time.

You might want to make sure Sts know what a *fence* is.

Play the audio once the whole way through for Sts to listen and complete the task.

EXTRA SUPPORT Read through the script and decide if you need to pre-teach any new lexis before Sts listen.

1B   21

1.16

(script in Student's Book on *p.122*)

A walk in the forest

I'm going to describe a situation and ask you some questions. Answer quickly without thinking about it too much – the first thing that comes into your head. Are you ready?

Imagine that you're walking through a beautiful forest. The sun is out; there's a light breeze. It's a really beautiful day. You're walking with one other person.

Question one: Who are you walking with?

***

As you walk through the forest, you come across an animal.

Question two: What kind of animal is it? A big animal or a small one? How do you interact with the animal?

***

Now you're walking deeper into the forest, and you come to a clearing, where there are no trees. There's a house in the middle of the clearing.

Question three: How big is the house? Does it have a fence around it or not?

***

You walk up to the door of the house and it's open. You go in, and you see a table.

Question four: What is there on the table? Are there any people sitting round it?

***

You finish looking around the house and you leave out of the back door. There's a huge garden behind the house. You go into the garden, and in the middle you find a cup.

Question five: What is the cup made of? Is it a ceramic cup? Metal? Plastic? Paper?

***

As you walk to the end of the garden, you come to some water. You must cross this water in order to get home.

Question six: What kind of water is it? A lake? A river? A small pond? How do you cross it? How wet do you get?

---

c Focus on the task and then play the audio again.

d **1.17** Focus on the task and the chart. Point out that the numbers in the chart correspond to the question numbers in **b**.

Now play the audio for Sts to listen and complete the explanations for 1–6.

Get Sts to compare with a partner, and then check answers.

EXTRA SUPPORT Read through the script and decide if you need to pre-teach any new lexis before Sts listen.

---

1 the person = an important person in your life
2 the animal = problems in your life
how you interact with it = how you deal with your problems
3 the house = your ambitions
no fence = you are open to new ideas
a fence = you often think you are right
4 the table = how you are feeling at the moment
5 the cup = how strong your relationship is with the person you are walking with
6 the water = your friends
how wet you get = how important your friends are to you
(very wet = very important)

1.17

(script in Student's Book on *p.123*)

What you have just done is a psychological test which analyses how you interact with other people. Now I'm going to tell you what your answers mean.

The person you were walking with is an important person in your life.

The animal represents problems in your life. The bigger the animal, the more problems you have.

How you interact with the animal represents how you deal with your problems. If you were aggressive or decisive, that means you confront your problems, try to solve them. If the interaction was peaceful, then you're a more passive person and often wait for problems to go away.

The house represents your ambitions. The bigger the house, the more ambitious you are. If there was no fence around the house, it means you're very open-minded, and welcome new ideas. If it had a fence, then you're more convinced that you're right, and tend to surround yourself by people who agree with you.

The table represents how you're feeling at the moment. If there was food or there were flowers on the table, and people sitting round it, this suggests that you're feeling happy in your relationships. No food, flowers, or people suggests that someone in your family, or a friend, is making you unhappy.

The cup represents how strong your relationship is with the person you're walking with, and how long the relationship will last. The harder and more resistant the material of the cup is, the stronger your relationship is.

The water represents your friends. If you saw a large river or lake, you have a big social circle and like to be surrounded by people. If you got very wet when you crossed it, your friends are very important for you. If you hardly got wet at all, it means that you depend less on your friends and are more self-sufficient.

---

e Focus on the first part of the task and give Sts time to look at their answers in **b** and the interpretation in **d**.

Now put Sts in pairs and tell them to discuss what they agree and disagree with.

You could elicit some feedback from various pairs.

EXTRA SUPPORT If there's time, you could get Sts to listen again with the scripts on *p.123*, so they can see exactly what they understood / didn't understand. Translate / Explain any new words or phrases.

f Focus on the task and make sure Sts understand the lexis in the bullet points. Elicit or model the pronunciation of the words in brackets, i.e. *graphology* /græˈfɒlədʒi/, *palmistry* /ˈpɑːmɪstri/, and *astrology* /əˈstrɒlədʒi/.

Do this as a whole-class activity, or put Sts in pairs or small groups and then get some feedback.

GRAMMAR IN CONTEXT

g Focus on **Grammar in Context** and tell Sts that this regular feature focuses on extra, smaller language points that come out of a reading or listening. Go through the examples and then the rules.

Highlight that:

- you mustn't separate the *more*, etc. from the adjective / adverb it goes with, e.g. *The more interesting the book is, the more slowly I read.* NOT ~~The more the book is interesting…~~

- occasionally we just use the two comparatives, e.g. *the sooner the better; the more the merrier*, especially when one of them is *better*.

Now focus on sentences 1–4 and elicit the first one from the class (*The **more you study**, the **more you learn***) and write the answer on the board.

Get Sts to do the other three.

1.18 Play the audio for Sts to listen and check.

Check answers. For 3, you could also accept *The more time you have, the more slowly you do things.*

22 **1B**

1.18
1 The more you study, the more you learn.
2 The more coffee I drink, the worse I sleep.
3 The more time you have, the slower you do things.
4 The fitter you are, the better you feel.

EXTRA SUPPORT Play the audio again, pausing after each sentence for Sts to listen and repeat. Tell them to try to copy the stress and rise–fall intonation.

h Focus on the task and give Sts time to complete each sentence. Monitor and help Sts, correcting any errors with the comparatives.

Get Sts to compare with a partner, and then elicit some ideas.

Possible answers
1 …the more I spend. / the more I save.
2 …the better I feel. / the worse I feel. / the more I do.
3 …the more difficult they are to understand.
4 …the thinner I get. / the hungrier I am. / the more bad-tempered I am.
5 …the more I enjoy it. / the easier it gets.
6 …the fitter i get. / the more I like it.

EXTRA IDEA Ask Sts if there are any common expressions in their language with this structure (like *the sooner the better*) and get them to work out how to say them in English.

5 VOCABULARY compound adjectives

a Tell Sts to look at the two extracts from the *A walk in the forest* listening. Give them time to work out what the missing words might be.

EXTRA CHALLENGE Elicit some ideas before playing the audio.

b **1.19** Play the audio for Sts to listen and check. Check answers.

1 minded   2 sufficient

1.19
1 If there was no fence around the house, it means you are very open-minded, and welcome new ideas.
2 If you hardly got wet at all, it means that you depend less on your friends and are more self-sufficient.

Now elicit whether the compound adjectives in **a** have a positive or negative meaning.

They both have a positive meaning.

Finally, focus on the **Compound adjectives** box and go through it with the class.

c **1.20** Play the audio for Sts to listen and decide which word has the main stress.
Check the answer.

The second word

1.20
See compound adjectives in Student's Book on *p.13*

EXTRA CHALLENGE Elicit the answer before playing the audio.

EXTRA SUPPORT After checking the answer, play the audio again for Sts to listen and repeat.

d Put Sts in pairs and get them to look at each compound adjective in **c** and then decide what it means and whether it describes a positive or negative characteristic.

Check answers. You may want to point out to Sts that *open-minded* and *narrow-minded* are opposites. *Laid-back* and *easy-going* are very similar in meaning: *laid-back* (informal) = calm and relaxed about everything; *easy-going* = relaxed and happy to accept things without worrying or getting angry.

You may also want to mention that depending on the context, some of the positive ones can be negative, e.g. if you say *He's a bit too laid-back*. Explain that *strong-willed*, though often negative, can also be used in a positive sense, depending on the context.

Positive
easy-going = relaxed and happy to accept things without worrying or getting angry
good-tempered = cheerful and not easily made angry
laid-back = calm and relaxed
open-minded = willing to listen to, think about or accept different ideas
well-balanced = sensible and emotionally in control
well-behaved = behaving in a way that other people think is polite or correct

Negative
absent-minded = tending to forget things, perhaps because you are not thinking about what is around you, but about something else
bad-tempered = often angry; in an angry mood
big-headed = having a very high opinion of how important and clever you are
narrow-minded = not willing to listen to new ideas or to the opinions of others
self-centred = tending to think only about yourself and not thinking about the needs or feelings of other people
strong-willed = determined to do what you want to do, even if other people advise you not to
tight-fisted = not willing to spend or give much money
two-faced = not sincere

EXTRA CHALLENGE Elicit a sentence to describe each of the adjectives, e.g. *A person who is bad-tempered gets angry easily, often about small things*, etc.

e Focus on the **Modifiers** box and go through it with the class. Highlight that *pretty* is more informal than *quite*, and that *rather* is more often used with negative adjectives, e.g. *rather self-centred*.

Now focus on the task and example, showing that Sts need to explain why they have chosen a particular characteristic for someone they know.

Give Sts a few minutes to think of people with the characteristics listed in *Do you know somebody who is…?*

Then put Sts in pairs and get them to tell each other about the people they have chosen.

Monitor and help if necessary.

Get some feedback from various pairs.

EXTRA SUPPORT You could choose one or two characteristics and tell the class about two people you know.

1B

1 Colloquial English Talking about… getting a job

Lesson plan

This is the first of five **Colloquial English** lessons featuring interviews and conversations commissioned and filmed specially for *English File*. In the first section, **The Interview**, there is an interview related to one or more of the topics in the preceding Files. The interviewees (Ryan Judd, Julia Eccleshare, Candida Brady, Simon Callow, and George Tannenbaum) all have unique first-hand experience in their field and offer interesting perspectives on what they do, as well as giving Sts an opportunity to engage with authentic, unscripted speech. In the second part of each Colloquial English lesson, **The Conversation**, there is an authentic unedited conversation between three people about an aspect of the same topic. The focus in this part is to encourage Sts to become more confident about following a conversation at natural speed. It is often hard for Sts to follow a conversation on audio when three (or more) people are speaking amongst themselves, and having these conversations on video will enable Sts to follow more easily who is saying what, and to focus on aspects of language related to such conversations, e.g. emphasizing a point, responding to an idea, etc. This part ends with Sts discussing further questions related to the topic in small groups. We suggest that Sts watch the video a final time with the script or subtitles, either in class after each section or at home. This will let them see what they did / didn't understand, and help them to further develop their awareness of features of spoken English such as elision, false starts, discourse markers, hesitation devices, etc.

In this lesson, the person interviewed is Ryan Judd, a recruitment advisor who works in Human Resources, and the focus is on formal language.

Then, in The Conversation, Sts watch three people discussing whether it is OK to slightly exaggerate on your CV when applying for a job. Sts then discuss this question as well as a couple of other questions related to the topic, focusing on ways to emphasize their ideas.

Teacher can find all the video for these lessons on the *Teacher's Resource Centre*. Sts can find all the video content on *Online Practice*.

These lessons can be used with *Class DVD* or *Classroom Presentation Tool*.

More materials

For teachers

Teacher's Resource Centre
Video Colloquial English 1
Quick Test 1
File 1 Test

For students

Workbook Colloquial English 1
          Can you remember? 1
Online Practice Colloquial English 1
                 Check your progress

OPTIONAL LEAD-IN (BOOKS CLOSED)

Ask Sts to brainstorm their top three tips for a friend who has a job interview the next day.

Elicit ideas and write them on the board.

1 ▶ THE INTERVIEW Part 1

a Books open. Focus on the photo and the biographical information about Ryan Judd. Either read it out loud or give Sts time to read it.

Do the question as a whole-class activity and elicit / explain that the HR department in a company deals with employing and training people.

b Focus on the task and go through the **Glossary** with the class.

Give Sts time to read 1–8.

Play the video (**Part 1**) once the whole way through for Sts to tick the things Ryan said.

Get Sts to compare with a partner, and then check answers.

EXTRA SUPPORT Before playing the video, go through the listening scripts and decide if you need to pre-teach / check any lexis to help Sts when they listen.

> Sts should have ticked: 1, 2, 3, 4, 6, 7, and 8.

I = interviewer, R = Ryan Judd
Part 1

I What's the first thing you're looking for in a candidate for a job?

R The first thing you're looking for with a job candidate is enthusiasm for the role. You're also looking for them to demonstrate experience…er…relevant to the position.

I How do you get candidates to relax in the interview?

R It's important to engage with the candidate straight away, so when you collect them from reception or from the…the front of the building – whatever it may be – you want to kind of greet them in a friendly manner. You want to ask them some general questions – just talking about their journey into the interview or, um, the weather, or have they been to the city before.

I And during the interview?

R During an interview, once it has commenced, I will always try to start the interview with some general questions, just to allow the candidate to talk about themselves, to talk about their CV, their background. Um, and often when a candidate is talking about something they know, which is themselves and what they've been doing, um, they're able to settle down much more quickly and have an element of confidence around…er…what they're talking.

I Is it important for candidates to ask the interviewer questions, and if so, what kind of questions should candidates ask?

R Questions can be related to anything, so I personally would encourage candidates to ask questions rated to any aspect of employment, and most recruiters would welcome that sort of interaction as an opportunity to actually give a little bit more information about the company.

I Is it OK for candidates to ask about the money or the salary at the interview?

R Of course, and candidates should be honest and realistic about their expectations, too. An interview is an appropriate environment to ask such a question, especially if salary, or…er… salary banding, was not identified in the job advert.

I How important are CVs and covering letters?

R CVs are very important to a recruiter because it actually provides an overview of a candidate's background, their employment,

24 **CE1**

what they've been doing to date. But a cover letter can actually be more important, because that's where a candidate will actually list and identify how they meet the criteria for the post, so it allows a candidate to be very specific about demonstrating what skills and experience they have that would be relevant – and often, that skill and experience may be missed on a CV when you're looking at a wider career history.

I What's the worst thing a job candidate can do when they're applying for a job?

R First thing is, obviously, to make mistakes on their application – um, that's always viewed negatively, depending on the role that they're applying for. Um, also coming to an interview late, coming to an interview unprepared.

c Focus on the three questions and give Sts time, in pairs, to see if they can remember any of the answers.

Play the video again the whole way through.

You could get Sts to compare with a partner before checking answers.

EXTRA SUPPORT You could pause the video after each question has been answered and, in pairs, get Sts to compare orally what they have understood.

> 1 He asks some general questions about their journey to the interview, the weather, or if they have been to Oxford before.
> 2 He asks some general questions about the candidate, their CV, their background.
> 3 Information which shows how the candidate meets the criteria for the post, including specific skills and experience they have that is relevant

EXTRA SUPPORT If there's time, you could get Sts to watch again with subtitles, so they can see exactly what they understood / didn't understand. Translate / Explain any new words or phrases.

d Either do this as a whole-class activity, or put Sts in pairs and then get some feedback.

▶ Part 2

a Focus on the task and play the video (**Part 2**) once the whole way through for Sts to answer the question.

Check answer.s

> One candidate thought they were being interviewed for a very different job.
> One candidate started eating a chocolate bar during the interview.
> One candidate arrived in their tennis clothes.

Part 2

I Can you give us an example of some of the more difficult interviews you've been involved in?

R I've been in interviews where candidates haven't been prepared and have not been able to, from the start, answer some of the questions. Um, one particular situation was when a candidate actually thought they were being interviewed for something completely different. Um, so again, you have to actually think how do you deal with that situation – do you stop the interview or do you carry on?

I Anything else that has surprised you during an interview?

R There was another situation where…er…a candidate actually produced food during the interview. Er…in the middle of answering a question, they stopped and rummaged in their bag to pull out a KitKat, um, which took both myself and the interviewing manager by surprise. We did ask and enquire as to what she was doing…er…at which point she actually advised she was a diabetic and just felt at that particular moment, um, that she just needed a little…er…something to eat to calm things –

which was absolutely fine, but again, during the interview, when she hadn't announced that's why she was doing it, it was a bit of a surprise.

I How important is the way a candidate dresses for an interview?

R A candidate's dress for interview is important because it shows how serious they take the situation. Um, however, I would always recommend that candidates would come to interview, um, in a dress that is appropriate for the role they're applying for. In today's modern…er…recruitment…er…environment, it's not always necessary for a…a guy to wear a suit to an interview. However, you would expect to see a shirt, you would expect to see a blazer, you would expect…expect to see appropriate footwear, and the same for a…a lady as well – um, certain clothes, certain types of footwear, would be inappropriate to come into an interview and may set a perception of that candidate which is perhaps incorrect.

I Have you ever had an interview with someone who was dressed very inappropriately?

R I had an interview on one occasion where a candidate actually arrived in tennis gear – a white T-shirt and shorts. They'd literally come straight from the tennis court and they had simply forgotten the interview was on that day, had suddenly had the reminder that actually they were due to be at the interview, so they thought they would come anyway as they were. Um, I did see the candidate and they were actually very impressive; we just had to move past the…the clothing aspect, but actually it was quite funny and allowed a real opportunity to engage with that particular candidate from the start.

I Did that person get the job?

R No, they didn't.

b Focus on the four questions and the **Glossary**. Now give Sts time, in pairs, to see if they can remember any of the answers.

Play the video again the whole way through.

Get Sts to compare with their partner, and then check answers.

EXTRA SUPPORT You could pause the video at appropriate places and, in pairs, get Sts to compare orally what they have understood.

> 1 He could have stopped the interview or carried on.
> 2 She was diabetic and needed to eat something to calm down.
> 3 Clothes that are appropriate for the role that they are applying for.
> 4 He had forgotten that he had the interview and had come directly from the tennis court in his tennis clothes. He didn't get the job.

EXTRA SUPPORT If there's time, you could get Sts to watch again with subtitles, so they can see exactly what they understood / didn't understand. Translate / Explain any new words or phrases.

c Either do this as a whole-class activity, or put Sts in pairs and then get some feedback.

▶ Part 3

a Focus on the task and give Sts time to read the two gapped questions.

Play the video (**Part 3**) once the whole way through for Sts to complete the task.

Check answers. Make sure Sts understand the situation in 2.

CE1 25

> 1 How would you describe **Facebook** to your **grandmother**?
> 2 Would you rather fight a horse-sized **duck** or a hundred duck-sized **horses**?

Part 3

I What can you tell us about extreme interviewing, that is, asking candidates very strange questions like *What dinosaur would you be?*

R OK. Um, extreme interviewing is a technique used by recruiters to put the candidate in a situation that they may not have been in before, um, or to put them…give them a scenario where they have to think quickly, where they have to digest information, where they perhaps have to problem-solve before giving an answer.

I Have you used it yourself?

R It's not something that I have direct experience of, but I am aware of some of the techniques that are used and some of the questions that could be used. Um, I was reading recently about, um, extreme interviewing techniques used for an insurance company. They asked candidates to describe if…they asked candidates during the interview how they would describe Facebook to their grandmother. What the recruiter was looking for was for that candidate to display an element of, um, technical skills and technical awareness, also to display communication skills and how they would explain Facebook to an audience or to somebody who doesn't understand modern technology or modern social media.

I Do you have any others?

R One I was reading about recently was posed to candidates during an interview…er…where they were looking to assess a candidate's ability to multitask. The candidates were asked whether they would want to fight a horse-sized duck or a hundred duck-sized horses. Depending on the answer – one or a hundred – that would potentially dictate whether that candidate was most comfortable multitasking or dealing with one…er… situation or one objective at a time.

I What would your answer to that question have been?

R I…when I read it, I had to re-read it four times, and that's just me reading it. In an interview, I would have had to have asked for that question to be repeated, and I'm not even sure if I would have been able to give an immediate response, because I would still be trying to understand what exactly they were asking of me. I guess for me personally, when I'd thought about it, I would have said one horse-sized duck, um, but that would potentially mean that I'm not able to multitask, so…!

b Focus on the task and give Sts time to read sentences 1–6. Remind them that they need to say why the F sentences are false.

Play the video again the whole way through for Sts to do the task.

Check answers.

EXTRA SUPPORT You could pause the video at the relevant places and, in pairs, get Sts to compare what they have understood before marking the sentences true or false.

> 1 T
> 2 F ('It's not something that I have direct experience of…')
> 3 T
> 4 F (It was to see if candidates had the ability to multitask.)
> 5 F (He would have had to have asked for the question to be repeated, and he probably wouldn't have been able to answer immediately.)
> 6 T

EXTRA SUPPORT If there's time, you could get Sts to watch again with subtitles, so they can see exactly what they understood / didn't understand. Translate / Explain any new words or phrases.

c Either do this as a whole-class activity, or put Sts in pairs and then get some feedback. You could also tell Sts your own answers. With a show of hands, you could find out how many Sts are good multitaskers according to the extreme interview question.

2 ▶ LOOKING AT LANGUAGE

This exercise focuses on an aspect of spoken language which is illustrated by the person being interviewed. Focus on the **Formal language** box and go through it with the class.

Now focus on the task and give Sts time to read extracts 1–7.

Play the video, pausing after each extract to give Sts time to write.

If necessary, play again and then check answers.

EXTRA CHALLENGE Ask Sts if they can remember any of the highlighted words or phrases before they listen to the extracts.

> 1 demonstrate   2 commenced   3 viewed   4 announced
> 5 appropriate footwear, a lady   6 am aware of   7 response

1 …you're also looking for them to demonstrate experience relevant to the position.
2 During an interview, once it has commenced, I will always try to start the interview with some general questions…
3 First thing is, obviously, to make mistakes on their application – um, that's always viewed negatively…
4 …but again, during the interview, when she hadn't announced that's why she was doing it, it was a bit of a surprise.
5 …you would expect…expect to see appropriate footwear. And the same for a…a lady as well…
6 It's not something that I have direct experience of, but I am aware of some of the techniques that they use…
7 …I'm not even sure if I would have been able to give an immediate response…

3 ▶ THE CONVERSATION

a Focus on the photo and tell Sts they are going to watch the three people answer the question, which they will see on the screen. Focus on the task and make sure Sts understand what they have to do. Make sure Sts understand *to exaggerate* (= to make sth seem larger, better, worse, or more important than it really is).

❗ Don't ask Sts their opinion yet, as they will be discussing this later in **c**.

Now play the video once the whole way through for Sts to write the initials in the appropriate place on the line.

Check answers by drawing the line on the board and writing the initials in the correct place.

EXTRA SUPPORT Before playing the video, go through the listening script and decide if you need to pre-teach / check any lexis to help Sts when they listen.

> S
> D
> A

26 **CE1**

Interviewer   When you're applying for a job, do you think it's OK to slightly exaggerate on your CV?

Alice
I think it's a terrible, terrible idea to even slightly exaggerate because I think it will always come back to hurt you. I think being as honest as you can – I think it doesn't matter if you, if you can't do something if you say 'I'm willing to learn, I'm a good learner, I, like, I have these skills, I'm really open to learning some new ones', but to go into an interview or, or write on your CV. Um, 'I can speak, you know, a very average amount of French' when you don't know anything, that… you might find yourself in a situation where you've wasted their time and you've just made yourself look really, really silly. I think it's a terrible idea and I would feel really uncomfortable – um, I'd say I'm quite an honest person so, if I can't do something, I'll just say it.

Sarah
I've definitely exaggerated on a CV! Um, I think you have to be – I mean, I would still consider myself an honest person and I'm not going to say I speak fluent Chinese when I don't – but I think I've done, I've done it when it wouldn't be an essential skill for the job, maybe just to pad – well, not even pad things out because I'm talking very small exaggerations here, but, where it's more for the optional side of things – just to make it look a bit more…like, I might put a language on there that, yeah I can read a postcard or I can understand an airport announcement, but if you asked me to actually speak it…but I wouldn't do that if I knew the job was going to require me *speaking* that language because, like you say, you're going to be potentially in a very awkward situation if that ever comes up, um, and I've had, I have had job interviews where they suddenly start speaking to you in another language to check, to check whether you speak the language or not, so…but I think, I think white lies are OK, personally.

Debbie
I swing between both. Um, you shouldn't outright lie because you *will* get caught out and if it's – a lot of the times it could cost a company a lot of money if they employ you to do a job and then when you turn up, you cannot do it or to the ability that you have told them you could, and there's a lot of people to be affected. So, you shouldn't lie because you will be asked to use it. But…the question didn't say where on the CV, so I agree with you because when you're talking about hobbies, that is to see what sort of person you are, whether they would like you to work with them, so if you're quite a boring person and you don't have many hobbies, I think you should exaggerate a few to make yourself look a little bit more interesting. So, I cook every single night, but that doesn't mean I enjoy cooking, but I'm happy to put down that I love cooking.

b Focus on the task and give Sts time to read sentence beginnings 1–6 and endings A–F.

Play the video again, pausing after each speaker to give Sts time to match their two sentence halves.

Get Sts to compare with a partner, and then play again if necessary.

Check answers.

> **1** D   **2** B   **3** A   **4** F   **5** E   **6** C

EXTRA SUPPORT   If there's time, you could get Sts to watch again with subtitles, so they can see exactly what they understood / didn't understand. Translate / Explain any new words or phrases.

c Either do the questions as a whole-class activity, or put Sts in pairs and then get some feedback.

d Focus on the task and give Sts time to read extracts 1–3.
Play the video for Sts to watch and complete the gaps.
Get Sts to compare with a partner, and then play again if necessary.
Check answers.

> **1** terrible terrible   **2** really really   **3** definitely

> **1** I think it's a terrible, terrible idea to even slightly exaggerate…
> **2** …you might find yourself in a situation where you've wasted their time and you've just made yourself look really, really silly.
> **3** I've definitely exaggerated on a CV.

Highlight that we often repeat an adjective or adverb to be more emphatic. We can also use *definitely* to stress that we are sure about something.

e Focus on the question and the extracts and give Sts time to read them.
Play the video for Sts to watch and complete the gaps.
Get Sts to compare with a partner, and then check answers.

> **1** speaking   **2** will

Now ask Sts what the speakers do to make the missing word more emphatic.

> They give the word extra stress.

> **1** …but I wouldn't do that if I knew the job was going to require me *speaking* that language…
> **2** …you shouldn't outright lie because you *will* get caught out and a lot of the times it could cost a company a lot of money…

EXTRA SUPPORT   Play the extracts in **d** and **e** again and get Sts to try to copy each speaker's stress and intonation.

f Put Sts in small groups of three if possible. Focus on the questions and check Sts understand what they mean. Then set a time limit for Sts to discuss them.

Monitor and help, and encourage them to use the different strategies focused on in **d** and **e** to emphasize what they think.

Get feedback from various groups. You could also tell the class what you think.

CE1   27

2A Doctor, doctor!

G present perfect simple and continuous
V illnesses and injuries
P /ʃ/, /dʒ/, /tʃ/, and /k/

Lesson plan

The topic of the lesson is medicine.

The first half of the lesson starts with a quiz on first aid – the Sts' own knowledge is tested and discussed. Sts then expand their vocabulary of medical words to describe symptoms, illnesses, and treatment. This is followed by a pronunciation focus on consonant sounds. Then Sts listen to three speakers talking about a time when someone needed first aid. Finally, Sts discuss whether they have ever received or given first aid, and what they could do in certain emergency situations.

The second half of the lesson starts with a light-hearted conversation between a doctor and a difficult patient, which leads into the grammar focus where Sts revise and extend their knowledge of the present perfect simple and continuous. These verb forms can be problematic for many Sts because of L1 interference. After practising the grammar, Sts read an article from *The Sunday Times* on cyberchondriacs, people who obsessively search for medical information online. Sts focus on summarizing each paragraph and on medical phrases, finishing with a discussion about hyperchondria and cyberchondria, and typical health concerns. Finally, the grammar and lexis are consolidated in the Writing Bank, where Sts write an informal email explaining to a friend why they haven't been well and saying what they have been doing recently.

More materials

For teachers

Photocopiables

Grammar present perfect simple and continuous *p.164*
Communicative Ask the doctor *p.194* (instructions *p.184*)
Vocabulary Illnesses and injuries *p.218*
(instructions *p.214*)

For students

Workbook 2A

Online Practice 2A

OPTIONAL LEAD-IN – THE QUOTE

Write the quote at the top of *p.16* on the board and the name of the person who said it, or get Sts to open their books and read it.

You could tell Sts that Erma Bombeck (1927–1996) was a journalist and author of 15 books. She was a popular humorist in the USA and Canada.

Ask Sts what they think the quote means and if they find it funny. You could ask them if there is anything else about a doctor or his / her surgery that would make them not want to go there.

1 VOCABULARY illnesses and injuries

a Focus on the title of the quiz, *Medical myths or first-aid facts?* Elicit the meaning of *myths* (= sth that many people believe, but that does not exist or is false) and *first aid* (= simple medical treatment that is given to sb before a doctor comes or before the person can be taken to a hospital).

Put Sts in pairs and give them time to read all six questions in the quiz and to decide what the highlighted words and phrases mean.

! Stress that Sts shouldn't answer the questions until they completely understand all the options.

Check answers by explaining / translating / miming, or by using the illustrations.

> **running water** = water from the tap
> **damp cloth** = slightly wet cloth
> **rub** (v) = to press two surfaces against each other and move them backwards and forwards
> **press** (v) = to push sth closely and firmly against sth
> **tip** (v) = to move so that one end or side is higher than the other
> **pinch** (v) = to hold sth tightly between the thumb and finger
> **bandage** (n) = a strip of cloth used for tying around a part of the body that has been hurt, in order to protect or support it

Now tell Sts to look at all six questions again with their partner and to mark whether options a, b, and c are myths (*M*) or facts (*F*). You might want to pre-teach / check some lexis, e.g. *sprained ankle*, *hypothermia*, etc.

Then get feedback from various pairs, but don't tell them yet if they are correct.

EXTRA SUPPORT Read the introduction as a class, making sure Sts understand the aim of the quiz.

b Put Sts in pairs, **A** and **B**, and tell them to go to **Communication Medical myths or first-aid facts?**, **A** on *p.106*, **B** on *p.111*, to each check the answers to half of the quiz.

When Sts have finished reading, ask them to close their books or to cover the answers and look at the illustrations on *p.16*, and tell their partner what the correct answer is for each one.

Check answers as a whole class, and find out how many Sts got the correct answers.

> **1** a and c are myths. **2** a is a myth. **3** a and b are myths.
> **4** a is a myth. **5** c is a myth. **6** c is a myth.

Finally, deal with any new vocabulary, and elicit or model the pronunciation.

c Tell Sts to go to **Vocabulary Bank Illnesses and injuries** on *p.152*.

28 2A

Vocabulary notes
Minor illnesses and conditions

Some of the words may be similar in Sts' L1, e.g. *diarrhoea*, but the pronunciation is likely to be quite different.

You might want to point out that *cough* is both a noun and a verb.

Highlight that *be sick = vomit*, but *feel sick = want to vomit*. *Sick* is also sometimes used as a synonym for *ill*, especially in American English. Also highlight the meaning of *swallow*.

You may want to point out that the adjective *swollen* comes from the verb *swell* (swelled, swollen).

Highlight also that *ache, hurt*, and *pain* can all be used to describe the same thing, e.g. *I have a pain in my back. / My back hurts. / My back aches*. There is a slight difference between *ache* and *hurt*: *ache* = a continuous, dull pain; *hurts* = often stronger (especially sudden) pain, e.g. *Ouch! That hurts! Ache* is used both as a noun and a verb, whereas *hurt* is normally used as a verb, and *pain* is normally used as a noun.

Phrasal verbs connected with illness

Other phrasal verbs related to illness that you may want to teach are *come down with* (e.g. *the flu*), *break out* (e.g. *an epidemic*), or *trip over*.

Focus on the title of the **Vocabulary Bank** and explain / elicit the difference between *illness* and *injury*:
– *illness* (n) = the general term for the state of being unwell, e.g. *My uncle has a serious illness*.
– *injury* (n) = harm done to an animal or person's body, e.g. in an accident

Focus on **1 Minor illnesses and conditions** and check that Sts know the meaning of *minor* /ˈmaɪnə/ (= not very large, important, or serious). Get Sts to do **a** individually or in pairs.

🔊 **2.1** Now do **b**. Play the audio for Sts to listen and check.

Check answers.

🔊 **2.1**
Illnesses and injuries
1 Minor illnesses and conditions, b
9 a cough
6 a headache
1 a rash
4 a temperature
2 sunburn
8 She's being sick. / She's vomiting.
10 She's sneezing.
3 Her ankle's swollen.
7 Her back hurts. / Her back aches.
5 Her finger's bleeding.

Now either use the audio to drill the pronunciation of the words and phrases, or model and drill them yourself. Give further practice of any words or phrases your Sts find difficult to pronounce.

Now get Sts to do **c** individually or in pairs.

🔊 **2.2** Now do **d**. Play the audio for Sts to listen and check.

Check answers. You may also want to teach *he has a runny nose* as another symptom of a cold.

🔊 **2.2**
d
1 B He has a sore throat. It hurts when he talks or swallows food.
2 D He has diarrhoea. He's been to the toilet five times this morning.
3 E He feels sick. He feels that he's going to vomit.
4 C He's fainted. It's so hot in the room that he's lost consciousness.
5 H He has a blister on his foot. He's been walking in uncomfortable shoes.
6 F He has a cold. He's sneezing a lot and he has a cough.
7 A He has flu. He has a temperature and he aches all over.
8 G He feels dizzy. He feels that everything is spinning round.
9 I He's cut himself. He's bleeding.

Give further practice of any words or phrases your Sts find difficult to pronounce.

EXTRA SUPPORT Tell Sts to cover the words / sentences in **a**, look at the pictures, and see if they can remember them.

Focus on **2 Injuries and more serious conditions** and make sure Sts know the meaning of *symptom* /ˈsɪmptəm/ (= a change in your body or mind that shows that you are not healthy). Get Sts to do **a** individually or in pairs.

🔊 **2.3** Now do **b**. Play the audio for Sts to listen and check. Check answers.

🔊 **2.3**
2 Injuries and more serious conditions
1 C He's unconscious. He's breathing, but his eyes are closed and he can't hear or feel anything.
2 G He's had an allergic reaction. He was stung by a wasp and now he has a rash and has difficulty breathing.
3 B He's sprained his ankle. He fell badly and now it's swollen.
4 D He has high blood pressure. It's one hundred and eighty over one hundred and forty.
5 E He has food poisoning. He ate some prawns that were off.
6 F He's choking. He was eating a steak and a piece got stuck in his throat.
7 A He's burnt himself. He spilt some boiling water on his hand.

Give further practice of any words or phrases your Sts find difficult to pronounce.

Focus on the **Common treatments for…** box and go through it with the class. You might want to point out that *bandage* here is a verb, but it can also be a noun. You could also elicit or model the pronunciation of *sprained*, *allergic*, and *antihistamine* /ˌæntiˈhɪstəmiːn/.

Finally, focus on **Activation** and tell Sts to cover the illnesses or conditions in **1a** and (1–9) in **1c** as well as the injuries or conditions (1–7) in **2a**, look at the pictures, causes, or symptoms, and say the injuries or conditions.

Now focus on **3 Phrasal verbs connected with illness** and get Sts to do **a** individually or in pairs.

🔊 **2.4** Now do **b**. Play the audio for Sts to listen and check.

Check answers, making sure Sts know the meaning of the new words / phrases.

🔊 **2.4**
3 Phrasal verbs connected with illness
1 *pass out* means *faint*
2 *lie down* means *put your body in a horizontal position*
3 *throw up* means *vomit, be sick*
4 *get over* means *get better, recover from something*
5 *come round* means *become conscious again*

2A 29

Now either use the audio to drill the pronunciation of the phrasal verbs, or model and drill them yourself. Give further practice of any words or phrases your Sts find difficult to pronounce

EXTRA SUPPORT Tell Sts to cover 1–5 and try to remember the meaning of the phrasal verbs.

EXTRA IDEA Sts can take it in turns to test each other. Sts **B** close their books and Sts **A** define or explain a word for **B** to try and remember, e.g. *What does the phrasal verb 'to pass out' mean?* After a few minutes, Sts can swap roles.
In a monolingual class, Sts could also test each other by saying the word in their L1 for their partner to say in English.

Tell Sts to go back to the main lesson **2A**.

EXTRA SUPPORT If you think Sts need more practice, you may want to give them the **Vocabulary** photocopiable activity at this point.

d Do this as a whole-class activity.

> **Possible answers**
> **eating out:** an allergic reaction, food-poisoning, diarrhoea, feeling sick, vomiting, stomach ache, choking
> **hiking in the mountains:** a blister, hypothermia, a sprained ankle, sunburn, be stung by an insect
> **doing sport:** backache, a sprained ankle, a swollen ankle, a blister
> **visiting a tropical country:** sunburn, be stung by an insect

2 PRONUNCIATION /ʃ/, /dʒ/, /tʃ/, and /k/

> **Pronunciation notes**
> **English sounds**
> Sts who have used previous levels of *English File* should recognize the sound pictures and be fairly confident with phonetic symbols. If your Sts are new to the series, you will need to explain to them that the sound pictures show the phonetic symbols and give a clear example of a word with the target sound to help them to remember the pronunciation of the symbol. There is one for each of the 44 sounds of English. Sts will see the chart and more example words when they go to the **Sound Bank** in **d**.

a Focus on the four sound pictures and elicit the words and consonant sounds (*shower* /ʃ/, *jazz* /dʒ/, *chess* /tʃ/, *key* /k/).

Then give Sts time to put the words in the correct column. You might want to tell them that this kind of exercise is easier if they say the words aloud to themselves.

Get Sts to compare with a partner.

b 🔊 **2.5** Play the audio for Sts to listen and check.

Check answers. You might want to remind Sts that *temperature* /ˈtemprətʃə/ has three syllables (the second *e* is silent).

🔊 **2.5**
shower /ʃ/   infection, pressure, rash, unconscious
jazz /dʒ/   allergic, bandage, emergency, injury
chess /tʃ/   choking, temperature
key /k/   ache, sick, stomach

Now play it again, pausing after each group of words for Sts to listen and repeat.

Then repeat the activity, eliciting responses from individual Sts.

Finally, get Sts, in pairs, to practise saying the words.

c Do this as a whole-class activity, or put Sts in pairs and then check answers.

> **1** *ti* (before *on*), *ss*, *sh*, *ci*; the most common is *sh*
> **2** /dʒ/
> **3** /k/ and /tʃ/; /tʃ/ is more common

d Now tell Sts to go to the **Sound Bank** on *pp.166–167*. Explain that here they can find all the sounds of English and their phonetic symbols, and also the typical spellings for these sounds, plus some more irregular ones.

Focus on the four sounds that Sts have just been working on and the typical spellings. Highlight that they have to be careful with *ch* because although it is usually pronounced /tʃ/, it can also be /k/, as in *ache*, or occasionally /ʃ/, as in *machine*. You may also want to point out when checking rule 2 that *g* before *y* can be /dʒ/ or /g/, e.g. *gym* /dʒɪm/ or *gynaecology* /ˌgaɪnəˈkɒlədʒi/.
Tell Sts to go back to the main lesson **2A**.

EXTRA SUPPORT If these sounds are difficult for your Sts, it will help to show them the mouth position. You could model this yourself or use the Sound Bank videos on the *Teacher's Resource Centre*.

e 🔊 **2.6** Focus on the task and give Sts a few moments to look at all the words.

EXTRA SUPPORT Let Sts use dictionaries, and get them to focus on the phonetics to see if the words are pronounced the same in English as in their L1.

Get Sts to compare with a partner.
Play the audio for Sts to listen and check.

EXTRA CHALLENGE You could also pause the audio before each word and get Sts to tell you how they think the word is pronounced, and then play the word.

Check answers and make sure that Sts know what all the words mean. Elicit or model pronunciation.

> **ch**olesterol = /k/   indi**gesti**on = /dʒ/, /tʃ/
> in**jecti**on = /dʒ/, /ʃ/   opera**ti**on = /ʃ/   s**cratch** = /k/, /tʃ/
> sur**ge**on = /dʒ/   syrin**ge** = /dʒ/
>
> **cholesterol** /kəˈlestərɒl/ = a substance found in blood, fat, and most tissues of the body. Too much cholesterol can cause heart disease.
> **indigestion** /ˌɪndɪˈdʒestʃən/ = pain caused by difficulty in digesting food
> **injection** /ɪnˈdʒekʃn/ = an act of injecting sb with a drug or other substance
> **operation** /ˌɒpəˈreɪʃn/ = the process of cutting open a part of a person's body in order to remove or repair a damaged part
> **scratch** /skrætʃ/ = cut or damage your skin slightly with sth sharp
> **surgeon** /ˈsɜːdʒən/ = a doctor who is trained to perform surgery (= medical operations that involve cutting open a person's body)
> **syringe** /sɪˈrɪndʒ/ = a plastic or glass tube with a long hollow needle that is used for putting drugs, etc., into a person's body or for taking a small amount of blood from a person

🔊 **2.6**
See words in Student's Book on *p.17*

Finally, play the audio again, pausing after each word for Sts to listen and repeat.

3 LISTENING & SPEAKING understanding
an anecdote – where they were, who with, what happened, how they felt

a Focus on the task and make sure that Sts understand the situation.

Put Sts in pairs and get them to tell their partner what they would do and why.

Get some feedback from various pairs. You could also have a class vote with a show of hands for each reaction, or simply tell the class what you would do.

b 🔊 **2.7** Focus on the task and give Sts time to quickly read the extracts.

Play the audio once the whole way through for Sts to listen and complete the gaps.

Get Sts to compare with a partner, and then play again if necessary.

Check answers. You might want to check Sts know the meaning of *pavement* and *stretcher*.

> 1 pulse, having a heart attack
> 2 calm her down, in shock
> 3 ambulance turned up
> 4 tripped and fell
> 5 was still conscious
> 6 very painful
> 7 fell backwards
> 8 called an ambulance
> 9 took him away

🔊 **2.7**
Jane
1 …he didn't have a pulse, so I thought he was probably having a heart attack.
2 …he took her to one side to calm her down, because obviously she was in shock.
3 I kept going until the ambulance turned up…
Daniel
4 …an old lady stepped off the pavement in front of me and she tripped and fell into the road.
5 She'd fallen heavily, but she was still conscious…
6 It was obviously an effort for her to sit up, it was very painful…
Alison
7 Then all of a sudden, he stopped walking and fell backwards…
8 Some teenagers in the queue called an ambulance…
9 …then they put him on a stretcher and took him away.

c 🔊 **2.8** Tell Sts they are now going to listen to the stories and must make a note of whether the speaker helped or not when the incident happened, and why. Make sure Sts know what an *incident* is (= sth that happens, especially sth unusual or unpleasant).

Now play the audio, pausing after each speaker to give Sts time to answer the questions.

Get Sts to compare with a partner, and then check answers.

EXTRA SUPPORT Read through the script and decide if you need to pre-teach any new lexis before Sts listen.

> **Jane:** Yes because she used to be a nurse.
> **Daniel:** Yes because it happened right in front of him.
> **Alison:** No because she didn't know what to do.

🔊 **2.8**
(script in Student's Book on *p.123*)
Jane
So, my husband and I were out shopping in our local town, and I saw a man lying on the ground. He was just a stranger, not someone I knew, and his wife was there, standing by him. And I used to be a nurse in A&E, so I went straight up to him to see if I could help. He was a bit blue; I felt his pulse and he didn't have a pulse, so I thought he was probably having a heart attack. I felt quite calm because I knew what to do – um, I started doing cardiac massage – you know, putting your hand on the chest and pressing down fast and at regular intervals – and my husband talked to the man's wife; he took her to one side to calm her down, because obviously she was in shock. I kept going until the ambulance turned up, and the man was still alive then, and they took him to hospital. I was really pleased that I could do something.
Daniel
So, I was cycling to work one morning, and just as I was coming round the corner, an old lady stepped off the pavement in front of me and she tripped and fell into the road. I just managed not to cycle into her, and I dropped my bike and I went over to see if she was OK. And it was busy in the street, as the shops were just opening and lots of people were around. She'd fallen heavily, but she was still conscious, and she told us she was sure she'd broken her arm. Somebody stopped the traffic, and I helped move her to the pavement, somebody else went and got a chair from one of the shops, and someone else called an ambulance, and we stayed with her until it came. It was obviously an effort for her to sit up, it was very painful, so I let her lean against me. I remember I was a bit worried because I'd left my rucksack on the bike with all my things in it, and I was worried someone was going to steal it, but I couldn't move because I was holding the woman up. Later, I went to visit her in hospital, and she'd actually broken her shoulder in two places and had to have an operation. I think, though, if I had just been walking past, I wouldn't necessarily have gone to help, but because it had happened right in front of me, I felt I had to do something, and now I'm, I'm glad I was able to do something – I felt quite good about it afterwards.
Alison
So, I was waiting for the bus at the end of my road, to go into work. A very big man – very tall man – walked past the bus stop, and I noticed him particularly because he was wearing very dirty clothes and he was walking in rather a strange way – and to be honest, I thought he was probably drunk. Then all of a sudden, he stopped walking and fell backwards, and hit the back of his head on the pavement. He fell so hard on the back of his head that it made a really loud noise. And then he just lay still. Some teenagers in the queue called an ambulance and I stood by the man. I felt completely helpless. He was breathing, but I didn't really know what to do. The ambulance arrived quite quickly, and the paramedic took the man's hand and talked to him, and then they put him on a stretcher and took him away. Afterwards, I thought I should've done more, I should've perhaps turned him on his side, or put a coat under his head – at least, I should have held his hand to show someone was there. I felt a bit ashamed because I think the reason why I didn't help him more was because he was a bit dirty, a bit scruffy, and I was scared of him.

d Tell Sts they are going to listen to the three stories again and this time they need to answer questions 1–5 for each story.

Give Sts time to read the questions and see if they can remember any of the information.

EXTRA CHALLENGE You could get Sts to explain why the speaker felt the way he / she did during and after the event (see answers in brackets in 5 in the answer key).

Before playing the audio, you might want to pre-teach *pulse* /pʌls/ (= the regular beat of blood as it is sent around the body, that can be felt in different places, especially on the inside part of the wrist).

Now play the first story, pausing at the end to give Sts time to answer the questions.

2A 31

Get Sts to compare with a partner, and then either check answers now for Jane's story, or repeat the process for the other two stories.

Check answers.

Jane
1 She was out shopping with her husband.
2 A man. He was lying on the ground.
3 She felt his pulse and started doing cardiac massage.
4 An ambulance came and took the man to hospital.
5 a) She felt quite calm (because she knew what to do).
   b) She felt pleased (because she was able to do something).

Daniel
1 He was cycling to work.
2 An old lady. She tripped and fell into the road.
3 He helped move her and then helped her sit up until the ambulance came.
4 She was taken to hospital and he visited her there.
5 a) He felt worried (because he thought someone might steal his rucksack.
   b) He felt glad (because he was able to do something).

Alison
1 She was waiting for the bus.
2 A big, tall man. He fell backwards and hit his head on the pavement.
3 She didn't really do anything.
4 An ambulance arrived, and the paramedics took him away on a stretcher.
5 a) She felt helpless (because she didn't know what to do).
   b) She felt ashamed of not helping the man (because he was a bit dirty).

EXTRA IDEA You could ask Sts *What do you think you would have done in the three situations?*

EXTRA SUPPORT If there's time, you could get Sts to listen again with the script on *p.123*, so they can see exactly what they understood / didn't understand. Translate / Explain any new words or phrases.

e Focus on the questions and make sure Sts understand all the lexis, e.g. *compulsory*, *severe*, and *epileptic seizure* /epɪˈleptɪk ˈsiːʒə/. Elicit or model the pronunciation.

Put Sts in small groups to ask and answer the questions.

Monitor and help with vocabulary if necessary.

Get some feedback for each question from various groups.

EXTRA SUPPORT Before Sts start, you could quickly elicit some expressions they saw in **1A** for reacting to what someone says, e.g. *Oh, really?*, *How awful!*, etc.

4 GRAMMAR present perfect simple and continuous

a 🔊 **2.9** Focus on the photo and the task. You could tell Sts to close their books and write the questions on the board.

Before playing the audio, you might want to tell Sts that *paracetamol* /pærəˈsiːtəmɒl/ is a type of painkiller – they saw *painkiller* in the **Vocabulary Bank**. Play the audio once the whole way through.

Check answers.

1 A cough, headaches, a temperature
2 A brain tumour
3 A blood test
4 He should wait a few days, take paracetamol, and go to bed early.

🔊 **2.9**
(script in Student's Book on *p.123*)
D = doctor, P = patient
D Hello again, Mr Payne. What's the problem this time?
P Doctor, I haven't been feeling well for a few days. I've been coughing a lot, and I keep getting headaches. I have a temperature today.
D What have you been taking for the headaches?
P Paracetamol. But I read on the internet that headaches can be the first symptom of a brain tumour.
D How many tablets have you taken today?
P I took two before breakfast.
D And have you taken your temperature this morning?
P Yes. I've taken it five or six times already. It's high.
D Let me see. Mmm…well, your temperature seems to be perfectly normal now.
P I think I need a blood test. I haven't had one for two months.
D Well, Mr Payne, you know, I think we should wait for a few days and see how your symptoms…um…develop. Take two more paracetamol and go to bed early tonight.
P But…
D Goodbye, Mr Payne. Goodbye.

b 🔊 **2.10** Focus on the task and then play the audio.

Check answers. Elicit / Explain the meaning of the informal idiom *a pain in the neck* (= a person or thing that is very annoying) and that a person like this is a *hypochondriac* /haɪpəˈkɒndriæk/ (= sb who worries all the time about their health and believes that they are ill / sick when there is nothing wrong with them). Elicit or model the pronunciation.

They think he's a pain in the neck.
We call someone who behaves like this 'a hypochondriac'.

🔊 **2.10**
(script in Student's Book on *p.123*)
R = receptionist, D = doctor
R Your next patient is Mrs Morris – here are her notes…
D How many times has Mr Payne been to the Health Centre this month?
R Er, six times, I think…
D That Mr Payne! He's a complete pain in the neck…

❗ Don't ask Sts yet if they know anyone who is a hypochondriac, as they will be asked this after the listening.

c 🔊 **2.11** Focus on the task and give Sts time to read 1–7.

Play the audio once the whole way through for Sts to listen and circle the correct form.

If they do them individually, get them to compare with a partner. Check answers. Now ask Sts if both options are possible in any of the sentences.

1 I haven't been feeling   2 I've been coughing
3 have you been taking   4 have you taken   5 have you taken
6 I've taken it   7 haven't had
In 1 and 3, the other option is possible although less common.

🔊 **2.11**
1 I haven't been feeling well for a few days.
2 I've been coughing a lot and I keep getting headaches.
3 What have you been taking for the headaches?
4 How many tablets have you taken today?
5 And have you taken your temperature this morning?
6 Yes. I've taken it five or six times already.
7 I think I need a blood test. I haven't had one for two months.

32 **2A**

EXTRA CHALLENGE Get Sts to circle the correct form(s) before they listen to the extracts. Elicit the answers and then play the audio for Sts to listen and check.

d Tell Sts to go to **Grammar Bank 2A** on *p.134*.

Grammar notes
Present perfect simple and continuous

Sts at this level should already have a reasonable grasp of the uses referenced here for the two tenses, but will still need more practice.

Highlight that the present perfect continuous emphasizes both the continuity and / or temporary nature of an action, e.g. *I've been waiting for you for two hours!* (= more common than *I've waited…*).

for and *since*

Sts should be very familiar with how these words are used (*for* = period of time, *since* = point of time), but you may want to highlight that *for* is omitted with *all day / morning / night*, etc., e.g. *I've been working all morning.* NOT …*for all morning*.

Focus on the example sentences for **present perfect simple: *have / has* + past participle** and play audio 🔊 **2.12** for Sts to listen and repeat. Encourage them to copy the rhythm. Then go through the rules with the class.

Repeat for **present perfect continuous: *have / has* + *been* + verb + -*ing*** 🔊 **2.13** and **present perfect simple or continuous?** 🔊 **2.14**.

Focus on the exercises and get Sts to do them individually or in pairs.

Check answers, getting Sts to read the full sentences.

a
1 ✓   2 phoned   3 been running   4 seen   5 met   6 been snowing   7 gone   8 ✓   9 been reading, read
b
1 We**'ve known** Jack and Ann for years.
2 You look really hot. **Have you been working out** at the gym?
3 Emily **hasn't done** her homework yet, so I'm afraid she can't go out.
4 They don't live in London – they**'ve moved**.
5 I hope they're getting on OK. They**'ve been arguing** a lot recently.
6 We**'ve been walking** for hours. Is this the right way?
7 Why is my laptop switched on? **Have you been using** it?
8 Oh no! I**'ve cut** my finger on this knife.

Tell Sts to go back to the main lesson **2A**.

EXTRA SUPPORT If you think Sts need more practice, you may want to give them the **Grammar** photocopiable activity at this point.

e This is an oral grammar practice activity. Focus on the task and questions. Point out that in question 6, Sts should choose between *school*, *work*, or *university*, as appropriate.

Check that Sts know what verb forms to use, and encourage them not to write the questions, but just use the prompts.

EXTRA SUPPORT Give Sts time to think what the questions are. Then demonstrate the activity by eliciting the questions from Sts and answering them yourself. If necessary, you could write the questions on the board.

1 Do you often get colds?
  How many colds have you had in the last three months?
2 Do you take any vitamins or supplements?
  How long have you been taking them?
3 Do you drink much water?
  How many glasses have you drunk today?
4 Do you do any exercise? What (do you do)?
  How long have you been doing it?
5 Do you eat a lot of fruit and vegetables?
  How many portions have you had today?
6 Do you walk to school / work / university?
  How far have you walked today?
7 How many hours do you sleep a night?
  Have you been sleeping well recently?
8 Are you allergic to anything?
  Have you ever had a serious allergic reaction?

Give Sts time to ask and answer the questions in pairs. Monitor and correct any mistakes with the present perfect.

Get some feedback.

5 READING & SPEAKING reading and summarizing

a Focus on the title of the article and elicit / explain the meaning of a *confession* /kən'feʃn/ (= a statement admitting sth that you are ashamed of or embarrassed about).

Put Sts in pairs and give them time to read the first paragraph.

When they have finished, they should complete the definition of a *cyberchondriac*. You could remind Sts of Mr Payne, the patient, in **Grammar**, and elicit that he was a hypochondriac.

Check the answer. You could elicit / explain the meaning of *compulsively* (= in a way that is difficult to stop or control).

Suggested answer
(real or imagined) symptoms of illness

Now ask Sts if they think the article is humorous or serious.

It's humorous, e.g. *Did I go straight there? Of course not.*, *Sadly, the problem with Dr Google is that he isn't exactly a comfort in times of crisis.*

b Tell Sts they are now going to read the whole article. Point out that 1–5 summarize each paragraph of the article. They must complete each summary with phrases a–e. Point out the **Glossary**.

Check answers.

EXTRA SUPPORT Before Sts read the article the first time, check whether you need to pre-teach any vocabulary, but <u>not</u> the highlighted phrases.

1 b   2 d   3 a   4 e   5 c

You could now ask Sts if they have changed their minds about the tone of the article.

c Sts now focus on some more medical phrases which appear in the article. Get Sts to first look at the highlighted phrases in context and guess their meaning.

2A 33

Then get Sts to match the highlighted phrases to definitions 1–7. You might want to point out that *IDM* in 3 stands for *idiom* (= a group of words whose meaning is different from the meanings of the individual words).

Check answers.

> **1** open-heart surgery   **2** miracle cures   **3** under the weather   **4** scare stories   **5** worst-case scenarios   **6** heart rate   **7** life-threatening illness

EXTRA CHALLENGE   Get Sts to cover the article and look at the definitions and try to remember the phrases.

d Tell Sts to read the article again and this time, after reading each paragraph, they should choose the best option for 1–5: a, b, or c. You might want to check that Sts know the meaning of the verb *rank* (= to give sth a position on a scale).

Get Sts to compare with a partner, and then check answers.

> **1** b   **2** b   **3** a   **4** a   **5** c

Deal with any other new vocabulary. Elicit or model the pronunciation of any tricky words.

e Give Sts time to read the two questions and their options.

Now put Sts in small groups and get them to discuss the questions.

Monitor and help if necessary.

Get some feedback from various groups. If you know anyone who is a hypochondriac or cyberchondriac, you could tell the class about them.

EXTRA SUPPORT   Before Sts start, you could quickly elicit some expressions they saw in **1B** for reacting to a story about something strange, e.g. *How weird! That's strange!* etc.

6 WRITING an informal email

This is the first time Sts are sent to the **Writing Bank** at the back of the Student's Book. In this section, Sts will find model texts with exercises and language notes, and then a writing task. We suggest that you go through the model and do the exercise(s) in class, but set the actual writing (the last activity) for homework.

Tell Sts to go to **Writing An informal email** on *p.115*.

a Focus on the task. Put Sts in pairs and tell them to look at each mistake highlighted in Anna's email. First, they need to decide what kind of mistake it is and then they must correct it.

Check answers.

> **1** haven't (punctuation)
> **2** temperature (spelling)
> **3** ~~since~~ for (grammar)
> **4** Luckily (spelling)
> **5** Anything exciting? (punctuation)
> **6** ~~are~~ is (grammar)
> **7** software company (punctuation)
> **8** they're (grammar)
> **9** May (punctuation)
> **10** recommend (spelling)
> **11** sightseeing (spelling)
> **12** you'll be able to show (grammar)

b Focus on the **Beginning an informal email** box and go through it with the class.

Then focus on the task. Tell Sts to read Anna's email again and to find the five sentences.

Check answers. Draw attention to how, in informal writing, we often leave out pronouns and use short questions, e.g. the follow-up question *Anything exciting?*

> emailed, messaged, or phoned. = been in touch
> reading and replying to = catching up on my emails
> Have you been doing anything fun? = What have you been doing? Anything exciting?
> I don't have any more news. = that's all for now
> send my best wishes to = give my regards to

c Tell Sts they are going to write an informal email to Anna to answer her questions. First, they need to complete some expressions in the **Useful language: an informal email** box. Get Sts to do this individually or in pairs.

If Sts worked alone, get them to compare with a partner.

Check answers.

> **1** for   **2** to   **3** not   **4** hope
> **5** hear   **6** to   **7** luck   **8** feel / are / get
> **9** for   **10** Give   **11** forward   **12** care   **13** Best
> **14** PS

d Go over the plan with the class.

EXTRA SUPPORT   Go over the plan, focusing on one point at a time. Give Sts time to read Anna's email again and check the answers.

> **1** How are you? What have you been doing? How are your family? Could you recommend a hotel? Do you think you'll be able to show me around?
> **2** brother's new job, the conference

e Tell Sts to answer Anna's questions and to use expressions from the **Useful language** box when they write the email.

You may like to get Sts to do the writing in class, or you could set it as homework. If you do it in class, set a time limit for Sts to write their email, e.g. 15–20 minutes.

f Sts should check their email for mistakes before giving it in.

34 **2A**

2B Act your age

G using adjectives as nouns, adjective order
V clothes and fashion
P vowel sounds

Lesson plan

The topic of this lesson is age.

The lesson begins with an article about friendship between people with a big age difference. This is followed by a speaking activity in which Sts discuss having a friend of a different generation and the advantages this can bring. The first half of the lesson ends with the grammar focus, where Sts extend their knowledge of how to use adjectives. They learn to use nationality adjectives as nouns when they talk about the people from a particular country (e.g. *the British*, *the French*) or a particular group of people (e.g. *the rich*, *the unemployed*), and they also focus on adjective order when two or more are used to describe a noun.

In the second half of the lesson, the angle is on age-appropriate dressing. It begins with a photo and article about how women of different generations can wear the same clothes, and this leads to a lexical focus on clothes and fashion. This is followed by Pronunciation, which looks at short and long vowel sounds and diphthongs. Sts then listen to a radio programme on whether men and women should dress their age. In Speaking, Sts work in groups, giving their opinion on clothes and fashion. This is followed by a writing task, bringing the lexis and grammar together, where Sts write two ads to sell items of clothing online. The lesson ends with a documentary film about a small Welsh company whose jeans have become a global fashion item.

More materials

For teachers

Photocopiables
Grammar adjectives as nouns, adjective order *p.165*
Communicative You're only as old as you feel *p.195*
(instructions *p.184*)
Vocabulary Clothes and fashion *p.219*
(instructions *p.214*)

Teacher's Resource Centre
Video Some very special jeans

For students

Workbook 2B

Online Practice 2B

OPTIONAL LEAD-IN – THE QUOTE Write the quote at the top of *p.20* on the board and the name of the person who said it, or get Sts to open their books and read it.

You could tell Sts that Hayao Miyazaki is one of Japan's greatest animation directors. Sts might have seen *Howl's Moving Castle*, *My Neighbour Totoro*, and *Spirited Away*.

Get Sts to discuss what they think it means. Do they agree with the quote?

1 READING & SPEAKING scanning several texts

a Focus on the task and on the list of adjectives, and make sure Sts know all of them.

Now give Sts time to think of someone and then circle the appropriate adjectives.

b Put Sts in pairs and get them to tell their partner about the person they chose in **a**. If you know of anybody, you could demonstrate the activity.

Get some feedback.

c Focus attention on the photo and elicit ideas from the class on how old the two women are. Tell Sts that both names are Welsh and that Sian (also spelled Siân) is pronounced /ʃɑːn/.

Dilys is 85. Sian is 37.

d Tell Sts they are going to read an article where each woman talks about the other, and explains how they met and became friends, and what they value in each other. Sts must then look at sentences 1–12 and decide which person / people each one is about. You could also elicit / explain the meaning of the title, *The joy of the age-gap friendship* (= the happiness of having friends of very different ages).

Quickly go through sentences 1–12, making sure Sts understand all the lexis, e.g. *to cheer sb up*, *an extreme sport*, etc. Point out the **Glossary**.

Get Sts to compare with a partner, and then check answers.

EXTRA SUPPORT Before Sts read the article the first time, check whether you need to pre-teach any vocabulary.

1 B	2 S	3 B	4 B	5 D	6 B	7 B	8 D	9 S	10 D
11 B	12 S								

Deal with any other new vocabulary. You might want to draw Sts' attention to the meaning of *just* (= *really*, *completely*) in *We just clicked*, *She was just a great person*, and compare it to other meanings of *just*, e.g. *recently* (*He's just arrived*) or *only* (*We have just one bottle left*). Elicit or model the pronunciation of any tricky words.

e Do this as a whole-class activity and elicit some ideas.

They have a lot in common and they admire each other.

f Now focus attention on the photo of the two men, and elicit ideas from the class on their age difference.

g Put Sts in pairs, **A** and **B**, and tell them to go to **Communication The joy of the age-gap friendship**, **A** on *p.107*, **B** on *p.111*.

Sts **A** read what Dave says about John and Sts **B** what John says about Dave.

When Sts have finished reading, they should cover their text and talk about each bullet point in **b**.

Finally, Sts discuss whether they would get on with Dave and / or John.

Get some feedback from Sts by eliciting the information they shared in **b**. Then find out if they think they would get on with either Dave or John, and why (not).

Finally, deal with any new vocabulary, and elicit or model the pronunciation.

Tell Sts to go back to the main lesson **2B**.

2B 35

h Focus on the task and the seven sentences from the four texts.

Tell Sts to complete as many gaps as they can remember.

Get Sts to compare with a partner, and then to look back at the texts to complete any words that they couldn't remember. When Sts have completed all the words, they should explain what the sentences mean.

Check answers and the meaning of the phrases.

> 1 clicked; to click = become friends with sb at once
> 2 hit; to hit it off = have a good friendly relationship with sb
> 3 gap; age gap = age difference
> 4 point, view; point of view = the particular attitude or opinion that sb has about sth
> 5 take; take sides = to express support for sb in a disagreement
> 6 care; couldn't care less = used to say, often rudely, that you do not think that sb / sth is important or worth worrying about
> 7 look; look up to = to admire or respect sb

i Focus on the task and put Sts in pairs to discuss the questions.

Monitor and help with vocabulary if necessary.

Get some feedback from various pairs.

2 GRAMMAR using adjectives as nouns, adjective order

a Focus on the sentences and give Sts time to tick or cross each option.

In pairs, they should discuss why they think some options are wrong.

Check answers, eliciting why the ✗ ones are wrong. In **1**, *b* is wrong because you can't use a definite article when you are talking about a group of people in general. In **2**, only *a* is correct because opinion adjectives, e.g. *lively*, go before descriptive adjectives, and colour, e.g. *dark-haired*, comes before origin, e.g. *Welsh*.

> 1 a ✓ b ✗ (no definite article needed) c ✓
> 2 a ✓ b ✗ (wrong word order) c ✗ (wrong word order)

b Tell Sts to go to **Grammar Bank 2B** on *p.135*.

Grammar notes
Adjectives as nouns
- **Rule 2: nationalities**

  Sts should already have a good knowledge of nationality adjectives in English, especially for the countries in their part of the world. However, the specific rules for talking about people from a country are quite complex, since where a noun for the people exists, this is often preferred.

  You may want to elicit more examples of nouns used to describe people from a particular country, e.g. Greece – *the Greeks*, Scotland – *the Scots*, Spain – *the Spaniards*, Mexico – *the Mexicans*, Thailand – *the Thais*, etc.

Adjective order

It's important to point out that in practice, people rarely use more than two adjectives (occasionally three) together, so Sts should not be put off by the chart showing adjective order. Encourage Sts to use their instinct as to what sounds correct, rather than try to memorize the chart, and to remember that opinion adjectives always come first.

Learning common combinations will also help them to remember the rule, e.g. *long fair hair*, *a big old house*, etc.

Focus on the example sentences for **adjectives as nouns** and play audio 🔊 **2.15** for Sts to listen and repeat. Encourage them to copy the rhythm correctly. Then go through the rules with the class.

Repeat for **adjective order** 🔊 **2.16**.

Focus on the exercises and get Sts to do them individually or in pairs.

If they do them individually, get them to compare with a partner. Check answers, getting Sts to read the full sentences.

> **a**
> 1 The Dutch 2 the sick 3 the blind 4 The French 5 the injured 6 The Swiss 7 the homeless 8 the unemployed 9 the dead 10 the deaf
>
> **b**
> 1 an attractive young man
> 2 dirty old shoes
> 3 a beautiful black velvet jacket
> 4 a tall teenage American girl
> 5 a long sandy beach
> 6 a magnificent 17th-century country house
> 7 a stylish Italian leather bag
> 8 huge dark eyes
> 9 a friendly old black dog
> 10 a striped cotton T-shirt

Tell Sts to go back to the main lesson **2B**.

EXTRA SUPPORT If you think Sts need more practice, you may want to give them the **Grammar** photocopiable activity at this point.

c This is an oral grammar practice exercise. Focus on the five statements and make sure Sts understand the lexis, e.g. *second home*, etc.

Put Sts small groups and tell them to discuss each statement, saying whether they agree or disagree, and why.

Get some feedback from various groups.

EXTRA SUPPORT Remind Sts of expressions for giving opinions by writing them on the board, e.g.:

IN MY OPINION,…

PERSONALLY, I THINK THAT…

I'D SAY THAT…

EXTRA IDEA Sts will be getting more practice with adjective order when describing clothes in the second half of the lesson, but if you want to give them more practice here, you could bring in some objects (or photos of objects) for them to describe with two or three adjectives, e.g. an old black leather wallet, a small brown wooden box, a pair of red plastic sunglasses, etc.

3 VOCABULARY clothes and fashion

a Focus on the task and check Sts understand the title, and elicit / explain its meaning (*Can the same clothes be worn by people of all ages?*). Do the question as a whole-class activity.

b Give Sts time to read the article and complete the seven gapped highlighted phrases with the items of clothing in the list.

Check answers, making sure Sts know the meaning of the adjectives in the article, e.g. *cropped*, *see-through*, etc.

36 **2B**

1 jeans **2** jacket **3** trainers **4** top **5** sandals **6** dress
7 sweater

You could ask if any Sts have now changed their minds about the answer they gave in **a**.

c Focus on the task and make sure Sts know what an *accessory* is (= a thing that you can wear or carry that matches your clothes, for example a belt or a bag). Do this as a whole-class activity, or put Sts in pairs and then get some feedback.

d Tell Sts to go to **Vocabulary Bank Clothes and fashion** on *p.153*.

Vocabulary notes
Describing clothes
Style
You may want to point out that *polo-neck* is normally used with *sweater*, but the others can go with any kind of top.

Adjectives to describe clothes and the way people dress
Remind Sts that in British English, *smart = well dressed*, but in American English it means *intelligent*.

Verbs and verb phrases
Make sure Sts are aware of the difference in meaning between *match*, *suit*, *fit*, and *get changed / dressed / undressed*. Highlight that the phrasal verb *dress up* means to wear smart clothes, or wear fancy dress. Elicit / Point out that *dress up*, *match*, *fit*, and *suit* are regular verbs and that *hang up* is irregular (past *hung up*).

You could elicit / point out the difference between *wear* and *dress*. *Wear* always needs an object (e.g. *I'm going to wear a jacket tonight*) and *dress* never has an object, but is normally used with an adverb, e.g. *well*, *badly*, etc. (e.g. *She dresses well*). You could give Sts the following extra examples:

*The English don't **dress** very stylishly. / The English don't **wear** very stylish clothes.*

*She usually **dresses in** black. / She usually **wears** black (clothes).*

*They **dress** their children **in** jeans and T-shirts. / The children **wear** jeans and T-shirts.*

Focus on **1 Describing clothes** and get Sts to do **a** individually or in pairs.

◆) 2.17 Now do **b**. Play the audio for Sts to listen and check.

Check answers.

◆) 2.17
Clothes and fashion
1 Describing clothes, b

Fit	Style	Pattern
2 loose	6 hooded	12 checked
1 tight	4 long-sleeved	10 patterned
	7 polo neck	8 plain
	3 sleeveless	11 spotted
	5 V-neck	9 striped

Now either use the audio to drill the pronunciation of the words, or model and drill them yourself. Give further practice of any words your Sts find difficult to pronounce. Get Sts to do **c** individually or in pairs.

◆) 2.18 Now do **d**. Play the audio for Sts to listen and check.

Check answers.

◆) 2.18
d, Materials
4 a cotton vest
9 a denim waistcoat
5 a fur collar
3 a lace top
1 a linen suit
7 a lycra swimsuit
8 a silk scarf
6 a velvet bow tie
2 a wool cardigan
11 leather sandals
10 suede boots

Now either use the audio to drill the pronunciation of the phrases, or model and drill them yourself. Give further practice of any words your Sts find difficult to pronounce.

Focus on **Activation** and tell Sts to cover the words and phrases, look at the photos, and describe them.

Look at **2 Adjectives to describe clothes and the way people dress**, and get Sts to do **a** individually or in pairs.

◆) 2.19 Now do **b**. Play the audio for Sts to listen and check.

Check answers.

◆) 2.19
2 Adjectives to describe clothes and the way people dress
1 She always wears **casual** clothes to work – she hates dressing formally.
2 He looks really **scruffy**. His clothes are old and a bit dirty.
3 Jane looked very **smart** in her new suit. She wanted to make a good impression.
4 That tie's a bit **old-fashioned**! Is it your dad's?
5 I like wearing **classic** clothes that don't go out of fashion.

Give further practice of any words your Sts find difficult to pronounce.

Now do **Activation** and tell Sts to name one item of clothing they have for each adjective in the list in **a**.

Look at **3 Verbs and verb phrases**, and get Sts to do **a** individually or in pairs.

◆) 2.20 Now do **b**. Play the audio for Sts to listen and check.

Check answers.

◆) 2.20
3 Verbs and verb phrases
1 C I'm going to dress up tonight. I'm going to a party.
2 A Please hang up your coat. Don't leave it on the chair.
3 F These jeans don't fit me. They're too small.
4 H That skirt really suits you. You look great in it.
5 G Your bag matches your shoes. They're almost the same colour.
6 B I need to get changed. I've just spilt coffee on my shirt.
7 E Hurry up and get undressed. It's bath time.
8 I Get up and get dressed. Breakfast is on the table.
9 D That tie doesn't really go with your shirt. They don't look good together.

Give further practice of any words or phrases your Sts find difficult to pronounce.

Now do **Activation** and tell Sts to cover the verbs and verb phrases in 1–9 and remember them by looking at matching sentences A–I.

2B 37

Tell Sts to go back to the main lesson **2B**.

EXTRA SUPPORT If you think Sts need more practice, you may want to give them the **Vocabulary** photocopiable activity at this point.

4 PRONUNCIATION vowel sounds

> **Pronunciation notes**
>
> Sts can improve their pronunciation by making an effort to distinguish between long and short vowel sounds, and diphthongs (a combination of two vowel sounds, e.g. the sound in *hair* /heə/).
>
> Many nationalities have problems with the silent *r*, i.e. when *r* comes after a vowel and lengthens the sound, e.g. *ir* as in *shirt*, or *ur* as in *fur*, and need reminding that there is no /r/ sound. Remind Sts that /ɪː/ = a long sound.

a Focus on the task and tell / remind Sts that English vowel sounds are either short, long, or diphthongs – a combination of two short sounds.

Get Sts to answer the question in pairs.

Check answers. Elicit each sound, and then model and drill it.

1 /ɪ/ = short   **2** /aɪ/ = diphthong   **3** /eɪ/ = diphthong
4 /ɜː/ = long   **5** /uː/ = long

b 🔊 **2.21** Point out to Sts that all the words in the five groups are related to clothes. They must find the word in each group in which the pink letters are a different sound. Remind Sts that this kind of exercise is easier if they say the words aloud to themselves.

Play the audio for Sts to listen and check.

Check answers.

1 striped   **2** plain   **3** leather   **4** scruffy   **5** wool

🔊 **2.21**
See words in Student's Book on *p.22*

EXTRA SUPPORT Play the audio again, pausing after each group of words for Sts to listen and repeat.

EXTRA CHALLENGE Put Sts in pairs and get them to identify the sound of the odd word out. Check answers.

1 str**i**ped /aɪ/   **2** pl**ai**n /eɪ/   **3** l**ea**ther /e/   **4** scr**u**ffy /ʌ/
5 w**oo**l /ʊ/

c 🔊 **2.22** Focus on the task and then play the audio, pausing after each phrase to see if anyone in the class is wearing the item described.

🔊 **2.22**
a loose linen shirt
brown suede shoes
a plain cotton T-shirt
a striped silk tie
red leather boots
dark blue denim jeans
a hooded sweatshirt
a long-sleeved V-neck sweater
a long patterned skirt

d Put Sts in pairs and get them to discuss what they would and wouldn't wear in each situation in the list.

Get some feedback for each situation.

5 LISTENING & SPEAKING understanding a discussion – opinions, explanations, examples

a Focus on the photos and elicit some opinions. Make sure Sts know what a *slogan* is (= a word or phrase printed on the item of clothing).

b 🔊 **2.23** Focus on the task and make sure Sts understand the topic of the radio programme.

Then get Sts to look at the clothing in 1–5 in **a** and the journalists' comments in A–F.

Play the audio once the whole way through for Sts to listen and match the photos to the sentences. Remind them that there is an extra comment.

Check answers.

EXTRA IDEA Before Sts listen, you could write on the board the names of the famous people the journalists mention (Meryl Streep, Catherine Deneuve, Helen Mirren, Jane Fonda, and Mick Jagger), and elicit some information about them, including how old Sts think they are and if Sts think they look good or dress well.

EXTRA SUPPORT Read through the script and decide if you need to pre-teach any new lexis before Sts listen.

A 3   **B** 5   **C** 2   **D** 4   **F** 1

🔊 **2.23**
(script in Student's Book on *p.123*)
P = presenter, L = Liza, A = Adrian
P Welcome to today's programme. The topic is age and fashion, and the question is: Do people nowadays dress their age, and should they? Our guests are both fashion journalists with well-known magazines. Hello, Liza and Adrian.
L & A Hello. Hi!
P Hi. Let's start with you, Liza.
L Well, the first thing I'd like to say to all the young people out there is next time you give your granny a warm cardigan and some fur slippers for her birthday, don't be surprised if she asks for the receipt because she'll probably want to go out and change them for something more exciting.
P So you think nowadays older women dress much younger than they used to?
L Oh absolutely. Think of women like Meryl Streep, Catherine Deneuve, Helen Mirren, Jane Fonda. When Jane Fonda was in her seventies, she appeared on a US talk show wearing a leather miniskirt – she looked fabulous. But of course…
A I have to say, I saw that programme and I thought Jane Fonda looked awful.
P Adrian, can you let Liza finish?
A Sorry. Sorry, go ahead.
L Well, what I was going to say was that it isn't just famous women who are dressing younger; some recent research says that nine out of ten women say that they try to dress younger than their years.
P What about younger women?
L Well, yes, of course it depends on your age. A lot of teenage girls try to dress older than they are, maybe to get into pubs and bars. But I would still say that from thirty onwards, most women try to dress younger than they are.
P And do you think there's anything wrong with that?
L Nothing at all; it's a question of wearing what suits you. And that could be anything, from current trends to classics. I mean, OK, there are a very few things which can look a bit ridiculous on an older woman, like, let's see, very short shorts…but not many.

38 **2B**

A I think very short shorts look ridiculous at any age – well, on anyone over fifteen or so.

P Adrian, what about men? Do you think they also try to look younger than their age?

A Well, interestingly, in the research Liza mentioned, only twelve per cent of the men who were questioned said that they had ever thought about dressing to look younger. But actually, I think a lot of them weren't telling the truth. Look at all those middle-aged men you see wearing jeans which are too tight, and T-shirts with slogans. I think they look terrible, as if they're trying to pretend they're still in their twenties.

L Sorry, but I don't agree. I think Mick Jagger looks great in tight jeans and T-shirts. They suit him!

A True, but Mick Jagger is one in a million. Most men of his age can't carry it off. Personally, I do think that men should take their age into account when they're buying clothes.

P Let's go back to the idea of dressing older than your age. Do you think that men do that, too?

A Yes, definitely, some do. Some men in their twenties look as if they were twenty years older by wearing blazers and chinos, or wearing a suit and a tie to work when nowadays most men don't dress like that.

L Maybe they've just started work and they want their bosses to take them more seriously?

A Well, perhaps.

P I think we're running out of time. So, to sum up, Liza, Adrian, what would your fashion rules be?

c Focus on sentences 1–6 and give Sts time to see if they can remember any of the information in the audio. If Sts don't know who Mick Jagger is, you could tell them that he is the lead singer of a group called The Rolling Stones.

Now play the audio again the whole way through and get Sts to mark the sentences *T* (true) or *F* (false). Remind them to correct the false ones. Play the audio again if necessary.

Get Sts to compare with a partner, and then check answers.

1 T
2 F (They sometimes dress older to get into pubs and bars.)
3 T
4 T
5 F (He looks great.)
6 F (Most men don't dress like that nowadays.)

d Focus on the task and put Sts in pairs to complete the two rules. You might want to tell them that the gaps do not represent one word only.

Elicit some ideas, but <u>don't</u> tell Sts if they are correct.

e 🔊 **2.24** Play the audio for Sts to listen and check. You might want to tell them that they will hear the presenter as well.

Check answers.

Liza **Wear whatever you think suits you** and makes you **feel good**.
Adrian **Dress for the age you are**, not for the age **you wish you were**.

🔊 **2.24**
(script in Student's Book on *p.124*)
P So, to sum up, Liza, Adrian, what would your fashion rules be? Liza?
L Wear whatever you think suits you and makes you feel good.
P And Adrian?
A Dress for the age you are, not for the age you wish you were.
P Liza, Adrian, thank you very much.

Now give Sts time in their pairs to discuss which journalist they agree with more.

Get some feedback.

EXTRA SUPPORT If there's time, you could get Sts to listen again to both parts of the audio with the scripts on *pp.123–124*, so they can see exactly what they understood / didn't understand. Translate / Explain any new words or phrases.

f Focus on the five statements and go through them, making sure Sts understand all the lexis, e.g. *vintage*.

Now focus on the **Managing discussions** and **Politely disagreeing** box and go through it with the class.

Put Sts in small groups of three and set a time limit. Each student in the group takes it in turn to be the presenter and to choose one of the topics and organize the discussion.

Monitor and help with vocabulary if necessary.

Get feedback from various groups and deal with any general vocabulary problems that arose.

6 WRITING

a Focus on the instructions and example. Ask Sts if they have ever bought or sold anything on eBay.

Give Sts time to write their two descriptions. Go round helping with vocabulary, and encourage Sts to describe their clothes in as much detail as possible.

When everyone is ready, get them to write their name on their adverts.

EXTRA IDEA You may want to set a time limit for Sts to write their descriptions in order to make it easier to manage stage **b**.

b Focus on the task and explain / elicit the meaning of the verb *bid* (= to offer to pay a particular price for sth).

Either get Sts to move around the class swapping adverts, or if possible, put the adverts on the class walls and get Sts to move around reading them. If they find an item of clothing they would like to bid for, they should make a note of it.

Stop the activity when you think most of the Sts have read all the adverts.

Get feedback to find out who would like to bid for something.

7 ▶ VIDEO LISTENING

This is the first of five **Video Listenings**, which are incorporated into the Student's Book. If you are unable to show the video in class, remind Sts that they can find the video on *Online Practice*, and ask them to watch the video and do the activities for homework.

a Tell Sts they are going to watch an interview about a Welsh company that makes jeans. Focus on the question and make sure Sts understand what a *USP* is (Unique Selling Point = a feature of a product or service that makes it different from all the others that are available and is a reason for people to choose it).

Play the video once the whole way through for Sts to watch and answer the question.

Get Sts to compare with a partner, and then check the answer.

2B 39

EXTRA SUPPORT Read through the script and decide if you need to pre-teach any new lexis before Sts watch the video.

> Each pair of jeans is made by hand.

Some very special jeans

N = narrator, D = David, C = Claudio

N *This is the factory floor of Hiut denim, a small company in the seaside town of Cardigan in West Wales. Whether they're cutting or stitching, everybody here shares the same goal – to produce a pair of simple but high-quality denim jeans.*

D Can I describe our jeans? I mean, our jeans are classic, you know, five pocket Western jean. And our design philosophy is to keep things as simple as we can. And we don't want to be high fashion because high fashion comes in and then it goes away. And so, we want to make a classic pair of jeans. We want to make, you know, one of the best jeans in the world. And we want to keep it as classic and as simple as we can because, like, classic doesn't come in or go out of fashion. It just stays.

N *The Hiut Denim Company was founded in two thousand and two by David and his wife Clare. Since then, it has become a cult fashion brand, selling to customers all over the world. The company has attracted the attention of the world's media, as well as some very famous celebrities. Meghan Markle, the Duchess of Sussex, even wore a pair of Hiut Dina jeans on a royal visit to Wales – a major moment for the small but ambitious business. However, this is not the first time jeans have been manufactured in Cardigan. David and Clare started their company with a particular mission in mind.*

D The reason we started is to try and get four hundred people their jobs back. Because, you know, for people out there to know the back story is, you know, this small town in West Wales used to have Britain's biggest jeans factory in it and it made thirty-five thousand pairs of jeans a week. I mean, that's a big number, but it did it for forty years. And then in two thousand and two, the factory closed because the economics had changed and, you know, the factory gates closed. And so, and the question myself and Clare asked was, 'Could we open those gates again and keep them open?'

N *Today, Hiut operates from the old factory and employs many of its former workers. They call these lifelong jean makers their 'Grand Masters', thanks to the skills and experience they bring to their craft.*

C My name is Claudio Belotti. I'm the Grand Master in cutting. Originally, I was born in Italy and then came over to this country when I was three years old and lived in this area ever since. It's something I've always done since the age of fifteen. I worked with Hiut from the start, David and Clare approached me and asked me if I'd like to help them start up a jeans factory again. To see jeans being made in Cardigan again was something I never thought I'd see.

N *And what does Claudio think makes a good pair of jeans?*

C I think it's the love you put into it and that's what it is. Unless you love doing what you're doing, then I think it's – don't get the reward for putting all that effort in.

N *Hiut is delighted to employ the former factory workers, but the company doesn't follow the original business model. Instead of the thirty-five thousand pairs of jeans a week that the old factory manufactured, the Hiut Jeans Company produces only around one hundred and eighty pairs. This is because, after Claudio and his team have cut the denim, each pair of jeans is made by hand, crafted from start to finish by one person. This focus on quality rather than quantity – as well as the importance they place on environmental sustainability – sets them apart from many others in the clothing industry. So, how does Hiut fit in today's world of 'fast fashion'?*

D We don't. I mean, I mean that's the thing. I mean, like, I think this throwaway culture is – I don't think it makes the human being actually feel very good because like, 'Oh, I've bought something, then I discard it.' How do I feel? I mean, after a while you don't think very much of either the environment or yourself. I think that ultimately messes with people. But also from an environmental point of view, you know, like, how does that work, you know, for the environment? And actually it

doesn't. You know, like, the biggest and best thing we can do for the environment is make something last as long as possible. And yes, we do free repairs for life and that means that those jeans last more and more time and that's good. So I think we're as far away from fast fashion as I, we, I can possibly get. And if we can get even further, I would love it.

N *The company also has a no-wash club, to help lower the jeans' environmental impact, even after they've been sold.*

D There's a reason for the, for the no-wash club and it's twofold. And one is to, you know, if you want to have a truly beautiful pair of jeans then if you don't wash it, you know, for three weeks, five weeks, you know, a couple of months, all those creases that you put in there, and those wrinkles, you know, when they, when you wash it once the dye goes out, and all, all those creases, and that imprint of you as a human being is there and it looks incredibly beautiful. So, so the second part is, you know, eighty per cent of the impact of a pair of jeans, you know, is by you and I washing it. So like, getting people to not wash a pair of jeans for three months or six months has a huge impact in the world. And so the greenest jean is the one that you don't wash.

N *Hiut's reputation for quality and craftsmanship, together with caring for the planet, has been key in its success. And this success is something that David, Clare, and their whole team can be proud of.*

D I'm proud of it. We…I love the fact we make one of the best pairs of jeans in the world. And that's good. And the Grand Masters downstairs, they're proud of it. They even sign each pair. And there's a thing on the pocket that says all artists sign their work because we must be one of the few companies in the world where they actually make it from start to finish. Like, I mean, the robots might be coming, but they're not coming to Cardigan anytime soon.

b Give Sts time to read the information in the chart and make sure that they understand all the lexis. Point out that the first one (*denim*) has been done for them.

Play the video again, pausing if necessary for Sts to make notes.

EXTRA CHALLENGE First, put Sts in pairs and tell them to try to remember any of the answers. Then play the video again. Check answers.

2 classic
3 Meghan Markle (the Duchess of Sussex)
4 In 2002 because the previous factory closed down and they wanted to get people's jobs back.
5 Many of the former factory's workers
6 180
7 They encourage people not to wash their jeans for 3 or 6 months.

EXTRA SUPPORT If there's time, you could get Sts to watch again with subtitles, so they can see exactly what they understood / didn't understand. Translate / Explain any new words or phrases.

c Do this as a whole-class activity, or put Sts in pairs and then get some feedback. You could also tell Sts if you would like a pair of Hiut jeans and if you would join the no-wash club.

1&2 Revise and Check

There are two pages of revision and consolidation after every two Files. These exercises can be done individually or in pairs, in class or at home, depending on the needs of your Sts and the class time available.

The first page revises the **grammar**, **vocabulary**, and **pronunciation** of the two Files. The exercises add up to 50 (grammar = 15, vocabulary = 25, pronunciation = 10), so you can use the first page as a mini-test on Files 1 and 2. The pronunciation section sends Sts to the Sound Bank on *pp.166–167*. Explain that this is a reference section of the book, where they can check the symbols and see common sound–spelling patterns for each of the sounds. Highlight the video showing the mouth position for each sound. If you don't want to use this in class, tell Sts to look at it at home and to practise making the sounds and saying the words.

The second page presents Sts with a series of skills-based challenges. First, there is a **reading** text which is of a slightly higher level than those in the File, but which revises grammar and vocabulary Sts have already learned. The **listening** is some unscripted street interviews, where people are asked questions related to the topics in the Files. Sts can either watch the interviews on video or listen to them on audio. You can find these on the *Teacher's Resource Centre*, *Classroom Presentation Tool*, *Class DVD*, and *Class Audio CDs* (audio only). Alternatively, you could set this section / activity as homework. Sts can find the video on *Online Practice*.

More materials
For teachers
Teacher's Resource Centre
Video Can you understand these people? 1&2
Quick Test 2
File 2 Test
For students
Online Practice Check your progress

GRAMMAR

a
1 about 2 did 3 does 4 Have 5 been
b
1 a 2 b 3 b 4 c 5 b 6 b 7 a 8 c 9 a 10 c

VOCABULARY

a
1 tempered 2 absent 3 fisted 4 confident 5 fashioned
b
1 bleed 2 swollen 3 bandage 4 toothache 5 rash
c
1 feel 2 sprained 3 fainted 4 fit 5 changed

d
1 plain (the others are a pattern)
2 smart (the others are a type of material)
3 collar (the others are adjectives)
4 lycra (the others are items of clothing)
5 scruffy (the others are positive adjectives)
e
1 over 2 down 3 throw 4 up 5 hang

PRONUNCIATION

a
1 ache /k/ 2 suede /s/ 3 striped /aɪ/ 4 wear /eə/
5 cough /ɒ/
b
1 incredibly 2 big-headed 3 antibiotics 4 swimsuit
5 fashionable

CAN YOU understand this text?

a
No, they don't.
b
1 b 2 c 3 b 4 c

▶ CAN YOU understand these people?

1 c 2 b 3 a 4 c

🔊 2.25
1
I = interviewer, S = Sean
I   Have you ever had an interview for a job or a place on a course?
S   Er, yeah, I actually have been in several interviews for jobs only. I haven't had one for school yet.
I   What kind of questions did they ask you?
S   Um, my last job interview, er, they asked me questions like what it's like to, what is it like to be a part of a team, um, to me. Um, they asked me what my favourite superhero was, er, which was interesting. Um, they asked me…'cause right now I'm a server at a restaurant, so they were asking me like, oh, what's, how's customer service and how important, er, is it to you and stuff like that.
I   Did you get the job or place?
S   Yes.
2
I = interviewer, H = Harry
I   Do you believe in ghosts or UFOs?
H   I do believe in ghosts. I believe in ghosts because I grew up in a house where there is a ghost. My mum has heard it, my dad has heard it, my brothers have heard it. And I heard it one night when I was at home on my own, with the dogs. I was sitting downstairs watching TV, in the house, on my own, with the dogs, and I heard footsteps go from one end of the house to the other, along the corridor above. But, no-one's scared of the ghost, we just know there's a ghost in the house.
3
I = interviewer, M = Maria
I   Have you ever given anyone first aid?
M   Er, yes, when I was sixteen, I was at home with my two younger brothers, um, and they were playing upstairs. I heard a loud bang, and, um, my little brother came downstairs crying and

Revise and Check 41

he'd hit his head on the door handle. Um, and there was quite a lot of blood, so I sat him on the sofa and got a wet cold flannel and put it on his head. Um, and, er, told him to sit, sit still a few minutes while I rang my mum who was working, um, a night shift, um, at the time. Um, and then while I was waiting for her to come home, I just checked his head, made sure that it wasn't bleeding too much. Um, and yeah, it was fine. Um, my mum came home, took him to the hospital, so, it was fine.

4

I = interviewer, T = Tom

I Are you good friends with anyone who is a lot older or younger than you?

T I have a really good friend who's a lot older than me. In fact, I just went to her sixtieth birthday party in London. Um, I won't say how old I am, but that's, that's a lot older than me.

I How did you meet?

T Uh, we met as a part of an amateur theatre group. And, um, she was the funniest person in it, so we stayed friends.

Revise and Check

3A Fasten your seat belts

G narrative tenses, past perfect continuous; so / such…that
V air travel
P irregular past forms, sentence rhythm

Lesson plan

The topic of this lesson is air travel, though both speaking activities cater for Sts who have never flown.

In the first half of the lesson, Sts listen to some announcements that are heard on planes and trains, and Vocabulary then focuses on lexis related to air travel. Sts read an article about where best to sit on a plane for comfort, safety, and service. In Grammar in Context, they also learn how to use so / such…that. Finally, they do a speaking activity on different aspects of travel.

In the second half, Sts listen to an interview with a pilot, who answers some of the questions air travellers frequently ask themselves. This is followed by a grammar focus on narrative tenses. Sts revise the three narrative tenses they already know (past simple, past continuous, and past perfect) and learn a new one: the past perfect continuous. The pronunciation which follows focuses on tricky irregular past verb forms as well as sentence rhythm. In the final speaking activity, Sts read and re-tell a couple of real stories about flying and then tell each other an anecdote related to travel.

More materials
For teachers
Photocopiables
Grammar narrative tenses: past simple, past continuous, past perfect, past perfect continuous *p.166*
Communicative Talk about it *p.196* (instructions *p.184*)
Vocabulary Air travel *p.220* (instructions *p.214*)
For students
Workbook 3A
Online Practice 3A

OPTIONAL LEAD-IN – THE QUOTE

Write the quote at the top of *p.26* on the board and the name of the person who said it, or get Sts to open their books and read it.

You could tell Sts that Al Gore was Vice President of the USA from 1993 to 2001. He has written several books on environmental issues and made documentaries on the same subject matter. In 2007, he was awarded the Nobel Peace Prize.

Ask Sts what they think the quote means.

1 LISTENING & VOCABULARY understanding formal language in announcements; air travel

a ◻ 3.1 Focus on the title of the lesson and ask Sts where they might hear this phrase (on a plane). Elicit the pronunciation of *fasten* /ˈfɑːsn/, pointing out the silent *t*, and drill its pronunciation. Check Sts understand what it means (= to close sth firmly).

Now focus on the instructions, and then play the audio, pausing after each announcement for Sts to write *T* (train) or *P* (plane).

Highlight that with announcements, the important thing is to understand what they need to do rather than every word of the announcements.

Check answers.

EXTRA SUPPORT Play the audio, pausing after each announcement. Check the answer, eliciting from Sts some of the words that helped them guess the answer.

EXTRA SUPPORT Read through the script and decide if you need to pre-teach any new lexis before Sts listen.

A P	B T	C T	D P	E P	F P	G T	H T	I P	J P

◻ **3.1**
(script in Student's Book on *p.124*)

A Good afternoon. This is your captain speaking. I'd like to welcome you all on board the Wings flight eight-six A to London Stansted. We are currently cruising at an altitude of thirty-three thousand feet, at an airspeed of four hundred miles per hour. The weather en-route looks good and we are expecting to land in London approximately fifteen minutes ahead of schedule. So, sit back, relax, and enjoy the rest of the flight.

B This is a platform alteration. The eleven thirty-two South-Eastern service to Margate will now depart from Platform thirteen. Passengers travelling on the eleven thirty-two South-Eastern service to Margate, please make your way to Platform thirteen, as the train is ready for boarding.

C We are sorry to announce that the fourteen fifteen South-Western service to Bournemouth has been cancelled. This is due to a signalling failure. South-Western Railways apologizes for the disruption to your journey today.

D Ladies and gentlemen, may we have your special attention for the following safety instructions? There are six emergency exits on this aircraft, all marked with exit signs. Take a minute to locate the exit closest to you. Note that the nearest exit may be behind you.

E This is the final boarding call for passengers Alice and Christopher Carter, booked on flight N-Y-three-seven-two-A to Las Vegas. Please proceed to Gate three immediately. I repeat: this is the final boarding call for Alice and Christopher Carter. Thank you.

F Ladies and gentlemen, welcome on board Flight M-A-four-B-seven to San Francisco. We are currently third in line for take-off and are expected to be in the air in approximately seven minutes' time. We ask that you please fasten your seat belts at this time and place all baggage securely underneath your seat or in the overhead compartments. We also ask that your seats and tray tables are in the upright position for take-off. Please turn off all personal electronic devices.

G The next train to arrive at Platform three will be the seventeen oh eight Great Western service to London Paddington, calling at Reading, Slough, and London Paddington. This train is formed of five coaches. First-class coaches are at the front of the train.

H This is a Northern Line train via Bank, terminating at Morden. The next station is London Bridge. Change here for the Jubilee Line.

I This is the pre-boarding announcement for flight F-S-eight-nine-B to Rome. We're now inviting those passengers with small children, and any passengers requiring special assistance, to begin boarding at this time. Please have your boarding pass and identification ready. Regular boarding will begin in approximately ten minutes' time. Thank you.

J We have now landed in London Gatwick. Please disembark by either the front or rear exits. Make sure you have all your personal belongings with you.

3A 43

b 🔊 **3.2** Tell Sts they are now going to listen to the announcements that are only related to train or Underground journeys, and focus on phrases 1–4. You could tell Sts that Margate and Bournemouth are towns on the southern coast of England; Paddington is a central train station in London as well as an Underground stop; and the Jubilee line is a line on the Underground.

Play the audio once the whole way through for Sts just to listen.

Now play it again, pausing after each announcement for Sts to write their answers.

Get Sts to compare with a partner, and then check answers.

1 The train will now leave from platform 13.
2 The train has been cancelled.
3 The first-class coaches are at the front of the train.
4 You need to change at the next stop (London Bridge).

🔊 **3.2**
1 This is a platform alteration. The eleven thirty-two South-Eastern service to Margate will now depart from platform thirteen. Passengers travelling on the eleven thirty-two South-Eastern service to Margate, please make your way to platform thirteen, as the train is ready for boarding.
2 We are sorry to announce that the fourteen fifteen South-Western service to Bournemouth has been cancelled. This is due to a signalling failure. South-Western Railways apologizes for the disruption to your journey today.
3 The next train to arrive at platform three will be the seventeen oh eight Great Western service to London Paddington calling at Reading, Slough, and London Paddington. This train is formed of five coaches. First-class coaches are at the front of the train.
4 This is a Northern Line train via Bank, terminating at Morden. The next station is London Bridge. Change here for the Jubilee Line.

c 🔊 **3.3** Tell Sts they are now going to listen to the announcements that are only related to plane journeys. Focus on the two questions.

Play the audio, pausing after announcement 1 for Sts to answer the two questions. Play it again if necessary and then check answers.

Repeat the same process for announcements 2–6.

1 On the plane. Relax and enjoy the flight.
2 On the plane. Pay attention to the safety instructions and locate your nearest emergency exit.
3 In the airport terminal. Go to Gate 3 immediately.
4 On the plane. Fasten your seat belts and place all baggage under your seat, put your seats and trays in the upright position, and turn off all electronic devices.
5 In the airport terminal. Passengers with children and needing special assistance can begin boarding; have boarding pass and ID ready.
6 On the plane. Please get off the plane by the front or rear exits; remember to take your belongings with you.

🔊 **3.3**
1 Good afternoon. This is your captain speaking. I'd like to welcome you all on board the Wings flight eight-six A to London Stansted. We are currently cruising at an altitude of thirty-three thousand feet, at an airspeed of four hundred miles per hour. The weather en-route looks good and we are expecting to land in London approximately fifteen minutes ahead of schedule. So, sit back, relax, and enjoy the rest of the flight.

2 Ladies and gentlemen, may we have your special attention for the following safety instructions. There are six emergency exits on this aircraft, all marked with exit signs. Take a minute to locate the exit closest to you. Note that the nearest exit may be behind you.
3 This is the final boarding call for passengers Alice and Christopher Carter, booked on flight N-Y-three-seven-two-A to Las Vegas. Please proceed to Gate three immediately. I repeat: this is the final boarding call for Alice and Christopher Carter. Thank you.
4 Ladies and gentlemen, welcome on board Flight M-A-four-B-seven to San Francisco. We are currently third in line for take-off and are expected to be in the air in approximately seven minutes' time. We ask that you please fasten your seat belts at this time and place all baggage securely underneath your seat or in the overhead compartments. We also ask that your seats and tray tables are in the upright position for take-off. Please turn off all personal electronic devices.
5 This is the pre-boarding announcement for flight F-S-eight-nine-B to Rome. We're now inviting those passengers with small children, and any passengers requiring special assistance, to begin boarding at this time. Please have your boarding pass and identification ready. Regular boarding will begin in approximately ten minutes' time. Thank you.
6 We have now landed in London Gatwick. Please disembark by either the front or rear exits. Make sure you have all your personal belongings with you.

d 🔊 **3.4** Focus on the task, and elicit / explain that announcements tend to use quite formal language. Put Sts in pairs and give them time to look at 1–6 and decide what the formal words and phrases mean.

Play the audio, pausing after each announcement for Sts to listen and complete the task.

Get Sts to compare with a partner, and then play the audio again if necessary.

Check answers, and elicit any other information given in the announcements.

1 about   2 find   3 go to   4 put, phones / iPads / laptops, etc.
5 needing   6 get off, back

🔊 **3.4**
1 The weather en-route looks good and we are expecting to land in London approximately fifteen minutes ahead of schedule.
2 Take a minute to locate the exit closest to you.
3 Please proceed to Gate three immediately.
4 We ask that you please fasten your seat belts at this time and place all baggage securely underneath your seat or in the overhead compartments…Please turn off all personal electronic devices.
5 We're now inviting those passengers with small children, and any passengers requiring special assistance, to begin boarding at this time.
6 Please disembark by either the front or rear exits.

EXTRA SUPPORT If there's time, you could get Sts to listen again with script 3.1 on *p.124*, so they can see exactly what they understood / didn't understand. Translate / Explain any new words or phrases.

e Tell Sts to go to **Vocabulary Bank Air travel** on *p.154*.

Vocabulary notes
At the airport
Highlight the difference between *luggage* and *baggage*:
- *luggage* (uncountable) = bags and (suit)cases you take with you when you travel. You can't use it in the plural, e.g. NOT ~~I have a lot of luggages.~~

3A

- *baggage* (uncountable) = a more formal word used by airlines and at airports, e.g. it is used in the expression *excess baggage* and in the sign *baggage reclaim*. In conversation we would normally use *luggage*.

On board

Highlight that:

- *aisle (seat)* = the seat next to the passage between seats on a plane. Point out the silent *s*.
- *turbulence* = sudden and sometimes violent movement of air
- *jet lag* = tiredness caused by long-haul flight, especially when there is a big time difference between where you depart from and your destination

Phrasal verbs related to air travel

Highlight that *drop sb off* = take someone somewhere by car and stop briefly to let them get out. You can also use *drop off + luggage* (= to deposit it somewhere), hence *bag drop*. Remind Sts that you can use *pick up* with *luggage* (= collect), but also with a person, e.g. *I'll pick you up at the airport*.

Focus on **1 At the airport** and get Sts to do **a** individually or in pairs.

🔊 **3.5** Now do **b**. Play the audio for Sts to listen and check.

Check answers.

🔊 **3.5**

Air travel

1 At the airport

1 A Airport terminal
2 D Bag drop
3 I Baggage reclaim
4 C Check-in desk
5 J Customs
6 B Departures board
7 G Gate
8 H Runway
9 E Security
10 F Lounge

Now either play the audio to drill the pronunciation of the words and phrases, or model and drill them yourself. Give further practice of any words your Sts find difficult to pronounce.

Focus on **Activation** and get Sts to cover words 1–10, look at definitions A–J, and try to remember the words.

Focus on **2 On board** and get Sts to do **a** individually or in pairs.

🔊 **3.6** Now do **b**. Play the audio for Sts to listen and check.

Check answers.

> **2** row **3** turbulence **4** cabin crew **5** seat belts **6** direct flights **7** connecting flight **8** long-haul flights **9** jet lag

🔊 **3.6**

2 On board

I often fly to Bolivia on business. I always choose an aisle seat, so that I can get up and walk around more easily. My favourite place to sit is the emergency exit row, so I have more legroom.
Sometimes there's turbulence when the plane flies over the Andes, which I don't enjoy, and the cabin crew tell the passengers to put their seat belts on.

There aren't any direct flights to La Paz from London, so I usually have to get a connecting flight in Madrid. Whenever I take long-haul flights, I always suffer from jet lag because of the time difference, and I feel tired for several days.

Give further practice of any words your Sts find difficult to pronounce.

Focus on **Activation** and get Sts to cover the words in the list and read the text aloud with the completed gaps.

EXTRA CHALLENGE Tell Sts to cover the text and try to remember the meaning of the words in the list.

Focus on **3 Travel, trip, or journey?** and get Sts to do **a** individually or in pairs.

🔊 **3.7** Now do **b**. Play the audio for Sts to listen and check.

Check answers.

🔊 **3.7**

3 Travel, trip, or journey?

1 Have a good trip! Hope the weather's great!
2 A Did you have a good **journey** here?
   B No, my flight was delayed for six hours.
3 Do you have to **travel** much in your job?
4 We're going on a five-day **trip** to the mountains.

Now either do the questions as a whole-class activity, or put Sts in pairs and then get some feedback.

> 1 **Travel** is normally used as a verb. However, it can be used as an uncountable noun.
> 2 **Journey** means the time when you travel from one place to another, but does <u>not</u> include the time you stay there.
> 3 The noun **trip** means to go somewhere and come back, including the time you stay there, e.g. a business trip.

EXTRA SUPPORT Get Sts to cover the sentences and remember what the words mean.

Focus on **4 Phrasal verbs related to air travel** and get Sts to do **a** individually or in pairs. You may want to point out the use of *travel* as a noun referring to travel in general (it is normally a verb) in the phrase *Air travel*.

🔊 **3.8** Now do **b**. Play the audio for Sts to listen and check.

Check answers.

🔊 **3.8**

4 Phrasal verbs related to air travel

1 My husband dropped me off at the airport two hours before the flight.
2 I **checked in** online the day before I was going to fly.
3 As soon as I **got on** the plane, I put my bag in the overhead locker.
4 The plane **took off** late because of the bad weather.
5 When I **picked up** my luggage at baggage reclaim, I bumped into an old friend who had been on the same flight.
6 I **filled in** the immigration form for the US, which the cabin crew gave me shortly before landing.
7 When I **got off** the plane, I felt exhausted after the long flight.
8 My flight arrived really late at night, but luckily, a friend **picked me up** at the airport.

EXTRA SUPPORT Tell Sts to cover the sentences and try to remember the meaning of the phrasal verbs in the list.

Tell Sts to go back to the main lesson **3A**.

3A 45

EXTRA SUPPORT If you think Sts need more practice, you may want to give them the **Vocabulary** photocopiable activity at this point.

2 READING using a diagram to understand a text

a Either do the questions as a whole-class activity, or put Sts in pairs and then get some feedback. If you have a preference, you could tell the class.

b Focus on the instructions and the diagram of the plane. Point out the eight seats with crosses and tell Sts they must read the article and then match each seat to one of the paragraphs. Tell them not to worry about the gaps in the article.

Get Sts to compare with a partner, and then check answers.

EXTRA SUPPORT Before Sts read the article the first time, check whether you need to pre-teach any vocabulary, but not the words in **c**.

> If you want a speedy exit 4C
> If you want to sleep 4L
> If you don't like turbulence 11C
> If you need more legroom 10L
> If you want a better dining experience 3J
> If you're safety-conscious 21B
> If you want to have an empty seat next to you 16J, 16L

c Tell Sts to read the article again and this time to complete the gaps with the words and phrases in the list.

Get Sts to compare with a partner, and then check answers.

> **1** overhead locker **2** altitude **3** cabin **4** low-cost
> **5** evacuation **6** special assistance **7** engine **8** tail

Deal with any other new vocabulary. Elicit or model the pronunciation of any tricky words.

d Do this as a whole-class activity.

GRAMMAR IN CONTEXT

e Go through the two examples and then the rules. Highlight that *that* is optional after *so / such*.

You may want to point out that we often use *so / such* simply for emphasis (i.e. without expressing a consequence), e.g. *That steak was so good. We had such a nice day!*

Elicit sentence 1 from the whole class and write the answer on the board (*so*).

Then get Sts to complete the rest of the gaps.

Check answers.

> **2** such a **3** so **4** so many **5** so much **6** such

3 SPEAKING

Focus on the questionnaire and point out the three sections, *If you have flown several times*, *If you have never / hardly ever flown*, and *Have you ever…* . Sts answer the questions in one or other of the first two sections, and then the third section. Elicit / Explain that *several* = more than two.

Put Sts in pairs to ask and answer the questions. Tell them to start by asking their partner *Have you ever flown?* and, if the answer is *yes*, ask *How many times?*, to help them decide which section to use to interview their partner.

Monitor and help while Sts ask and answer the questions. Sts could either both answer each question as they go through the questionnaire, or take it in turns to talk about their travel experiences.

Get some feedback and deal with any general vocabulary problems that arose.

4 LISTENING

a Focus on the task and questions 1–6. Make sure Sts can remember the meaning of *device* and how to pronounce the plural *devices* /dɪˈvaɪsɪz/.

Now give Sts time to discuss the six questions in pairs and predict how the pilot will answer.

Elicit some ideas, but don't tell Sts if they are correct or not.

b 🔊 **3.9** Play the audio once the whole way through for Sts to listen and see how many questions in **a** they predicted correctly.

You could get Sts to compare with their partner, before checking answers by eliciting brief responses at this stage.

Ask Sts how many they guessed correctly.

EXTRA SUPPORT Read through the script and decide if you need to pre-teach any new lexis before Sts listen.

> **1** When the wind changes direction suddenly.
> **2** No.
> **3** Take-off is slightly more dangerous.
> **4** So they aren't distracted.
> **5** Yes, definitely.
> **6** No, never.

🔊 **3.9**
(script in Student's Book on *p.124*)
I = interviewer, R = Richard
I With me in the studio today I have Richard, who's a pilot, and he's going to answer some of the most frequently asked questions about flying and air travel. Hello, Richard.
R Hello.
I So, Richard, the first question is: what weather conditions are the most dangerous when flying a plane?
R Probably the most dangerous weather conditions are when the wind changes direction very suddenly. Er…this tends to happen during thunderstorms and typhoons, and it's especially dangerous during take-off and landing. But it's quite unusual – I've been flying for twenty-five years now, and I've only experienced this three or four times.
I What about turbulence? Is that dangerous?
R It can be very bumpy and very uncomfortable, but it isn't dangerous. Even strong turbulence won't damage the plane. Pilots always try to avoid turbulence, but it can sometimes occur without any warning, which is why we always advise passengers to wear their seat belt all the time during the flight.
I Which is more dangerous, take-off or landing?
R Both take-off and landing can be dangerous. They are the most dangerous moments of a flight. Pilots talk about the 'critical eight minutes' – the three minutes after take-off and the five minutes before landing. Most accidents happen in this period. But I would say that take-off is probably slightly more dangerous than landing. There is a critical moment just before take-off when the plane is accelerating, but it hasn't yet reached the speed to be able to fly. If the pilot has a problem with the plane at this point, he has very little time – maybe only a second – to abort the take-off.

46 **3A**

I Why are passengers asked to switch off their electronic devices during take-off and landing?

R It's mainly because they don't want passengers to be distracted, in case there's an emergency. It's nothing to do with the devices interfering with aircraft controls. I mean, aircraft control systems are so sophisticated now that they wouldn't cause any interference. Incidentally, that's also the reason why people have to put their tray tables up. If we had to abandon take-off or have an emergency evacuation, a tray table could cause a passenger injury or prevent other passengers from getting out easily.

I Is it really worth listening to safety demonstrations?

R Definitely. I can tell you for a fact that when pilots are passengers in a flight, they always identify the nearest emergency exit and count how many rows in front or behind it is.

I Do you ever get scared?

R I've been asked this many times, and the answer is no – hand on heart. I've been flying since I was sixteen and there's never been a single occasion where I've felt scared in the air. Bear in mind you've been asking me about dangerous situations, but these are incredibly rare.

I Thanks very much, Richard.

---

c Play the audio again for Sts to listen for more detail, pausing as necessary to give Sts time to write their notes. Play the audio again if necessary.

Get Sts to compare with a partner, and then check answers.

> 1 When the wind changes direction very suddenly, especially during take-off and landing
> 2 No, it isn't, though passengers should wear their seat belts.
> 3 They're both dangerous, but take-off is slightly more dangerous.
> 4 Because the crew don't want passengers to be distracted if there's an emergency, and they don't want the tray tables to get in the way if there's an evacuation.
> 5 Yes, definitely, especially to identify the nearest emergency exit
> 6 No, never, and he has been flying since he was 16.

EXTRA SUPPORT If there's time, you could get Sts to listen again with the script on *p.124*, so they can see exactly what they understood / didn't understand. Translate / Explain any new words or phrases.

d Do this as a whole-class activity.

5 GRAMMAR narrative tenses, past perfect continuous

a Focus on the newspaper article and tell Sts that this is a true story from a British newspaper called *The Independent*. Now focus on the task and make sure Sts know the meaning of *deny* /dɪˈnaɪ/ (= to say that sth is not true).

Set a time limit for Sts to read the story and answer the questions. Tell them not to worry about 1–8 in the newspaper story.

Check answers.

> The *Daily Mail* said that the pilot had told passengers they would probably have to fly with just one engine working and asked if they wanted to stay on the plane or get off.
> In fact, the pilot just asked the passengers if they wanted to get off the plane or not, while he was trying to start the engines.

b Get Sts to read the article again and this time they should circle the correct form of the verbs in 1–8.

Check answers.

> 1 boarded   2 were sitting   3 asked   4 was trying   5 had asked   6 said   7 provided   8 landed

c In pairs, Sts look at the sentence and answer the questions. Sts should be able to work out the tense because of the auxiliary verb *had* and the *-ing* form *staying*.

Check answers.

> Thursday and Friday
> Past perfect continuous

EXTRA SUPPORT Do this as a whole-class activity.

d Tell Sts to go to **Grammar Bank 3A** on *p.136*.

Grammar notes
Narrative tenses

- **Rules 1–3**

  This should all be revision for Sts at this level.

- **Rule 4: past perfect continuous**

  This will probably be new for most Sts. It has the same form as the present perfect continuous, except that *had* is used instead of *have / has*.

Past perfect simple or continuous?

The past perfect continuous is like all other continuous tenses in that it is used for actions that take place over a period of time, and is only used with action verbs.

In the examples given in the box, highlight that *she'd been reading a book* = she might have just finished reading or still have been reading the book when she started crying. *She'd read the book* = she had finished the book.

Focus on the example sentences for **narrative tenses** and play audio 🔊 **3.10** for Sts to listen and repeat. Encourage them to copy the rhythm. Then go through the rules with the class.

Repeat for **past perfect simple or continuous?** 🔊 **3.11**.

Focus on the exercises and get Sts to do them individually or in pairs.

Check answers, getting Sts to read the full sentences.

> a
> 1 were checking in   2 had won   3 had been looking forward to   4 had forgotten   5 had arrived   6 ran   7 went   8 was filling in   9 hurried   10 got
> b
> 1 I was really fed up because we**'d / had been queuing** for hours.
> 2 She went to the police to report that someone **had stolen** her bag.
> 3 It**'d / had been raining** all morning.
> 4 She got to work late because she**'d / had left** her phone at home and **had had to** go back and get it.
> 5 He**'d / had changed** a lot since I last saw him.
> 6 They**'d / had been sitting** in the sun all morning and they **hadn't put on** any sun cream.
> 7 I could see from their expressions that my parents **had been arguing**.
> 8 Jess had a bandage on her arm because she**'d / had fallen** off her bike that morning.
> 9 I was amazed because I**'d / had never seen** such an enormous plane before.
> 10 How long **had** you **been walking** before you realized that you were lost?

Tell Sts to go back to the main lesson **3A**.

3A   47

EXTRA SUPPORT If you think Sts need more practice, you may want to give them the **Grammar** photocopiable activity at this point.

e Focus on the task and get Sts to work either in pairs or groups of three. Set a time limit and remind Sts that they have to try to use the four different narrative tenses in the endings.

Get feedback and accept all correct meaningful sentences.

> **Some possible ways to complete the sentences**
> 1 …didn't have his lights / seat belt on.
>   …was using his mobile.
>   …had gone through a red (traffic) light.
>   …had been driving too fast.
> 2 …it was very hot.
>   …my neighbours were making a noise.
>   …I had had a cup of coffee after dinner.
>   …I had been worrying about work.

6 PRONUNCIATION irregular past forms, sentence rhythm

> **Pronunciation notes**
> This exercise focuses on commonly mispronounced irregular past verb forms. Sometimes, Sts at this level still have some ingrained pronunciation problems with some of the trickier irregular past and past participle forms, e.g. the -ought / -aught endings.
>
> There is also a focus on sentence rhythm with narrative tenses, and Sts get the opportunity to practise reading a short paragraph aloud.

a Focus on the picture words and elicit the eight sounds.

Then focus on the past simple verb in column **3** and elicit that it has the same vowel sound. Do the same with the verb in column **8**.

Now get Sts to look at all the verbs in the list, think of the past simple form for each one, and write it in the correct column.

EXTRA SUPPORT Check answers to **a** before doing **b**, by getting Sts to spell the verbs to you.

> 1 /uː/ flew, threw
> 2 /ɪ/ hid
> 3 /ɔː/ fought, thought
> 4 /ɜː/ heard, hurt
> 5 /əʊ/ drove, rode, told, wrote
> 6 /ʌ/ cut
> 7 /e/ fell, held, kept, left, read, said, slept
> 8 /eɪ/ lay

Or get Sts to do **a** and **b** in pairs.

b Now tell Sts to look at all the verbs in **a** again and decide which have a past participle form that is not the same as the past simple form. They must then write the past participles in the chart as well. You could do the first one with them (*become*, which should go in column **6**).

Get Sts to compare answers.

c 🔊 **3.12** Now play the audio for Sts to listen and check. Check spelling by eliciting the answers and writing the verbs on the board in a chart.

> 🔊 **3.12**
> 1 boot /uː/ flew, threw
> 2 fish /ɪ/ hid, driven, hidden, ridden, written
> 3 horse /ɔː/ caught, fought, thought, fallen
> 4 bird /ɜː/ heard, hurt
> 5 phone /əʊ/ drove, rode, told, wrote, flown, thrown
> 6 up /ʌ/ cut, become
> 7 egg /e/ fell, held, kept, left, read, said, slept
> 8 train /eɪ/ became, lay, lain

Remind Sts that:
* verbs ending in -aught are pronounced exactly the same as ones which end in -ought, e.g. *caught, fought, thought*.
* the *ea* in *read* is irregular and pronounced /e/.

Play the audio again, pausing after each group of words for Sts to listen and repeat.

EXTRA IDEA At this point, or perhaps at the end of the lesson, you may want to revise other common irregular verbs. Refer Sts to the **Irregular verbs** list on *p.165* and explain that this is their reference list. Get Sts to go through the list quickly in pairs, checking that they know what the verbs mean. Encourage them to highlight verbs they didn't know or whose past forms they had forgotten. Test the class, or get Sts to test each other.

d Focus on the task and make sure Sts can remember what an *anecdote* is (= a short, interesting, or amusing story about a real person or event).

Put Sts in pairs and get them to read the anecdote and guess what the missing verbs might be.

e 🔊 **3.13** Play the audio for Sts to listen and check. Check answers.

> 1 happened 2 flying 3 reading 4 watching 5 heard 6 turned 7 having 8 came 9 born

> 🔊 **3.13**
> This happened when my wife and I were on a flight to New York, and we'd been flying for a few hours. I was reading, and my wife was watching a film, when suddenly we heard an announcement – 'Is there a doctor on board?' It turned out that a woman was having a baby! Luckily, two doctors came forward, and the baby was born safely.

Tell Sts they are going to practise sentence rhythm now. Tell them to listen to the extract and notice that the **bold** words are stressed and the others aren't. Remind Sts that the stressed words are the 'content' ones (e.g. verbs and nouns) – the ones that convey important information.

Play the audio again once the whole way through for Sts just to listen.

Now put Sts in pairs and get them to practise reading the anecdote, concentrating on getting a good rhythm.

Get some Sts to read a sentence each to the class.

EXTRA SUPPORT Play the audio again, pausing at intervals, for Sts to listen and repeat.

48 **3A**

7 SPEAKING

a Put Sts in pairs, **A** and **B**, and tell them to go to **Communication Flight stories**, **A** on *p.107*, **B** on *p.112*.

Tell Sts they are each going to read a true story about a flight. Go through the instructions and make sure Sts know what they have to do.

Give Sts time to read their stories.

Now tell them to cover their story and use the information under *Setting the scene*, *The main events*, and *What happened in the end* to help them retell their story to their partner as if they had been a passenger on the plane.

Then Sts decide which situation was more scary.

You could get a show of hands for which story was more scary.

Finally, deal with any new vocabulary, and elicit or model the pronunciation.

Tell Sts to go back to the main lesson **3A**.

b Focus on the task and go through the instructions with the class.

Then focus on the **Telling an anecdote** box and go through it with the class.

Tell Sts to look at the topics and to choose one. If they have a real story, they can tell it as it happened. If not, they should invent the details. Later, their partner will have to decide if he / she thinks the story was true or not.

Give Sts plenty of time to plan how they are going to tell their stories, and go round checking whether they need any help with vocabulary.

EXTRA SUPPORT Tell one of the stories yourself first and elicit responses and questions from the class. Then ask Sts if they think the story is true or invented.

c Put Sts in pairs, **A** and **B**, and focus on the example. Sts **A** start by telling their story and Sts **B** should show interest and ask for more information. If necessary, remind them of the phrases for reacting to what someone says in **1A** on *p.7*.

Monitor and help, correcting any misuse of narrative tenses and encouraging the listener to listen actively.

EXTRA SUPPORT Tell Sts to look back at *p.11* to remind them of ways of reacting to a story about something strange.

When Sts **A** have finished telling their story, Sts **B** must guess whether or not it is true.

Sts then swap roles.

Get some Sts to tell their stories to the class. Deal with any general vocabulary problems that arose.

EXTRA IDEA Get Sts to write up their story for homework, using the same prompts as in **Communication** (*Setting the scene*, etc.) to help them with paragraphing.

3A

3B A really good ending?

G the position of adverbs and adverbial phrases
V adverbs and adverbial phrases
P word stress and intonation

Lesson plan

The topic of this lesson is stories and reading.
The lesson starts with a grammar focus on adverbs and adverbial phrases, and their position in sentences, which is presented through four 50-word stories with a twist. This is followed by a vocabulary focus on certain pairs of adverbs which are often confused, and in Pronunciation the focus is on word stress and emphatic intonation on certain adverbs. Sts then write their own 50-word stories.

In the second half of the lesson, Sts begin by talking about their reading habits, or about why they don't read for pleasure. They then read and listen to a short story by the French author Guy de Maupassant. The ending of the story is on the audio, in order to create more suspense. Finally, Sts go to the Writing Bank to prepare for writing longer stories.

More materials
For teachers
Photocopiables
Grammar the position of adverbs and adverbial phrases *p.167*
Communicative Tell the story *p.197* (instructions *p.185*)
Vocabulary Adverbs and adverbial phrases *p.221* (instructions *p.214*)
For students
Workbook 3B
Online Practice 3B

OPTIONAL LEAD-IN – THE QUOTE

Write the quote at the top of *p.30* on the board and the name of the person who said it, or get Sts to open their books and read it.

You could elicit / tell Sts that Chuck Palahniuk is most famous for his novel *Fight Club*, which also was made into a popular film of the same name.

Ask Sts if they agree with the quote.

1 GRAMMAR the position of adverbs and adverbial phrases

a Focus on the title of the lesson and on the name of the website. Explain that the stories submitted to the website have to tell a story in exactly 50 words.

Now focus on the task and put Sts in pairs.

Set a time limit for Sts to read the stories, and tell them to use the pictures to help them. Tell them not to worry about the highlighted words or the number of words. You may want to remind them of the use of the present tense for dramatic storytelling even when the actions took place in the past.

Elicit some predictions from various pairs for each story.

b Now tell Sts that sentences A–D are the final sentences of each story. They must read the stories again and this time match the correct ending to each one.

Check answers.

1 D	**2** A	**3** B	**4** C

Get Sts to say what they think each story is about. Do story 1 with the whole class. Elicit / Explain the meaning of *chat-up lines* (= sth you say in a friendly way to sb you are attracted to). Then elicit the story from Sts by asking, e.g. *Where does the story take place?* (on a train) *Who are the characters?* (a man and a woman) *What does the man always do to chat women up?* (He asks them a simple question and pays them a compliment.) *Why didn't it work this time?* (Because the woman is reading her divorce papers.)

Then get Sts to explain the other three stories in pairs.

Get feedback, encouraging Sts to use their own words to explain each story. Find out which story they think has the best ending.

You might want to explain that although the stories deal with potentially 'dark' themes, such as male predatory behaviour, death, loneliness, and anger, the authors make their stories end in an unexpected and humorous way.

c Focus on the instructions and go through the five categories of adverbs. Make sure Sts understand the categories by focusing on the examples.

Get Sts to write the adverbs in the chart individually or in pairs.

If Sts worked alone, get them to compare with a partner, and then check answers.

Time: at once, at last
Manner: carefully, silently, angrily
Degree: much, absolutely
Comment: unfortunately
Frequency: always

d Explain that one of the problems with adverbs is where to put them in a sentence, and elicit / explain that there are three possible positions: at the beginning or end of the phrase / sentence, or in the middle (usually before the main verb). Tell Sts that although the rules may seem a bit complicated, they will probably have a good instinct for where adverbs should go, and to try to see which position sounds best.

In pairs, Sts put the adverbs in the sentences.

Check answers.

1 He speaks French and Spanish **fluently**.
2 I **hardly ever** use public transport.
3 I thought I'd lost my phone, but **fortunate**ly it was in my bag.
4 It's **extremely** important that you arrive on time.
5 When I find out, I'll tell you **immediately**.

e Tell Sts to go to **Grammar Bank 3B** on *p.137*.

Grammar notes
The position of adverbs and adverbial phrases

This is an area of grammar where practice and Sts' own instinct as to what sounds correct will probably be more useful in the long run than memorizing rules. A useful tip to tell Sts is that with adverbs that don't end in *-ly* (e.g. *even*, *just*, etc.), if in doubt, to put them in mid-position, e.g. before the main verb.

- **Rule 1: adverbs of manner**

  In spoken English, adverbs of manner usually go after the verb or verb phrase, e.g. *He opened the door quietly*. However, in written English, e.g. a novel, they are sometimes used before the verb for dramatic effect, e.g. *He quietly opened the door and came in. Jane quickly explained why she was leaving.*

  You could give Sts some more examples of adverbs of manner in passive sentences: *Their house is beautifully designed. It's a well-written story.*

- **Rule 4: *a lot* and *much***

  You may want to expand this information and tell Sts that we can use *a lot* as an adverb after a verb (+ object) or verb phrase, e.g. *She goes out a lot, He loves her a lot*. We can also use *much* in the same way in questions and negatives, e.g. *Does he drink much? I didn't sleep much last night*. In [+] sentences we can use *very much*, usually after a noun or pronoun, e.g. *Thank you very much. We enjoyed the play very much.*

Now focus on the example sentences and play audio ◆ **3.14** for Sts to listen and repeat. Encourage them to copy the rhythm. Then go through the rules with the class.

Focus on the **Other adverbs** box and go through it with the class.

Focus on the exercises and get Sts to do them individually or in pairs.

Check answers, getting Sts to read the full sentences.

a
1 <u>a lot</u> ✗ She liked the present a lot.
2 <u>very late</u> ✗, <u>last night</u> ✗ Mark came home very late last night.
3 <u>after a few minutes</u> ✓
4 <u>badly</u> ✗ A young man was badly hurt and was taken to hospital.
5 <u>incredibly</u> ✓
6 <u>a bit</u> ✗ She's a bit lazy about doing her homework.
7 <u>almost</u> ✗, <u>fortunately</u> ✗ I almost forgot your birthday, but fortunately, my sister reminded me.
8 <u>luckily</u> ✗, <u>straight away</u> ✓ Luckily, we had taken an umbrella because it started to rain straight away.
9 <u>always</u> ✓, <u>healthily</u> ✓, <u>often</u> ✓
10 <u>apparently</u> ✗ Apparently, John has been sacked.

b
1 Their house was **badly** damaged in the fire **last week**.
2 Ben is **often** at his friend's house **in the evening**.
3 My father **usually** has a nap **in the afternoon**.
4 Julia left **early** and she didn't **even** say goodbye.
5 Martin **always** eats **incredibly** quickly.
6 **Apparently**, his brother **nearly** died in a skiing accident.
7 We're **probably** going to the cinema **tonight**.
8 I **rarely** send emails **nowadays**.
9 I've **just** bought a **really** beautiful new coat.
10 **Eventually**, Karen realized that she was **never** going to learn to drive.

Tell Sts to go back to the main lesson **3B**.

EXTRA SUPPORT If you think Sts need more practice, you may want to give them the **Grammar** photocopiable activity at this point.

f ◆ **3.15** This is an oral grammar practice activity. Focus on the instructions and tell Sts the sound effects and conversations will tell them what is happening in each situation and they then need to complete each sentence using the adverb in **bold**. Demonstrate by playing the audio and pausing after 1.

Now continue, pausing the audio after each sound effect or conversation to give Sts time to write the sentences. Play each situation again if necessary.

Check answers.

Possible answers
1 …had **just** left.
2 …**suddenly** the music stopped / the electricity went off.
3 …**luckily**, he found it in his pocket / it was in his pocket.
4 …in fact, they have **never** met.
5 …it was raining (so) **hard**, etc.
6 …he was speaking **incredibly** fast / quickly.

◆ **3.15**
1 *sound effects of bus leaving, followed by rushed footsteps*
  Woman   Oh no!
2 *sound effects of a party with music, which suddenly stops*
3 Woman   Can I see your boarding pass?
  Man   Oh no, I've lost it. Where is it? Where is it?
  Woman   I'm afraid you can't fly if you haven't got your boarding pass.
  Man   Oh, here it is…
4 Woman   Tom, this is Andrea – but you two know each other, don't you?
  Tom   Actually, we don't, but I've heard about you. Hi, Andrea. Nice to meet you at last.
  Andrea   Hello.
5 *sound effects of rain*
  Man   I can't see a thing. I think we'd better stop for a bit.
6 Frenchman   Excuse me. Please could you tell me how to get to the train station?
  Taxi driver   Yeah, mate. Straight down the high street, left at the lights, straight through the underpass, then it's right in front of you.
  Frenchman   Pardon?

---

2 VOCABULARY adverbs and adverbial phrases

a Focus on the task and give Sts time to read the story.
Elicit the answer. You could point out to Sts the use of the present simple for storytelling.

Dad

b Put Sts in pairs and get them to discuss the difference between the highlighted adverbs.
Check answers.

a *near* = close to, *nearly* = almost
b *late* = near the end of a period of time, *lately* = recently

EXTRA SUPPORT Do this as a whole-class activity.

c Tell Sts to go to **Vocabulary Bank** Adverbs and **adverbial phrases** on *p.155*.

3B   **51**

Vocabulary notes
Confusing adverbs and adverbial phrases
Highlight that:

- *actually* does not mean *now* or *at the present moment* (it's a false friend for some nationalities). It means *in fact* and is used to emphasize a fact or comment, or to say that something is really true.
- *especially* = above all (you can't use *specially* here; *specially* is only used with an adjective or participle, e.g. *It's a specially designed umbrella* NOT ~~especially designed~~)
- *at the end* = when something has finished, e.g. *at the end of the class / film*, etc., or to describe the furthest point, e.g. *at the end of the street*.
  In the end = finally, after a period of time or series of events, e.g. *It took me two years, but in the end, I passed my driving test*.
- *yet* goes at the end of a phrase and *still* in the mid position, e.g. *He hasn't found a job yet. He still hasn't found a job* (*still* = more emphatic). You may want to tell Sts that *still* can also be an adjective meaning *not moving*.

Focus on **1 Confusing adverbs and adverbial phrases** and get Sts to do **a** individually or in pairs. Make sure they understand what they have to do. Remind Sts to write in the *Adverbs* column on the right-hand side, <u>not</u> in the sentences.

🔊 **3.16** Now do **b**. Play the audio for Sts to listen and check.

Check answers.

🔊 **3.16**
Adverbs and adverbial phrases
1 Confusing adverbs and adverbial phrases
1 He trains very hard – at least three hours a day.
  It's incredibly foggy. I can **hardly** see anything.
2 I hate it when people arrive **late** for meetings.
  I haven't heard from Mike **lately**. He must be very busy.
3 **At the end** of a film, I always stay and watch the credits roll.
  I didn't want to go, but **in the end** they persuaded me.
4 I love most kinds of music, but **especially** jazz.
  My wedding dress was **specially** made for me by a dressmaker.
5 She looks younger than me, but **actually** she's two years older.
  At the moment they're renting a flat, but they're hoping to buy one soon.
6 I've **nearly** finished my book. I'm on the last chapter.
  Excuse me, is there a bank **near** here?
7 Have you found a job **yet**?
  He's thirty-five, but he **still** lives with his parents.
8 Have you **ever** been to the USA?
  I've been all over the USA – I've **even** been to Alaska!

Give further practice of any words or phrases your Sts find difficult to pronounce.

Do **Activation** and get Sts to cover the *Adverbs* column on the right, look at sentences 1–8, and see if they can remember the missing adverbs or adverbial phrases.

Focus on **2 Comment adverbs** and get Sts to do **a** individually or in pairs.

🔊 **3.17** Now do **b**. Play the audio for Sts to listen and check.

Check answers.

🔊 **3.17**
2 Comment adverbs
1 ideally
2 in fact
3 basically
4 obviously
5 gradually
6 apparently
7 certainly
8 eventually

Now either play the audio to drill the pronunciation of the adverbs, or model and drill them yourself. Give further practice of any words your Sts find difficult to pronounce.

Do **Activation** and get Sts to cover definitions 1–8, look at the sentences on the left, and see if they can remember the meaning of the adverbs.

Tell Sts to go back to the main lesson **3B**.

EXTRA SUPPORT If you think Sts need more practice, you may want to give them the **Vocabulary** photocopiable activity at this point.

3 PRONUNCIATION word stress and intonation

Pronunciation notes
Comment adverbs and adverbs of degree are often given extra stress and intonation in a sentence to add emphasis to their meaning, e.g. *It's incredibly easy* (extra emphasis and intonation on *incredibly*).

a 🔊 **3.18** Focus on the adverbs and give Sts time to underline the stressed syllable.

EXTRA SUPPORT Put Sts in pairs and get them to say each adverb aloud, so they can work out which syllables are stressed.

Play the audio for Sts to listen and check.

Check answers by writing the adverbs on the board and underlining the stressed syllable.

<u>ab</u>solutely	<u>ac</u>tually	a<u>pp</u>arently	<u>ba</u>sically	<u>de</u>finitely
es<u>pe</u>cially	e<u>ven</u>tually	<u>for</u>tunately	<u>gra</u>dually	i<u>de</u>ally
in<u>cre</u>dibly	<u>luck</u>ily	<u>ob</u>viously	unfor<u>tu</u>nately	

🔊 **3.18**
See words in Student's Book on *p.31*

EXTRA SUPPORT Play the audio again, pausing after each adverb for Sts to listen and repeat.

b 🔊 **3.19** Play the audio once the whole way through for Sts just to listen.

🔊 **3.19**
See sentences in Student's Book on *p.31*

Now play the audio again, pausing after each sentence for Sts to listen and repeat.

Then repeat the activity, eliciting responses from individual Sts.

52 **3B**

4 WRITING

a If there is time, do this activity in class. If not, set it for homework. Focus on the instructions.

Then put Sts in pairs and get them to choose a title.

b Get Sts to think of their plot together.

Give them time to write the first draft, and tell them not to count the words yet.

EXTRA CHALLENGE Encourage them to write the first draft individually and then continue working individually through the next stage.

c Now give Sts time to edit their stories together to get the correct number of words. Remind them that they have to include at least two adverbs, and that contracted forms (*I'm, don't,* etc.) count as one word.

Monitor and help as they write, suggesting ways they could cut down or expand their stories.

d When Sts have finished, get them to swap stories with two other pairs.

Get some feedback.

EXTRA IDEA You could put corrected stories on the wall of your classroom or on your class website for other Sts to read.

5 SPEAKING

a Put Sts in pairs and focus on the *Reading habits* questions. Make sure Sts understand all the text types, e.g. *comics, classics, manuals,* etc.

Put Sts in pairs and get them to go through the different types of reading matter and discuss each one, saying whether they ever read them and how often. Monitor and encourage Sts to ask for more information when possible.

b Tell Sts to go to **Communication Reading habits** on *p.108*.

Go through the instructions with them carefully.

Put Sts in pairs, **A** and **B**. Sts **A** (book open) start by interviewing Sts **B** (book closed), then they swap roles.

Finally, Sts discuss how similar their reading habits are.

Get some feedback, and find out how many Sts in the class read for pleasure.

Finally, deal with any new vocabulary, and elicit or model the pronunciation.

Tell Sts to go back to the main lesson **3B**.

6 READING & LISTENING reading for pleasure

a 🔊 **3.20** Tell Sts they are going to read and listen to a story in parts and then answer a few questions. You could tell them that the short story is by a famous French novelist called Guy de Maupassant (1850–1893).

Focus on the **Reading for pleasure** box and go through it with the class.

Now play **Part 1** on the audio for Sts to read and listen at the same time. Point out the **Glossary**.

Then focus on 1–8, and give Sts time to continue the sentences with a partner. They can do this either orally or in writing.

Elicit continuations from various pairs.

EXTRA SUPPORT Before Sts read **Part 1** of the story the first time, check whether you need to pre-teach any vocabulary.

Suggested answers
1 she was socially ambitious, but poor.
2 she was jealous of her life of luxury.
3 he had got an invitation to a party at the Ministry.
4 she had nothing to wear to the party.
5 his wife didn't want to go to the party and he had gone to a lot of trouble to get the invitation.
6 he had already saved the money for himself.
7 she didn't have any jewellery.
8 she lent her a beautiful necklace to wear.

🔊 **3.20**
See **Part 1** in Student's Book on *p.32*

Focus on the questions in **bold** and make sure Sts know the meaning of the verb *sympathize* /ˈsɪmpəθaɪz/ (= to feel sorry for sb). Elicit ideas. Tell Sts that the story is set in France at the end of the 19th century.

Deal with any vocabulary problems that arose.

❗ Sts may query why, in **Part 1**, Mathilde says *'…whose wife has better clothes than I'* rather than *'better clothes than me'*. Explain that this is grammatically correct (it leaves out the second *have = 'better clothes than I [have]'*), but is now considered very formal / correct English. The more usual expression nowadays is *better clothes than me*.

b 🔊 **3.21** Focus on the **Glossary** and go through it with the class.

Give Sts time to read questions 1–7, making sure they understand the phrase *raise money*.

Play **Part 2** on the audio for Sts to listen.

Then give Sts time to see if they can answer some of the questions.

Play the audio again, pausing to give Sts time to note their answers.

Get Sts to compare with a partner, and then check answers.

EXTRA SUPPORT Read through the script and decide if you need to pre-teach any new lexis before Sts listen.

---

1 Yes, she did. She was the prettiest of all, all the men admired her, she danced all night.
2 They walked and then got a cab.
3 That she had lost Madame Forestier's necklace.
4 Her husband went out to look for the necklace.
5 They decided to buy another necklace.
6 They used their savings and borrowed the rest.
7 She reacted coldly and told Mathilde she should have returned the necklace sooner.

🔊 **3.21**
(script in Student's Book on *p.124*)
N = narrator, L = Mr Loisel, M = Mathilde Loisel, F = Madame Forestier
Part 2
N *The day of the party arrived. Mathilde was a success. She was the prettiest of them all, elegant, smiling, and mad with joy. All the men stared at her, asked her name, and asked to be introduced. She danced all night in a cloud of happiness.*
They left at about four in the morning. It was a cold night, and her husband could not find a cab.
They walked towards the Seine, shivering, and finally found one. When they got home, Mathilde took off her cloak, but as she glanced at the mirror to see herself one last time, she suddenly gave a cry. Her husband, half undressed already, asked…
L What is the matter with you?

3B 53

N *She turned to him, in terror.*
M The necklace. I have lost Madame Forestier's diamond necklace!
N *He jumped up, frightened.*
L What? How? It is not possible!
N *They searched everywhere, but they did not find it. They had no way of contacting the cab driver. Her husband rushed out and retraced their steps from the Ministry to where they had caught the cab. He came back at about seven o'clock in the morning. He had found nothing. He went to the police, to the newspapers, and to the cab companies to offer a reward, hoping against hope that it would be found.*
L You must write to your friend…
N *…he said…*
L …that you have broken the clasp of her necklace and that you are having it repaired. That will give us time to decide what to do.
N *By the end of the week they had lost all hope. The next day they went from jeweller's to jeweller's, looking for a necklace like the one Mathilde had borrowed.*
In a shop in the Palais Royal, they found a diamond necklace that seemed to them absolutely identical. The price was thirty-six thousand francs.
Monsieur Loisel had eighteen thousand francs, which he had inherited from his father. He borrowed the rest, asking a thousand francs from one friend, five hundred from another, doing business with money lenders, and signing promises to pay which he was not sure he would be able to keep. Finally, he was able to raise the eighteen thousand more that they needed.
When Mathilde took the necklace back to Madame Forestier, she said, coldly…
F You should have brought it back sooner. I might have needed it.

Finally, focus on the question in **bold** and elicit some ideas.

Deal with any vocabulary problems that arose.

EXTRA SUPPORT If there's time, you could get Sts to listen again with the script on *p.124*, so they can see exactly what they understood / didn't understand. Translate / Explain any new words or phrases.

c 🔊 **3.22** Tell Sts they are now going to read and listen to **Part 3**.

Give Sts time to read questions 1–4, and also get them to look at the **Glossary**.

Play **Part 3** for Sts to read and listen at the same time.

Get Sts to discuss the questions with a partner.

Check answers.

EXTRA SUPPORT Before Sts read **Part 3** of the story the first time, check whether you need to pre-teach any vocabulary.

1 They moved to a small attic with no servant. She had to do all the housework and shopping, and wear worn-out clothes.
2 He worked in the evening and at night.
3 They had paid everything back that they owed.
4 Mathilde now looked like an old woman.

🔊 **3.22**
See **Part 3** in Student's Book on *p.33*

Finally, focus on the questions in **bold** and elicit some ideas.

Deal with any other vocabulary problems that arose.

d 🔊 **3.23** Tell Sts that they are now going to hear the end of the story. Focus on the task and the **Glossary**, and go through it with the class.

Now play **Part 4** once the whole way through.

Get Sts to discuss what they understood and then play the audio again as necessary.

Get some feedback.

Now focus on the questions in **bold** and elicit ideas.

EXTRA IDEA You may want to pause the audio before Madame Forestier's last line and get Sts to predict what they think she is going to say.

Suggested answer for the message of the story
The moral of the story is that you should be happy with what you have.

🔊 **3.23**
Part 4
N *One Sunday, after a hard week's work, Mathilde decided to go for a walk in the Champs-Élysées. As she was walking, she saw a woman with a child. It was Madame Forestier, still young, still beautiful, still seductive.*
Mathilde felt moved. Should she speak to her? Yes, certainly. And now that they had paid off the debt, she would tell her everything. Why not?
M Good morning, Jeanne.
N *Madame Forestier did not recognize her. She hesitated.*
F But, madame, I don't know you. Are you not making a mistake?
M No. I am Mathilde Loisel.
N *Her friend gave a cry.*
F Oh, my poor Mathilde, how changed you are.
M Yes, I have had hard times since I last saw you, and many troubles, and all because of you.
F Because of me? How can that be?
M You remember that diamond necklace that you lent me, to go to the party at the Ministry?
F Yes. I remember.
M Well, I lost it.
F That's not possible. You brought it back to me.
M I brought you back another one just like it. And for the last ten years we have been paying for it. You will understand that it was not easy for us; we had no money…But it's paid for at last.
N *Madame Forestier stared at her.*
F You say that you bought a diamond necklace to replace mine?
M Yes. You did not even notice it, did you? They were exactly alike.
N *Madame Forestier, much moved, took her by both hands.*
F Oh, my poor Mathilde. But my diamonds were false; they were imitation. At most they were worth five hundred francs!

EXTRA SUPPORT You could give Sts some useful language to respond to a story, e.g. *I was really surprised / disappointed, I didn't expect…, The ending was a real surprise, I thought it would end like that*, etc.

EXTRA SUPPORT If you photocopy script 3.23 from here, Sts could read and listen to the whole story.

7 WRITING a short story

This writing stage focuses on using the narrative tenses practised in **Lesson A** and also on using adjectives and adverbs to make a story more vivid. Tell Sts to go to **Writing A short story** on *p.116*.

a Focus on the task and give Sts time to read the story and answer the two questions. Tell them not to worry about the gaps.

Check answers.

He wrote an email which had a negative comment about his boss's wife in it and he accidentally sent it to his boss.
He was sacked.

EXTRA IDEA Ask Sts a few more questions about the story, e.g. *What company did he work for? Why didn't he like his boss's wife?* etc.

54 **3B**

b Focus on the instructions. Remind Sts to think about both the meaning and the position of the gap when they are choosing which word to complete it with.

Check answers.

> **2** quite **3** well **4** aggressive **5** frequently **6** new
> **7** fond **8** quick **9** immediately **10** An hour later

c Focus on the instructions. Remind Sts that in a story, they can either use reported speech or direct speech, i.e. dialogue, but that if they use dialogue, they must punctuate it properly.

Give Sts time to write out the sentence with the correct punctuation. Remind them to look at the dialogue in the story to help them.

Check answers either by getting a student to write the text with punctuation on the board, or writing it yourself.

> 'I want to talk to you about an email you sent,' Mr Simpson said coldly.

Highlight that inverted commas go outside any other punctuation, e.g. full stops, commas, and question marks. Inverted commas can be single or double (").

d Focus on the **Useful language: time expressions** box and give Sts time to complete the time expressions.

Check answers.

> **1** **At** that moment **2** As soon **as** **3** Ten minutes **later**
> **4** **One** morning in September **5** just **in** time

e Go through the instructions. Then put Sts in pairs and give them time to choose which story to write and to discuss what the plot is going to be.

f Focus on the plan and go through points 1–3 with the class. When looking at 1, make sure Sts do not think they have to write another story that is exactly 50 words.

g If Sts wrote a 50-word story in class, it would probably be best to set this longer one for homework.

h Sts should check their short story for mistakes before giving it in.

2&3 Colloquial English Talking about… books

Lesson plan

In The Interview, the person interviewed is Julia Eccleshare, a British journalist and author on the subject of children's books.

In The Conversation, Sts watch three people discussing whether there are any books that they think everyone should read. Sts then discuss this question as well as a couple of other questions related to the topic, focusing on vague language (e.g. *I mean, sort of*, etc.) and phrases to refer to what someone else has said (e.g. *as you were saying*, etc.).

More materials
For teachers
Teacher's Resource Centre
Video Colloquial English 2&3
Quick Test 3
File 3 Test
For students
Workbook Colloquial English 2&3
Can you remember? 2&3
Online Practice Colloquial English 2&3
Check your progress

OPTIONAL LEAD-IN (BOOKS CLOSED) Write some characters from famous British and American children's books you think your Sts might have read, and see if, in pairs, they can name the book:

1 CHRISTOPHER ROBIN

2 CAPTAIN HOOK

3 HERMIONE

4 LYRA AND WILL

5 PETER, SUSAN, EDMUMD, AND LUCY

6 LAURA INGALLS

> 1 *Winnie-the-Pooh* by AA Milne
> 2 *Peter Pan* by J.M. Barrie
> 3 the Harry Potter series by J.K. Rowling
> 4 His Dark Materials trilogy by Philip Pullman
> 5 *The Lion, the Witch and the Wardrobe* by C.S. Lewis
> 6 *Little House on the Prairie* by Laura Ingalls Wilder

1 ▶ THE INTERVIEW Part 1

a Books open. Focus on the biographical information about Julia Eccleshare. Either read it out loud or give Sts time to read it.

Do the question as a whole-class activity and find out if Sts have read any of the books.

b Focus on the task and go through the **Glossary** with Sts.

Play the video (**Part 1**) once the whole way through for Sts to do the task.

Check answers.

EXTRA SUPPORT Before playing the video, go through the listening scripts and decide if you need to pre-teach / check any lexis to help Sts when they listen.

> *Warrior Scarlet* was her favourite book when she was a child.
> Her mother read *Little House on the Prairie* to her brother.
> Her father read *Mouse House* to her when she was a child.
> *Northern Lights* is a classic book by Philip Pullman, who is her favourite children's writer.

I = interviewer, J = Julia Eccleshare

Part 1

I What was your favourite book when you were a child?

J It's always very difficult thinking back to one's favourite book as a child because…er…different times were different favourite books, but the book that I remember best that I go back to in times of wanting to have a quiet moment of…er…reflection is a book by Rosemary Sutcliffe called *Warrior Scarlet*, and why it appealed to me is very hard to say. It's about a boy with a withered arm in the Iron Age, who can't get his place in the tribe because he can't kill a wolf. I probably read it once a year even now.

I Even now?

J Well, yes, because there is a special thing about reading a book that you loved as a child – it takes you back to that time. You… typically if you ask people about their favourite book as…as a child or the book that made them a reader – which I think is another way of looking at it – they can remember a fantastic amount about it. They can often remember who gave it to them, or who read it to them, or where they read it, or…and I have exactly that experience with…with that book.

I When you were a small child, who read to you: your mother or your father?

J Well, I'm third of four children and – this is a terrible thing to say – I don't think anybody read to me. I think I remember listening in on my older sisters being read to. So I was the youngest of three girls, and then I've got a younger brother. And I very much remember my mother reading the Laura Ingalls Wilder *Little House on the Prairie* sequence to my brother, and that's when I heard them, too; I certainly never had them read to me. And then my father read me Rumer Godden's *Mouse House*, and again, this is a very profound memory, probably because he didn't actually very often read aloud, so it's logged in my brain as something that he read to me.

I And who read to your children: you or your husband?

J Well, that's interesting, because if I think back to it, I think, perhaps because I worked in books and my husband didn't, he seems to have done more of the reading aloud than I did. Um, he loved reading aloud; he has incredible stamina for it, and he would read for an hour quite happily, I think, at the end of a working day. It was quite a nice thing for him to do.

I Do you have a favourite children's writer?

J I think my favourite author at the moment is Philip Pullman. I think he gave us a classic book in *Northern Lights*, the first of His Dark Materials trilogy, which opened up to a very wide range of children what imaginative fiction can be at its best, and there's nothing that Philip has written that isn't interesting, beautifully crafted, um, surprising, and a story that you reflect on. He…he raises so many questions, giving openings for children to think – that's the best kind of writing as far as I'm concerned. So if you ask me now of a contemporary writer, he would be the person who I think is the greatest.

---

c Focus on the task and give Sts time to read sentences 1–5. Remind them that they have to correct the ones that are false.

Play the video again the whole way through for Sts to mark each statement *T* (true) or *F* (false).

Get Sts to compare with a partner, and then check answers.

CE2&3

EXTRA SUPPORT You could pause the video at the relevant places and, in pairs, get Sts to compare orally what they have understood, before marking the sentences *T* or *F*.

1 F (She reads it once a year.)
2 T
3 F (She doesn't think her mother read to her and can only remember her father reading one book to her aloud.)
4 F (He loved reading aloud and was very happy to do it when he came home from work.)
5 T

EXTRA SUPPORT If there's time, you could get Sts to watch again with subtitles, so they can see exactly what they understood / didn't understand. Translate / Explain any new words or phrases.

d Do the questions as a whole-class activity, or put Sts in pairs and then get some feedback. You could demonstrate the activity by talking about your childhood.

▶ Part 2

a Focus on the task and play the video (**Part 2**) once the whole way through for Sts to number the photos.
Get Sts to compare with a partner, and then check answers.

1 B   2 A   3 C

Part 2

I What do you think is the one big thing that helps to make a child a reader?

J One of the extraordinary things about reading that isn't talked about enough, I think, there's a lot of…of talk about how children learn to read and all of this, but actually – and what strategy might be best – but actually, what makes a reader, a book, it's finding the book that you really want to read. And so that's the chemistry – that's the chemical moment, when the child finds something that they really want to read.

I Teenagers can also be quite negative about reading. What do you think can help inspire teenagers to read?

J Well, I think the biggest inspiration that I…I would…I mean, I would like to say again – to get back to the idea that it is the right book – but I think there are lots of ways into reading, and one of the things that's very evident is that, um, good films, far from putting children off reading the book, often take children or teenagers to read the book. You take a book like *The Beach* – all right, it wasn't a book that was written for children, but it was a, you know, it was a great teen novel. It was a sort of…almost a teen anthem novel and, um, a lot of teenagers read the book after they'd seen the film.

I How do you feel about children reading books which are badly written?

J What I certainly wouldn't do is make judgements about quality of writing. One of the weirdest things that happens in children's books is that as soon as a child finds an author that they love, the parents tend to think it's not suitable because they think if the child is loving it, it's too easy, or too trivial, or too whatever. And Jacqueline Wilson is a very good example of this. She is an author who girls particularly found and loved for years, and it's taken the parents a very long time to realize that she is a very good author. And what do you say about someone like J.K. Rowling, who is, you know, not a great literary stylist, but has some really remarkable qualities in her books and will be credited – probably over three more generations – for having made children readers? I wouldn't want to say children shouldn't have read her books because they're not a great literary quality.

b Focus on the five sentences and the **Glossary**. Now give Sts time, in pairs, to see if they can remember any of the answers before they watch again.
Play the video again the whole way through.
Get Sts to compare with a partner, and then check answers.

EXTRA SUPPORT You could pause the video at appropriate places and, in pairs, get Sts to compare orally what they have understood.

1 finding the right book   2 often   3 should   4 children, parents   5 shouldn't

EXTRA SUPPORT If there's time, you could get Sts to watch again with subtitles, so they can see exactly what they understood / didn't understand. Translate / Explain any new words or phrases.

c Do the questions as a whole-class activity, or put Sts in pairs and then get some feedback. You could demonstrate the activity by talking about when you learned to read and your reading habits as a teenager.

▶ Part 3

a Focus on the task and give Sts time to read the three questions. You might want to check that Sts know what a *BlackBerry* is (= a type of smartphone or tablet).
Play the video (**Part 3**) once the whole way through for Sts to do the task.
Check answers.

1 Both.   2 No   3 Yes

Part 3

I For the most part, do you read paper books or eBooks?

J Ah, I'm…I'm almost entirely a print-book reader – but that's not out of prejudice, that's just out of, um, the fact that I get sent all the books, so it's easy for me to find the book I want to read and pick it up. Um, I read on my, um, iPad sometimes. Um, I think we are…ought to, sort of, stop seeing the two in polarity. I think, you know, everybody is going to read both. I read the newspaper online and I read it in print at the weekends. I think we are all just going to get very used to reading in different ways.

I Has all the new media made young people read less?

J When television first hit, as it were, everyone said children would stop reading, and the curious thing is that children's books, and even books for teenagers, are stronger now – much stronger than they were when television – children's television – first took hold. Children's television has slightly dwindled; books have increased. So the book has always been under threat from these other media, but somehow reading survives, so there must be something very important about it, or it would have gone – we would all have taken to seeing things in film, which is a much easier way of accessing the same wonderful stories. Or, I…I always think the thing that really threatens reading is listening to music. I know you can do both, but most people don't. But, you know, even with the explosion of music that children have access to, they still have found time for reading.

I Do you still read for pleasure?

J Well, I still do read for pleasure, um, but it's harder to get back to that magical experience, which I do remember very clearly from childhood. I do remember that being totally absorbed in the book, but as you get older, it's just harder to carve out time like that, and there is always something else pressing. And of course, that's got more so with…you know, I have a BlackBerry; I look at it all the time, and…er…I have to stop myself doing that if I'm going to enter this amazing fictional world. So for me, the place that it really works best is a long train journey, 'cause I don't have to look at anything; I can be out of my ordinary life and I can just have

CE2&3 57

that experience of getting completely lost in the story. But it only really works when the story comes to you, and you have that kind of chemical moment when the story grabs you and you know you're not going to stop until you've got to the end of it, or whatever. You know, you know you want to read it as long as possible. So I can still read for pleasure, but I have to find the right book.

b Focus on the task and give Sts time to read sentences 1–5. Play the video again the whole way through.

Get Sts to compare with a partner, and then check answers.

> **EXTRA SUPPORT** You could pause the video at appropriate places and, in pairs, get Sts to compare orally what they have understood.

> 1 She is referring to paper books and eBooks.
> 2 When television first started, people said that children would stop reading and watch TV.
> 3 Reading and listening to music at the same time
> 4 It's harder to find time to get absorbed in a book, as you always have other things you have to do.
> 5 She means that you suddenly get a feeling that you must know how the story finishes and that you will carry on reading until you do.

> **EXTRA SUPPORT** If there's time, you could get Sts to watch again with subtitles, so they can see exactly what they understood / didn't understand. Translate / Explain any new words or phrases.

c Do the questions as a whole-class activity, or put Sts in pairs and then get some feedback. You could demonstrate the activity by talking about your reading habits.

2 ▶ LOOKING AT LANGUAGE

This exercise focuses on a common feature of speech – giving yourself time to think. Focus on the **Ways of giving yourself time to think** box and go through it with the class. You could ask Sts if they do the same in their own language; in a monolingual class, if you know the Sts' L1, you could elicit examples of this.

Focus on the task and give Sts time to read extracts 1–6. Point out that the first one (*Well*) has been done for them.

Play the video, pausing after each extract to give Sts time to write.

Get Sts to compare with a partner, and then check answers.

> **EXTRA CHALLENGE** Ask Sts if they can remember any of the missing words or phrases before they listen to the extracts.

> 2 actually   3 I mean   4 all right   5 sort of   6 you know

> **EXTRA SUPPORT** You could get Sts to read completed sentences 1–6 aloud, to give them practice using the ways of giving yourself time to think.

1 Well, that's interesting, because if I think back to it…
2 …I think there's a lot of, of talk about how children learn to read and all of this, but actually, and what strategy might be best, but actually what makes a reader…
3 Well, I think the biggest inspiration that I…I would…I mean, I would like to say again…
4 You take a book like *The Beach* – all right, it wasn't a book that was written for children…
5 …it was a sort of…almost a teen anthem novel…
6 And what do you say about someone like J.K. Rowling, who is, you know, not a great literary stylist…

3 ▶ THE CONVERSATION

a Focus on the photo and tell Sts they are going to watch these three people discuss a question, which they will see on the screen. Focus on the task and make sure Sts understand what they have to do.

Play the video and pause after the question. Then play the video once the whole way through for Sts to answer the question.

Check answers.

> **EXTRA SUPPORT** Before playing the video, go through the listening script and decide if you need to pre-teach / check any lexis to help Sts when they watch.

> D recommends one book.
> E recommends more than one book.
> I doesn't recommend a specific book.

I = interviewer, E = Emma, Id = Ida, D = David
I   Are there any books that you think everybody should read?
E   I think that's really tough because it depends a lot on the person, I think. But, I think the one thing I would say I think everybody should read is Harry Potter.
I & D   Hmm.
E   I think, from, like, all of my friends that are my age, we all kind of read it when we were young and it just becomes, like, everyone knows what you mean when you talk about your Hogwarts house, for example.
I   Yeah.
E   And you just kind of lose yourself in this fantasy. The book that you read as a child, I still kind of re-read it every few years and a lot of people have said that it's helped them deal with, like, grief and…
D   Wow!
E   …things like that. So, I think it's actually quite powerful.
I   I think also because, like you were saying, you, you, sort of grew up with it. So you grew up with the characters and, and they kind of become part of some larger literal, literary, literary, sorry, family.
E   Yeah!
I   And everybody knows what everybody else is talking about
E   Mmmhmm.
D   But then having said that, I've, I've never read it. I've never seen the films.
E   Now I'm shocked.
D   And then when people are talking about it – in the office or, or when I'm out – I haven't got a clue what they're talking about. And I feel a little bit out of it and maybe, maybe I should read it.
E   Mmm, you should!
D   Mmm…er…
I   I think only for, from a sort of social perspective. It's so huge and it's influenced so many people in every country – not just in the UK, or not just Western countries – but all over the world that I think it becomes, like you were saying, a common language of sorts. And also becomes a, almost like a social history in a way.
E   Yeah.
I   It sort of becomes – it's more than a book. It's a kind of a, a common experience.
D   I, I once read…*The Diving Bell and the Butterfly*, that was a good book. Very short book. And it was about a…
I   I've never heard of it.
D   …a gentleman, he had a stroke and he only could communicate the book, er, through blinking an eye…
E   Oh, OK!
D   …an eyelid.
I   Oh right, OK.
D   And, er, it was quite a moving thing to read, but also uplifting as well at the same time. I'd definitely recommend it.
E   Things like that are great because it's learning about other people's experiences…
D   Yeah.
E   … and kind of finding empathy or…
I & D   Yeah.

CE2&3

E …just experiencing 'Oh my goodness this has happened to someone'.

D Yeah.

E Um, so, I read a great book recently by Dolly Alderton – just about her life and her growing up and things and just, it's kind of like a real celebration of, like, female friendship. And I just wanted to recommend it to all my friends.

D What period was that set in then?

E It's, it's present day, so it's about her growing up. It's called, um, *Everything I Know About Love*.

D Mmmhmm, mmmhmm.

I I think that what you said there about empathy and understanding other people's experiences, I think that is the key to any good book. And I think that is what makes books so important.

E Mmm.

I Not only to expand people's imagination, and their minds, and, and practical knowledge, but the idea of empathy, particularly in the world we live in today, it's sort of…

D Hmm…more so than ever…

I …allowing that time to understand other people's experiences is, is vital, I think.

b Focus on the task and the three book titles. Give Sts time to read the questions.

Play the video again for Sts to listen and answer the questions with a book.

Get Sts to compare with a partner, and then play again if necessary.

Check answers.

> **1** C **2** B **3** B **4** A **5** A **6** C **7** B **8** B **9** C

EXTRA SUPPORT If there's time, you could get Sts to watch again with subtitles, so they can see exactly what they understood / didn't understand. Translate / Explain any new words or phrases.

c Either do the questions as a whole-class activity, or put Sts in pairs and then get some feedback. You could tell Sts what you think, too.

d Focus on the task. Give Sts time to read the extracts.

Play the video for Sts to listen and circle the option they hear.

Check answers.

> **1** like **2** kind of **3** things like that **4** sort of

Now put Sts in pairs and get them to decide if the other option is also possible.

Check answers.

> **1** no **2** yes **3** yes **4** yes

Highlight that:
– *like* is used frequently nowadays as a filler, to give you time to think (Emma uses it in this way before *all of my friends*). Note that some people find the overuse of *like* annoying.
– *kind of* and *sort of* are synonyms.
– *stuff* = similar to *things*, a word we use for a substance or group of things when we don't want to specify exactly what. It is only used in the singular.

EXTRA IDEA Dictate these sentences. Then get Sts to decide how they could use use the vague language from **d** and where they would put it.

1 *I really enjoyed reading science fiction when I was younger.*

2 *I grew up with the internet.*

3 *I sometimes forget where I am when I'm reading.*

> **Suggested answers**
> **1** I really enjoyed reading (like) science fiction and stuff / things like that when I was younger.
> **2** I like / kind of / sort of grew up with the internet.
> **3** I mean / Like, I sometimes kind of forget where I am when I'm reading.

E I think, from, like, all of my friends that are my age, we all kind of read it when we were young and it just becomes, like, everyone knows what you mean when you talk about your Hogwarts house, for example.

I Yeah.

E And you just kind of lose yourself in this fantasy. The book that you read as a child, I still kind of re-read it every few years and a lot of people have said that it's helped them deal with, like, grief and…

D Wow!

E …things like that. So, I think it's actually quite powerful.

I I think also because, like you were saying, you, you, sort of grew up with it.

e Put Sts in small groups of three if possible. Focus on the questions, and check Sts understand what they mean. Then set a time limit for Sts to discuss them.

Monitor and help, and encourage them to use the different examples of vague language focused on in **d** where appropriate.

Get feedback from various groups. You could also tell the class what you think.

CE2&3 59

4A Stormy weather

G future perfect and future continuous
V the environment, weather
P vowel sounds

Lesson plan

The topic of this lesson is the environment and climate change.

The first half of the lesson begins with a quiz to see if Sts are as environmentally friendly as they think. They then look at an infographic with predictions related to the environment. This leads into the grammar focus, which is on two tenses that will be new for most Sts: the future perfect and future continuous.

In the second half of the lesson, Sts expand their weather vocabulary. This is followed by a pronunciation focus on combinations of vowels which can be pronounced in different ways, e.g. *ea* and *oo*. Sts then read an article from a website called the Climate Stories Project, in which six people from different continents talk about how they are affected by climate change. Sts listen to an interview with a meteorologist, and finally they talk about their own experiences of climate change and extreme weather conditions.

More materials
For teachers
Photocopiables
Grammar future perfect and future continuous *p.168*
Communicative In 20 years' time *p.198* (instructions *p.185*)
Vocabulary Weather *p.222* (instructions *p.215*)
For students
Workbook 4A
Online Practice 4A

OPTIONAL LEAD-IN – THE QUOTE

Write the quote at the top of *p.36* on the board and the name of the person who said it, or get Sts to open their books and read it.

Elicit / Explain what an *anthropologist* is (= a person who studies the human race, especially its origins, development, customs, and beliefs). You could tell Sts that Jane Goodall is also an animal rights activist and is known for her work with chimpanzees.

Ask Sts what they think Jane Goodall was saying in the quotation and whether they agree with her.

1 SPEAKING

a Focus on the task and elicit from the class what *environmentally friendly* means (= doing things that help the environment, e.g. recycling).

Now ask Sts if they can think of any synonyms, and elicit *eco-friendly* and *green*.

Finally, explain to Sts that on a scale of 1–10, 1 means *not at all* and 10 means *very*. Give them a few minutes to put their friends and family on the scale, and then the people in their town.

! Don't ask Sts to put themselves on the scale, as they will be doing this later in the lesson.

Put Sts in pairs and get them to tell their partner their opinion on how environmentally friendly everyone is, and then get some feedback.

b Focus on the title of the questionnaire. Ask a few Sts how environmentally friendly they are and to give examples of what they do.

Point out the two sections of the questionnaire, **A** *Your 'values'* and **B** *Your 'actions'*. Focus on the instructions in both sections, and make sure Sts understand what they have to do.

Give Sts time to do the questionnaire individually and work out their scores.

When they have finished, they should compare their answers and scores with a partner, giving examples and reasons.

EXTRA SUPPORT Before Sts do the questionnaire, focus on the *Your overall score* section, and quickly review the mathematical terms, i.e. *average, add up, divide,* and *subtract*.

c Tell Sts to go to **Communication Your score** on *p.108*.

Give them time to read about their score and then compare the meaning of their score with their partner's.

Get some feedback from various Sts. With a show of hands, find out how many Sts were really as environmentally friendly as they thought they were.

Finally, deal with any new vocabulary, and elicit or model the pronunciation.

Tell Sts to go back to the main lesson **4A**.

2 GRAMMAR future perfect and future continuous

a Focus on the task and make sure Sts know what an *infographic* is (= information or data that is shown in a chart, diagram, etc., so that it is easy to understand).

Now focus on the question and the words in the list.

Either do the question as a whole-class activity, eliciting predictions from the class, or put Sts in pairs and then get some feedback.

EXTRA IDEA Write the categories on the board and get Sts to close their books before they make their predictions, to avoid them reading the ones in **b**.

EXTRA SUPPORT Write Sts' predictions on the board to help with **b**.

b Put Sts in pairs and tell them to read the infographic to see if their predictions are mentioned. Give them time to discuss each prediction and say how likely they think they are.

Elicit some opinions from the class.

c Focus on the instructions. Sts should look at the highlighted verbs in the predictions and decide whether they refer to an action or situation that will be finished or still in progress in the future.

Get them to compare with a partner, and then check answers.

60 4A

a all the ones beginning with *will have*, e.g. *will have installed, will have stopped*, etc.

b all the ones with *will be + -ing* form, e.g. *will be recycling, will be cycling*, etc.

Elicit / Explain the basic difference between the future perfect and the future continuous:

- the future perfect + time expression = an action will be finished (at the latest) by that time
- the future continuous + time expression = an action will be in progress at that future time.

Highlight that *by + time expression = that time at the latest.*

d Tell Sts to go to **Grammar Bank 4A** on *p.138*.

Grammar notes

Although Sts will probably have seen the future perfect and future continuous passively in reading, they are likely not yet part of their active knowledge.

If Sts have the same or similar tense in their L1, it will be worth drawing comparisons. If not, then you will need to make sure the concept is clear. Both tenses are projections into the future in the speaker's mind.

If we use **the future perfect** instead of the simple future, we are **emphasizing the certain completion of the action**. However, the difference between the two tenses is often quite small.

The future continuous, though often used for an action in progress at a future time, is also very commonly used as an alternative to *going to* or the present continuous to ask about future plans or arrangements, e.g. *Will you be going out this evening?*

Focus on the example sentences for **future perfect: *will have* + past participle** and play audio 🔊 **4.1** for Sts to listen and repeat. Encourage them to copy the rhythm. Then go through the rules with the class.

Repeat for **future continuous: *will be* + verb + -*ing*** 🔊 **4.2**.

Focus on the exercises and get Sts to do them individually or in pairs.

If they do them individually, get them to compare with a partner. Check answers, getting Sts to read the full sentences. You could get two strong Sts to read out the conversation in **b**.

a
1 At 10.00 they**'ll / will be flying** to Geneva.
2 By the end of the year, I**'ll / will have saved** €2,400.
3 At 7.00 tomorrow, she**'ll / will be driving** to work.
4 Don't call me at 2.30 because we**'ll / will be having** a meeting.
5 By June, he**'ll / will have paid** for his car.
6 By the end of May, they**'ll / will have finished** their exams.
7 By the end of this week, she**'ll / will have written** five chapters.
8 It's 7.00 and she**'ll / will be working out** at the gym.

b
1 won't be lying   2 'll / will be working   3 will have disappeared   4 will have doubled   5 will have moved
6 will have grown   7 will have run out   8 will have invented
9 'll / will be getting

Tell Sts to go back to the main lesson **4A**.

EXTRA SUPPORT If you think Sts need more practice, you may want to give them the **Grammar** photocopiable activity at this point.

e This is an oral practice activity. Focus on the **definitely, probably, and *likely / unlikely*** box and go through it with the class. Point out that the opposite of *likely* is *unlikely*, which is often used instead of *not likely*, e.g. *He's unlikely to come now. / He isn't likely to come now.* However, we <u>don't</u> use *improbably*. Instead, we say *probably not*, e.g. *He probably won't come now.*

Now focus on the first prediction, ask the class what they think, and elicit ideas.

Get Sts to continue in pairs.

Monitor and help Sts, correcting any mistakes with future forms.

Get some feedback.

EXTRA IDEA You could elicit some more personalized oral practice with the futures by asking individual Sts:

What will you be doing a) *in two hours' time?* b) *this time tomorrow?*

When do you think you will have finished your studies?, etc.

f Focus on the task and topics in the list. To help Sts, you could write on the board IN 20 YEARS' TIME, I THINK…

Give Sts time in their pairs to make at least one prediction for each topic (or more if they can).

Elicit some predictions for each topic. Ask the other Sts if they agree each time. If not, ask why not.

3 VOCABULARY   weather

a Focus on the photos and ask the two questions to the class.
b Tell Sts to go to **Vocabulary Bank Weather** on *p.156*.

Vocabulary notes
What's the weather like?
Highlight that with the weather, it's important to be sure whether the word you are using is an adjective or a noun.

- Compare ***It's** windy* (adj) with ***There's a** strong wind* (n).
- The difference between *chilly* and *cool* is a question of how pleasant / unpleasant it is; 12°C may be cool for one person and chilly for another. This may also vary depending on the part of the world where Sts are.

Elicit / Explain the literal meaning of *boiling* (= 100°C).

Adjectives to describe weather
Point out that:

- despite having similar meanings, certain adjectives are only used with certain nouns, e.g. you can say *strong winds*, but <u>not</u> *strong rain* (you have to say *heavy rain*), and we say *bright sunshine* (<u>not</u> *strong sunshine*).
- *settled* is the opposite of *changeable*.

Focus on **1 What's the weather like?** and point out that the phrases in the top row of the chart refer to <u>not very</u> cold / hot / rainy / windy weather, and the phrases in the bottom row refer to <u>very</u> cold / hot / rainy / windy weather.

Get Sts to do **a** and **b** individually or in pairs.

4A 61

4.3 Now do **c**. Play the audio for Sts to listen and check.

Check answers to **a** and **b**.

◖)) 4.3
Weather
1 What's the weather like?
a
1 It's cool.
2 It's chilly.
3 It's freezing.
4 It's below zero.
5 It's mild.
6 It's warm.
7 It's boiling. It's scorching.
8 It's humid.
9 It's damp.
10 It's drizzling.
11 There are showers.
12 It's pouring.
13 There's a breeze.
b
When the weather's foggy or misty, or there's smog, it's difficult to see.
Mist isn't usually very thick, and often occurs in the mountains or near the sea.
Fog is thicker and can be found in towns and in the country.
Smog is caused by pollution and usually occurs in big cities.

Now either use the audio to drill the pronunciation of the sentences, or model and drill them yourself. Give further practice of any words your Sts find difficult to pronounce.

EXTRA SUPPORT Tell Sts to look at the words in the list and try to remember what sort of weather they are associated with.

Focus on **2 Extreme weather** and get Sts to do **a** individually or in pairs.

◖)) 4.4 Now do **b**. Play the audio for Sts to listen and check.
Check answers.

◖)) 4.4
2 Extreme weather
1 heatwave
2 drought
3 hail
4 lightning
5 thunder
6 blizzard
7 flood
8 hurricane
9 monsoon

Now either use the audio to drill the pronunciation of the words, or model and drill them yourself. Give further practice of any words your Sts find difficult to pronounce, e.g. *drought*, which is very irregular.

Do **Activation** and get Sts to cover the weather words on the left, look at definitions 1–9, and see if they can remember the weather words.

Focus on **3 Adjectives to describe weather** and get Sts to do **a** individually or in pairs.

◖)) 4.5 Now do **b**. Play the audio for Sts to listen and check.
Check answers.

---

2 heavy   3 thick   4 icy   5 clear   6 bright   7 changeable
8 sunny   9 settled

◖)) 4.5
3 Adjectives to describe weather
In the north of England and Scotland, it will be very cold, with strong winds and heavy rain. There will also be thick fog in the hills and near the coast, though it should clear by midday. Driving will be dangerous, as the roads will be icy. However, the south of England and the Midlands will have clear skies and it will be bright and sunny, though the temperature will still be quite low. Over the next few days, the weather will be changeable, with some showers, but occasional sunny periods. It should become more settled over the weekend.

Do **Activation**. If your Sts are all from the same place, do the question as a whole-class activity. If your Sts live in different places with different seasons, put them in pairs to discuss the question, and then get some feedback.

EXTRA SUPPORT Tell Sts to look at the words in the list and try to remember what sort of weather they are associated with.

Tell Sts to go back to the main lesson **4A**.

EXTRA SUPPORT If you think Sts need more practice, you may want to give them the **Vocabulary** photocopiable activity at this point.

4 PRONUNCIATION vowel sounds

Pronunciation notes
You may want to give Sts the following rules:
- The letters *ow* can be pronounced /aʊ/ or /əʊ/, though they are more commonly /əʊ/ when they come at the end of a word.
- The letters *ea* are usually pronounced /iː/ or sometimes /e/, e.g. *head*. They can occasionally be /eɪ/, as in *break* and *great*.
- The letter *i* between consonants is usually /ɪ/, but sometimes /aɪ/, e.g. *mild*.
- The letters *oo* are usually pronounced /uː/ or /ʊ/, but they are occasionally /ʌ/, e.g. in *blood* and *flood*.
- *ought* is usually /ɔːt/ – *drought* is an exception.
- The letter *u* between consonants is usually /ʌ/, but can be /juː/, e.g. *music*.
- The letters *or* are usually pronounced /ɔː/, but /ɜː/ after *w*.

a Focus on the instructions and point out that the first one (*owl*) has been done for them. Encourage Sts to say the words out loud to help them to identify the sound of the pink letters in each word.

b **◖)) 4.6** Play the audio for Sts to listen and check.
Check answers.

---

2 phone   3 boot   4 up   5 egg   6 tree   7 horse   8 fish
9 bike   10 ear

◖)) 4.6
See groups of words in Student's Book on *p.38*

Play the audio again, pausing after each group of words for Sts to listen and repeat.

EXTRA SUPPORT You may want to give Sts the rules in the **Pronunciation notes**.

EXTRA SUPPORT If these sounds are difficult for your Sts, it will help to show them the mouth position. You could model this yourself or use the Sound Bank videos on the *Teacher's Resource Centre.*

5 READING scanning for examples

a Focus on the task and either read the introduction as a class, or give Sts time individually to read it.

Ask the question to the class.

> It's about sharing stories about how climate change has affected people in different parts of the world.

b Focus on the task and put Sts in pairs.

Give Sts time, individually, to read the six stories. Then they should discuss in their pairs where they think each person might be from. Encourage them to look at the names and photos, and to look for clues about the places where they live in the texts.

Check answers.

EXTRA SUPPORT Before Sts read the six stories the first time, check whether you need to pre-teach any vocabulary.

> Diana Maciaga is from **Poland**.
> Umberto Crespo Palmarito is from **Cuba**.
> Nadine Lefort is from **Canada**.
> Harou Abass Hadiza is from **Niger**.
> Efleda Bautista is from the **Philippines**.
> Jordan Hamada is from **the USA**.

c Give Sts time to read the stories again, and this time find items 1–6 and say who mentions them and why.

Get Sts to compare with a partner, and then check answers. If you have any Sts who speak Polish, you could ask them how to pronounce the word in 5. It is /pʃedˈviːɔːʃnie/.

> 1 Efleda – They had one month's rainfall in one or two days and everywhere was flooded.
> 2 Umberto – They used to say that 21st September was when the weather changed.
> 3 Jordan – Los Angeles and Manhattan will eventually be underwater – a scary thought.
> 4 Harou – The river used to be deep and green and they used to swim in it, but now it's dusty and dirty.
> 5 Diana – This means the period between winter and spring, which doesn't really exist any more.
> 6 Nadine – Many beautiful properties and parks on the coasts will disappear because of erosion.

Deal with any other new vocabulary. Elicit or model the pronunciation of any tricky words.

d Do this as a whole-class activity.

6 LISTENING understanding examples

a Focus on the task and questions 1–7. Make sure Sts understand all the lexis, but <u>don't</u> explain what a *meteorologist* is, as Sts need to answer that question in 1. You could elicit or model its pronunciation /miːtiəˈrɒlədʒɪst/.

Now put Sts in pairs and get them to predict what Mike Bench is going to say for questions 1–7.

Elicit some answers, but <u>don't</u> tell Sts if they are correct.

b 🔊 **4.7** Play the audio once the whole way through for Sts to listen and check their predictions in **a**.

Check answers. Find out if any Sts got all seven answers correct.

EXTRA SUPPORT Read through the script and decide if you need to pre-teach any new lexis before Sts listen.

EXTRA SUPPORT You could pause the audio after the meteorologist has answered each question, to give Sts time to write.

> 1 A meteorologist collects the data, and a weather presenter presents the information on radio or TV.
> 2 Five to seven days
> 3 Not in detail, but they can give a general trend.
> 4 Thunderstorms
> 5 Because it affects everything they do, because the weather changes all the time.
> 6 He doesn't think it has changed significantly – there's a bit more extreme weather and it's a bit warmer.
> 7 Pessimistic

🔊 **4.7**
(script in Student's Book on *pp.124–125*)

P = presenter, M = Mike Bench

P And moving on to our next guest… We all know that one of the favourite topics of conversation here in the UK is the weather, especially after the scorching temperatures we've been having recently. Now we have with us in the studio meteorologist Mike Bench, and earlier in the show we asked listeners to tweet us any questions they had about the weather, and now Mike's going to answer some of them for us. Welcome to the show, Mike.

M Thanks, Jennie.

P So, the first question for you from our listeners is: What's the difference between a meteorologist and a weather presenter?

M Well, basically, a meteorologist collects all the data, whereas a presenter, well, is given the information and presents it on the radio or on TV, or wherever. Mind you, a few presenters are also trained meteorologists, but not many.

P How far ahead can you accurately predict the weather?

M I think, typically, we can forecast about five to seven days ahead on average. But some weather is more predictable than others. If there's high pressure, with not much changing, we could forecast, maybe, seven to ten days ahead. On other occasions, it can be very uncertain, we don't know even over just a few hours, so for example, if there's a lot of low cloud at airports, it will be very difficult for us to know when the cloud is going to clear enough for aircraft to take off or land.

P Are long-term forecasts ever accurate?

M In terms of forecasting as far ahead as next summer or winter, there's a very new system where we can see how what's happening in one part of the world might affect another weather system somewhere else. So, like, weather in the Arctic and in the Indian Ocean both make a difference to the weather in the UK. So we can't get real detail that far ahead, but we can get a general trend.

P What's your favourite kind of weather?

M Thunderstorms, especially at night, because they're very exciting. You can see things like the lightning moving around inside the clouds, especially at night, when the lightning really

4A 63

highlights the shape of the clouds. You never quite know what weather might come out of a thunderstorm; it's a kind of 'weather factory', really. It can generate large amounts of rain of tremendous intensity; it can bring very strong winds, large hail, snow sometimes…There's just incredible power and majesty in thunderstorms.

P Why do you think the British talk about the weather so much?

M Because it affects absolutely everything we do, every day. So, for instance, driving to and from work, what to wear when we're going out, whether we heat our house or not. It can affect what's in the shops, even how we feel – it just absolutely affects everything. Another reason is that in the UK, the weather changes all the time. We might not get global extremes of weather, but we get pretty much everything, so there's always something to talk about.

P In what ways have you noticed that the weather has changed in the last ten years?

M Well, in fact, over the last ten years, I don't think the weather has changed an awful lot. This year we've had an intense heatwave and also quite a lot of snow. It's unusual, yes – these are quite extreme for the UK, I suppose – but it's not unprecedented; both have happened before, and both will happen again. There's evidence to show that maybe extreme weather is happening a little bit more frequently; certainly globally, looking at the science, it tends to have got more extreme than it has been in the past, and it's obviously becoming a bit warmer as well, so yeah, but I've not necessarily noticed it myself day to day.

P Are you optimistic or pessimistic about climate change?

M I'm fairly pessimistic about it. I think in the UK, it will probably lead to more frequent, more extreme heatwaves, potentially colder and longer winters, and some more extreme weather as well, more intense rainfall, and a greater risk of extreme flooding.

P Mike, thank you very much for coming and answering our questions.

c Focus on the task and give Sts time to read 1–6.

Play the audio again, pausing if necessary to give Sts time to write the examples.

Get Sts to compare with a partner, and then play the audio again if necessary.

Check answers.

> 1 Low cloud at airports, knowing when it's going to clear
> 2 The weather in the Arctic and the Indian Ocean can affect the weather in the UK.
> 3 You can see lightning moving inside the clouds, showing the shape of the clouds.
> 4 Driving to and from work, what to wear when we're going out, putting the heating on, what's in the shops, how we feel
> 5 An intense heatwave
> 6 More extreme heatwaves, colder and longer winters, more rain and flooding

EXTRA SUPPORT If there's time, you could get Sts to listen again with the script on *pp.124–125*, so they can see exactly what they understood / didn't understand. Translate / Explain any new words or phrases.

d Do this as a whole-class activity.

> **Suggested answer**
> Yes because he's very enthusiastic, almost poetic, about his favourite kind of weather (thunderstorms), and about how the weather affects almost every aspect of people's lives.

7 SPEAKING

Focus on the **Modifiers with strong adjectives** box and go through it with the class. Remind Sts that *really* can be used with both normal adjectives, e.g. *It's really cold*, and strong adjectives, e.g. *It's really freezing*. Remind Sts too that we normally say these adjectives with extra stress and intonation.

Get Sts to focus on the questions, making sure they understand all the lexis, e.g. *mood*.

Put Sts in pairs and tell them to ask and answer all the questions in the first section, and then tell their partner about any information they can for the questions in *Have you, or has anyone you know, ever been somewhere when…?*

Monitor and correct any misuse of modifiers.

Deal with any general vocabulary problems that arose.

When Sts have finished, get some feedback.

EXTRA SUPPORT Demonstrate first by telling Sts about an experience of your own.

4B A risky business

G zero and first conditionals, future time clauses
V expressions with *take*
P linked phrases

Lesson plan

The topic of this lesson is risk.

In the first half, Sts listen to four people answering the question *Are you a risk-taker?* and they then interview each other to find out if they too are risk-takers. This is followed by the grammar focus on conditionals. Sts expand their knowledge of future time clauses and real conditionals, and see the variety of tenses that can be used apart from the present simple and future simple. In Pronunciation, Sts look at linked phrases, such as *and above all*, *as far as*, etc.

In the second half of the lesson, Sts read an article about the rise in popularity of extreme sports. This is followed by a vocabulary focus on common collocations with *take* (e.g. *take a risk*, *take seriously*). Then Sts go to the Writing Bank to focus on for and against essays. Finally, Sts watch a documentary about a young Irish surfer who talks about the risks and rewards of the sport.

More materials
For teachers
Photocopiables
Grammar zero and first conditionals, future time clauses *p.169*
Communicative Finish the sentences *p.199* (instructions *p.185*)
Teacher's Resource Centre
Video Riding the waves
For students
Workbook 4B
Online Practice 4B

OPTIONAL LEAD-IN – THE QUOTE

Write the quote at the top of *p.40* on the board and the name of the person who said it, or get Sts to open their books and read it.

You might want to tell Sts that Eleanor Roosevelt (1884–1962) also served as the First Lady of the United States during her husband President Franklin D. Roosevelt's four terms in office, making her the longest-serving First Lady of the United States.

Ask Sts why they think Eleanor Roosevelt said this and whether they agree with it.

1 LISTENING focusing on the main points

a Focus on the instructions and the list, making sure Sts know the meaning of all the items.

Give Sts time, individually, to score each item in the list from 1–5.

Now put Sts in small groups of three or four and get them to compare their scores.

Get some feedback by finding out if there were any strong disagreements on how risky some of the things are.

b 🔊 **4.8** Focus on the task and make sure Sts understand what they have to do. Explain, if necessary, that ✓ / ✗ is for people who answer both *yes* and *no*.

Play the audio once the whole way through for Sts to listen and do the task.

Check answers.

EXTRA SUPPORT Read through the script and decide if you need to pre-teach any new lexis before Sts listen.

1 ✗, a sport
2 ✓, money
3 ✓ / ✗, a job
4 ✗, a relationship

🔊 **4.8**
(script in Student's Book on *p.125*)
P = presenter, H = Holly, K = Karen, T = Tom, J = Jeanie

1 **Holly**
P Are you a risk-taker?
H Generally, definitely not, and I think that started early in life when I was a little girl. I hated getting hurt, therefore I thought, 'If I don't take any risks, I won't get hurt', and so I think even to this day I'm not really a risk-taker.
P Can you give me an example of a risk you *have* taken?
H Well, as I said, I don't usually take risks , for example, I hate flying. I only fly if there's no alternative, and I drive safely – carefully – because I don't want to put myself or my family in any danger. But once, someone persuaded me to try scuba-diving. I was very worried in the beginning, until I knew what I was doing. My mum was absolutely horrified that I was going to try it, so maybe it's a personality thing. In my family, my children are the same. But anyway, in the end I was very pleased I did the scuba-diving; it's one of the best things I've ever done! That's quite interesting, isn't it? So even for me, I can see that sometimes taking a risk has a positive outcome.

2 **Karen**
P Are you a risk-taker?
K I'd say that, on the whole, perhaps I am.
P Can you give me an example of a risk you've taken?
K Well, something I do a lot is buy things on eBay. And there, you're buying something you, you've never seen. You're relying on what the seller says about it, but you're going to calculate the risk based on their description, and how much you're paying, so if it only costs five pounds, it's not a great risk. However, if it's an expensive item, you might lose some money. But I reckon that's something that most people take a risk on now.

3 **Tom**
P Are you a risk-taker?
T I am in some ways – I mean, I've done some things that were physically dangerous – but when it comes to things like money, then I think I'm much more conservative.
P Can you give me an example of a risk you've taken?
T Well, when I finished university, my mum and dad just wanted me to apply for a normal kind of job – for example, working for a company – but I decided that I wanted a bit more fun while I was that age, so I decided to spend some time working as a bar manager, and I worked at loads of different food and drinks festivals all over the UK. I knew it would affect my CV because employers are always asking you questions about why you chose to do that, how was that useful to you, and just saying it seemed like a fun idea isn't a very good answer. After two or three years, I realized that it was going to be very difficult for me to continue doing the job past the age of about thirty. But now I'm glad I did it, and actually maybe it gave me what they call soft skills, like being flexible and dealing with people, which are really useful in

4B 65

my job now – I work in sales in a computer software company –
so on balance, I think the risk was worth it in the end.

4 Jeanie
P Are you a risk-taker?
J Um, not really, no, I don't think I am. Though once I took a really
big risk.
P What was it?
J When I left university, I went into a well-paid job straight away,
um, and after about two years, I was doing really well and
enjoying it a lot. And then, through some friends, I met this guy,
Richard, and we fell in love immediately. I know people think love
at first sight doesn't really happen, but it did. Anyway, um, he
was – is – a scientist, a marine biologist, um, and, um, after we'd
been going out for not very long, he was offered a job working
in Australia, and he said, 'Come with me.' I did think about it a
bit, but not much, and I left my well-paid job to follow a man I'd
known less than three months to the other side of the world. My
parents were horrified. I was a bit horrified myself, actually. Um,
but I married him, and we are still together. So it was definitely
worth it, but on the other hand, um, I haven't really had a career
as such, and if I hadn't gone with him then, maybe I would have
had a different kind of life. Who knows?

c Tell Sts they are going to listen to the audio again, and this
time they must decide who 1–8 is about. Give them time
to read the questions and see if they can remember any of
the answers.

Play the audio again, pausing after each speaker.

If necessary, play again, and then check answers.

> **1** H **2** K **3** J **4** H **5** K **6** T **7** J **8** T

EXTRA SUPPORT If there's time, you could get Sts to listen
again with the script on *p.125*, so they can see exactly what
they understood / didn't understand. Translate / Explain any
new words or phrases.

d Do this as a whole-class activity.

❗ Don't ask Sts who they identify with most, as they will be
seeing whether they are risk-takers in the next activity.

2 SPEAKING

a Focus on the task and instructions, making sure Sts
understand what they have to do.

Put Sts in pairs, **A** and **B**, and get them to interview each
other. Stress that Sts should explain their answers and not
just say *Yes* or *No*.

Monitor and help whilst Sts are talking.

b When Sts have finished, get them to look at all the circles
they have written an *R* in and decide in which areas of life
their partner is a risk-taker.

Sts share their results and discuss whether or not they
agree with the conclusions.

Finally, they should decide which of them is the bigger
risk-taker.

Get some feedback and deal with any general vocabulary
problems that arose.

3 GRAMMAR zero and first conditionals, future time clauses

a Focus on the sentence halves and give Sts time to match
them.

Check answers.

> **1** B **2** D **3** C **4** G **5** F **6** E **7** H **8** A

b Give Sts time, in pairs, to answer the questions.
Check answers.

> **1** Any present form, e.g. present simple, present continuous,
> present perfect, or an imperative
> **2** Any future form, e.g. *will*, *going to*, present continuous – with
> future meaning (H), future perfect, future continuous, or an
> imperative (D)

EXTRA SUPPORT Do **b** and **c** as a whole class.

c Focus on the task and questions.
Give Sts time to do the task.
Check answers.

> **1** a **2** b

d Tell Sts to go to **Grammar Bank 4B** on *p.139*.

Grammar notes

Zero conditional

This kind of conditional has not previously been focused
on, but Sts are likely to have seen it. Emphasize here that
a zero conditional is used to generalize or give facts, e.g.
If you heat water, it boils.

Although zero conditionals are usually based on present
tenses, they can also be used in the past, e.g. *If people
didn't have money, they didn't eat.*

First conditional

Up to now, Sts have probably been given a simplified
version of the first conditional (i.e. that we always use
present simple in the *if*-clause, and the future with *will*
in the main clause). In this lesson, they learn that a much
wider variety of forms is possible (including in the main
clause the two new tenses they have just studied in **4A** –
the future perfect and continuous).

Remind Sts that although a present tense is used after *if*,
the meaning here is future.

Future time clauses

Perhaps the most important point to emphasize is that
a future tense can never be used after *if* or after *when*, *as
soon as*, *until*, *unless*, *before*, *after*, and *in case*.

Typical mistakes are:

* *I'll be ready as soon as* ~~I'll have had a shower~~.
  I'll have dinner as soon as ~~I'll get home~~.
* *We'll probably be watching the cup final when* ~~you'll arrive~~.

in case

This expression may be new to Sts. Be careful that they do
not confuse it with *in case of*, which is sometimes seen in
notices, e.g. *In case of fire, break glass.*

You may want to point out that *in case* can also be used
in the past tense, e.g. *I took a jacket in case it got cold later.*
Also point out that unlike the other expressions, *in case*
cannot be used at the beginning of a sentence.

Focus on the example sentences for **zero conditional**
and play audio 🔊 **4.9** for Sts to listen and repeat.
Encourage them to copy the rhythm. Then go through
the rules with the class.

Repeat for **first conditional** 🔊 **4.10** and **future time
clauses** 🔊 **4.11**.

Focus on the exercises and get Sts to do them individually
or in pairs.

66 **4B**

If they do them individually, get them to compare with a partner.

Check answers, getting Sts to read the full sentences.

a
1 aren't feeling **2** 'll have sold **3** have **4** have scored
5 'll be bathing **6** won't get **7** aren't wearing **8** 'll catch
9 always gets **10** won't go

b
1 I'm going to pack my suitcase **before** I go to bed.
2 Take your phone with you **in case** you get lost.
3 I'll be leaving work early tomorrow **unless** there's a last-minute crisis.
4 Let's meet **when** I'm in London next week.
5 There's a crisis! Please call me **as soon as** you possibly can.
6 **If** I'm late tomorrow, start the meeting without me.
7 Lily will have packed some sandwiches **in case** we get hungry.
8 Dan will be playing football in the park **until** it gets dark.
9 Then, **after** we've eaten, we could go for a walk.
10 Don't call the emergency number **unless** it's a real emergency.

Tell Sts to go back to the main lesson **4B**.

EXTRA SUPPORT If you think Sts need more practice, you may want to give them the **Grammar** photocopiable activity at this point.

e Focus on the sentence stems and get Sts to complete them in pairs. Elicit ideas for sentence 1 from the whole class to demonstrate the activity.

Get feedback. You could write the phrases on the board and get the class to vote for the best tips.

Suggested answers
1 …you're sure it's in good condition.
2 …you're afraid of needles.
3 …someone has an accident.
4 …they are at least 14 years old.
5 …you have a problem when you're on holiday.
6 …destroy the old one immediately.
7 …you've told someone where you're going.
8 …you'll need to learn the language.

4 PRONUNCIATION linked phrases

Pronunciation notes

The way words are linked in English can often cause problems in understanding when Sts hear several words run together so that they sound like one word, e.g. Sts sometimes hear *festival* when someone is saying *first of all*. Here, Sts get more practice in deciphering linked phrases. They should know the two main rules for linking which are revised here, i.e. a) a word ending in a consonant sound followed by a word beginning with a vowel, e.g. *some eggs*, or b) a word ending in a consonant sound followed by a word which begins with the same sound, e.g. *some money*.

Sts may need reminding that with the second rule, /s/ and /z/ are considered the same sound, and /t/ and /d/. So for example, the words *is singing* are linked, and the words *wanted to* are linked.

a 🔊 **4.12** Focus on the task.

First, play the audio the whole way through for Sts to listen and complete the sentence.

Check the answer.

as soon as

Now give Sts time, individually or in pairs, to answer the question.

Check the answer.

a) *As* and *soon* are linked because *as* finishes with the /z/ sound and *soon* starts with the very similar sound /s/.
b) *Soon* and *as* are linked because *soon* ends with a consonant sound (/n/) and *as* begins with a vowel sound (/æ/).

🔊 **4.12**
I'll call you as soon as my shopping's been delivered.

EXTRA CHALLENGE Get Sts to complete the task before playing the audio.

b 🔊 **4.13** Focus on the task and give Sts time to quickly read 1–8. Tell Sts that each gapped phrase is three words and contractions count as one word.

Play the audio, pausing after each sentence to give Sts time to complete the gaps.

Check answers.

1 unless it's an **2** far as I'm **3** and above all
4 such an amazing **5** short time ago **6** worth it in
7 First of all **8** In an ideal

🔊 **4.13**
1 Don't call me unless it's an emergency.
2 As far as I'm concerned, you have to be mad to want to do an extreme sport.
3 Be careful with your wallet, and above all, don't use your phone in the street.
4 It was such an amazing experience that I've never forgotten it.
5 I dyed my hair blue a short time ago, and I hated it!
6 I was quite scared at first, but it was worth it in the end.
7 First of all, let's try to find a cheap hotel.
8 In an ideal world, everyone would earn a salary.

c Focus on the task and then put Sts in pairs.

Give Sts time to practise saying all the highlighted phrases, linking the words.

EXTRA SUPPORT You could use the audio or model and drill the phrases to help Sts before giving them time to practise in pairs.

Then tell Sts to make as many sentences as possible about themselves, using the highlighted phrases.

EXTRA SUPPORT Give Sts time to write some sentences before they tell their partner.

Get some Sts to tell the class their sentences.

5 READING summarizing an argument

a Focus on the task and then give Sts a few minutes to label the photos with the sports in the list and to think of other extreme sports. If Sts don't know what an extreme sport is, get them to guess by looking at the photos (= a sport that is extremely exciting to do and often dangerous).

Check answers and elicit some other extreme sports onto the board. Elicit or model pronunciation.

1 wingsuit flying **2** bungee jumping **3** skydiving
4 paragliding

4B 67

b Focus on the title of the article, *Why are deadly extreme sports more popular than ever?*, and make sure Sts understand it.

Now focus on reasons 1–6, and make sure Sts know the phrasal verb *to take sth up* (= to learn or start to do sth, especially for pleasure). You might also want to point out that *live* in 5 is the adjective /laɪv/. Point out the **Glossary** and go through it with the class.

Before Sts start reading, you could tell them that 110 mph (miles per hour) is 177 kmph (kilometres per hour).

Give Sts time to read the article and tick the three reasons they find.

Check answers.

EXTRA SUPPORT Before Sts read the article the first time, check whether you need to pre-teach any vocabulary.

> Sts should have ticked 2, 4, and 5.

c Focus on the task and make sure Sts understand what they have to do.

Give Sts time to first work out whether 1–7 need a name or number, and then to read the article to complete the gaps.

EXTRA SUPPORT Before Sts read the article, looking for the missing information, elicit what kind of information is missing. Then give Sts time to find the information in the article.

> **1** a number **2** a number **3** two names **4** a number
> **5** a number **6** a name **7** a name

Check answers.

> **1** 110 mph **2** 33 **3** Dean Potter, Graham Hunt **4** 59,679
> **5** 36% **6** Jess Cox **7** Steph Davis

d Do this as a whole-class activity, or put Sts in pairs and then get some feedback.

> He means that people need to learn to do them better, e.g. more elegantly, rather than more dangerously.

Again, either elicit Sts' opinions as a whole-class activity, or put Sts in pairs and then get some feedback.

Deal with any other new vocabulary. Elicit or model the pronunciation of any tricky words.

EXTRA SUPPORT Look at the writer's quote as a class and work out the meaning. Then put Sts in pairs and get them to tell each other whether they agree with the quote or not. Finally, elicit some opinions.

e Put Sts in pairs to answer the questions.

Get some feedback. If you have ever done an extreme sport, you could tell the class about it.

6 VOCABULARY expressions with *take*

a 🔊 **4.14** Focus on the task and give Sts time to read the six questions. Tell them they are going to hear Sophie Rees speaking – they will not hear the questions she is answering, but there will be a small space between her answers.

Play the audio once the whole way through for Sts to listen and match the questions to Sophie's answers.

Check answers.

EXTRA SUPPORT Read through the script and decide if you need to pre-teach any new lexis before Sts listen.

> **1** What's the first extreme sport you did? When was it?
> **2** What other extreme sports have you done?
> **3** Why do you enjoy extreme sports?
> **4** Are you ever afraid that you might get injured or killed?
> **5** Why do you think extreme sports are becoming more popular?
> **6** Do you think extreme sports are more popular with men than with women?

🔊 **4.14**
(script in Student's Book on *p.125*)
Skiing was the first extreme sport that I did. I started when I was six and I haven't really stopped since. I take after my dad – we're both sports-mad. He got me into skiing so he could take me on winter holidays.

***

I've done a lot of extreme sports in the mountains, such as mountain biking, and rock climbing, and ice-walking across glaciers. I've also done white-water rafting recently. It's very hard work, but really worth the energy.

***

I think it's because I love taking risks; I love the adrenaline rush.

***

I don't really think about getting injured or killed. I've never had a bad accident, but I've had some scary moments, where I knew if I made a mistake, I could get seriously hurt. But I've never really thought there was a chance I could die.

***

I think more and more people are taking part in extreme sports because they're becoming more accessible, and there's much more exposure than before on TV and on social media. Like I said before, it's the adrenaline rush that people really enjoy – you can't always get that in your everyday life.

***

A few years ago, I would have said men were much more associated with extreme sports. However, I think it's becoming a bit more equal between men and women. Extreme sportswomen are really appreciated because they're going against the gender stereotype, but men do still seem to dominate, maybe because they were more involved when the sports were first recognized.

b Focus on the task and give Sts time to see if they can remember any of the information.

Play the audio again, pausing after each of Sophie's responses to give Sts time to write.

Get Sts to compare with a partner, and then play again if necessary.

Check answers.

> **1** Skiing; when I was six
> **2** Mountain biking, rock climbing, ice-walking, white-water rafting
> **3** I love taking risks; I love the adrenaline rush.
> **4** I don't really think about getting injured or killed.
> **5** Because they're becoming more accessible, and there's much more exposure than before on TV and on social media. It's the adrenaline rush that people really enjoy.
> **6** I think it's becoming a bit more equal between men and women, but men still dominate.

c Focus on the three extracts from the interview and give Sts time to see if they can remember any of the missing words.

Check answers.

1 after **2** risks **3** part

Elicit the meaning of each phrasal verb or idiom.

1 **take after sb** = to look or behave like an older member of your family, especially your mother or father
2 **take risks** = to do sth even though you know that sth bad could happen as a result
3 **take part in** = to be involved in sth

EXTRA SUPPORT If there's time, you could get Sts to listen again with the script on *p.125*, so they can see exactly what they understood / didn't understand. Translate / Explain any new words or phrases.

d Focus on the task and point out the two sections, *Expressions with 'take'* and *Phrasal verbs with 'take'*.

Put Sts in pairs and give them time to work out the meaning of the highlighted words by looking at the context.

Check answers, either explaining in English, translating into Sts' L1, or getting Sts to check in their dictionaries.

Vocabulary notes

You may want to explain that *take advantage of* can also mean to make use of sb / sth in a way that is unfair or dishonest, e.g. *He took advantage of my generosity and asked for much more than I had intended to give him.*

1 **take care of** = care for sb / sth / yourself; to be careful about sth
2 **take advantage of** = make use of sth well; to make use of an opportunity
3 **take place** = happen, especially after previously being arranged or planned
4 **take your time** = use as much time as you need without hurrying
5 **take into account** = consider particular facts, circumstances, etc. when making a decision about sth
6 **take no notice** = pay no attention
7 **take pity on** = show compassion, feel sorry for
8 **take off** = remove; leave the ground and begin to fly
9 **take up** = learn or start to do sth, especially for pleasure
10 **take to** = start liking sb
11 **take against** = to start not liking sb / sth for no clear reason
12 **take out** = go to a restaurant, theatre, club, etc. with sb you have invited; remove

EXTRA SUPPORT Give Sts a few minutes to read the sentences again and check their answers. Then put Sts in pairs, **A** and **B**. Sts **A** (book open) read a sentence to Sts **B** (book closed), using *beep* to represent the blanks, e.g.:
A *My neighbour beep beep beep my son while I'm at work.*
B *takes care of*
Then they swap roles.

e Put Sts in pairs, **A** and **B**, preferably face-to-face. Tell them to go to **Communication I'll take a question**, **A** on *p.108*, **B** on *p.114*.

Go through the instructions carefully.

Give Sts time to complete the phrasal verbs or expressions in 1–5.

Check answers by only eliciting the missing words, <u>not</u> the whole question.

Sts A
1 after **2** care of **3** advantage of **4** place **5** notice
Sts B
1 your time **2** up, up **3** into account **4** to, against **5** out

Before giving Sts time to ask and answer their questions in their pairs, get them to focus on the **Giving examples** box.

In their pairs, Sts now ask and answer their questions.

Finally, when Sts have finished, deal with any new vocabulary, and elicit or model the pronunciation.

Tell Sts to go back to the main lesson **4B**.

7 WRITING for and against

Tell Sts to go to **Writing For and against** on *p.117*.

a Focus on the task. Give Sts time to read the blog post and answer the question. Tell them not to worry about the gaps.

Elicit opinions.

b Tell Sts to read the blog post again and to complete gaps 2–10 with the linking expressions from the list. Point out that two of the expressions are interchangeable (can be swapped around).

Get Sts to compare with a partner, and then check answers.

2 for example **3** Another advantage **4** Furthermore / In addition **5** On the other hand **6** Although **7** for example **8** Because of **9** Furthermore / In addition **10** To sum up

c Focus on the **Useful language: linking expressions** box and get Sts to complete the chart with the linking expressions from **b**.

Check answers.

To list advantages / disadvantages: another advantage
To add more points to the same topic: furthermore, in addition
To introduce an example: for example
To make contrasting points: on the other hand, although
To give a reason: because of
To introduce the conclusion: to sum up

d Focus on the task and give Sts time to choose which topic they want to write about in their post.

e Focus on the task and go through points 1–3 with the class.

f Focus on the instructions, making sure Sts know what *colloquial expressions* means.

Then either get Sts to write their blog post in class (set a time limit of, e.g. 20 minutes) or get them to write it at home for homework.

g Sts should check their post for mistakes before giving it in.

8 ▶ VIDEO LISTENING

a Focus on the task and go through the **Glossary** with the class.

Play the video once the whole way through for Sts to watch and answer the question.

EXTRA SUPPORT Read through the script and decide if you need to pre-teach any new lexis before Sts watch the video.

4B 69

Check the answer.

Surfing helped her to relax and get her mind off her problems.

Tell Sts to go back to the main lesson **4B**.

Riding the waves

N = narrator, G = Grace

N *Tramore is a small town on the south coast of Ireland. Its long and unspoilt stretch of coastline makes it very popular with tourists, and the sea plays an important role in life here. Just ask local resident Grace Doyle. Grace is a qualified maths teacher, but she decided to take a career break to pursue her lifelong love of surfing.*

G So, I started surfing at maybe eleven or twelve years old. But I always used to be in the ocean and playing on a bodyboard and I used to always know what surfing was and wanted to do it. My oldest brother got a surfboard lesson for his twenty-first birthday. And that eventually just got passed down to me as I grew up because my other brother started doing it. And then I wanted to do it naturally.

N *Each day Grace checks the weather conditions online. If the waves are good, she packs her boards, and drives to one of her favourite spots. Luckily, the Irish coastline offers plenty of places to surf due to its position in the Atlantic Ocean, attracting surfers from all over the world. Surfing as a sport is growing rapidly in Ireland, and reflects a global trend. Grace's success in competitive surfing has led to several sponsorship deals, allowing her to chase waves all over the world.*

G I've been to a lot of places around the world – Central America, Indonesia, Europe. The best wave I've ever surfed is probably in Indonesia. So, the water's warm, the waves are crystal clear and super clean. Part of it is because they're bigger so I enjoy the bigger waves.

N *Today, there are an estimated thirty-five million surfers around the world and the industry has annual revenues of around one hundred billion dollars. How does Grace account for this growth in popularity?*

G There's a lot of media coverage lately, a lot more than there used to be. So you've got like Facebook, and Instagram and YouTube and everything is just being put out there now, whereas years ago it would be quite hard, you'd have to wait for the magazines to come out to see the footage. People are seeing how healthy surfing is as a lifestyle. So if you surf, you're out with nature, you're exercising, you're having fun, you're getting everything in one go. So I think people are drawn to that because it's something healthy and fun at the same time.

N *But surfing can be dangerous too.*

G I guess the scariest thing that's happened to me as a surfer is being held down for quite a long time under the water. So you might fall off a wave and it's quite a big wave. So it just holds you down for quite a long time. Once it happened to me in Indonesia, and I just thought that maybe it was the end, but then you always just come up. I've learned to relax. So when it happens, you know it's going to be a long hold down. So you just have to rely on holding your breath and relax because if you panic, then you're going to run out of breath faster.

N *Does Grace enjoy the element of danger?*

G To a point, like, it's part of the adrenaline rush. So I would enjoy the element of danger in the sense of, like, I'm out in big waves and I know if I wipe out there's a high risk, I'm going to get injured. But there's also a high risk I'm going to get the best wave of my life. So I, I like that adrenaline rush.

N *And Grace knows that this can go too far.*

G I have seen people that are out in waves that they shouldn't be out in. And you can see before it even happens, that stuff is going to happen to them. It's a fine line in that sense that they're putting everything and everything around them at risk, like, in terms of losing them, if they die. Because that's…at that level of big wave surfing, if you wipe out, like, in those kind of waves it's like, are you going to die or not? It's not like, are you going to hurt yourself? It's more like, are you going to come up?

N *As with all extreme sports, this element of danger is part of the attraction and it can be extremely addictive. Does Grace consider herself an adrenaline junkie?*

G Yeah, definitely because when you're addicted to surfing, you're addicted to that adrenaline rush. It's just something you want to keep going back for more and more of. So you have a really, really good surf and you think you're satisfied for like a week. But no, the next day, you're like, 'I want to do the same again.' It's definitely something that you're drawn to time and time again. And I don't think it's just the adrenaline. It's being out in nature and water. Like several times surfing has gotten me over difficult times in my life. So I lost my dad when I was sixteen. And surfing is what got me through that, surfing with my friends and people around here. There's something about being in nature that sort of relaxes you and just gets your mind off everything else.

N *Grace has managed to organize her life around surfing. For her, and many others like her, it isn't just an extreme sport, it's a way of life.*

b Focus on the task and give Sts time to read 1–10.

Play the video again, pausing if necessary for Sts to complete the gaps.

EXTRA CHALLENGE First, put Sts in pairs and tell them to try to remember any of the answers. Then play the video again.

Check answers.

1	Ireland
2	maths teacher
3	older brother
4	Europe, Indonesia
5	hundred, dollars
6	more popular
7	healthy, fun
8	breath, relax
9	best wave
10	hurt, killed

EXTRA SUPPORT You could get Sts to watch the video again with subtitles, so they can see exactly what they understood / didn't understand. Translate / Explain any new words or phrases.

c Focus on the questions and make sure Sts know the meaning of an *adrenaline rush* (= an increase in the substance produced in the body when you are excited, afraid, or angry. It makes the heart beat faster and increases your energy and ability to move quickly).

Do this as a whole-class activity, or put Sts in pairs and then get some feedback. You could also tell Sts what you think and what you do that is both healthy and fun.

EXTRA SUPPORT Do these as open-class questions.

70 **4B**

3&4 Revise and Check

For instructions on how to use these pages, see *p.41*.

More materials

For teachers

Teacher's Resource Centre
Video Can you understand these people? 3&4
Quick Test 4
File 4 Test

For students

Online Practice Check your progress

GRAMMAR

a
1 a **2** c **3** a **4** a **5** c **6** c **7** a **8** c **9** b **10** b

b
1 'll / will be lying **2** will, have started **3** has landed / lands
4 drink **5** finish / 've finished

VOCABULARY

a
1 gate **2** baggage reclaim **3** aisle **4** turbulence **5** jet lag

b
1 trip **2** lately **3** even **4** hard **5** especially

c
1 blew **2** dropped **3** poured **4** got **5** took

d
1 blizzard (the others only relate to wind)
2 chilly (the others relate to hot temperatures)
3 damp (the others are nouns)
4 bright (the others relate to cold temperatures)
5 drought (the others relate to storms)

e
1 in **2** off **3** up **4** after **5** place

PRONUNCIATION

a
1 w**i**ndy /ɪ/ **2** cl**ear** /ɪə/ **3** l**ou**nge /aʊ/ **4** h**u**mid /uː/
5 troll**ey** /iː/

b
1 e<u>ven</u>tually **2** <u>gra</u>dually **3** e<u>spe</u>cially **4** <u>pa</u>ssenger
5 <u>hu</u>rricane

CAN YOU understand this text?

a Mount Misti

b **1** N **2** T **3** N **4** M **5** T **6** M

CAN YOU understand these people?

1 b **2** b **3** a **4** c

4.15

1

I = interviewer, N = Nora

I Have you ever flown long-haul?

N Yes, I've flown to Hong Kong. I was flying from Dublin, but I had a stock-, a stopover in Stockholm. Uh, but still, Stockholm to Hong Kong I think was thirteen hours. So quite long.

I How was the flight?

N Er, it was OK. But it was, it was very long, and, er, can get a bit tiring I think, just sitting down and wondering when you're going to land. Er, but I watched films on the plane to distract myself and fell asleep.

2

I = interviewer, R = Rafael

I What kind of things to you enjoy reading?

R I like to read. I'm a slow reader, but I love reading, so I like to read, um, besides everything about everything, everybody, every subject. I like biographies, and, er, and I like, er, true testimonies, and, er, it varies, I like poetry a lot, and very occasional fiction, which I know is a challenge to write well.

I Do you prefer reading in print or online?

R I still prefer to read in print, but online saves time.

3

I = interviewer, D = Diarmuid

I Have you ever experienced extreme weather?

D Er, I lived in Japan, um, I lived in Japan and every year, er, Japan has a typhoon season. Um, and it was quite soon into my stay there that we had several typhoons, one after the other. Um, and it was quite extreme.

I What happened?

D Um, er, we had, we were all told to stay indoors. Um, they were very used to it, so they had drills. Um, and it did cause some damage in the town, I think like broken roofs and things like that. Um, but they did deal with it very well.

4

I = interviewer, J = Julia

I Have you ever done a dangerous sport?

J Er, yeah, I guess waterskiing is the most dangerous sport I've done.

I Did you enjoy it?

J I did, but mostly because I just didn't realize that you can die from it. So I went really, I went really, really quickly and was like, this is great. And then afterwards my sister told me about a relative of ours who like, broke their leg from waterskiing. So…but it's fine, yeah.

5A I'm a survivor

G unreal conditionals
V feelings
P word stress in three- or four-syllable adjectives

Lesson plan

The topic of this lesson is survival.
In the first half, Sts talk about how they think they would react in an emergency situation and they read about a British reality TV show in which groups of participants have to survive on a remote uninhabited island. Sts then listen to an interview with one of the participants talking about the best and worst experiences on the island. The vocabulary focus is on feelings, e.g. *devastated*, *stunned*, etc., and Pronunciation looks at word stress in three- or four-syllable adjectives.

The second half of the lesson is based on the true story, later made into a documentary for Discovery TV, of three young backpackers and their guide who got lost in the Amazon jungle. Sts read and listen to the story. The grammar focus is on unreal conditionals, i.e. second and third conditionals. Sts should have seen both these structures before, but will still need practice in using them, especially third conditionals. Finally, Sts go to the Writing Bank and focus on writing a blog post.

More materials
For teachers
Photocopiables
Grammar unreal conditionals *p.170*
Communicative Would you survive? *p.200*
(instructions *p.186*)
Vocabulary Feelings *p.223* (instructions *p.215*)
For students
Workbook 5A
Online Practice 5A

OPTIONAL LEAD-IN – THE QUOTE

Write the quote at the top of *p.46* on the board and the name of the person who said it, or get Sts to open their books and read it.

You could point out that Bear Grylls was an SAS serviceman and is now an adventurer, TV presenter, writer, and survival instructor. Although his real name is Edward, he was nicknamed Bear by his sister when he was one week old, and the name stuck. He is currently involved in a TV survival series called *The Island*.

Ask Sts whether they agree with him.

1 SPEAKING

a Focus on the six survival questions, making sure Sts understand all the situations, e.g. *hear an intruder*, *ski off-piste*, etc.

Put Sts in pairs and give them time to read each question and simply say how they would feel in that situation: *calm*, *nervous*, *scared*, or *terrified*. You could write the four adjectives on the board to remind Sts. Tell them <u>not</u> to

look at options a–c. You could demonstrate by telling the class how you would feel for the first two questions.
Get some feedback.

b Now quickly focus on options a–c for each question and make sure Sts understand all the situations, e.g. *confront an intruder*, *neutral / lower gear*, etc.

Now tell Sts to choose an answer for all six questions.

Put Sts in small groups of three and get them to compare their answers. Remind them to give reasons for their answer.

Get some feedback.

c Focus on the task and then tell Sts to continue working in their group of three, **A**, **B**, and **C**. Tell them to go to **Communication It's an emergency!**, **A** on *p.108*, **B** on *p.112*, and **C** on *p.114*.

Monitor and help while Sts are reading the answers to the situations. Then give them time to make notes under the headings *You should…* and *You shouldn't…*

When they are ready, each student should tell the other two people in their group what they should and shouldn't do in that particular situation. Encourage Sts to do this in their own words, without looking at the text.

Get feedback for each emergency situation.

Finally, deal with any new vocabulary, and elicit or model the pronunciation.

Tell Sts to go back to the main lesson **5A**.

d Finally, get Sts to quickly look back at their answers to the six questions in **b** to see if they chose the correct answers.
Check answers.

1 c **2** b **3** a **4** b **5** a **6** a

With a show of hands, find out how many Sts chose the correct answers.

2 READING & LISTENING recognizing positive and negative experiences

a Focus on the task and either give Sts time to read the description individually, or read it as a class.

EXTRA SUPPORT Ask Sts some comprehension questions to check understanding. Tell them to use their own words when answering, e.g. *What kind of island do the participants go to?* (An island that is far away and has no people living on it) *Is Bear Grylls with them?* (No, they are alone.) *What was different about series 5?* (The participants were put into groups according to how much money they earn.), etc.

Ask the class if they have a similar programme in their country. If so, have they watched it, and did they enjoy it?

b Focus on the interview and the image. Tell Sts that the photo is of Ali Brookes – a participant in series 5 of *The Island* – and elicit what else they can see in the image.

Give Sts time to read the interview and tell them not to worry about the gaps.

Give Sts time individually to think of their answers to the two questions.

72 **5A**

Get Sts to compare with a partner, and then elicit some feedback.

EXTRA SUPPORT Before Sts read the interview the first time, check whether you need to pre-teach any vocabulary.

c Give Sts time to read the interview again and this time complete gaps 1–10. For each gap, there are three choices, and they must choose the best one. Encourage them to look carefully at the surrounding context and to try the sentence out with each of the alternatives before choosing the one they think fits best.

Get Sts to compare with a partner and explain their choices.

d 🔊 **5.1** Play the audio for Sts to listen and check. Tell them the person on the audio is Ali Brookes.

Check answers.

1 challenge	**2** so	**3** actually	**4** easy	**5** through	**6** sick
7 if	**8** Although	**9** as well	**10** definitely		

🔊 **5.1**
See text in Student's Book on *p.47*

Now ask Sts if they think that Ali was mostly positive or negative.

On balance, she was positive.

Deal with any other new vocabulary. Elicit or model the pronunciation of any tricky words.

e Tell Sts they are going to listen to the second part of the interview. Look at the seven things they will hear Ali talk about, and make sure Sts understand them.

Give Sts time to tick and cross each item that Ali mentions according to whether they think she enjoyed it or found it difficult.

f 🔊 **5.2** Play the audio for Sts to listen and check.

Check answers, and if Sts are doing the **Extra challenge**, elicit reasons (see script).

Find out with a show of hands how many people predicted all Ali's answers correctly.

EXTRA CHALLENGE Tell Sts when they listen they should also make a note why the experiences were positive or negative.

EXTRA SUPPORT Read through the script and decide if you need to pre-teach any new lexis before Sts listen.

✗ most of what we ate was yucca, which is a bit like a potato
✗ the water we had to wash in was the sea
✗ when it rained
✗ we were meeting all these new people we'd never met before
✓ (He) threw us out of the boat and told us to swim to the island.
✓ we had a sports day and we had a talent show
✓ leaving the island

🔊 **5.2**
(script in Student's Book on *pp.125–126*)
I = interviewer, A = Ali
I What was the most difficult or challenging part of your experience?
A Well, because you're, um, put on the island with just the clothes on your back and a few basic tools, it means that anything you eat you have to find, catch, and kill, if necessary. So, for the first

week, we didn't eat anything at all except a few coconuts. Um, so I lost four kilos in just a week. Um, after that, most of what we ate was yucca, which is a bit like a potato, grows in the ground. But you have to walk a lot to find it, um, and even then it would only be the equivalent of having a small potato each, um, every day. So we were still hungry. We were able to catch some fish, um, and then we did manage to kill a wild boar. And also because of the lack of food we became really weak, so it was hard you, – hard even to go out for a stroll along the beach. That became really difficult. It was also difficult being dirty all the time, because the water we had to wash in, er, was the sea. So you're obviously salty and covered in sand and you never really feel clean. Um, when it rained, which was all the time, the ground would become really muddy and everything would just get absolutely filthy. We had a couple of weeks where the weather was really bad, so we were completely soaked, really freezing cold, wet, miserable, and hungry. Um, and the other thing that was really difficult was the tension between the groups and also within our group, because everyone was very stressed and hungry and tired, it didn't take much for arguments to occur, and there's nowhere to escape from on the desert island.
I What were the highlights?
A So at first, even just landing on the island was a highlight, um, because we were so excited and we were meeting all these new people, um, we'd never met before, and we were full of enthusiasm and energy. Um, and we just had lunch, so we weren't hungry. Um, so when Bear Grylls picked us up on his boat and drove us round the island, um, and then he stopped in the middle of the sea and threw us out of the boat and told us to swim to the island, um, which was so exciting. Um, and the last week was also a real highlight for me because the two groups came together and we built a communal shelter in the middle of the beach so everyone – for everyone to sleep in and to enjoy, and we had a really good time. The weather at this point, um, had turned really good and so, we had a sports day and we had a talent show, and even a wedding! It was a really fun week. Um, but I think probably leaving the island was the real highlight – best day of my life, even. Um, it was so brilliant to know that we'd survived for thirty-five days. And seeing Bear pull up on his boat, er, to come and collect us was just an amazing feeling. I felt both really proud and super relieved.
I Out of the sixteen people that landed on the island, thirteen, including Ali, managed to last the whole five weeks. Two participants decided to leave before the end, and unfortunately, one had to go to hospital with an eye injury. By the last week, the participants had all realized that they were much more effective working together as one big team than trying to survive in separate groups. How much money they earned, or what their background was, turned out to be completely irrelevant. Both teams worked hard, kept their morale high, and survived.

g Focus on items 1–5 and make sure Sts know what they are.

Play the audio again for Sts to listen and make a note of what Ali says about each item (this time the items are mentioned in the order given).

Get Sts to compare with a partner, and then check answers.

1 For the first week, they didn't eat anything except a few coconuts.
2 They managed to kill a wild boar.
3 There was tension between the two groups, and it didn't take much for arguments to occur.
4 The two groups came together, and they built a communal shelter on the beach in the last week.
5 Ali survived for 35 days (five weeks) on the island.

EXTRA SUPPORT If there's time, you could get Sts to listen again with the script on *pp.125–126*, so they can see exactly what they understood / didn't understand. Translate / Explain any new words or phrases.

5A 73

h Ask Sts the first two questions and check answers.

> **13**
> They learned that they were much more effective working together as one big team.

Finally, either do the last question as a whole-class activity, or put Sts in pairs and then get some feedback. Ask Sts to give examples of what they would enjoy, what they would find difficult, and what they would miss. You could tell the class if you think you could survive on the island.

3 VOCABULARY & PRONUNCIATION
feelings; word stress

a ◗ **5.3** Focus on the task and give Sts time to read the two extracts.

> **EXTRA CHALLENGE** Elicit some possible adjectives for the gaps before Sts listen, but <u>don't</u> tell them if they are correct. Sts then listen and check.

Play the audio for Sts to listen and write the missing adjectives that describe how Ali was feeling.

Check answers, making sure Sts know what all the adjectives mean. Elicit or model pronunciation.

> **1** stunned **2** thrilled **3** proud **4** relieved

◗ 5.3
So, I was absolutely stunned when they told me they wanted me to go on the, on the programme, but at the same time, um, I was thrilled. …seeing Bear pull up on his boat, er, to come and collect us was just an amazing feeling. I felt both really proud and super relieved.

b Tell Sts to go to **Vocabulary Bank Feelings** on *p.157*.

Vocabulary notes
Adjectives

Make sure Sts are clear about the meaning of the new words. *Nervous* may be a false friend for your Sts, depending on their L1. In English it means anxious, worried, or frightened about something that is going to happen in the future, e.g. a job interview, an exam, etc.

You might want to explain / elicit the difference between *fed up* and *upset*:

- *fed up* = bored or frustrated and unhappy (especially with a situation which has gone on too long), e.g. *I'm really fed up with my job. I think I'm going to quit.* Point out that *fed up* is always followed by *with*, e.g. *I am fed up **with** this awful weather*.
- *upset* = unhappy when something bad happens, e.g. *Carol was terribly upset when her dog disappeared*.

Strong adjectives

You might want to remind Sts that you <u>can't</u> use *a bit*, *quite*, or *very* with these adjectives. NOT ~~I was very astonished.~~ If you want to use an intensifier, use *really / absolutely / totally / completely*.

Informal words and expressions

Highlight that words like *gobsmacked* and *gutted* would only be used in very informal situations, e.g. talking with friends.

Focus on **1 Adjectives** and get Sts to do **a** individually or in pairs.

◗ **5.4** Now do **b**. Play the audio for Sts to listen and check.

Check answers.

◗ 5.4
Feelings
1 Adjectives
1 B I feel really miserable.
2 F I feel a bit homesick.
3 E I'm quite disappointed.
4 G I'm very lonely.
5 I I'm incredibly proud.
6 H I'm really fed up.
7 C I'm very grateful.
8 A I'm very upset.
9 D I'm so relieved.
10 J I'm very offended.

Now either use the audio to drill the pronunciation of the adjectives, or model and drill them yourself. Give further practice of any words your Sts find difficult to pronounce.

> **EXTRA SUPPORT** Tell Sts to cover 1–10, look at situations A–J, and try to remember the adjectives.

Focus on **2 Strong adjectives** and get Sts to do **a** individually or in pairs.

◗ **5.5** Now do **b**. Play the audio for Sts to listen and check.

Check answers.

◗ 5.5
2 Strong adjectives
1 stunned
2 devastated
3 thrilled
4 delighted
5 astonished
6 desperate
7 overwhelmed
8 bewildered
9 horrified

Now either use the audio to drill the pronunciation of the adjectives, or model and drill them yourself. Give further practice of any words your Sts find difficult to pronounce.

Now do **Activation**. Get Sts to choose five adjectives from **1a** and **2a** and make true sentences about themselves. They could write their sentences or do it orally with a partner.

Get some feedback.

> **EXTRA SUPPORT** Tell Sts to cover definitions 1–9, look at the strong adjectives in the list, and try to remember what each one means.

Focus on **3 Informal words and expressions** and get Sts to do **a** and **b** individually or in pairs.

◗ **5.6** Now do **c**. Play the audio for Sts to listen and check their answers to **a** and **b**.

Check answers.

74 **5A**

◉ 5.6

3 Informal words and expressions
1 B I was scared stiff when I heard the bedroom door opening.
2 A You look a bit down. What's the problem?
3 D I'm absolutely shattered. I want to relax and put my feet up.
4 F I was completely gobsmacked when I heard that Tina was getting married!
5 E I'm sick of hearing you complain about your job.
6 C When England missed the penalty in the last minute, we were absolutely gutted.

Give further practice of any words your Sts find difficult to pronounce.

Now do **Activation** and get Sts to cover sentences 1–6 in **a**, look at feelings A–F in **b**, and try to remember what they mean.

Tell Sts to go back to the main lesson **5A**.

EXTRA SUPPORT If you think Sts need more practice, you may want to give them the **Vocabulary** photocopiable activity at this point

---

Pronunciation notes

Word stress

There are not many clear rules to give Sts regarding the pronunciation of three- and four-syllable adjectives, and the stress may fall on the first, second, or third syllable. It is worth reminding Sts that prefixes and suffixes are not stressed, e.g. *dishonest*, *ungrateful*, etc.

It is also worth reminding Sts that the unstressed /ə/ sound often occurs after or before the stressed syllable in multi-syllabic words, and may even occur twice, e.g. *desperate* /ˈdespərət/.

---

c ◉ 5.7 Focus on the task and tell Sts that each line in 1–9 is a response to part of a conversation. Give Sts time to read 1–9.

EXTRA CHALLENGE Get Sts to decide which they think is the stressed syllable in each **bold** adjective before they listen (but <u>not</u> to underline it yet). Remind them that this kind of exercise is easier if they say the adjectives out loud to themselves.

Play the audio for Sts to listen to the nine conversations and underline the stressed syllable in the **bold** adjectives.

Check answers by writing the adjectives on the board and underlining the stressed syllables. Elicit what the context was in each mini conversation.

1 <u>des</u>perate   2 of<u>fen</u>ded   3 disap<u>poin</u>ted   4 be<u>wil</u>dered
5 as<u>ton</u>ished   6 de<u>ligh</u>ted   7 de<u>vas</u>tated   8 <u>hor</u>rified
9 over<u>whelmed</u>

◉ 5.7
1
A Hi, Sue. What's the matter?
B I've just been robbed! Please come quickly. I'm desperate.
2
A You weren't offended by what I said, were you?
B Yes, actually, I was. I don't like you criticizing my family.
3
A What did you think of the film?
B To be honest, I was a bit disappointed.

4
A What don't you understand in the report?
B I'm completely bewildered by so much information.
5
A Were you surprised to hear that the boss is leaving?
B I was astonished. I really wasn't expecting it.
6
A So can you come to dinner next week?
B Yes, we'd be delighted to. Thank you so much.
7
A How did your parents react when you told them you and Rita had separated?
B They were devastated. It was such a shock.
8
A How did you feel when you heard the news about the plane crash?
B I was absolutely horrified. It was an awful accident.
9
A Do you like the necklace?
B I love it. I'm overwhelmed – it's stunning!

---

d Now put Sts in pairs and get them to practise saying the sentences, paying attention to intonation and stress in the adjectives. Make sure they swap roles.

e Focus on the task and give Sts time to choose their three adjectives from **c** and to think of what they want to tell their partner.

In their pairs, Sts tell each other their situations for the three adjectives they have chosen. Get them to give as many details as possible.

Get some feedback.

4 READING & LISTENING understanding mood and feelings

a Focus on the six sentences about the Amazon rainforest.

Put Sts in small groups of three or four and tell them to complete as many gaps as they can in 1–6.

Check answers and make sure Sts understand all the lexis, e.g. *canopy*, *indigenous*. For 5, you could tell Sts that there are around 400–500 indigenous tribes living in the Amazon rainforest altogether.

1 Australia   2 Brazil, Peru, Colombia   3 second-longest
4 dark   5 tribes, contact   6 snakes, frogs, spiders

b Focus on the beginning of the story and the photos. Explain that the people in the first photo are two of the four men, plus a local man, taken before they went into the jungle. Stress that this is a true story which happened some years ago. Set a time limit for Sts to read the beginning of the story and answer the questions.

Get Sts to compare with a partner, and then check answers to 1–3, and elicit from Sts their own ideas for the questions in **bold**.

EXTRA SUPPORT Before Sts read the whole story the first time, check whether you need to pre-teach any vocabulary.

1 To go deep into the jungle for seven days and visit an undiscovered Indian village
   After seven days, they still hadn't found the village and there were tensions in the group, so they decided to turn around and go back to Apolo, their starting point.

5A 75

2 a The three friends started to suspect that Karl (the guide) didn't know where the village was.

b Marcus was complaining about everything, especially his feet.

3 Kevin was angry with Marcus because he thought it was his fault that they were having to cut the trip short; Kevin and Yossi decided to raft down the river, but didn't want Marcus to come. Marcus and Karl decided to go back to Apolo on foot.

Now check whether there is any vocabulary Sts couldn't guess and elicit / explain the meaning. Encourage Sts to write down any new lexis.

EXTRA SUPPORT If you want to check that Sts have really understood the first part, you could ask them the following comprehension questions before moving on to the listening: *What did Karl promise the three friends? What promise did they make to each other? How do you think the three friends felt before going into the jungle? What decision did Kevin take? etc.*

c ◀) **5.8** – ◀) **5.13** Now focus on the instructions and photos. Get Sts to look at the photos first, and use them to pre-teach *jaguar* and *footprint*.

◀) **5.8** Play the audio for Sts to listen to the first part. Then play it again and get Sts to answer the questions orally in pairs.

Check answers and elicit opinions for the questions in **bold**. Make sure Sts use the correct verb form *I would rather have been in X's situation…*

EXTRA SUPPORT Read through the scripts and decide if you need to pre-teach any new lexis before Sts listen.

1 They were both thrown into the water when the raft hit a rock.

2 He swam to the river bank and found their backpack floating in the river, with food, insect repellent, a lighter, and the map.

◀) **5.8**

(script in Student's Book on *p.126*)

Yossi and Kevin soon realized that going by river was a big mistake. The river got faster and faster, and soon they were in rapids.

The raft was swept down the river at an incredible speed until it hit a rock. Both men were thrown into the water. Kevin was a strong swimmer and he managed to swim to land, but Yossi was swept away by the rapids.

But Yossi didn't drown. He was carried several kilometres downriver by the rapids, but he eventually managed to swim to the riverbank. He was totally exhausted. By an incredible piece of luck, he found their backpack floating in the river. The backpack contained a little food, insect repellent, a lighter, and most important of all…the map. But the two friends were now separated by a canyon and six or seven kilometres of jungle.

You may want to ask a few more questions before moving on to the next part to make sure Sts got all the details (e.g. *Can you remember what was in the backpack?*).

◀) **5.9** Repeat the process for **Part 2**.

3 Kevin was feeling desperate and responsible for what had happened to Yossi. Yossi was feeling quite optimistic because he was sure he would find Kevin.

4 A jaguar came near him, but he frightened it away.

◀) **5.9**

(script in Student's Book on *p.126*)

Kevin was feeling desperate. He didn't know if Yossi was alive or dead, but he started walking downriver to look for him. He felt responsible for what had happened to his friend because he had persuaded him to go with him on the river.

Yossi, however, was feeling quite optimistic. He was sure that Kevin would look for him, so he started walking upriver, calling his friend's name. 'Kevin! Kevin!' But nobody answered.

At night Yossi tried to sleep, but he felt terrified. The jungle was full of noises. Suddenly, he woke up because he heard a branch breaking. He turned on his flashlight. There was a jaguar staring at him…

Yossi was trembling with fear. But then he remembered something that he had once seen in a film. He used the cigarette lighter to set fire to the insect repellent spray…and he managed to scare the jaguar away.

◀) **5.10** Repeat the process for **Part 3**.

5 Because he was exhausted and starving. Then he saw footprints which he thought were Kevin's and followed them. Then he realized they were his own.

◀) **5.10**

(script in Student's Book on *p.126*)

After five days alone, Yossi was exhausted and starving. Suddenly, as he was walking, he saw a footprint on the trail – it was a hiking boot. It had to be Kevin's footprint! He followed the trail until he discovered another footprint and then another. But suddenly he realized that the footprints weren't Kevin's footprints. They were his own. He had been walking around in a circle. At that moment, Yossi realized that he would never find Kevin. In fact, he felt sure that Kevin must be dead. He felt totally depressed and on the point of giving up.

◀) **5.11** Repeat the process for **Part 4**.

6 He had been looking for Yossi.

7 He decided to save himself and let himself float down the river.

8 He was rescued by two (Bolivian) hunters.

◀) **5.11**

(script in Student's Book on *p.126*)

But Kevin wasn't dead. He was still looking for Yossi. But after nearly a week, he was also weak and exhausted from lack of food and lack of sleep. He decided that it was time to forget Yossi and try to save himself. He had just enough strength left to hold onto a log and let himself float down the river.

Kevin was incredibly lucky – he was rescued by two Bolivian hunters who were travelling downriver in a canoe. The men only hunted in that part of the rainforest once a year, so if they had passed by a short time earlier or later, they wouldn't have seen Kevin. They took him back to the town of San José, where he spent two days recovering.

◀) **5.12** Repeat the process for **Part 5**.

9 He went to an army base and asked them to look for Yossi.

10 Because the plane had to fly too high over the dense forest, so they couldn't see anything..

11 He paid a local man with a boat to take him up the river.

76 **5A**

5.12
(script in Student's Book on *p.126*)

As soon as Kevin felt well enough, he went to a Bolivian army base and asked them to look for Yossi. The army officer he spoke to was sure that Yossi must be dead, but in the end, Kevin persuaded them to take him up in a plane and fly over the part of the rainforest where Yossi might be. But the plane had to fly too high over the rainforest, and the forest was too dense. They couldn't see anything at all. It was a hopeless search. Kevin felt terribly guilty. He was convinced that it was all his fault that Yossi was going to die in the jungle. Kevin's last hope was to pay a local man with a boat to take him up the river to look for his friend.

5.13 Repeat the process for **Part 6**. Encourage Sts to use *must have*, *might have*, etc. when they speculate about what happened to Marcus and Karl.

12 Three weeks. He was starving, exhausted, and losing his mind.
13 A bee. It was the engine of the boat Kevin was in.

5.13
(script in Student's Book on *p.126*)

By now, Yossi had been on his own in the jungle for nearly three weeks. He hadn't eaten for days. He was starving, exhausted, and slowly losing his mind. It was evening. He lay down by the side of the river, ready for another night alone in the jungle.

Suddenly, he heard the sound of a bee buzzing in his ear. He thought a bee had got inside his mosquito net. But when he opened his eyes, he saw that the buzzing noise wasn't a bee…

It was a boat. Yossi was too weak to shout, but Kevin had already seen him. It was a one-in-a-million chance that Kevin would find his friend, but he did – Yossi was saved.

When Yossi had recovered, he and Kevin flew to the city of La Paz and they went directly to the hotel where they had agreed to meet Marcus and Karl.

But Marcus and Karl were not at the hotel. The two men had never arrived back in the town of Apolo. The Bolivian army organized a search of the rainforest, but Marcus and Karl were never seen again.

EXTRA SUPPORT If there's time, you could get Sts to listen again to all parts of the audio with the scripts on *p.126*, so they can see exactly what they understood / didn't understand. Translate / Explain any new words or phrases.

d Do this as a whole-class activity.

You might like to tell Sts that Yossi Ghinsberg now works giving talks at conferences about motivation, based on his experience. He has also devoted a lot of time and raised money to help protect the rainforest where he got lost. He lives in both Australia and Israel. Kevin Gale works as a manager of a gym. The documentary made about their experience is based on Yossi's book *Lost in the Jungle* and can be seen on the Discovery Channel as part of the series called *I Shouldn't Be Alive*.

5 GRAMMAR unreal conditionals

a Focus on the task and tell Sts to complete the gaps.
Get Sts to compare with a partner, and then check answers.

1 were hiking, got lost   **2** 'd / would call, wouldn't confront
3 had been   **4** would have died

b Either get Sts to do this individually, or do it as a whole-class activity. Before they start, make sure Sts know the meaning of *hypothetical*.
If Sts worked alone, check answers.

3 and 4 refer to a hypothetical situation in the past.
1 and 2 refer to a hypothetical situation in the present or future.

c Tell Sts to go to **Grammar Bank 5A** on *p.140*.

Grammar notes
Unreal conditionals

Sts will have studied both the second and third conditionals separately, but here they are contrasted. Sts should be fairly confident with the concept of both, although they will probably still have problems using them orally with fluency, especially the third conditional. Sts also widen their knowledge of the second and third conditionals by seeing how other forms can be used in either clause.

Second or third conditional?

The point to emphasize here is that the second conditional refers to a hypothetical situation in **the present or future**, which can sometimes be changed and sometimes not, e.g. *If she were taller, she could get a job as a model* (situation can't be changed). *If you studied more, you would pass the exam* (situation could be changed).

The third conditional refers to hypothetical situations in the past **which didn't happen**, e.g. *If we had known you were in hospital, we would have visited you* (we didn't know, so we didn't visit you).

Mixed conditionals

Sometimes the second and third conditionals are mixed. We suggest that you draw Sts' attention to this for passive recognition, but this is not practised in the exercises.

Focus on the example sentences for **second conditional sentences: *if + past simple, would / wouldn't + infinitive** and play audio **5.14** for Sts to listen and repeat. Encourage them to copy the rhythm. Then go through the rules with the class.

Repeat for **third conditional sentences: *if + past perfect, would / wouldn't have + past participle* 5.15** and **second or third conditional? 5.16**.

Now go through the **Mixed conditionals** box with Sts.

Focus on the exercises and get Sts to do them individually or in pairs.

If they do them individually, get them to compare with a partner. Check answers, getting Sts to read the full sentences.

a
1 I **wouldn't have made** so much food if you'd told me you weren't hungry.
2 If I were you, I **wouldn't lend** money to members of your family.
3 If Jack were here, I**'d / would ask** him to help me.
4 Joe **wouldn't have had** an accident if he hadn't been driving so fast.
5 I'd run a half-marathon if I **were / was** a bit fitter.
6 If you**'d / had looked** (or **had been looking**) where you were going, you wouldn't have fallen over.
7 I'm sure you**'d / would enjoy** dancing if you came to the classes with me.
8 We'd go to the local restaurant more often if they **changed** the menu from time to time.
9 Nina wouldn't have gone abroad if she**'d / had been able** to find a job here.
10 If you**'d / had asked** for a discount in the shop, they might have given you one.

5A 77

b

1 If Luke **hadn't missed** the train, he **wouldn't have been** late for the interview.
2 Millie **would have bought** the top if she**'d / had had** enough money.
3 If it **hadn't started** snowing, we**'d / would have reached** the top.
4 If Rebecca **didn't drink** so much coffee, she **wouldn't sleep** (so) badly.
5 I**'d drive / would drive** to work if **there weren't / wasn't** so much traffic.
6 If Matt **worked** harder, he**'d / would get** promoted.
7 If we **hadn't run** for the bus, we **wouldn't have caught** it.

Tell Sts to go back to the main lesson **5A**.

EXTRA SUPPORT If you think Sts need more practice, you may want to give them the **Grammar** photocopiable activity at this point.

d Focus on the task and the example. Point out the chain – the end of one sentence becomes the beginning of the next, with a change in the verb form.

Put Sts in pairs and give them time to complete the two conditional story chains. Remind them that one should be in the second conditional and the other in the third.

Monitor and help with verb forms if necessary.

e Put two pairs together and get them to read their stories to each other.

Get various groups to read their favourite story to the class.

6 WRITING a blog post

Tell Sts to go to **Writing A blog post** on *p.118*.

a Focus on the task and the three pictures.

Elicit ideas from the class, or get Sts to discuss the question in pairs.

If Sts worked in pairs, elicit ideas, but <u>don't</u> tell them if they are correct or not.

Now give Sts time to read the blog to check.

Check answers.

The parents should have kept the knives in drawers that children can't reach.
They shouldn't have put a bed under a window.
They shouldn't have put medicine where children can reach it.

b Focus on the task and make sure Sts understand what they have to do. Point out that the first one (the blue slash after …*to prevent accidents*) has been done for them.

Get Sts to compare with a partner, and then check answers.

New paragraph after …*the child falls out.*
New paragraph after …*keep them in a locked cupboard.*
New paragraph after …*liquids are in high or locked cupboards.*

c Focus on the task and give Sts time, in pairs, to choose which topic they want to write about in their blog.

d Focus on the task and go through points 1 and 2 with the class.

Give Sts time, in pairs, to brainstorm possible tips and an introductory sentence.

e Focus on the **Useful language: giving advice** box and go through it with the class.

Then either get Sts to write their article in class (set a time limit of, e.g. 20 minutes), or get them to write it at home for homework.

f Sts should check their blog post for mistakes before giving it in.

5B Wish you were here

G *wish* for present / future, *wish* for past regrets
V expressing feelings with verbs or *-ed* / *-ing* adjectives
P sentence rhythm and intonation

Lesson plan

The topics in this lesson are things that people would like to be different, or which annoy them in their daily lives, and regrets people have about the present and the past. They provide the context for Sts to learn to use *I wish…* To make it easier for Sts to assimilate the grammar, it has been split into two separate presentations, and so there are two visits to the Grammar Bank in this lesson. This is quite a tricky grammar point, especially the difference between *wish + past simple* and *wish + would*, so do not expect your Sts to assimilate how it is used immediately.

The first half of the lesson starts with the grammar presentation of the construction *I wish + past simple*, using different kinds of social media to express things you would like to be different, and *wish + would* to express annoyance. This is followed by a vocabulary and speaking focus on different ways of expressing feelings, with a verb or with an *-ed* or *-ing* adjective, e.g. *It annoys me. / I'm annoyed. / It's annoying.*

In the second half of the lesson, Sts read an article in which a journalist asked people to tweet about their biggest regrets, followed by the second grammar focus using *wish + past perfect* to express past regrets. The pronunciation focus is on sentence rhythm and intonation, and Sts then practise the new structure talking in small groups about some past regrets. The lesson ends with a poem about regret, which Sts listen to before writing their own.

More materials
For teachers
Photocopiables
Grammar wish for present / future, *wish* for past regrets *p.171*
Communicative Wishes pp.201–202 (instructions *p.186*)
For students
Workbook 5B
Online Practice 5B

OPTIONAL LEAD-IN – THE QUOTE

Write the quote at the top of *p.50* on the board and the name of the person who said it, or get Sts to open their books and read it.

You could tell Sts that Jim Rohn (1930–2009) was also an author and motivational speaker.

Ask Sts what his quote means and if they agree with it.

1 GRAMMAR *wish* for the present / future

a Focus on the task and make sure Sts know what Pinterest is (*a photo-bookmarking website*).

Give Sts time to read all the wishes and see if they can identify with them.

Get some feedback. You could tell the class if you ever wish any of the things in the posts, and if so, which ones.

b Focus on the messages and ask Sts if they have any groups on social media like WhatsApp which they share with friends.

Then focus on the task and make sure Sts know the meaning of *annoy* (= to make sb irritated or angry).

Give Sts time to read the WhatsApp messages and tick the ones that also annoy them.

c Focus on the **Expressing annoyance** box and go through it with the class. Elicit or model the intonation in the three phrases which express annoyance.

Get Sts to choose their top three and then to compare with a partner, using the expressions in **Expressing annoyance**.

Get some feedback and tell the class your top three, too. You could find out which is the top annoying habit for the whole class.

d Focus on the task and explain that Sts should compare the structure after *wish* in the Pinterest posts and in the WhatsApp messages. Give Sts time to complete the two rules.

Check answers.

> **1** past simple   **2** *would / wouldn't* + infinitive

e Tell Sts to go to **Grammar Bank 5B** on *p.141*.

Grammar notes

wish for present / future

Sts often have problems distinguishing between these two structures, and it may help them to compare how they express the different concepts in their L1.

wish + past simple

You may want to point out that unlike with *wish + would*, this structure is often used with *I* or *we* for things you would like to be different for you, e.g. *I wish I / we could / had / was…*, etc.

Point out to Sts that the use of the past simple with a future meaning is the same as in second conditionals, e.g. *I wish I had more money. If I had more money, I'd buy a new phone.*

wish + would / wouldn't

The contracted form of *would* (*'d*) is often used after *wish*.

Highlight the fact that we only use this structure to talk about things we would like <u>other people</u> (or things) to do or not to do. We <u>don't</u> use this structure with *I* or *we*, e.g. NOT ~~I wish I would have more money.~~

5B 79

Focus on the example sentences for **wish + past simple** and play audio 🔊 **5.17** for Sts to listen and repeat. Encourage them to copy the rhythm. Then go through the rules with the class.

Repeat for **wish + would / wouldn't** 🔊 **5.18**.

Focus on **a** <u>only</u>, and get Sts to do it individually or in pairs. If they do them individually, get them to compare with a partner. Check answers, getting Sts to read the full sentences.

a
1 I wish I was / were fitter.
2 I wish my sister didn't share a room with me.
3 I wish I could / was able to dance.
4 I wish my grandmother wasn't dead.
5 I wish I lived in a country with a better climate.
6 I wish shop assistants would be more polite.
7 I wish you wouldn't turn the heating up all the time.
8 I wish my brother would tidy our room.
9 I wish the neighbour's dog wouldn't bark at night.
10 I wish it would stop raining.

Tell Sts to go back to the main lesson **5B**.

❗ Don't use the **Grammar** photocopiable activity at this point, as it includes *wish* for past regrets, which Sts see in the second half of the lesson.

f Focus on the task. Tell Sts individually to first think of two things which annoy them and that they would like people to change, and to write messages similar to the ones in **b** for each one, using *I wish* + person / thing + *would / wouldn't*.

Then they should think of two things they would like to be different about themselves and write two posts similar to the Pinterest ones in **a**, using *I wish + I / we* + past simple.

Help with any vocabulary Sts may need.

g Now put Sts in pairs or small groups to compare what they've written.

Get feedback from the whole class and write some of the best examples on the board. You could tell Sts about things that annoy you or that you would like to be different about yourself.

2 VOCABULARY & SPEAKING expressing feelings with verbs or *-ed* / *-ing* adjectives

In the previous lesson, Sts learned adjectives for describing how people feel (*shocked*, *disappointed*, etc.). In this lesson, other ways of talking about feelings are covered, e.g. using *It* structures with verbs like *annoy* (*It really annoys me when…*).

a Focus on the **Ways of talking about how we feel** box and go through it with the class.

EXTRA SUPPORT Give Sts another example, as follows:

verb: ***to bore***; adjectives: ***bored / boring***, e.g. *This programme **bores** me. / This programme is **boring**. = I'm **bored** with watching this programme.*

Then focus on the instructions, making sure Sts know the meaning of all the verbs in **bold**. Highlight that the **bold** words are all verbs. Do the first one with the class as an example (*It really **infuriates** me when people drive close behind me*).

Give Sts time to do the task either individually or in pairs.

b 🔊 **5.19** Play the audio for Sts to listen and check.

Check answers. Elicit or model any adjectives your Sts might find difficult to pronounce. You could use the audio to do this, or model and drill them yourself. Remind Sts that the rules for pronouncing *-ed* adjectives are the same as for regular past tense verbs, e.g. *annoyed* = /d/, *irritated* = /ɪd/, and *depressed* = /t/.

You could focus on stress and intonation in feelings here.

2 frustrated   3 embarrassing   4 exhausting   5 disappointed
6 amazes   7 terrifying   8 inspired   9 confuse   10 thrilled

🔊 **5.19**
1 It really infuriates me when people drive close behind me.
2 I get very frustrated when something goes wrong with my internet connection and I don't know how to fix it.
3 It's so embarrassing when I can't remember someone's name, but they can remember mine.
4 I used to love shopping in the sales, but now I find it exhausting. After an hour, I just want to go home.
5 I'm often disappointed with my birthday presents. My expectations are obviously too high!
6 It amazes me that some people still don't do their banking online.
7 I find speaking in public absolutely terrifying. I hate doing it.
8 I've often been inspired by reading about how some successful people have overcome difficulties.
9 I never find instructions for electronic devices helpful – in fact, usually they just confuse me.
10 When I travel, I'm always thrilled if I manage to communicate something in a foreign language.

Put Sts in pairs and get them to look at each sentence and say whether or not it is true for them. They should give examples or reasons whenever possible.

Get some feedback.

c Focus on the **Feelings adjectives that have an *-ed* form, but not an *-ing* form** box and go through it with Sts.

Now look at the example (number 1) together and elicit the meaning. Elicit or model pronunciation of the two adjectives and elicit which syllable is stressed (the second).

Give Sts time to complete the gaps.

Check answers, and elicit which syllable is stressed. Elicit or model the pronunciation of the adjectives.

2 <u>stress</u>ful   3 <u>scary</u>   4 de<u>light</u>ful   5 o<u>ffen</u>sive

EXTRA CHALLENGE You could call out the sentences in **c** in random order, saying *blank* instead of the adjective / verb and getting the class to call out the missing word, e.g.

T *I get very stressed at work. My new job is very BLANK.*
Sts *stressful*

d Focus on the task, which activates orally some of the adjectives in **a** and **c**.

Give Sts a couple of minutes to think about which three of the subjects they can talk about.

Now put them in pairs and tell them to take turns to talk. The first student can start by saying *I'm going to tell you about…*

Monitor and help.

Deal with any general vocabulary problems that arose.

80 **5B**

Find out if any pairs felt exactly the same way about certain things.

You could tell Sts some of your own experiences / feelings, too.

3 READING & SPEAKING checking hypotheses

a Focus on the task and the words in the list.

Now give Sts time to choose the three areas of life they think people might have most regrets about.

Elicit some ideas, asking Sts to explain why.

b Give Sts time to read the article to check their answers to **a** and to find out how the writer changed someone's life.

Get Sts to compare with a partner, and then check answers.

EXTRA SUPPORT Before Sts read the article the first time, check whether you need to pre-teach any vocabulary.

> education, career, love
> By retweeting one of the replies to someone who had very few followers; she now has more than 900.

c Tell Sts to read the article again and to complete gaps 1–6 with tweets A–F. You might want to check Sts know the meaning of *dyslexic* in D.

Check answers.

> **1** D **2** E **3** B **4** F **5** C **6** A

Then tell Sts to read all the tweets again and try to work out what kind of words have been left out in some of the tweets.

Get Sts to compare with a partner, and then check answers.

> Pronouns, e.g. *I* (in A, *Moved to France…* instead of *I moved…*); *it* (in A, *Still scary…* instead of *It's still scary*).

Deal with any other new vocabulary. Elicit or model the pronunciation of any tricky words. Highlight that after *regret*, you can use an infinitive or perfect infinitive (*I regret doing / having done…*) or a *that*-clause (*I regret that I didn't…*).

d Tell Sts to look at the eight highlighted words in the article and decide whether they are nouns or adjectives. If it is a noun, they must write the adjective, and if it is an adjective, they must write the noun.

Now give Sts time to do the task individually or in pairs.

Check answers.

EXTRA SUPPORT First, go through the article with the class, eliciting whether each highlighted word is a noun or an adjective. Then put Sts in pairs and get them to write the other version of the word.

> **Nouns:** sorrow (adj: sad), anger (adj: angry), fear (adj: afraid)
> **Adjectives:** honest (n: honesty), brave (n: bravery), encouraging (n: encouragement), excited (n: excitement), enthusiastic (n: enthusiasm)

e Focus on the task and example.

Give Sts time to think of their biggest regret.

Remind Sts that when they are asked a personal question that they don't want to answer, they can say *Actually, I*

prefer not to say. Tell Sts they can use this here or they could simply choose a regret they are happy to talk about.

Put Sts in small groups or get them to mingle, telling each other their biggest regret.

Find out if any Sts found a classmate with the same or similar regret.

4 GRAMMAR *wish* for past regrets

a ◑ 5.20 Focus on the task and play the audio for Sts to listen and answer the question.

Get Sts to compare with a partner, and then check answers.

EXTRA SUPPORT Read through the script and decide if you need to pre-teach any new lexis before Sts listen.

> **Speaker 1** Not asking a girl out
> **Speaker 2** Not spending more time with her grandmother
> **Speaker 3** Not changing schools

◑ **5.20**
(script in Student's Book on *p.126*)

1
One thing I really regret is not being brave enough to ask out a girl who I met at a party last summer. I really liked her, but I was just too scared to invite her on a date in case she said no. I wish I'd tried. I'm absolutely positive we would have got on well. Now it's too late – she's engaged to another guy!

2
Um, I wish I'd had more time with my grandmother. She died when I was twelve, and since then, I've discovered that she must have been a really fascinating person, and there are so many things I would love to have been able to talk to her about. She was Polish, but she was in Russia, in St Petersburg, during the Russian Revolution, and she knew all sorts of interesting people at the time: painters, writers – people like that. I was only a kid, so I never asked her much about her own life. Now I'm discovering all about her through reading her old letters and papers, but I wish she'd lived longer so that I could have talked to her about those times face-to-face.

3
When I was sixteen, I got the chance to change schools and go to a better school to do my last two years. My parents were really keen for me to change because they thought I'd probably get better marks in the exams and so have a better chance of going to university. But I was totally against the idea because I didn't want to leave all my friends behind and I didn't know anyone at the other school. So, in the end, I managed to convince them and I stayed at my old school. I did OK in my exams, but not brilliantly. Um, now I wish I'd listened to my parents. It would have been much better for my future career, but at the time I just couldn't see it.

b Focus on the task and then play the audio again for Sts to listen and complete each sentence stem. Pause the audio after each speaker to give Sts time to write.

Check answers.

> **1** I wish I**'d tried**.
> **2** I wish I**'d had more time with my grandmother**.
>   I wish she**'d lived longer**.
> **3** I wish I**'d listened to my parents**.

Now ask Sts which tense is used after *wish* to talk about a regret.

> The past perfect

5B 81

c Tell Sts to go to **Grammar Bank 5B** on *p.141*.

Grammar notes
wish for past regrets

Remind Sts that both *would* and *had* can be contracted to *'d*, so they will need to focus on the main verb to see what the structure is. Compare:

*I wish he**'d come**. (= would come – you want him to come)*

*I wish he**'d come**! (= had come – you're sorry that he didn't come)*

Point out to Sts that the use of the past perfect here is similar to its use in third conditionals, e.g. *I wish we hadn't bought such an expensive car. If we hadn't bought it, we wouldn't have got into debt.*

The information about *if only* in the box applies to all uses of *wish*. *If only* is a stronger and more dramatic way of expressing a wish, e.g. *If only it would stop raining!* We normally use an exclamation mark after *If only…!*

Focus on the example sentences for **wish + past perfect** and play audio 🔊 **5.21** for Sts to listen and repeat. Encourage them to copy the rhythm. Then go through the rules with the class.

Now focus on **b** and get Sts to do it individually or in pairs. Check answers, getting Sts to read the full sentences.

b
1 I wish **I'd / had seen Prince live**.
2 He wishes **he'd / had learned to cook at school**.
3 Do you wish **you hadn't bought a second-hand car**?
4 Jenny wishes **she hadn't married her first husband**.
5 My parents wish **they hadn't moved to the country**.
6 Does Tom wish **he'd / had studied law**?
7 I wish **I hadn't had my hair cut so short**.
8 They wish **they'd / had gone to the wedding**.

Tell Sts to go back to the main lesson **5B**.

EXTRA SUPPORT If you think Sts need more practice, you may want to give them the **Grammar** photocopiable activity at this point.

d Focus on the task and give Sts time to write their four regrets. Remind Sts that these regrets must be about the past. You could give an example for the first one, e.g. *I wish I'd been kinder to my sister when we were growing up*.

Get Sts to exchange pieces of paper, so they can read each other's regrets.

Get feedback. You could find out if any Sts had the same regrets or if they found any regrets surprising.

5 PRONUNCIATION & SPEAKING sentence rhythm and intonation

a 🔊 **5.22** Focus on the task and play the audio once the whole way through for Sts just to listen.

Then play it again, pausing after each sentence to give Sts time to write.

Finally, play the audio once more for Sts to check their sentences.

Check answers by writing the sentences on the board.

🔊 **5.22**
1 I wish I hadn't eaten two pieces of cake.
2 I wish I'd gone to university.
3 I wish I'd bought those shoes I saw in the sales.
4 I wish I hadn't told Anna about seeing her boyfriend with another woman.
5 I wish we hadn't said we'd go to Simon's party tonight.
6 I wish I'd been at the match!

EXTRA SUPPORT Play the audio for Sts to listen and repeat the sentences, trying to copy the rhythm.

b Focus on the task and give Sts time to match the six *I wish* sentences they wrote in **a** to A–F. You could do the first one with the class as an example (*1D*).

c 🔊 **5.23** Play the audio for Sts to listen and check. Check answers.

> 1 D 2 C 3 E 4 F 5 A 6 B

🔊 **5.23**
1 D
A I wish I hadn't eaten two pieces of cake.
B Yes, you should have had more self-control!
2 C
A I wish I'd gone to university.
B Well, it isn't too late. You're only twenty-two.
3 E
A I wish I'd bought those shoes I saw in the sales.
B Why don't you go back to the shop and see if they still have them?
4 F
A I wish I hadn't told Anna about seeing her boyfriend with another woman.
B Yes, it was a bit tactless. I hope she's not too upset.
5 A
A I wish we hadn't said we'd go to Simon's party tonight.
B Do you want me to phone and make an excuse?
6 B
A I wish I'd been at the match!
B Yes, watching it on TV is never as exciting.

Now put Sts in pairs and get them to practise the six two-line conversations. Encourage them to concentrate on getting the rhythm correct by stressing the longer 'content' words, especially in the *I wish…* sentences.

Get some pairs to practise in front of the class.

d Focus on the topics and make sure Sts can remember what a *live event* is (= of a performance, given or made when people are watching, not recorded).

Put Sts in small groups of three or four and get them to discuss a few of their regrets. Encourage them to give reasons for their answers.

Deal with any general vocabulary problems that arose.

Get some feedback from the class about some of their regrets. You could tell Sts about some of your regrets, too.

6 LISTENING & WRITING understanding a poem

a 🔊 **5.24** Focus on the task and make sure Sts know what a *verse* in a poem is (= a group of lines that form a unit).

Play the audio once the whole way through for Sts to listen and write the first line of each verse.

Check the answer.

> I wish I had said

82 **5B**

◉ 5.24

I wish

I wish I had said
Nothing at all
Everything that came out
Of my mouth was wrong
The words didn't help much

I wish I had said
That I love you
Everything that I said
Was not what I meant
All I want is for you to
Forgive me

I wish I had said
Something to make everything
Go right
The only thing I should have
Said was what I really felt

I wish I had said
That I love you with all my heart
And that I'm sorry for
Everything that went wrong
Between us

b Play the audio again, pausing after each verse to give Sts time to write as many words as they can.

c Put Sts in pairs. Get them to compare what they have written and try to reconstruct the poem.

EXTRA SUPPORT Write the skeleton of the poem with the first word(s) of each line on the board for Sts to try to complete:

I WISH I HAD SAID

NOTHING _____ _____

EVERYTHING _____ _____ _____

OF MY _____ _____ _____

THE WORDS _____ _____ _____

I WISH I HAD SAID

THAT _____ _____ _____

EVERYTHING _____ _____ _____

WAS NOT _____ _____ _____

ALL _____ _____ _____ _____ _____ _____

_____ _____

I WISH I HAD SAID

SOMETHING TO _____ _____

_____ _____

THE ONLY THING _____ _____ _____

SAID WAS WHAT _____ _____ _____

I WISH I HAD SAID

THAT _____ _____ _____ _____ _____ _____ _____

AND THAT _____ _____ _____

EVERYTHING _____ _____ _____

_____ _____

d Finally, play the audio again for Sts to listen and check their version.

Check answers by eliciting the poem onto the board line by line.

See script 5.24

e In their pairs, Sts now write their own poem with at least three verses starting with *I wish I had / hadn't*. They could use the first verse of the poem as an example of how they could construct their own.

Monitor and help if necessary whilst Sts write their poems.

f Ask each pair to read their poem aloud to the class – they can take turns to read the verses, as on the audio.

With a show of hands, get Sts to vote for their favourite poem.

EXTRA IDEA If you don't have time for Sts to read their poems, or if you think they might not want to, you could get Sts to hand in their poems. Number them and put them around the classroom for Sts to read.

5B

4&5 Colloquial English Talking about… waste

Lesson plan

In The Interview, the person interviewed is Candida Brady, a British journalist and film-maker.

In The Conversation, Sts watch three people discussing whether they think we will ever be plastic free. Sts then discuss this question as well as a couple of other questions related to the topic, focusing on different ways that people respond to what another person has said.

More materials
For teachers
Teacher's Resource Centre
Video Colloquial English 4&5
Quick Test 5
File 5 Test
Progress Test Files 1–5
For students
Workbook Colloquial English 4&5
Can you remember? 4&5
Online Practice Colloquial English 4&5
Check your progress

OPTIONAL LEAD-IN (BOOKS CLOSED)
Write the name JEREMY IRONS on the board and ask Sts if they know him and what nationality he is (he is a British actor), and if they have seen him in any films or TV series (e.g. *The Borgias, The Man in the Iron Mask, The Kingdom of Heaven, Eragon, Beautiful Creatures, The Man Who Knew Infinity, Assassin's Creed, Red Sparrow, Watchmen,* etc.)

1 ▶ THE INTERVIEW Part 1

a Books open. Focus on the biographical information about Candida Brady. Either read it out loud, or give Sts time to read it.

Focus on the question and do it as a whole-class activity.

b Focus on the task and give Sts time to read sentences 1–6. Remind Sts that they do not need to correct the false ones at this stage.

Go through the **Glossary** with the class.

Play the video (**Part 1**) once the whole way through for Sts to watch the interview and write *T* (true) or *F* (false) for each sentence.

Get Sts to compare with a partner, and then check answers.

EXTRA SUPPORT Before playing the video, go through the listening scripts and decide if you need to pre-teach / check any lexis to help Sts when they watch.

1 T 2 F 3 T 4 F 5 T 6 F

I = interviewer, C = Candida Brady

Part 1

I What were you hoping to do by making the film *Trashed*?

C Well, I think, um, the role of the film, um, for me was to raise awareness, um, on the topic and get it into the press so that people could start having a…a meaningful conversation about waste, which, um, is not a particularly, um, attractive subject, let's say.

I How many countries did you film in?

C We ended up actually filming in eleven countries, um, but the stories that I've chosen are universal, and obviously I spoke to… to people in communities, um, in more countries, um, than we actually filmed in. Um, but their stories are certainly not isolated: they were repeated around the world, sadly, wherever you kind of want to pick, actually.

I How did you persuade Jeremy Irons to get involved in the film?

C I had worked with Jeremy some years ago on a…on a different film, and I was generally aware that he doesn't like waste, either. Um, he will, you know, wear his jumpers until they're worn out; he'll keep his cars until they're falling apart, you know; he'll repair everything – so he's always seen, you know, the value in reusing things. It's just something natural to him as well, so he just felt like a natural, um, first approach, and…and so I sent him the treatment and amazingly he…he loved it.

I How did you get Vangelis to write the soundtrack?

C Well, Jeremy and Vangelis have been friends for years, so, um, Jeremy sent him the rough cut of the film and Vangelis absolutely loved it. He…he is also a committed environmentalist, so he's always been aware. Um, he was aware because he worked with, um, Cousteau – sort of various people, you know – he was aware of issues for the seas and so on, um, but generally, again, he was very shocked, um, by the film and really wanted to get involved, so…

I What research did you do before you started making the film?

C I spent about a year, um, talking to communities, talking to experts, um, you know, obviously reading an awful lot, um, and, um, just ingesting it all, because obviously, again, it's such an enormous topic to take on.

---

c Focus on the task and play the video again the whole way through for Sts to correct sentences 2, 4, and 6.

Check answers.

> 2 Jeremy Irons keeps things a long time, until they are worn out, e.g. jumpers, car. He doesn't like waste.
> 4 Vangelis is Jeremy's friend.
> 6 She spent a year talking to people – communities and experts.

EXTRA SUPPORT If there's time, you could get Sts to watch again with subtitles, so they can see exactly what they understood / didn't understand. Translate / Explain any new words or phrases.

d Do the questions as a whole-class activity, or put Sts in pairs and then get some feedback. You could demonstrate the activity by telling Sts about any documentaries on the environment that you have seen, and what you learned.

84 **CE4&5**

▶ Part 2

a Give Sts time to read the two questions and play the video (**Part 2**) once the whole way through for Sts to watch and answer the questions.

Check answers.

> **1** trying not to make it too depressing   **2** sea

Part 2

I Rubbish isn't very attractive visually. Was that a problem for you as a film-maker?

C Er…yes and no, um, strangely enough. Obviously, I had a wonderful, um, DOP – Director of Photography – so, um, he can pretty much make anything look beautiful, I think. But, um, I wanted to choose – as…as I've said earlier, um, you know, I did a lot of research, and so sadly, these things were repeatable and… and in every country around the world – so I wanted to choose, um, beautiful places wherever possible, um, that had been ruined, unfortunately, by, um, man-made rubbish. So, um, the ancient port of Saida in Lebanon – um, the fact that, you know, you've got this huge mountain of waste which was formerly a flat sandy beach.

I Documentaries about how we're destroying the planet can be very depressing. Was that also a challenge for you?

C A huge challenge, yes. Um, I would have preferred to make a much more cheerful, um, documentary than, um, I think *Trashed* is. I think it has got hope, um, I think 'cos we were very much aware that we wanted to offer solutions at the end of it, but you are…um, the subject is not a cheerful subject. Um, I could have gone further, I think, with it, but I didn't want to because actually, you know, you could sort of end up feeling that you just want to go and shoot yourself, which is not what I wanted. I wanted to feel that, you know, people feel that they can make a difference to this topic.

I In the film, you focus on air pollution, land pollution, and water pollution – which do you think is the most worrying?

C Um, if I had to pick one, um, which I would be reluctant to do… er…it would be water, without a doubt. I think that what has happened to all of the oceans – and beaches, actually, as well – um, in the world in the last thirty years is astonishing in the scale and the speed. Um, you know, there are certain places in the world, that, you know…that you have to dig down on a beach, um, over a foot before you'll find sand that doesn't have plastic in it. Unfortunately, what's happened with the way that soft plastic degrades in water is that, um, the pieces become so fragmented that they're the same size as the zooplankton, um, which obviously is in the food chain.

b Go through the six sentences and the **Glossary** with the class.

Play the video again the whole way through for Sts to complete the gaps. Play again if necessary.

Get Sts to compare with a partner, and then check answers.

EXTRA SUPPORT When playing the video the second time, pause after each question has been answered to give Sts time to write the missing words.

> **1** wonderful   **2** ruined   **3** cheerful   **4** solutions   **5** plastic
> **6** food

EXTRA SUPPORT If there's time, you could get Sts to watch again with subtitles, so they can see exactly what they understood / didn't understand. Translate / Explain any new words or phrases.

c Do the question as a whole-class activity.

▶ Part 3

a Give Sts time to read the three questions, making sure they know the meaning of *blame*. Go through the **Glossary** with the class.

Play the video (**Part 3**) once the whole way through for Sts to watch and answer the questions.

Get Sts to compare with a partner, and then check answers.

EXTRA SUPPORT You could pause the video at appropriate places and, in pairs, get Sts to compare answers.

> **1** She tries not to blame one person.
> **2** Because San Francisco shows that zero waste can be achieved on a big scale.
> **3** No.

Part 3

I Who do you think is mostly to blame for the problems we have with waste?

C I tried very hard, actually, not to blame one person or things, um, in the film – actually quite deliberately, because I think in a way, um, it lets us off the hook, um, and it also, um…I think we all need to work on the…the problem together because it's too complicated to blame one person or one thing or one act, or, um, you know, I think it's…it's multi-faceted, unfortunately.

I Your film finishes on an optimistic note with the example of San Francisco's zero-waste policy. Can you tell us a bit about that?

C Well, I…I actually in the film ended up, um, using San Francisco as the example because I wanted to show…er…that zero waste could be achieved on a big scale. When you go and stay in San Francisco in your hotel room, you'll have four different bins, and you'll have signs on the wall of what goes into each bin, so it's very, very easy to…to recycle, and I think that's a huge part of what we should be doing.

I Has the film changed your own habits regarding waste?

C I don't think the film has particularly changed my own habits dramatically, um, because I've always been thrifty, um, by nature because, um, I was lucky enough to spend a lot of time with my grandparents when I was growing up, and the post-war, sort of, philosophy of never wasting anything, it just, you know, it was instilled in me.
I ride the same bicycle that I've had since I was fifteen years old, and over the years obviously had it repaired and repaired, but I take tremendous pride in the fact that I've always, um, ridden the same bike, and, you know, I have lovely memories of it, so – and with it – so, um, I think…I think we need a slight change of mindset to make things cool the longer you have them, in a way, than actually this perpetual thing of buying new things for the sake of it.

b Focus on the task and give Sts time, in pairs, to see if they can remember why Candida mentioned the three things.

Play the video again the whole way through.

Get Sts to compare with their partner, and then check answers.

EXTRA SUPPORT You could pause the video at appropriate places and, in pairs, get Sts to compare orally what they have understood.

> **1** They have four different bins, and signs on the wall of what goes into each bin, so it's very easy to recycle.
> **2** She spent a lot of time with her grandparents when she was growing up. They taught her not to waste anything, as they had lived through the war.
> **3** She still rides the bike she got when she was 15.

CE4&5   85

EXTRA SUPPORT If there's time, you could get Sts to watch again with subtitles, so they can see exactly what they understood / didn't understand. Translate / Explain any new words or phrases.

c Do the questions as a whole-class activity, or put Sts in pairs and then get some feedback.

2 ▶ LOOKING AT LANGUAGE

This exercise focuses on a common feature of spoken English – the use of comment adverbs. Focus on the **Comment adverbs** box and go through it with the class.

Now focus on the task and give Sts time to read extracts 1–7.

Play the video, pausing after each extract to give Sts time to write the missing adverbs.

Check answers.

> **1** actually **2** obviously **3** amazingly **4** generally
> **5** strangely **6** sadly **7** Unfortunately

---

1 We ended up actually filming in eleven countries…
2 …but the stories that I've chosen are universal and, obviously, I spoke to, to people in communities, um, in more countries, um, than we actually filmed in…
3 …and so I sent him the treatment and amazingly he, um, he loved it.
4 …but generally, again, he was very shocked, um, by the film and really wanted to get involved.
5 …yes and no, um, strangely enough. Obviously, I had a wonderful DOP – Director of Photography, so, um, he can pretty much make anything look beautiful…
6 I did a lot of research, and so sadly, these things were repeatable and, and in every country around the world…
7 Unfortunately, what's happened with the way that soft plastic degrades in water is that, um, the pieces become so fragmented…

---

3 ▶ THE CONVERSATION

a Focus on the photo and tell Sts they are going to watch these three people answer a question, which they will see on the screen. Focus on the task and make sure Sts understand what they have to do.

Play the video and pause after the question. Elicit / Explain that *plastic free* = will not be contaminated by plastic because people will have stopped using it.

Then play the video once the whole way through for Sts to circle the correct option in the conclusion.

Check the answer.

EXTRA SUPPORT Before playing the video, go through the listening script and decide if you need to pre-teach / check any lexis to help Sts when they listen.

> possible but difficult

I = interviewer, J = Joanne, S = Simon, Sy = Syinat

I Do you think we will ever be plastic free?
J That's such a huge topic…
S That's a massive topic.
J …isn't it? But actually it's an area – we've got to be plastic free ultimately. We've certainly, if we don't, if we're not plastic free, we need to find an alternative, don't we?
S I think, um, businesses particularly – perhaps in the food and beverages industry – are already starting. I noticed in a pub the other day, they've changed the straws from plastic to cardboard – sorry, to, to paper – which is a step in the right direction…
J It's a step, it's a step.
S It's a small step, but it's a step, but at least they're taking notice and doing things like that.
J Yeah, agreed. I think it's got to be customer-led though, don't you?
S Yeah.
Sy Yeah, yeah.
J We consumers have got to push it.
Sy Yeah, yeah.
J Because if we don't demand paper straws and we keep saying actually no we have to have plastic…
S Yeah absolutely.
J …they're going to keep producing plastic.
S I mean, I don't know about you, but I recycle, it seems like a bag a week of plastic – I can't believe how much plastic there is.
J I know, mmm. It's really awful actually.
Sy Yeah. And it's very hard to be plastic free.
J It is actually.
S It is.
J I mean, if you try really hard – and I do try hard – um, if you go and you shop in supermarkets, it's incredibly hard to…
Sy Yeah.
J …buy organic in non-plastic.
Sy Everything is wrapped.
S I think there are some businesses now that you can take your plastic items with you to the shop and fill up with goods rather than taking plastic away from – I think that's a good start, but it's such a small thing. It needs to be much bigger.
Sy But that'd be very difficult on a large scale, I believe.
S It would be a lot – it would be difficult because mass consumers wouldn't want to do that. Especially…
Sy Yeah, no, but if you think about it, eight billion people, three meals a day…yeah, so, food and beverages would be…
S I was reading a story the other day – apparently, we sent some plastic to China and they've now sent it back to us in containers saying 'Actually, we're not recycling your plastic, you need to, you need to do it where you are rather than sending it to us.'
J Yes, and that gets us onto the other topic: it's not just stopping using new plastic, it's recycling what's already out there, because the the, amount that's out there at the moment is just scary.
S And the amount that's killing whales or getting caught in whales or, or dolphins or fish is just…
Sy Turtles, yeah.
J Oh my goodness and did you see, the, you know the Mariana Trench?
Sy Yeah!
J The deepest place on the planet…
S It's full of plastic.
J …and they found plastic. I mean, that's just so depressing, isn't it?
S It's depressing. So…
J I think, I think the awareness is there now and that's got to be positive, right?
Sy Yeah!
S So plastic free, I think there has to be some sort of – if you said plastic free five years, that's never going to happen, if you said ten years, that's probably not gonna happen, but if you said maybe twenty years, potentially it could happen, but there has to be new ways of recycling plastic – and then not just not using it, that's the hardest thing I suppose.
Sy I'm sure, I'm sure you guys have heard the fact that there's more plastic in the sea by weight than there are fish.
J Yes, isn't that awful?
S Yeah, it's very scary!

86 **CE4&5**

J Actually, it's the time frame, I think, is quite significant as well. That actually this has happened really since my grandmother was a child – she never had plastic.

Sy Yeah, we're talking past century.

J Yeah! Really, less. More like a half-century. I can't remember the exact date, but something like that – it's a reasonably short time, and we've really got less than that, a lot less than that to turn it around, so we have to come up with alternatives. But surely we can do that!

Sy I have some positive news for you.

S Go on.

Sy So they have found bacteria that have evolved to digest nylon plastic…

S Yes, I knew about that.

Sy …just naturally. That's amazing!

J So we could get there.

S So plastic munchers that can munch plastic – is that what you're saying?

Sy Yes.

J Yeah.

S Cool!

J And you can get plastic bottles – I read you can get plastic bottles now – that are on sale somewhere in London, one of the museums I think – plastic bottles that actually you can then eat the plastic.

S Oh wow. OK.

Sy Really?

J I think that's just so amazing.

S That sounds pretty, that sounds pretty cool.

J So yes, we think we could be plastic free, it's possible, but…

Sy But it'd take a lot of work.

S I think it will. Cool.

S Yeah.

b Focus on the task and give Sts time to read the nine questions, and make sure they understand them.

Play the video again for Sts to answer the questions.

Get Sts to compare with a partner, and then play again if necessary.

Check answers.

1 S	**2** J	**3** J	**4** S	**5** S	**6** Sy	**7** J	**8** Sy	**9** J

EXTRA SUPPORT If there's time, you could get Sts to watch again with subtitles, so they can see exactly what they understood / didn't understand. Translate / Explain any new words or phrases.

c Either do the questions as a whole-class activity, or put Sts in pairs and then get some feedback.

d Focus on the task and give Sts time to read 1–3 and A–G.

Play the video for Sts to listen and do the matching task.

Get Sts to compare with a partner, and then play again if necessary.

Check answers.

1 E, C	**2** A, D	**3** B, F, G

1 J The deepest place on the planet…
  S It's full of plastic.
  J …and they found plastic. I mean, that's just so depressing, isn't it?
  S It's depressing. So…
2 Sy …there's more plastic in the sea by weight than there are fish.
  J Yes, isn't that awful?
  S Yes, it's very scary!
3 J …plastic bottles that actually you can then eat the plastic.
  S Oh wow.
  Sy Really?
  J I think that's just so amazing.
  S That sounds pretty, that sounds pretty cool.

e Put Sts in pairs and give them time to put responses A–G into the appropriate category.

EXTRA SUPPORT Do this as a whole-class activity.

Check answers.

Responding to sth positive B, F, G
Responding to sth negative A, C, D, E

EXTRA IDEA Put Sts in groups of three. Sts **A** (book open) read an extract from **d**, Sts **B** and **C** (books closed) respond with an appropriate expression. Make sure they swap roles.

EXTRA CHALLENGE Elicit more possible responses to something positive or negative, e.g.

+

How / That's fantastic / brilliant / really good, etc.
What a great idea, etc.

−

How / That's awful / terrible / sad, etc.
What a pity / a shame / a nightmare / bad luck, etc.

f Put Sts in small groups of three if possible. Focus on the questions, and check Sts understand them. Then set a time limit for Sts to discuss them. Monitor and help, and encourage them to respond to what other people say.

Get feedback from various groups. You could also tell the class what you think.

CE4&5

6A Night night

G *used to, be used to, get used to*
V sleep
P /s/ and /z/

Lesson plan

The context of this lesson is several different angles on sleep.

At the start of the first half of the lesson, Sts listen to three people who all have some kind of sleep problem. Sentences taken from the listening provide the context for the grammar presentation, which revises the use of *used to* to talk about repeated past actions, and introduces *be used to* and *get used to* (doing something) to talk about actions or activities which have become, or are becoming, familiar. The pronunciation focus is on the sounds /s/ and /z/ in *used to*. Sts then read an article about the benefits of segmented sleep (i.e. sleeping for a few hours, waking up for a couple of hours, and going back to sleep), followed by short articles, which they read separately and tell each other about, on what some people do in their waking hours in the middle of the night.

The second half of the lesson starts with a vocabulary focus on words and phrases related to sleep (e.g. *yawn, be a light sleeper*). This is followed by a listening podcast given by a sleep expert. Finally, the lesson finishes with a speaking activity to recycle the new lexis.

More materials
For teachers
Photocopiables
Grammar used to, be used to, get used to p.172
Communicative usually, used to, get used to p.203
(instructions *p.186*)
For students
Workbook 6A
Online Practice 6A

OPTIONAL LEAD-IN – THE QUOTE

Write the quote at the top of *p.56* on the board and the name of the person who said it, or get Sts to open their books and read it.

You could tell Sts that Anthony Burgess (1917–1993) is best known for his novel *A Clockwork Orange*, which was made into a famous film.

Ask Sts what they think the quote means and if they think it's funny. Do they agree with it?

1 GRAMMAR *used to, be used to, get used to*

a Do this as a whole-class activity, or put Sts in pairs and then get some feedback.

b 🔊 **6.1** Focus on the task and the two questions.

Play the audio, pausing after each speaker to give Sts time to answer the questions.

Get Sts to compare with a partner, and then play the audio again if necessary.

Check answers.

Speaker 1 (Rafa) Because his bedroom isn't completely dark.
Speaker 2 (Mike) Because he does shift work (one weeknights, the next weekdays).
Speaker 3 (Steph) Because she takes a lot of long-haul flights.
None of them have really solved the problem.

🔊 **6.1**
(script in Student's Book on *pp.126–127*)
I = interviewer, R = Rafa, M = Mike, S = Steph

1 Rafa
I Why do you have problems sleeping?
R Well, I'm Spanish, but I moved to London a few years ago when I married a British woman. I've been living here for three years now. I have a lot of problems getting to sleep at night because our bedroom just isn't dark enough. I can't get used to sleeping in a bedroom where there's light coming in from the streetlights outside. In Spain, I always used to sleep in complete darkness, because my bedroom window had blinds and when I went to bed I used to close the blinds completely. But here in England, our bedroom window just has curtains, and curtains don't block out the light properly. It takes me a long time to get to sleep at night, and I always wake up more often than I used to do in Spain.
I So why don't you just get thicker curtains?
R Because my wife doesn't like sleeping in a completely dark room. She says that she feels claustrophobic if the room is too dark.
I Ah yes, some people do feel like that.

2 Mike
I Why do you have problems sleeping?
M Well, I'm a policeman, so I have to do shift work, which means I work at night every other week – so I start work at ten o'clock at night and finish at six in the morning the following day. The main problem is that my body's used to sleeping at night, not during the day. So it's very hard to get used to being awake all night and trying to work and concentrate when your body is just telling you to go to bed.
I But isn't it something you eventually get used to?
M Actually, no, because I work during the day for one week and then the next week I work at night – which means that just when my body has got used to being awake at night, then I go back to working in the day. And then of course I can't get to sleep at night because my body thinks it's going to have to work all night. The other problem is that when I get home after working a night shift, everyone else is just starting to wake up, so that means that it can be really noisy. The neighbours put on the radio, and bang doors, and shout to wake their children up. So even though I'm really tired, it's just very hard to get to sleep.
I How many hours do you usually sleep?
M Before I became a policeman, I used to sleep about eight or nine hours a night, but I think now I probably don't sleep more than six hours.

3 Steph
I Why do you have problems sleeping?
S I have a lot of problems sleeping because of jet lag. I have to travel a lot in my job, and I take a lot of long-haul flights. I fly to New York quite often and I arrive maybe at six in the evening my time, but when it's only one o'clock in the afternoon in New York. So at five in the afternoon New York time, I'll be feeling tired and ready for bed because it's my bedtime, but I can't go to sleep because I'm probably still working or having dinner with my American colleagues. Then when I do finally get to bed at, say, midnight, I find that I wake up in the middle of the night because my body thinks that it's morning, because it's still working on UK time.
I And can you get back to sleep when you wake up?

88 **6A**

S No, that's the problem – I can't get back to sleep. And then the next day, when I have meetings, I feel really sleepy. It's very hard to stay awake all day. And just when I'm finally used to being on New York time, then it's time to fly back to the UK. And flying west to east is even worse.

I Oh! Why's that?

S Because when I get off the plane, it's early morning in the UK. But for me, on New York time, it's the middle of the night. It takes me four or five days to recover from one of those trips.

I Gosh, that must be really difficult for you.

S Yeah, it is.

c 🔊 **6.2** Focus on the six gapped extracts and give Sts time to read them.

Play the audio, pausing after each extract to give Sts time to write. They should complete each gap with a phrase. Check answers.

> 1 sleeping in a bedroom   2 sleep in complete darkness
> 3 sleeping at night   4 being awake   5 sleep about eight or
> nine   6 being on New York time

🔊 **6.2**
Rafa
I can't get used to sleeping in a bedroom where there's light coming in from the streetlights outside.
I always used to sleep in complete darkness.
Mike
The main problem is that my body's used to sleeping at night, not during the day.
It's very hard to get used to being awake all night.
Before I became a policeman, I used to sleep about eight or nine hours a night.
Steph
And just when I'm finally used to being on New York time, then it's time to fly back to the UK.

d Put Sts in pairs to focus on the target grammar. Tell them to look at the highlighted phrases in **c** and answer questions 1–3. Make sure Sts understand *accustomed to* if this is not an L1 cognate.

Check answers.

> 1 b
> 2 *be old*, etc. = you are like this
>   *get old*, etc. = you are becoming like this
> 3 We use the infinitive after *used to* and the *-ing* form after *be* / *get used to*.

e Tell Sts to go to **Grammar Bank 6A** on *p.142.*

Grammar notes

used to / didn't use to + infinitive

At this level, Sts should be confident about using *used to (do sth)* to talk about past habits. They may still make mistakes with usage, like using *I use to…* instead of *I usually…* to describe a present habit, which can cause misunderstanding, as a listener may understand *I used to…* (i.e. a past habit). Sts may also make mistakes with form, e.g. *I didn't used to…*

- **Rule 2: would**
  Remind Sts of the contraction of *would* to *'d*, i.e. in example sentence 2, *We'd buy them every morning…*

be used to / get used to + gerund

These structures are introduced for the first time. Their similarity in form to *used to* means that they sometimes get mixed up in Sts' minds.

be used to / get used to + gerund

These structures are introduced for the first time. Their similarity in form to *used to* means that they sometimes get mixed up in Sts' minds. A very common mistake is to use these structures with the infinitive instead of the gerund (e.g. *I'm used to ~~wake up~~ early*). Point out to Sts that *to* here is a preposition, and can be followed by either a gerund or a noun (e.g. *I'm used to living in London now; I'm used to the weather here now*).

The meaning of *be used to doing something* may not be immediately obvious to Sts. A formal equivalent would be *be accustomed to doing something*.

You may also want to point out that the difference between *be used to* and *get used to* is like the difference between *be angry* and *get angry*, and that *get* here = *become.*

Focus on the example sentences for **used to / didn't use to + infinitive** and play audio 🔊 **6.3** for Sts to listen and repeat. Encourage them to copy the rhythm. Then go through the rules with the class.

Repeat for **be used to / get used to + gerund** 🔊 **6.4**.

Now focus on the exercises and get Sts to do them individually or in pairs.

If they do them individually, get them to compare with a partner Check answers, getting Sts to read the full sentences.

> **a**
> 1 ✗ we didn't use to like
> 2 ✗ we couldn't get used to having
> 3 ✓
> 4 ✓
> 5 ✓
> 6 ✗ Paul used to have / had
> 7 ✗ I usually get up
> 8 ✓
> 9 ✗ to get used to living
> 10 ✓
> **b**
> 1 When Nathan started his first job, he couldn't **get used to getting up** at 6 a.m.
> 2 I didn't recognize you! You **used to have** blonde hair, didn't you?
> 3 Isabelle **used to rent** a flat when she was at university, but now she has a house of her own.
> 4 When we were children, we **used to spend** all day playing football in the park.
> 5 Jasmine has been a nurse all her life, so she **is used to working** nights.
> 6 I've never worn glasses before, but now I'll have to **get used to wearing** them.
> 7 Ameila is an only child. She **isn't used to sharing** her things.
> 8 Although I've lived in Spain for years, I've never **got used to having** dinner at nine or ten o'clock at night.
> 9 I **didn't use to like** spinach, but now I love it.
> 10 If you want to get fit, then you'll have to **get used to exercising** more.

Tell Sts to go back to the main lesson **6A**.

EXTRA SUPPORT If you think Sts need more practice, you may want to give them the **Grammar** photocopiable activity at this point.

6A 89

f This exercise recycles the grammar orally. Put Sts in pairs and get them to discuss 1–3, encouraging them to give as much information as possible.

Get some feedback.

EXTRA SUPPORT Demonstrate the activity by answering some of the questions yourself.

2 PRONUNCIATION /s/ and /z/

> ### Pronunciation notes
>
> At lower levels, Sts will have been exposed to the sounds /s/ and /z/, especially in plural noun endings and third person verb endings; however, the focus will have been more on recognizing when *es* = /ɪz/, as in *pieces*, or just /z/, as in *lives*.
>
> Although the difference between these two sounds is small, there are pairs of words where the only difference is whether there is a /s/ or /z/ sound, and this section raises awareness of the comprehension problems that might occur if Sts don't discriminate successfully between the sounds when they hear them, or if they don't produce them precisely.
>
> Sts start by focusing on the difference in meaning between *used to* with /s/, e.g. *We used to live in the country*, and *used to* with /z/, e.g. *It's used to make furniture*. They then practise final /s/ or final /z/ sounds in pairs of words with very different meanings, and finally they have a go at pronouncing specific words accurately.

a ◑ **6.5** Focus on the task.

Play the audio once the whole way through for Sts just to listen.

◑ **6.5**
See sentences in Student's Book on *p.56*

Now ask Sts to identify the sentence in which *used* is pronounced differently, and then to explain the difference in meaning.

3 is pronounced /juːzd tuː/ (= this is what we use it for), but 1 and 2 are pronounced /juːstuː/ (1 = past habit, 2 = get accustomed to).

b ◑ **6.6** Focus on the list of words and make sure Sts know the different meanings in each pair.

Play the audio once the whole way through for Sts to listen and repeat.

◑ **6.6**
See words in Student's Book on *p.56*

EXTRA CHALLENGE You might want to point out that there are a few words where the difference in pronunciation between /s/ and /z/ marks the difference between the noun and the verb, e.g. *use* /s/ = noun, *use* /z/ = verb. Other examples are *abuse*, *excuse*, and *advice / advise*.

EXTRA SUPPORT Put Sts in pairs and get them to practise saying all the words.

c ◑ **6.7** Focus on the instructions and make sure Sts understand that in sentences 1–4, the extra information will help them work out which word they are hearing, but that in 5–8 both meanings would fit the context, so they have to really concentrate on the sounds.

Play the audio for Sts to listen to the sentences and choose which word from **b** they hear.

Get Sts to compare with a partner, and then check answers.

1 a **2** b **3** a **4** b **5** a **6** a **7** b **8** b

◑ **6.7**
1 Pyjamas should always be **loose**, never tight.
2 There was a real **buzz** when she arrived.
3 Who's doing this **course**?
4 She has nice **eyes**.
5 Are we going to have a **race**?
6 They made **peace**.
7 The **prize** was a hundred pounds.
8 We saw the **plays** last week.

---

d Put Sts in pairs, **A** and **B**. For each pair of words, Sts **A** say one of the words, and Sts **B** have to say if they heard word *a* or word *b*. Then Sts swap roles.

EXTRA SUPPORT If these sounds are difficult for your Sts, it will help to show them the mouth position. You could model this yourself or use the Sound Bank videos on the *Teacher's Resource Centre*.

3 READING using contextual clues

a Focus on the task and either read the title and first paragraph as a class, or give Sts time to do it alone.

Elicit what *segmented sleep* is.

It is a sleep pattern when you go to bed, then wake up for a few hours during the night, then go back to sleep again.

b Tell Sts to read the whole article and to answer questions 1–3.

Get Sts to compare with a partner, and then check answers.

EXTRA SUPPORT Before Sts read the article, check whether you need to pre-teach any vocabulary.

1 Meditate, think about vivid dreams, visit sick family, do housework, steal from the neighbours
2 Yes, doctors thought it had medical benefits. And people thought it was a good thing, as it was a time when they could do whatever they wanted, undisturbed.
3 Because of artificial light

Deal with any vocabulary problems that arose.

c Focus on the task and give Sts time to read Brennan's text and to answer the two questions. Tell them not to worry about the gaps. Point out to Sts that the text is in American English, but their answers should be in British English.

Get Sts to compare with a partner, and then check answers.

6A

EXTRA SUPPORT Before Sts read the text, check whether you need to pre-teach any vocabulary.

> 1 Three or four hours
> 2 He takes photographs in San Francisco, frames his photos, marks (grades) students' work, watches a film, runs.

d Tell Sts to read the text again and complete gaps 1–9.

Get Sts to compare with a partner, and then check answers.

> 1 used   2 between   3 got   4 would   5 light   6 myself
> 7 windy   8 leave   9 ended

Deal with any vocabulary problems that arose.

e Focus on the task and get Sts, in pairs, to tell each other why Brennan mentioned each item in the list.

EXTRA CHALLENGE You could get Sts to cover the text and look at the words and phrases in the list, or write them on the board and get Sts to close their books.

Get feedback for each item.

> the sun: When he lived in Bolivia, the people used to follow the patterns of **the sun**, i.e. go to bed when it is dark and get up when it got light again.
> 100 pages: He would sometimes read **100 pages** of a book between midnight and 3.00 a.m.
> one bedroom: He and his wife lived in a **one-bedroom** apartment in San Francisco.
> the woods: He sometimes went to **the woods** in the middle of the night.
> Angel Island: One of his favourite photos is of **Angel Island**.
> grading: He is a teacher, so has to **grade** (= mark) students' work.
> the street corner: He would meet his running partner at the **street corner** and run for an hour.
> young kids: He has **young kids**, who depend on him, so he can't follow his sleep pattern.

Finally, deal with any new vocabulary, and elicit or model the pronunciation.

f Do this as a whole-class activity. You could tell the class what you think you would do.

Elicit whether Sts think segmented sleep is generally a good or a bad idea.

4 VOCABULARY sleep

a Ask Sts whether they think that men yawn more than women, or the other way round. Tell Sts they are going to read some facts about sleep.

Give Sts time to read all the facts.

Find out which fact(s) Sts found the most surprising and if they already knew some of them.

b Put Sts in pairs and tell them to look at the **bold** words in **a**. Get Sts to decide what part of speech they are, and then work out what they mean from the context.

Check answers, either explaining in English, translating into Sts' L1, or getting Sts to check in their dictionaries. Elicit or model pronunciation.

yawn /jɔːn/ = open your mouth wide and breathe in deeply through it, usually because you are tired or bored
nap /næp/ = a short sleep, especially during the day
sleepy /ˈsliːpi/ = needing sleep; ready to go to sleep
snore /snɔː/ = breathe noisily through your nose and mouth while you are asleep
blankets /ˈblæŋkɪts/ = large covers, often made of wool, used especially on beds to keep people warm
sheets /ʃiːts/ = large pieces of thin cloth used on a bed to lie on or lie under
pillow /ˈpɪləʊ/ = a square or rectangular piece of cloth filled with soft material, used to rest your head on in bed
duvet /ˈduːveɪ/ = a large cloth bag that is filled with feathers or other soft material and that you have on top of you in bed to keep yourself warm
insomnia /ɪnˈsɒmniə/ = the condition of being unable to sleep
sleeping pills /ˈsliːpɪŋ pɪlz/ = pills containing a drug that helps you to sleep

c Tell Sts that the words and phrases in the list are all related to sleep. In pairs, they must try to work out what they think they mean. Tell them to use individual words or parts of words in the phrases to help them.

Check answers, either explaining in English, translating into Sts' L1, or getting Sts to check in their dictionaries. Elicit or model pronunciation. Point out that we can also say *be a heavy sleeper*. You could tell Sts that people sometimes say *sleep like a baby* instead of *sleep like a log*.

be a light sleeper = be easily woken up
fall asleep = go / get to sleep
be fast asleep = be sleeping deeply
have nightmares = have unpleasant or frightening dreams
keep you awake = make you stay awake
oversleep = sleep longer than you intended
set the alarm = prepare or arrange the alarm clock so that it is ready to wake you up at the time you need
sleep like a log = sleep very well, sleep deeply
sleepwalk = walk around while you are asleep

d **Vocabulary race** Put Sts in pairs. Focus on the task and the example word (*sleepy*). Elicit / Explain the difference between *sleepy* and *tired*. Then demonstrate the activity, pointing out that the example word *sleepy* comes from the text in **a**.

Say *Go* and wait for the first finishing pair to put their hands up. Then stop the activity.

e 🔊 **6.8** Play the audio for Sts to listen and check.

Check answers and make sure Sts understand all the words and phrases.

> 2 yawn   3 pillow   4 duvet   5 sheets, blankets   6 insomnia
> 7 sleeping pills   8 snore   9 nap   10 sleeps like a log
> 11 light sleeper   12 have nightmares   13 keep you awake
> 14 fast asleep   15 sleepwalk   16 set the alarm   17 oversleep
> 18 fall asleep

🔊 **6.8**
1 Most people start feeling sleepy at around eleven p.m.
2 When people are tired, they often open their mouth and yawn.
3 When they get into bed, they put their head on the pillow.
4 In bed, many people sleep under a duvet filled with feathers or synthetic material.
5 Other people prefer to sleep under sheets and blankets.
6 Some people can't sleep because they suffer from insomnia.

6A   91

7 People sometimes have to take sleeping pills to help them go to sleep.
8 Some people who are asleep make a loud noise when they breathe, i.e. they snore.
9 In hot countries, it's common to have a short nap in the afternoon.
10 A person who sleeps well 'sleeps like a log'.
11 Someone who doesn't sleep very deeply is a light sleeper.
12 Some children have nightmares if they watch scary films before bedtime.
13 If you drink coffee in the evening, it may keep you awake.
14 In the middle of the night, most people are fast asleep.
15 As many as fifteen per cent of people sleepwalk during the night, getting out of bed and even getting dressed or eating.
16 When people need to get up early, they often set the alarm.
17 If you don't hear your alarm, you might oversleep.
18 According to one study, four point seven per cent of Americans fall asleep while driving.

Finally, ask the pair who finished first how many answers they got correct. Then find out if any other pairs got more correct answers.

EXTRA SUPPORT Get Sts to cover the words in the right-hand column, and then to try to remember them by reading sentences 1–18 again and saying the missing words from memory. Alternatively, if there's time, you could quickly elicit the words from the whole class to wrap up the activity.

5 LISTENING understanding reasons

a Focus on the task and make sure Sts know what a *podcast* /ˈpɒdkɑːst/ is (= a digital audio file that can be downloaded or streamed from the internet and played on a computer, smartphone, iPod, etc.). Explain that they're going to think about what a sleep expert might say about a good bedtime routine.

Now put Sts in pairs and get them to discuss how to complete the gaps in 1–8. You might want to point out that all the missing words are nouns except for 7, which is a number. Tell Sts <u>not</u> to write the words in yet.

b 🔊 **6.9** Play the audio once the whole way through for Sts to listen and complete the gaps in 1–8 in **a**.

Get Sts to compare with a partner, and then check answers. Find out if Sts had guessed any correctly.

EXTRA SUPPORT Read through the script and decide if you need to pre-teach any new lexis before Sts listen.

---

1 bedroom 2 materials 3 pillows 4 window 5 dinner
6 coffee 7 9.5 8 read a book

🔊 6.9
(script in Student's Book on *p.127*)
I know a lot about sleep. I've been involved in sleep research for over thirty-six years. I call myself a sleep expert, and I think that if you are going to give advice about sleep, you should follow your own rules. So here are some things you should know about my sleep habits.
Number one: I sleep in a different bedroom from my partner.
Everyone should sleep alone. It's much better, if you can, to have your own room. You can wake refreshed, rather than be cross because your partner snored all night. My partner wasn't offended when I suggested we had separate rooms. In fact, she found she slept much better. Apparently, I make funny noises in my sleep.
Number two: I sleep under natural materials.
I wouldn't dream of getting into a bed made with hot, sweaty, man-made fibres. If you're really hot, it's hard to fall asleep or stay asleep. This is why we turn over at night – not just to relieve pressure, but to

find a cool spot. To sleep well, we need to lose one degree of body temperature, and cotton is excellent at keeping us cool.
Number three: I'm obsessive about pillows.
Pillows are really necessary for good sleep. It's essential that your body is in the right position, and a pillow should fill the gap between your shoulder and neck, to keep the neck and spine aligned when you lie on your side. I have two pillows because I'm tall and that works for me, but if one pillow holds you in the correct position, that's fine, too. I wash my pillows every six months and dry them outside.
Number four: I sleep with the window open.
Fresh air is good for sleep, and a build-up of carbon dioxide disturbs it. It's the warmth under the duvet that's important, not the warmth of the room. So keep your bedroom door open, and open the window at least a centimetre every night, all year round. Even if it's minus five degrees, I keep the window open, and curl up with a hot-water bottle.
Number five: I don't have dinner late.
I prefer to eat before seven p.m. If you have a large meal too close to bedtime, your body will still be working to digest it, and not resting. Eating your main meal three or four hours before bed is ideal.
Number six: I drink coffee in the evenings.
After dinner in a restaurant, I will happily order an espresso. Many people are insensitive to caffeine. Unless you know that you are sensitive to caffeine, it's actually the worrying that you've drunk caffeine that keeps you awake, not the caffeine itself.
Number seven: I need nine and a half hours' sleep.
It's a myth that you need an average of eight hours' sleep. Sleep need is genetic – some people might need four hours, others eleven. The right amount of sleep for you is something you can work out based on how many hours you need to feel alert during the day. That figure stays the same for you throughout your life. I always wake up at the same time early every morning, so to get the amount of sleep I need, I know I need to be in bed by nine thirty p.m.
Number eight: I read a book before going to sleep.
Everyone should have a way to relax before going to sleep. I read a non-thrilling book, often short stories, or a book with short chapters. You don't want something where every chapter ends on a cliffhanger, because that makes you want to read on.

Now ask Sts if they are surprised by any of the things Dr Neil Stanley does, and elicit some answers.

Finally, elicit what kind of person they think Dr Neil Stanley is (e.g. *fussy, rich, annoying*, etc.). You could tell the class what you think, too.

c Tell Sts they are going to listen to the podcast again and this time they need to complete Dr Stanley's reasons for his bedtime routine. Point out that reasons 1–8 here are related to sentences 1–8 in **a**.

Play the audio again, pausing after each prompt to give Sts time to write.

Get Sts to compare with a partner, and then play the audio again if necessary.

Check answers.

---

1 get disturbed / have to listen to your partner snoring.
2 you're really hot, and cotton is cooler.
3 sleep in the right position.
4 fresh air, even if it's cold outside.
5 will still be digesting the meal when you go to bed.
6 affected by caffeine.
7 that's right for him; everybody needs a different amount.
8 relaxing before going to sleep.

EXTRA CHALLENGE You could focus on some of the language related to sleep problems from the podcast, e.g. *sweaty man-made fibres, fill the gap, curl up with a hot-water bottle, insensitive to caffeine, feel alert, a cliffhanger*, etc.

6A

EXTRA SUPPORT If there's time, you could get Sts to listen again with the script on *p.127*, so they can see exactly what they understood / didn't understand. Translate / Explain any new words or phrases.

d Give Sts time to look at the list of completed rules in **a** and tick any they normally do. (If you think that Sts might not want to give personal information, tell them just to tick any that they are comfortable with.) They could underline the ones they would like to be able to do.

Now put Sts in pairs and get them to compare their lists.

Find out if any Sts already follow some of Dr Stanley's rules, and if there are any they would like to be able to do. You could tell the class about your own sleeping habits.

6 SPEAKING

Focus on the task and the questions. Give Sts time to read through them, and check they know all the lexis, e.g. *blinds*, *recurring dreams*, etc.

Put Sts in pairs, **A** and **B**. Sts **A** ask Sts **B** the green questions, and Sts **B** ask Sts **A** the red ones. Encourage Sts to ask for and give plenty of information in their answers. If you have time, you could ask Sts to return the questions with *What about you?*

Monitor and help whilst Sts ask and answer the questions.

Deal with any general vocabulary problems that arose.

Get some feedback from various pairs.

6A

6B Music to my ears

G gerunds and infinitives
V music
P words from other languages

Lesson plan

The topic of this lesson is music and how it affects our emotions.

In the first half of the lesson, Sts listen to an interview with a music psychologist, who explains why we listen to music and how music can affect us emotionally. Sts then talk about what kinds of music they listen to when they are in certain moods. The lesson continues with a grammar focus on the uses of gerunds and infinitives. Sts revise the basic rules about when to use a gerund or an infinitive after a verb, and then learn about certain verbs (e.g. *remember*, *try*) which can be followed by either a gerund or an infinitive, but with a change in meaning. The vocabulary and pronunciation focus is on words related to music, including 'borrowed' words such as *cello*, *choir*, and *ballet*, and on other foreign words which are used in English.

The second half of the lesson begins with a text about some research on the importance of finding the right music for the right task. Sts then read what four surgeons say about playing music while they work. This is followed by a speaking activity in which Sts discuss some statements about music. The lesson finishes with a documentary about pianist Isata Kanneh-Mason and her large family, all of whom are very talented musicians.

More materials
For teachers
Photocopiables
Grammar gerunds and infinitives *p.173*
Communicative Gerund or infinitive? *p.204*
(instructions *p.186*)
Teacher's Resource Centre
Video Music in the family
For students
Workbook 6B
Online Practice 6B

OPTIONAL LEAD-IN – THE QUOTE

Write the quote at the top of *p.60* on the board and the name of the person who said it, or get Sts to open their books and read it.

You could tell Sts that G.K. Chesterton (1874–1936) is probably best known for his series·about the priest-detective Father Brown, who appeared in 50 stories.

Ask Sts if they agree with the quote.

1 LISTENING & SPEAKING understanding a talk
(explanations and examples)

a Put Sts in pairs and get them to ask and answer the questions, giving as much information as possible. You could demonstrate the activity by telling Sts about yourself.

Get some feedback for each question from various Sts.

EXTRA SUPPORT Before Sts start talking in pairs, elicit different types of music, e.g. *classical*, *hip-hop*, *rap*, *reggae*, *jazz*, etc.

b 🔊 **6.10** Tell Sts that they are going to listen to the music psychologist John Sloboda talking about why we listen to music. Point out that he is the author of the book in the photo. Focus on the task and tell Sts that the first time they listen, they should try to complete reasons and examples 1–3 with key words or phrases. They will then compare notes with a partner and listen a second time. Make sure Sts know the meaning of *intensify*.

Play the audio once the whole way through and give Sts time to write their notes. You could pause after each reason and example is given.

EXTRA SUPPORT Read through the script and decide if you need to pre-teach any new lexis before Sts listen.

🔊 **6.10**
(script in Student's Book on *p.127*)
Part 1
I think it's very interesting that human beings are the only animals which listen to music for pleasure. A lot of research has been done to find out why we listen to music, and there seem to be three main reasons. Firstly, we listen to music to make us remember important moments in the past, for example when we met someone for the first time. Think of Humphrey Bogart in the film *Casablanca* saying, 'Darling, they're playing our song.' When we hear a certain piece of music, we remember hearing it for the first time in some very special circumstances. Obviously, this music varies from person to person. Secondly, we listen to music to help us to change activities. If we want to go from one activity to another, we often use music to help us make the change. For example, we might play a certain kind of music to prepare us to go out in the evening, or we might play another kind of music to relax us when we get home from work. That's mainly why people listen to music in cars, and they often listen to one kind of music when they're going to work and another kind when they're coming home. The same is true of people on buses and trains.

The third reason why we listen to music is to intensify the emotion that we're feeling. For example, if we're feeling sad, sometimes we want to get even sadder, so we play sad music. Or we're feeling angry and we want to intensify the anger – then we play angry music. Or when we're planning a romantic dinner, we lay the table, we light candles, and then we think, 'What music would make this even more romantic?'

EXTRA SUPPORT Focus on the task and tell Sts that they will be listening to the audio twice: the first time they listen, they should try to complete sentences 1–3 with a phrase. The second time, they should try to listen for at least one example for 1–3.

Play the audio and then check answers for reasons 1–3.

94 6B

1 remember important moments in the past
2 change activities
3 the emotion that we're feeling

Then play the audio again for Sts to listen to the examples.

c Get Sts to compare with a partner, and then play the audio again for Sts to add any extra information.

Check answers.

1 to make us **remember important moments in the past**, e.g. when we met someone for the first time (like Humphrey Bogart in *Casablanca* saying, 'Darling, they're playing our song.').
2 to help us to **change activities**, e.g. to prepare us to go out in the evening, to relax us when we get home from work.
3 to intensify **the emotion that we're feeling**, e.g. if we're feeling sad, we want to get sadder; if we're feeling angry, we want to intensify the anger; if we're having a romantic dinner, we use music to make it more romantic.

EXTRA SUPPORT If there's time, you could get Sts to listen again with the script on *p.127*, so they can see exactly what they understood / didn't understand. Translate / Explain any new words or phrases.

d Put Sts in pairs and give them time to discuss the two questions.

Elicit times Sts listen to music for each of the three reasons given in the interview, as well as the various kinds of music they listen to.

e ◗ **6.11** Focus on the task and the four pieces of music. Ask Sts if they know any of the music. Point out that 4 is a piece of film music, and ask Sts if they have heard of or seen the film.

Now play the audio, pausing after each piece of music, and ask Sts how it makes them feel.

◗ **6.11**
See the four pieces of music in Student's Book on *p.60*

EXTRA SUPPORT Before playing the music extracts, elicit from Sts how music can make you feel, e.g. *happy*, *sad*, *angry*, *frightened*, etc. Write all the adjectives they suggest on the board. Then play each piece of music one at a time.

f ◗ **6.12** Focus on the task and give Sts time to look at the incomplete notes. Make sure they understand the meaning of the noun *pitch* in music (= how high or low a sound is, especially a musical note). Explain that the purpose of the activity is to try to get as much information as they can in one listening. Point out that in the third section (*Emotions related to pieces of music*), they should be looking for the emotion word / how you feel (*sad*, etc.).

Play the audio, pausing between each section to give Sts time to complete their notes (see *** in script 6.12).

Get Sts to compare with a partner. If Sts really need to listen again, play the audio a second time.

Check answers. You might want to remind Sts in answer 4, under *Emotions related to pieces of music*, of the difference between *terrifying*, which they heard on the audio (…*the music makes it absolutely terrifying*), and the answer *terrified*, which is how the music makes people feel.

EXTRA SUPPORT Read through the script and decide if you need to pre-teach any new lexis before Sts listen.

The human voice:
1 happy = people speak **faster**, the voice is **higher**
2 sad = people speak **more slowly**, the voice is **lower**
3 angry = people **raise** their voice or **shout**
Music copies the human voice:
1 **faster**, **high-pitched** music sounds happy
2 **slow** music with **falling** pitches sounds sad
3 **loud** music with **irregular** rhythms sounds angry
Emotions related to pieces of music:
1 **happy** = the Beethoven
2 **angry** = the Holst
3 **sad** = the Albinoni
4 **terrified** = the film music from *Psycho*

◗ **6.12**
(script in Student's Book on *p.127*)
Part 2
Let's take three important human emotions: happiness, sadness, and anger. When people are happy, they speak faster and their voice is higher. When they are sad, they speak more slowly and their voice is lower, and when people are angry, they raise their voices or shout. Babies can tell whether their mother is happy or not simply by the sound of her voice, not by her words.
***
What music does is it copies this, and it produces the same emotions. So faster, higher-pitched music will sound happy. Slow music with lots of falling pitches will sound sad. Loud music with irregular rhythms will sound angry. It doesn't matter how good or bad the music is – if it has these characteristics, it will make you experience this emotion.
***
Let me give you some examples. For happy, for example, the first movement of Beethoven's *Seventh Symphony*. For angry, say *Mars*, from *The Planets* by Holst. And for sad, something like Albinoni's *Adagio for Strings*.
Of course, the people who exploit this most are the people who write film soundtracks. They can take a scene which visually has no emotion and they can make the scene either scary or calm or happy, just by the music they write to go with it. Think of the music in the shower scene in Hitchcock's film *Psycho*. All you can see is a woman having a shower, but the music makes it absolutely terrifying.

EXTRA SUPPORT If there's time, you could get Sts to listen again with the script on *p.127*, so they can see exactly what they understood / didn't understand. Translate / Explain any new words or phrases.

g Focus on the questions and example. Then put Sts in pairs and set a time limit for Sts to go through them and compare answers and choices of music. Encourage Sts to specify not just the kind of music they would play, but also the name of the artist or song / piece of music.

Monitor and help whilst Sts do the task.

Deal with any general vocabulary problems that arose.

Get some feedback from individual Sts.

EXTRA IDEA If Sts have examples of music on their phones, which they would listen to in any of these situations, you could get them to play a short extract to the class and see if they agree.

2 GRAMMAR gerunds and infinitives

a Focus on the task and extracts 1–3 and give Sts a couple of minutes to put the verbs into the infinitive (with or without *to*) or the gerund.

Get them to compare with a partner.

6B 95

b 🔊 **6.13** Now play the audio for Sts to listen and check. Check answers.

1 remember	**2** hearing	**3** to go, make	

🔊 **6.13**
1 Firstly, we listen to music to make us remember important moments in the past.
2 When we hear a certain piece of music, we remember hearing it for the first time…
3 If we want to go from one activity to another, we often use music to help us make the change.

c This exercise introduces a new grammar point, i.e. that certain verbs can use either the gerund or the infinitive, but that the meaning changes depending on which form is used.

Focus on the task and give Sts time to try and work out the difference between the two sentences.

Check answers.

A 2	**B** 1	

d Tell Sts to go to **Grammar Bank 6B** on *p.143*.

Grammar notes

Sts have previously learned about the use of gerunds and infinitives (with and without *to*) after certain verbs. Here they revise and expand their knowledge of verbs which can take the gerund and those which take the infinitive with or without *to* – something that even the most advanced Sts make mistakes with. They then learn to use verbs which can take either form, but with a change in meaning.

Verbs followed by the gerund and verbs followed by the infinitive

- **Rules 1–5**

  A full list of the most common verbs which take the gerund or infinitive is included in the **Appendix – Verb patterns: verbs followed by the gerund or the infinitive** on *p.164*. After reminding Sts of the three verb patterns (rules 1–4), take a few minutes to go through the **Appendix** and make sure Sts know the meaning of the verbs. You could ask Sts to revise the three groups as self-study and test them on the material.

- **Rule 4:** *make* and *let*

  Highlight that the verb form following *make* depends on whether the sentence is active or passive. In the passive, *make* is followed by the infinitive with *to*. Compare:

  *They **made** us **wear** a uniform at school.*

  *We **were made to wear** a uniform at school.*

Verbs that can be followed by the gerund or infinitive with a change in meaning

This rule for verbs where the meaning changes will be new to most Sts. In Sts' L1, some of these concepts may be covered by using two different verbs, so if you know your Sts' L1, you can use it to make the meaning clear.

- **Rule 3:** *try* + gerund is often used in advice, e.g. *Why don't you try changing the battery?*
- **Rule 4:** with *need to do / needs doing*, highlight that *needs doing* is an alternative to a passive construction, e.g. *The house needs painting / to be painted*.

Focus on the example sentences for **verbs followed by the gerund and verbs followed by the infinitive** and play audio 🔊 **6.14** for Sts to listen and repeat. Encourage them to copy the rhythm.

Then go through the rules with the class.

Now focus on the *like, love, hate,* **and** *prefer* box and go through it with the class. You could give Sts the additional example: *I prefer cycling to driving.* (general) *You don't need to give me a lift to the station. I prefer to walk.* (specific)

Repeat for **verbs that can be followed by the gerund or infinitive with a change in meaning** 🔊 **6.15**.

Focus on the exercises and get Sts to do them individually or in pairs.

If they do them individually, get them to compare with a partner Check answers, getting Sts to read the full sentences.

a
1 I suggest **taking** a taxi to the airport tomorrow.
2 Even though the snow was really deep, we managed **to drive** to the local shop and back.
3 We'd better **do** some shopping…
4 i'm very impatient. I can't stand **waiting** in queues.
5 A young man kindly offered **to carry** my bags.
6 My parents used to make me **tidy** my room.
7 We threatened **to call** the police if the boys didn't stop throwing stones.
8 Do you feel like **coming** to the gym with me?
9 I'd prefer **to eat out** instead of getting a takeaway.
10 I don't mind **working** late tonight if you want me to.
b
1 seeing 2 to call 3 taking 4 locking 5 to turn
6 painting 7 to send 8 to reach

Tell Sts to go back to the main lesson **6B**.

EXTRA SUPPORT If you think Sts need more practice, you may want to give them the **Grammar** photocopiable activity at this point.

e Put Sts in pairs for this oral grammar practice activity and focus on the task. Give Sts time to think and plan what they are going to say, before getting them to speak.

Monitor and help Sts, correcting any errors with gerunds and infinitives.

Get some feedback.

3 VOCABULARY & PRONUNCIATION music; words from other languages

a 🔊 **6.16** Tell Sts they are going to hear some musical extracts and they have to match them to the words in the two lists, *instruments* or *musicians*.

Play the audio once or twice as necessary.

🔊 **6.16**
(sounds for the following:)
1 a cello
2 drums
3 a bass guitar
4 a saxophone
5 a flute
6 a keyboard
7 a violin
8 a conductor
9 a choir
10 a soprano
11 an orchestra

96 **6B**

b 🔊 **6.17** Now play the audio for Sts to listen and check.
Check answers.

🔊 **6.17**
1 (sound effects) a cello
2 (sound effects) drums
3 (sound effects) a bass guitar
4 (sound effects) a saxophone
5 (sound effects) a flute
6 (sound effects) a keyboard
7 (sound effects) a violin
8 (sound effects) a conductor
9 (sound effects) a choir
10 (sound effects) a soprano
11 (sound effects) an orchestra

Now either use the audio to drill the pronunciation of the words, or model and drill them yourself. Give further practice of any words your Sts find difficult to pronounce.

Put Sts in pairs and get them to practise saying the words.

Give Sts, in their pairs, a few minutes to think of any other words they know for instruments and musicians.

Elicit answers on the board in two columns headed INSTRUMENTS and MUSICIANS. Get Sts to spell the words, and then elicit / model pronunciation where necessary.

Possible suggestions
Instruments: trumpet, triangle, recorder, harp, harmonica, banjo, trombone, clarinet, organ, etc.
Musicians: cellist, drummer, bass guitarist, pianist, violinist, keyboard player, saxophonist, rapper, tenor, singer-songwriter, composer, lead singer, band, etc.

Finally, find out if Sts can play any of the instruments mentioned, or if they sing.

Pronunciation notes
English has borrowed many words from other languages. Some of them have been anglicized, e.g. *boeuf* (French) to *beef*. Others are unchanged, e.g. *cello*. Where English uses a foreign word, the consonants are often pronounced in a way which is similar to the language of origin, e.g. in *cello* the *c* is pronounced /tʃ/ – similar to the Italian pronunciation. On the other hand, vowels are usually anglicized, e.g. the final *o* in *cello* is pronounced /əʊ/, as in English.

Note: in borrowed French words which include the letters *en*, e.g. *genre*, the vowel is pronounced in a similar way to French, and sounds like the *o* in *on* /ɒn/.

c Focus on the **Foreign words that are used in English** box and go through it with the class.

Now put Sts in pairs and tell them to look at all the words in the *Borrowed from…* chart, try to say them to each other using an 'English' pronunciation, and underline the stressed syllable.

d 🔊 **6.18** Play the audio for Sts to listen and check.
Check answers.

con**ce**rto   **me**zzo-soprano
chorus   **rhy**thm   **sym**phony
ballet   **en**core   **gen**re

🔊 **6.18**
See words in Student's Book on *p.61*

Now play the audio again, pausing after each group of words. Elicit how the pink letters are pronounced. Refer Sts to the phonetics for each word.

The second letter *c* in *concerto* is pronounced /tʃ/.
The letters *zz* in *mezzo* are pronounced /ts/.
The letters *ch* in *chorus* are pronounced /k/.
The letters *rhy* in *rhythm* are pronounced /rɪ/.
The letters *ph* in *symphony* are pronounced /f/.
The letters *et* in *ballet* are pronounced /eɪ/.
The letters *en* in *encore* are pronounced /ɒŋ/.
The letter *gen* in *genre* are pronounced /ʒɒn/.

Play the audio again, pausing after each group of words for Sts to listen and repeat.

Then repeat the activity, eliciting responses from individual Sts.

e Focus on the task and point out that these words are not related to music. You might want to highlight that Sts have seen a lot of these words in previous lessons.

Put Sts in pairs, get them to say the words to each other using an 'English' pronunciation if possible, and then guess their origin. Tell Sts that there are six words in each group.

Say each word in turn and ask Sts which language they come from and their meaning. Elicit or model pronunciation as necessary.

f 🔊 **6.19** Now play the audio for Sts to find out which language the words come from.
Check answers.

🔊 **6.19**

From Italian	barista, cappuccino, graffiti, macchiato, paparazzi, villa
From Greek	architecture, hypochondriac, microphone, philosophy, psychic, psychologist
From French	bouquet, chauffeur, chef, chic, croissant, fiancé

Play the audio again, pausing after each group of words for Sts to listen and repeat.

Then repeat the activity, eliciting responses from individual Sts.

Finally, give Sts time to practise saying them.

g Do this as a whole-class activity.

EXTRA IDEA You might like to extend the speaking practice by asking more questions using words from other languages, e.g. *Have you ever been to see a live performance of a ballet? Do you know anyone who can play the cello? How long should people be with their fiancé / fiancée before getting married? When was the last time you bought someone a bouquet of flowers?* etc. With a strong class, Sts could write and ask their own questions.

4 READING scanning across several texts

a Do this as a whole-class activity. You could get a show of hands for how many Sts in class listen to music when working / studying. Elicit whether any Sts never listen to music in these situations.

b Focus on the task and then set a short time limit for Sts to read the article once and choose the best summary for the results of the research mentioned. Tell them not to worry about the gaps.

6B 97

Check the answer. Focus on paragraph 3 and elicit the difference between what the research calls *divergent thinking* (thinking creatively, spontaneously coming up with new ideas) and *convergent thinking* (doing problem-solving, using logic to solve existing problems).

EXTRA SUPPORT Before Sts read the article the first time, check whether you need to pre-teach any vocabulary.

> 2

c Quickly go through phrases A–F, checking Sts know the meaning of all the lexis, e.g. *stimulate*, *mood*, *uplifting*, etc.

Now get Sts to read the article again and complete gaps 1–6.

Get Sts to compare with a partner, and then check answers.

> **1** B **2** F **3** D **4** A **5** C **6** E

Deal with any vocabulary problems that arose.

d Do this as a whole-class activity and elicit opinions from various Sts.

e Focus on the task. Put Sts in pairs and get them to look at the photo and answer questions 1–2.

Get some feedback from various pairs. For question 1, you could get a show of hands for Sts' opinions. For question 2, you could elicit all the advantages and disadvantages onto the board to help Sts with **f**.

f Focus on the first part of the task, and before Sts read the article, you could focus on the four different surgeons and check Sts know what kind of surgery they do.

Give Sts time to read the article to check their answers to **e**.

Elicit whether the article mentioned any of the points Sts talked about in **e**.

Now focus on the second part of the task. Elicit / Explain the meaning of *general consensus* /ˈdʒenrəl kənˈsensəs/ (= the opinion that most or all members of a group agree with). Then ask what the general consensus is regarding playing music whilst operating.

EXTRA SUPPORT Before Sts read the article the first time, check whether you need to pre-teach any vocabulary.

> The consensus would probably be 'have music while you work'.

You might like to focus on some of the words and phrases in the text that refer to types of music: *crowd-pleasers* (= music that everyone likes), *easy listening* (= pleasant or relaxing music, but that some people think is quite boring), *sing-along tracks* (= songs that people enjoy singing out loud to), *playlist* (= a personal selection of songs and pieces of music), *lift music* (= background music of the kind you hear in a lift, usually very bland / uninteresting).

g Focus on the task and point out that the letters are the surgeons' initials.

Give Sts time to read the article again and do the task. Check answers.

> **1** SN **2** RT **3** RT **4** SA **5** GW **6** SA **7** SN **8** GW

Deal with any other new vocabulary. Elicit or model the pronunciation of any tricky words.

h Put Sts in pairs and then give them time to create a playlist. Tell them to be as precise as possible, e.g. they should name the specific song and singer, etc., that they would like to listen to.

Get Sts to mingle and share their playlists, or put them on the classroom walls and get Sts to read them.

You might want to ask Sts to (create and) present their playlists to the class, and explain their choices using *because* clauses.

5 SPEAKING

Focus on the questions, making sure Sts understand all the lexis, e.g. *lyrics*, *decade*, etc.

Before Sts start the activity, give them time to think about their own individual opinions for each statement, e.g. by marking each one on a scale from 'strongly agree' to 'strongly disagree'.

Put Sts in small groups of three or four and tell them to take turns to start the discussion for each statement.

EXTRA SUPPORT Before Sts start the discussion, remind them of the expressions they saw for **Managing discussions** and **Politely disagreeing** in **Lesson 2B**.

Monitor and help if necessary.

Deal with any general vocabulary problems that arose.

Finally, get some quick feedback from various groups on some of the statements.

6 ▶ VIDEO LISTENING

a Tell Sts they are going to watch an interview with a famous pianist called Isata Kanneh-Mason. Give Sts time to read the two questions.

Play the video once the whole way through for Sts to watch and answer the questions.

Check answers.

EXTRA SUPPORT Read through the script and decide if you need to pre-teach any new lexis before Sts watch the video.

> Her parents and siblings are all talented musicians.
> Because they are all professional musicians or about to become professionals.

Music in the family

N = narrator, I = Isata

N *This is Isata Kanneh-Mason. A talented pianist studying at London's prestigious Royal Academy of Music. She's quickly gaining a strong reputation in the world of classical music. It's easy to see, and hear, why, but how did this young prize-winning artist first become interested in classical music?*

I So, I first became interested in music because my parents were massive classical music fans. And they were always playing classical music around the house and I just always listened to it. And it was always part of my childhood so, I feel like I've always been interested in music.

N *Isata herself started playing an instrument when she was very young.*

I Well, I actually started playing the recorder when I was three years old. And then when I was six, I had my first piano lesson, and I've been playing since then.

N *It wasn't long before Isata's remarkable talent was noticed. At the age of nine she started studying at the Junior Royal Academy of Music. When she was seventeen, she was awarded the Elton John scholarship to continue her undergraduate studies at the Royal Academy of Music, and actually performed with the pop legend.*

I Playing with Elton John was amazing. I was seventeen years old and I played with him in LA, I actually played the viola for that concert. And it was, it was just such a fun experience because it wasn't classical music so, it was nice to do something different. And it was also just amazing to be part of that energy on stage. He's a very charismatic person and I just really enjoyed the whole thing.

N *But Isata hasn't made this journey alone. Incredibly, she is the eldest of seven siblings that all share Isata's talent and passion for classical music. There's Braimah, Sheku, Konya, Jeneba, Aminata, and Mariatu. Between them they play a variety of instruments, in fact, her brother Sheku, who is a cellist, won the BBC Young Musician Award in twenty sixteen and performed at the royal wedding in twenty eighteen. What was it like growing up in such a musical family?*

I I've always loved growing up in a musical family, but it's quite hard to say what it was like because I don't really know it any other way. But, I do know that it was always very noisy, very busy, um, and the house is just always full of music. I think growing up in a musical family definitely helps me as a musician because I think it's so important to just be surrounded by music, and to always be listening. And also my siblings and I, we always give each other advice and help each other with our practice. So, I'd definitely say that being part of a musical family has really helped me grow as a musician.

N *With so many talented siblings, are they competitive?*

I I wouldn't say we're competitive because we were lucky enough that we all chose different instruments. And, although several of us play the piano, the ages are quite far apart so there's never been any competition. There's always just been a sense of spurring each other on and a sense of support.

N *Isata and several of her siblings are already well on the road to being professional musicians – but it is not an easy career choice.*

I I think if you have a career in classical music, it's always going to be a sacrifice. For my siblings and I, we definitely felt that at school, sometimes you can't go out with your friends or go to parties because you have to practice. And not everyone may always understand that but I think if you love music enough, which we all definitely did, then the sacrifice is so worth it. And I think if you want to succeed in anything, you have to make sacrifices, so, I think we got used to that.

N *What is the most important thing for you when you're choosing a piece to perform?*

I For me, the emotion of a piece is extremely important. I think there's of course, a massive intellectual side to classical music, and you need to analyse the music you're playing. But at the end of the day, when you go to a concert, you go because you want to feel something special. So, I think the emotion of the piece completely defines it for me.

N *And the importance of emotion is easy to hear in Isata's playing.*

I I think for me, playing has always been a release from everyday life. I think there's so much emotion and there's just so much in music and so playing has always been kind of an escape for me. So, I'm just so lucky that my escape is what I do.

N *This piece, by nineteenth century composer Clara Schumann, appears on Isata's debut album. Both Isata and Sheku already have contracts with the prestigious record label Decca, and it seems likely that other siblings will follow in their footsteps. For the Kanneh-Mason family, the future looks bright.*

b Give Sts time to read questions 1–8 and make sure that they understand all the lexis.

Play the video again, pausing if necessary for Sts to write their answers.

EXTRA CHALLENGE First, put Sts in pairs and tell them to try to remember any of the answers. Then play the video again.

Check answers.

1 When she was growing up her parents were always playing classical music around the house.
2 She won the Elton John scholarship, so she could continue her studies at the Royal Academy of Music. She also performed with Elton John.
3 She is the eldest child.
4 He plays the cello. He won the BBC Young Musician Award in 2016 and performed at Prince Harry and Meghan Markle's wedding.
5 They have a very good relationship. as they give each other advice and help each other.
6 They couldn't always go out or go to parties. They got used to it.
7 The emotion because she thinks people want to listen to music to make them feel something special.
8 She feels she is lucky that her job is also what helps her escape everyday life.

EXTRA SUPPORT You could get Sts to watch again with subtitles, so they can see exactly what they understood / didn't understand. Translate / Explain any new words or phrases.

c Do this as a whole-class activity, or put Sts in pairs and then get some feedback. You could also tell the class if you know any such people or families.

100

5&6 Revise and Check

For instructions on how to use these pages, see *p.41*.

More materials

For teachers

Teacher's Resource Centre
Video Can you understand these people? 5&6
Quick Test 6
File 6 Test

For students

Online Practice Check your progress

GRAMMAR

a
1 hadn't found 2 didn't work 3 wouldn't have gone
4 wouldn't be 5 I could speak 6 'd learned to play 7 you
wouldn't leave 8 used to driving 9 to have 10 to getting
up
b
1 meeting 2 cutting 3 to get 4 not to be 5 working

VOCABULARY

a
1 proud 2 homesick 3 grateful 4 guilty 5 stunned
b
1 exhausting 2 shocked 3 embarrassed 4 stressful
5 annoys 6 disappointing 7 amazes 8 horrified
9 offensive 10 scary
c
1 pillow 2 snore 3 nap 4 nightmare 5 set
d
1 a conductor 2 a band / a choir 3 a cello 4 a soprano
5 a keyboard

PRONUNCIATION

a
1 delighted /ɪ/ 2 yawn /ɔː/ 3 eyes /z/ 4 homesick /s/
5 chic /ʃ/
b
1 absolutely 2 devastated 3 infuriating 4 insomnia
5 sleepwalk

CAN YOU understand this text?

a
Music that has a rhythm of 60–80 beats, without lyrics
b
1 b 2 a 3 c 4 a 5 b 6 a 7 b 8 b 9 c 10 c

▶ CAN YOU understand these people?

1 c 2 b 3 a 4 b

◀)) 6.20

1
I = interviewer, C = Christopher
I   How well do you think you'd survive if you were left alone on a
    desert island?
C   Not very! I did the boy scouts, and so I know a little bit of basic
    survival. But it would be, I would, hopefully, hopefully be found
    rather quickly after my, my abandonment there.
I   What would you do?
C   Um, probably, kind of what you see in all the movies – build a
    bonfire, and see if I had any mirror or anything to attract a plane
    or a passing boat. Just try to find shelter and, and whatever
    type of food's on the island.

2
I = interviewer, L = Lemuel
I   What kind of things do people do that really annoy you?
L   Walking slowly in public. Um, tapping their pencils on tables
    during lectures as well, yeah.
I   Do you think you do anything that annoys other people?
L   Um, biting my nails. Um, yeah, not much else.

3
I = interviewer, M = Mary
I   Do you ever have problems sleeping?
M   Most of the time I don't have a problem sleeping, but
    sometimes if I, I'm either really cold or I'm really excited about
    something that's happening, or I'm really sad about something
    that has happened, then I have problems sleeping.
I   What do you do if you can't sleep?
M   I normally read a book, because any time I read a book in bed I
    will fall asleep.

4
I = interviewer, M = Martina
I   On a typical day, do you listen to music?
M   Yes, I listen to music every day.
I   When and where?
M   First thing in the morning, outside on my patio.
I   Do you listen to different kinds of music at different times of
    day?
M   I listen to different types of music no matter what time of day.
I   What makes you choose one kind of music over another?
M   Um, I choose sort of spa, new age music in the morning to wake
    up. I choose country to just get going during the day and a little
    soul at night.

Revise and Check

7A Let's not argue

G past modals: *must have*, etc.; *would rather*
V verbs often confused
P weak form of *have*

Lesson plan

The topic of this lesson is arguments: what causes them, how to argue, and how to win online arguments.

The first half of the lesson starts with the grammar presentation, where Sts listen to some people arguing, a context in which past modals of deduction can naturally occur. Your Sts will have learned to use present modals of deduction (*must / might / can't* + infinitive) and *should* (+ infinitive) for advice at Intermediate level. In this lesson, they learn how to use these same modals to make deductions or speculate about the past (e.g. *You must have taken a wrong turning*, *Somebody might have stolen it*) and to make criticisms (e.g. *You shouldn't have said that*). The pronunciation focus is on weak forms of *have* in sentences with past modals (e.g. *You should have told me*). Then in Reading & Speaking, Sts read an article aimed at helping students in shared accommodation avoid arguments, and discuss the solutions.

In the second half of the lesson, Sts start by role-playing an argument. They then listen to a psychologist talking about how to argue in a sensible and controlled way, and then Sts put the advice into action in another role-play. Grammar in Context focuses on the use of *would rather*, and is followed by a vocabulary focus on verbs which are sometimes confused, e.g. *argue* and *discuss*. The lesson finishes with an article about the best ways to win an online argument, which Sts put into practice by simulating an online discussion.

More materials
For teachers
Photocopiables
Grammar past modals *p.174*
Communicative Guess my verb *p.205* (instructions *p.187*)
Vocabulary Verbs often confused *p.224* (instructions *p.215*)
For students
Workbook 7A
Online Practice 7A

OPTIONAL LEAD-IN – THE QUOTE

Write the quote at the top of *p.66* on the board and the name of the person who said it, or get Sts to open their books and read it.

You could tell Sts that Desmond Tutu is a South African Anglican archbishop and human rights activist.

Ask Sts to tell you what the quote means.

1 GRAMMAR past modals: *must have*, etc.

a Put Sts in pairs and tell them to focus on the photo and guess who the people are, where they are, and what they might be arguing about. Encourage them to follow the style of the example and use *can't be*, *must be*, or *could be*. Elicit ideas, but don't tell Sts if they are correct or not.

EXTRA SUPPORT Do this as a whole-class activity. Either focus on the example, or write CAN'T BE, COULD BE, and MUST BE on the board to help Sts.

b 🔊 7.1 Play the audio for Sts to listen and check. Ask Sts who the 'guilty' person is.

> The people are flatmates, and they are in the kitchen of their shared house. One girl is accusing the others of using her milk. The others defend themselves, but in the end, it is established that Jack (M2) used her milk in his coffee.

🔊 7.1
(script in Student's Book on *p.127*)
W = woman, M = man
W1 Where's my milk? It's not here.
M1 I haven't seen it. You must have finished it.
W1 I definitely didn't finish it. I was keeping a bit for my cereal this morning. One of you must have used it.
W2 It can't have been me. I only drink my soya milk. Could you have drunk it last night and then forgotten? Did you have something before going to bed?
W1 No, I didn't. I just drank a glass of water.
M1 Someone might have given it to the cat.
W1 Oh, come on. We all know she drinks water, not milk. I'm telling you, last night I know there was some milk in the fridge. *My* milk.
M1 Well, I don't know what's happened to it. In any case, you should have put your name on it.
W1 I did put my name on it! In capital letters!
W3 And it wasn't me, because I stayed at Mike's last night, and I had breakfast there before getting back here.
W1 What are you drinking, Jack?
M2 Just coffee.
W1 Yes, white coffee. That's where my milk went. You didn't have any milk of your own in the fridge.
W2 Ooh, Jack, you naughty boy!
W1 Well, you can go to the supermarket and get me some more.
M2 OK, OK, calm down. I'll go and get you some milk.

c 🔊 7.2 Focus on the instructions and the gapped extracts. Give Sts time to read the extracts. Then play the audio, pausing after each extract for Sts to complete the sentences. Play the audio again, as necessary. Check answers.

> 1 must have 2 must have 3 can't have 4 Could…have
> 5 might have 6 should have

🔊 7.2
1 You must have finished it.
2 One of you must have used it.
3 It can't have been me.
4 Could you have drunk it last night…?
5 Someone might have given it to the cat.
6 …you should have put your name on it.

7A 101

d Focus on the task and give Sts time to do it in pairs.

Check answers and elicit that A = *must have*, B = *could* or *might have*, C = *can't have*, and D = *should have*.

A 1,2 **B** 4,5 **C** 3 **D** 6

EXTRA SUPPORT You could play audio 🔊 7.2 again and get Sts to listen and repeat, copying the rhythm and intonation.

e Tell Sts to go to **Grammar Bank 7A** on *p.144*.

Grammar notes

must, may / might / could, can't / couldn't + have + past participle

Sts have previously seen these modal verbs to make deductions about the present, e.g. *John must be ill. She might be French*. Here they learn to use the same modals to make deductions about the past (*You must have made a mistake*).

- **Rule 1: *must have***

Sts may sometimes try to use *mustn't have* (which doesn't exist) instead of *can't have*, e.g. *You can't have seen me yesterday. I was in bed all day*. NOT ~~You mustn't have…~~

- **Rule 2: *might / may / could + have***

Remind Sts that *may have* and *might have* in these sentences are interchangeable (although *might have* must be used in reported speech). Highlight also that *could have* is interchangeable with *might / may have*, but *couldn't have* (see rule 3) isn't interchangeable with *might / may not have*.

should have / ought to have + past participle

Sts are familiar with *should* and *ought to* to give advice or to express an opinion (*You should get a new phone. The government ought to change the law*). Here they learn to use *should have / ought to have* to criticize somebody's actions (*You should have turned left. You ought not to have spoken to her like that*).

Focus on the example sentences for ***must, may / might / could, can't / couldn't + have + past participle*** and play audio 🔊 7.3 for Sts to listen and repeat. Encourage them to copy the rhythm. Then go through the rules with the class.

Repeat for ***should have / ought to have* + past participle** 🔊 7.4.

Focus on the exercises and get Sts to do them individually or in pairs.

If they do them individually, get them to compare with a partner. Check answers, getting Sts to read the full sentences.

a
1 She might have had an argument with her boyfriend.
2 Ben must have read my email.
3 They can't have got lost.
4 You can't have seen Ellie yesterday.
5 John might not have seen you.
6 Lucy must have bought a new car.
7 Alex can't have been very ill.
8 They might not have been invited.
9 You must have used too much sugar.
10 It can't have been my phone.

b
1 You **should have / ought to have written** it down.
2 You **shouldn't have / oughtn't to have driven** here.
3 You **shouldn't have / oughtn't to have invited** her.
4 You **shouldn't have / oughtn't to have bought** so many shoes.
5 I **should have / ought to have gone** to bed earlier last night.
6 You **should have / ought to have taken** it out of the freezer earlier.
7 You **shouldn't have / oughtn't to have sat** in the sun all afternoon without any sunscreen.

Tell Sts to go back to the main lesson **7A**.

EXTRA SUPPORT If you think Sts need more practice, you may want to give them the **Grammar** photocopiable activity at this point.

2 PRONUNCIATION weak form of *have*

Pronunciation notes

When *have* is an auxiliary verb, not a main verb, it usually has a weak pronunciation, e.g. *I might have lost it* (*have* = /əv/). Sts may sometimes misunderstand this as the weak form of *of*, and many native speakers sometimes misspell weak *have* as *of*.

To encourage Sts to use the weak form of *have*, tell them that the most important thing for Sts is to stress the modal and the participle strongly, and not to stress *have* at all.

a Do this as a whole-class activity. Elicit ideas.

Now focus on the **Weak form of *have*** box and go through it with the class.

Check the answer.

Because the weak (unstressed) form of *have*, e.g. in *must have*, sounds like the weak form of *of*.

b 🔊 **7.5** Play the audio for Sts to listen and repeat the six sentences.

🔊 **7.5**
1 He must have left his bag at school.
2 You must have known it would happen.
3 It can't have been a very good concert.
4 Could you have left it on the bus?
5 There might have been some witnesses.
6 You should have phoned me.

c 🔊 **7.6** Focus on the task and play the audio, pausing after each sentence to give Sts time to write.

Get Sts to compare with a partner, and then check answers by eliciting the sentences onto the board. Remind Sts that they can only understand whether it's *have* or *of* from the meaning and context of the sentence, not from the pronunciation.

🔊 **7.6**
1 Where have you been all morning?
2 I woke up in the middle of the night.
3 Of course I'll be there on time!
4 We can't have gone the wrong way!
5 I'll have finished in about ten minutes.
6 What's the point of arguing?

102 **7A**

EXTRA SUPPORT Play the audio again, pausing after each sentence for Sts to underline the stressed words. Check answers and elicit that the auxiliaries *have* and *of* are never stressed.

1 <u>Where</u> have you <u>been</u> <u>all</u> <u>morning</u>?
2 I <u>woke</u> up in the <u>middle</u> of the <u>night</u>.
3 Of <u>course</u> I'll <u>be</u> <u>there</u> on <u>time</u>!
4 We <u>can't</u> have <u>gone</u> the <u>wrong</u> <u>way</u>!
5 I'll have <u>finished</u> in about <u>ten</u> <u>minutes</u>.
6 <u>What's</u> the <u>point</u> of <u>arguing</u>?

d Focus on the task and the example. Highlight that in 2–4, Sts are given the modal verb, but in 5–8 they have to choose an appropriate one. Point out that Sts can use *may have* instead of *might have*.

Give Sts time in pairs to complete **B**'s responses.

Elicit ideas from different pairs. Accept responses which are grammatically correct and make sense in the context.

Possible answers
2 left it at work
3 forgotten
4 gone to bed so late last night
5 You should have practised more.
6 One of them might have met someone else.
7 He might have been ill.
8 We should have left earlier.

Then get Sts to read their conversations in pairs, practising stressing the correct words and using the weak form of *have*.

Finally, check their pronunciation by getting a different pair to read each conversation.

3 READING & SPEAKING identifying solutions to problems

a Focus on the task and give Sts time, individually, to number the words in the list, from 1 = least likely to cause an argument to 5 = most likely to cause an argument. If Sts don't have any experience of sharing a flat or house with friends, get them to think of things that cause problems in their family home.

Put Sts in pairs or small groups and get them to share their opinions.

Find out if any pairs / groups disagreed.

b Focus on the title of the article, *Classic student house arguments – and how to avoid them*, and elicit a synonym for *classic* here (= *typical*).

Now focus on the task and the **Glossary**.

Give Sts time to read the article to find the answer to the question.

Check the answer.

EXTRA SUPPORT Before Sts read the article the first time, check whether you need to pre-teach any vocabulary.

who gets the biggest room, taking too long in the bathroom

c Focus on sentences A–H, making sure Sts understand all the lexis, e.g. *ear plugs*, *wax*, and *rota*.

Now set a time limit for Sts to read the article again and to match the solutions (A–H) to the problems. Encourage them to look at each problem and then choose an appropriate solution from the list.

Get Sts to compare with a partner, and then check answers.

1 B **2** E **3** H **4** A **5** F **6** D **7** G **8** C

Deal with any other new vocabulary. Elicit or model the pronunciation of any tricky words.

d Put Sts in pairs and get them to answer the two questions. Monitor and help if necessary.

For question 1, find out which solution Sts thought was better for each problem – you could simply do this with a show of hands and ask a couple of Sts to give reasons. Then elicit from the class if there are any other solutions. For question 2, elicit a few opinions and experiences from various Sts.

4 LISTENING & SPEAKING understanding advice

a Focus on the situation and read it as a class.

Put Sts in pairs, **A** and **B**, preferably face-to-face. Tell them to go to **Communication Argument!**, **A** on *p.109*, **B** on *p.113*.

Get Sts to read their role in the role-play and decide what they are going to say. When they are ready, tell Sts **A** to start.

Stop the role-play when you think it has gone on long enough. Elicit whether any pairs managed to agree on a course of action for resolving the problems.

Finally, deal with any new vocabulary, and elicit or model the pronunciation.

Tell Sts to go back to the main lesson **7A**.

b 🔊 **7.7** Tell Sts they're now going to listen to some advice about how to argue better. Focus on the task and make sure Sts understand it.

Give Sts time to read sentences 1–4. You might want to check Sts know the meaning of *mediate* (= try to end a disagreement between two or more people or groups by talking to them and trying to find things that everyone can agree on).

Play the audio once the whole way through for Sts to listen and choose the two general points the psychologist makes.

Check answers.

EXTRA SUPPORT Read through the script and decide if you need to pre-teach any new lexis before Sts listen.

Sts should have ticked 2 and 3.

7A 103

◀)) 7.7

(script in Student's Book on *pp.127–128*)

In life, we sometimes have disagreements with people. It could be with your partner, with your boss, with your parents, or with a friend. When this happens, the important thing is to try not to let a difference of opinion turn into a heated argument. But of course, it's easier said than done.

The first thing I would say is that the way you begin the conversation is very important.

Imagine you live with your partner, and you're feeling annoyed because you feel that you always do most of the housework. If you say, 'Look, you're not doing your share of the housework,' you're beginning the conversation in a very negative way, and the discussion will very soon turn into an argument. It's much more constructive to say something like, 'I think we'd better have another look about how we divide up the housework. Maybe there's a better way of doing it.'

My second piece of advice is simple. If you're the person who's in the wrong, just admit it! This is the easiest and best way to avoid an argument. Just apologize – say to your flatmate, your parents, or your husband, 'Sorry, it was my fault,' and move on. The other person will have more much respect for you if you do that.

The next tip is, don't exaggerate. Try not to say things like, 'You always forget our wedding anniversary,' when perhaps this has only happened once before, or, 'You never ever remember to turn the lights off.' This will just make the other person get very defensive because what you're saying about them just isn't true.

If you follow these tips, you may often be able to avoid an argument. But if an argument does start, it's important to keep things under control, and there are ways to do this.

The most important thing is not to raise your voice. Raising your voice will just make the other person lose their temper, too. If you find yourself raising your voice, stop for a moment and take a deep breath. Say, 'I didn't mean to shout. I'd rather we didn't argue, but this is very important to me,' and continue calmly. If you can talk calmly and quietly, you'll find the other person will be more ready to think about what you're saying.

It's also very important to stick to the point. Try to keep to the topic you're talking about. Don't bring up old arguments, or try to bring in other issues. Just concentrate on solving the one problem you're having, and leave the other things for another time. So, for example, if you're arguing about the housework, don't suddenly say, 'And another thing, I was really disappointed with my birthday present – you didn't make any effort at all.'

And my final tip is that, if necessary, call 'Time out,' like in a sports match. If you think that an argument is getting out of control, then you can say to the other person, 'Listen, I'd rather talk about this tomorrow, when we've both calmed down.' You can then continue talking about it the next day, when perhaps both of you are feeling less tense and angry. That way, there's much more chance that you'll be able to reach an agreement. You'll also probably find that the problem is much easier to solve when you've both had a good night's sleep.

But I want to say one last thing which I think is very important. Some people think that arguing is always bad, but that isn't true. Conflict is a normal part of life, and dealing with conflict is an important part of any relationship, whether it's three people sharing a flat, a married couple, or just two good friends. If you don't learn to argue properly, then when a real problem comes along, you won't be prepared to face it together. Think of all the smaller arguments as training sessions. Learn how to argue cleanly and fairly. It will help your relationships become stronger and last longer.

c Get Sts to focus on the seven sentences from typical arguments and see if they can remember what the psychologist said about each.

Play the audio again the whole way through. You might want to pause it from time to time to give Sts time to tick or cross the sentences and note why each item is correct or wrong.

Get Sts to compare with a partner, and then check answers.

> 1 ✗ Because you're beginning the conversation in a very negative way.
> 2 ✓ It's more constructive.
> 3 ✓ If you're the person who's in the wrong, just admit it.
> 4 ✗ Because it may only have happened once, and it will make the other person get very defensive.
> 5 ✓ If you can talk calmly and quietly, the other person will be more responsive.
> 6 ✗ Concentrate on solving the problem you're having now.
> 7 ✓ This can stop an argument that's getting out of control.

EXTRA SUPPORT The first time Sts listen, tell them just to tick or cross 1–7 according to the psychologist's advice. Check answers. Then play the audio again and get Sts to write down the reasons the psychologist gives.

EXTRA SUPPORT If there's time, you could get Sts to listen again with the script on *pp.127–128*, so they can see exactly what they understood / didn't understand. Translate / Explain any new words or phrases.

d Give Sts time to look at the sentences they ticked in **c** (2, 3, 5, and 7) and remind them that the psychologist recommends using these sentences in an argument.

Now tell Sts they are going to do the role-play they did in **a** again. Elicit the situation in **a** from the class.

Put Sts in new pairs, **A** and **B**, preferably face-to-face. Tell them to go to **Communication Argument!**, **A** on *p.109*, **B** on *p.113*. The focus is on arguing better, so ideally, Sts should take the same **A** or **B** role as they did last time round, and try to improve their approach.

Get Sts to re-read their role in the role-play. Then tell Sts **B** to start. Monitor to see if Sts are doing what the psychologist said they should.

Stop the role-play when you think it has gone on long enough, and get feedback to see if Sts think they were able to solve their issues better this time.

Tell Sts to go back to the main lesson **7A**.

GRAMMAR IN CONTEXT

e Focus on the two examples and read the rules with the class.

Now give Sts time to rewrite sentences 1–5 with *would rather*.

Check answers.

> 1 I'd rather go to the cinema
> 2 I'd rather not go to the party
> 3 Would you rather meet
> 4 I'd rather you didn't
> 5 I'd rather your parents stayed

EXTRA IDEA To give Sts more oral practice, get them, in pairs or round the class, to take turns to look again at sentences 1–5 and say them aloud using *would rather*.

f Focus on the task and put Sts in pairs. Tell them to take turns asking and answering each question. Remind them to start with *Would you rather…?* when asking their partner a question, and to answer with *I'd rather*, and give a reason.

104 7A

Monitor and help, correcting any errors of the use of *would rather*.

Get some feedback.

5 VOCABULARY   verbs often confused

a ⏺ **7.8** Focus on the task and explain to Sts that they are going to hear six extracts of conversations, and for each one, they must write a sentence using a verb in the list. Go through the list, making sure Sts know the meaning of all the verbs.

Focus on the example and ask Sts what they might hear on the audio (e.g. a man saying 'I didn't do it').

Play the first extract and then pause the audio to make sure Sts understand what they have to do.

Play the audio again, pausing after each extract to give Sts time to write their sentences.

Get Sts to compare with a partner, and then check answers.

> **2** They're discussing something.
> **3** She's warning someone about something.
> **4** They're arguing about something.
> **5** She's advising someone about something.
> **6** He's refusing to do something.

⏺ **7.8**

1
A So what do you have to say for yourself?
B I didn't do it! It definitely wasn't me that did it. It must have been somebody else who stole the phone.

2
A OK, so who would like to go first? James?
B Well, one idea is to make this new marketing campaign entirely digital, and just have online advertisements.
C Interesting. Though I'm not sure that would work. What do you think, Sarah?
D Well, I'm not too sure about that...

3
A Don't even think of swimming here. There are crocodiles! Look, there's a sign over there.
B What?! Let's get out of here…

4
A The A-two-four-five? Oh no! We must have gone the wrong way.
B Of course we've gone the wrong way. You should have taken the second exit at the roundabout. What's the point of having a satnav if you don't do what it says?
A Well, if you knew the way to your cousin's house, then we wouldn't have to use the satnav. Why didn't you phone her before we left? It's always me who has the responsibility.
B That is so not true...

5
A …so I just don't know what to do.
B Well, I think maybe you ought to talk to her. She probably doesn't realize how much she upset you and how offended you feel.

6
A OK, so lunch with my parents next Sunday.
B Sorry, but no. I'm not going. You can go if you like, but I'm absolutely not prepared to go to another family Sunday lunch.

EXTRA SUPPORT   Put Sts in pairs to do the activity.

EXTRA CHALLENGE   Do the activity orally, and elicit sentences from Sts after pausing the audio.

b Tell Sts to go to **Vocabulary Bank Verbs often confused** on *p.158*.

Vocabulary notes
There are various reasons why Sts may confuse different pairs of verbs, e.g. L1 interference, different verbs existing in English where Sts' L1 just uses one, or the fact that the form of two different verbs is very similar.

Make sure Sts get as much practice as possible with the verbs which are confusing for them.

Get Sts to do **a** individually or in pairs. Remind them they might need to change the form of the verb and to write their answers in the *verbs* column.

⏺ **7.9** Now do **b**. Play the audio for Sts to listen and check.

Check answers.

⏺ **7.9**
Verbs often confused
1 I need to **discuss** the problem with my boss.
2 I often **argue** with my parents about doing housework.
3 I didn't **realize** you were so unhappy.
4 I didn't **notice** that Karen had changed her hair colour.
5 Jack always tries to **avoid** arguing with me.
6 My dad can't **prevent** me from seeing my friends.
7 When are you going to pay me back the fifty pounds that I **lent** you?
8 Could I **borrow** your car tonight? I know you're not using it.
9 My parents don't **mind** if I stay out late.
10 It doesn't **matter** if we're five minutes late.
11 Can you **remind** me to call my mum later?
12 **Remember** to turn off the lights before you go.
13 I **expect** that Daniel will forget our anniversary. He always does.
14 We'll have to **wait** half an hour for the next train.
15 I **wish** I was a bit taller!
16 I **hope** that you can come on Friday. I haven't seen you for ages.
17 Arsenal **won** the match five–two.
18 Arsenal **beat** Manchester United five–two.
19 Tom always **refuses** to discuss the problem.
20 Tom always **denies** that he has a problem.
21 The cost of living is going to **rise** again this month.
22 It's hard not to **raise** your voice when you're arguing with someone.
23 Go and **lie** on the bed if you're tired.
24 I usually **lay** my baby on the bed to change his nappy.
25 The men had been planning to **rob** the bank.
26 If you leave your bike unlocked, somebody might **steal** it.
27 I think I should **warn** you that Liam doesn't always tell the truth.
28 My teachers are going to **advise** me what subjects to study next year.

Now focus on **Activation** and get Sts to cover the *verbs* column, look at the sentences, and see if they can remember the missing verbs.

Tell Sts to go back to the main lesson **7A**.

EXTRA SUPPORT   If you think Sts need more practice, you may want to give them the **Vocabulary** photocopiable activity at this point.

c Focus on the task and give Sts a few minutes, either in pairs or individually, to complete the gaps with the **bold** verbs. Remind them that they may need to change the form of the verb.

Check answers.

> **1** mind, matter   **2** remember, remind   **3** robbed, stolen
> **4** advise, warn   **5** prevent, avoid   **6** borrow, lent   **7** won, beaten

7A   105

Now put Sts in pairs and get them to ask each other the questions. Encourage them to ask for more information where appropriate.

Deal with any general vocabulary problems that arose.

Get feedback from different pairs.

6 READING & WRITING contributing effectively in online exchanges

a Before Sts look at the article, ask them if they ever read any comments people have made online, e.g. in forums, in response to news articles, or on social media sites. Do they ever write any comments / take part in online discussions? Elicit examples of things they've commented on, if any.

Focus on the task and the title of the article, *How to win an online argument*. Go through the **Glossary** with the class. Elicit or model the pronunciation of *thread* /θred/.

Give Sts time to read the article and answer the two questions.

Get some feedback.

EXTRA CHALLENGE You could get Sts to cover the article, and elicit some ideas, before they read.

EXTRA SUPPORT Before Sts read the article the first time, check whether you need to pre-teach any vocabulary.

> **Suggested answers**
> Get your timing right   Be polite   Use evidence
> Show consideration for others' opinions   Know when to give up

Now ask Sts which tips they think are the most important and why.

b Focus on the task and elicit from the class what ChangeMyView is (*a website where users invite others to challenge their views and present alternative opinions*).

Give Sts time, in pairs or individually, to improve the highlighted phrases.

Check answers.

> **Suggested answers**
> 1 Be polite. ➜ 'I'm sorry, I don't agree.'
> 2 Use evidence. ➜ 'According to some research I read,...'
> 3 Show consideration for others' opinions. ➜ 'It may be true that a lot of young people…'

Deal with any other new vocabulary. Elicit or model the pronunciation of any tricky words.

c Focus on sentences 1–4 and make sure Sts understand all the lexis, e.g. *private school, abolish, vegan*, etc.

Now put Sts in groups of four. Assign each student a number 1–4, and make sure they have a piece of paper each to write on.

Tell Sts to either write the number of the statement or the statement itself at the top of the paper. Then tell each student to look at the argument for their number and to write a short response. They can agree or disagree with the statement, and they should give a brief reason.

Monitor and help with vocabulary. Remind Sts to try to use the advice from the article they've just read in their responses.

d Now tell Sts to pass their piece of paper to the next person in their group. They must read their classmate's comment and respond to it.

Repeat this process three more times, until Sts get back their original piece of paper. Remind Sts that they can respond not only to the original post, but to other comments in the thread as well (as in an authentic online forum discussion).

Now give Sts time to read all the comments. They should decide who wrote the best arguments and why they were effective.

Get some feedback from various groups.

7B It's all an act

G verbs of the senses
V the body
P silent consonants

Lesson plan

The general topic of this lesson is body language.

The first half of the lesson starts with the grammar presentation on verbs of the senses and how they are used grammatically. Sts also look at uses of *as*, e.g. *He works as a builder. She's as slim as me. I enjoy activities such* as *swimming and jogging*, etc. They then look at film stills of actors in well-known films and discuss who the people are, how they are feeling, and what they are doing, using *She looks…*, *He looks like…*, *She looks as if…*. Sts then practise using the same structures with sounds, feels, tastes, etc. This is followed by Reading & Listening, where Sts read an exercise on how to improve their acting skills, and then try it out. They then listen to three more exercises and complete the instructions. Finally, Sts do the three acting exercises which they listened to.

In the second half of the lesson, Sts extend their vocabulary related to the body, first revising facial features, and then learning, in addition to new body parts, verbs and verb phrases connected to the body. Sts then do a speaking activity where they describe photos to each other and put the grammar and vocabulary into practice. The pronunciation focus which follows is on silent consonants, e.g. in *calf* and *thumb*. Then Sts read an article about how to spot a liar, and do a speaking activity in which they have to work out if their partner is telling the truth or lying. The lesson ends with Sts writing a description of a photo.

> ### More materials
>
> **For teachers**
> **Photocopiables**
> *Grammar* verbs of the senses *p.175*
> *Communicative* Two photos *p.206* (instructions *p.187*)
> *Vocabulary* The body *p.225* (instructions *p.215*)
> **For students**
> Workbook 7B
> Online Practice 7B

OPTIONAL LEAD-IN – THE QUOTE

Write the quote at the top of *p.70* on the board and the name of the person who said it, or get Sts to open their books and read it.

Check Sts understand the meaning of the quote.

Ask Sts if they agree with Rachel Weisz.

1 GRAMMAR verbs of the senses

a Focus on the task and make sure Sts understand what they have to do.

Give Sts a few minutes to choose an adjective or two from the list and think how they are going to mime it.

Put Sts in pairs and get them to do the activity.

EXTRA SUPPORT Tell Sts to go to the **Vocabulary Bank Feelings** on *p.157* if they can't remember the meaning of some of the adjectives.

b Focus on the task and the film still at the top. If Sts don't know Keira Knightley, tell them that she is a very successful and popular British actress.

Ask Sts what kind of film they think it is, and if anyone has seen it. Don't tell them if they are correct or not at this point.

Then get Sts to look closely at the film still and, in pairs, choose the best options to complete sentences 1–3. Tell them that more than one option may be possible.

Elicit some opinions, but don't tell Sts if they are correct or not.

c 🔊 **7.10** Play the audio for Sts to listen and check.

Check answers. Elicit some of the details about the scene from various Sts to check that Sts have understood the 'story'.

EXTRA SUPPORT Before Sts listen, write the following proper names from the film on the board and say them aloud: CECILIA TALLIS /səˈsiːlɪə tælɪs/, CAMBRIDGE /ˈkeɪmbrɪdʒ/, ROBBIE /ˈrɒbi/, BRIONY /ˈbraɪəni/.

> **1** a **2** a **3** c

🔊 7.10
(script in Student's Book on *p.128*)

This still is from the film *Atonement*, a period drama set in the nineteen thirties. It shows Keira Knightley, who plays Cecilia Tallis, the elder daughter of a wealthy family, and James McAvoy who plays Robbie, the son of the family's housekeeper. Cecilia is studying at Cambridge University, and, unusually, Robbie is too, his studies being paid for by Cecilia's father. Despite moving in very different circles at university, they have always been close and they are now back at the family home for the holidays. This evening, there's going to be a dinner party, to which Robbie has been invited. In this shot, he is following her in to dinner. She is feeling anxious and indecisive, because she has just realized that she is in love with him, but knows that their relationship would be frowned on given their difference in status. Despite this, soon after they declare their love for each other. The film was one of Knightley's first big starring roles. It won several awards and was nominated for several others, including costume design. This green dress is one of the stunning outfits she appears in.

d Focus on the task and do it as a whole-class activity.

> *looks like* + noun
> *looks* + adjective
> *looks as if* + clause

e Tell Sts to go to **Grammar Bank 7B** on *p.145*.

7B 107

Grammar notes
look / feel / smell / sound / taste

Sts have previously studied *look* + adjective and *look like* + noun. Here Sts learn to use these structures with the other verbs of the senses and also the structure *as if* (e.g. *He looks as if he needs a holiday*). They also focus on the difference between *look* and *seem*.

* **Rule 3: *look, feel,* etc. + *as if* + clause**

Point out to Sts that we sometimes use *like* instead of *as if* (e.g. *He looks like he needs a holiday*) in conversation. In written English, *as if* or *as though* are usually preferred.

You may want to point out that *smell* and *taste* are also often used with *of* when we think something <u>really</u> <u>is</u> what it smells / tastes of, e.g. *Open the window – it smells of gas in here. This strawberry ice cream really tastes of strawberries.* When we use these verbs with *like*, we are saying that something smells or tastes <u>similar</u> to something else, e.g. *Does rabbit taste like chicken?*

Focus on the example sentences for ***look / feel / smell / sound / taste*** and play audio 🔊 **7.11** for Sts to listen and repeat. Encourage them to copy the rhythm. Then go through the rules with the class.

Go through the ***feel like*** and ***as*** box with the class.

Focus on the exercises and get Sts to do them individually or in pairs.

If they do them individually, get them to compare with a partner. Check answers, getting Sts to read the full sentences.

> **a**
> **2** G **3** A **4** L **5** K **6** J **7** C **8** E **9** D **10** I **11** H **12** B
>
> **b**
> **1** look as if **2** smells **3** sounds like **4** taste like **5** sound as if **6** feels **7** seem **8** feels like **9** tastes **10** smells as if

Tell Sts to go back to the main lesson **7B**.

EXTRA SUPPORT If you think Sts need more practice, you may want to give them the **Grammar** photocopiable activity at this point.

f Put Sts in pairs, and get them to match the stills to the film genres in the list. Tell them to guess if they don't know.

Elicit ideas, but <u>don't</u> tell Sts if they are correct yet. Ask them if they know the names of the films the stills are from, and anything about any of them.

g Now, with Sts in the same pairs, focus on the instructions. Give Sts time to read 1–3, and then check they understand what they have to do.

Monitor, checking for correct use of the target language structures.

h 🔊 **7.12** Play the audio for Sts to listen and check their ideas in **f** and **g**.

Play the audio again if necessary.

Elicit some of the ideas from the class for each film still, and check who got the closest answers.

> **A** historical drama (*The Queen*)
> **B** fantasy (*Fantastic Beasts and Where to Find Them*)
> **C** comedy (*Burn after Reading*)
> **D** horror (*Get Out*)
>
> Sts' own answers (see script 7.12)

🔊 **7.12**
(script in Student's Book on p.128)
A

Helen Mirren won a well-deserved Oscar for her performance as Queen Elizabeth II in *The Queen*. The film is about how the Royal Family responds to the tragic death of Diana, Princess of Wales, in a car crash in nineteen ninety-seven. The Queen had had a troubled relationship with Diana, who had divorced Prince Charles. When Diana dies, she feels the death is a private affair, and wants to protect her grandchildren, Princes William and Harry, from the paparazzi, so she keeps them at her castle in Scotland. However, there is a massive outpouring of grief from the general public, who surround Buckingham Palace with flowers, and both the Prime Minister and Prince Charles think the Queen should return to London. At first, she refuses, but in the end, she is persuaded to come back, and in this scene, the climax of the film, she inspects the thousands of flowers outside the palace. Her expression shows a mixture of feelings: sadness, perhaps some surprise at the strength of the public's love for Diana, and perhaps relief that she had made the right decision in the end to come back to London.

B

This is a scene from the fantasy film *Fantastic Beasts and Where to Find Them*, which is a prequel to the Harry Potter films. Set in nineteen twenty-six, the film stars Eddie Redmayne as the wizard Newt Scamander, who comes to New York with a suitcase containing several magical creatures. When he's at the bank, one of the creatures escapes from the suitcase. In this scene, he is desperately trying to recapture it, and is watching, horrified, as it starts stealing things from people in the bank. J.K. Rowling herself both wrote the script and co-produced the film, and it was the first film set in Harry Potter's wizarding world to win an Oscar.

C

Frances McDormand, who won an Oscar for best actress in *Three Billboards Outside Ebbing, Missouri*, is without doubt one of the most versatile actresses of her generation. This still is from the Coen brother's black comedy *Burn After Reading*, which also starred George Clooney and Brad Pitt. McDormand plays the role of Linda Litzke, a personal trainer who, with her co-worker Chad, tries to steal money from a retired CIA worker. Linda is in desperate need of money, mainly because she's obsessed with expensive cosmetic surgery. In this scene, she's discussing with the doctor the work she wants done. During the discussion, the doctor has suggested that she have an operation to get rid of her crows' feet – the lines and wrinkles around the eyes. Linda protests that they're baby, tiny crow's feet, and as the doctor explains the procedure, she feels more and more unsure and indecisive about what to do. The genius of McDormand's acting is that although the character of Linda is self-centred, superficial, and not very bright, McDormand manages to portray her as a true American heroine.

D

This still shows Daniel Kaluuya in the two-thousand-seventeen American horror movie *Get Out*. Daniel plays the role of Chris, a young black photographer who goes to meet the parents of his white girlfriend Rose, who live in a large house in the country. Although the parents try to make it clear that they are not at all racist, Chris quickly realizes that there is something very strange about them, and about the black servants they employ. In this scene, Rose's mother, a psychiatrist who practises hypnotherapy, is hypnotizing him. Although in theory it is to help him to stop smoking, here she gets him to relive the horror and the shock of the evening when he was six years old and his mother was killed in a car accident. Kaluuya was nominated for an Oscar for his performance, and the movie won the Oscar for best screenplay.

108 7B

i 7.13 Focus on the instructions. Tell Sts they are going to hear some sounds which they have to identify. You could do this as a whole-class activity and get Sts to call out answers as you play each sound, or get Sts in pairs to silently write down their answers, and check answers at the end.

Point out that Sts may feel they are missing some of the vocabulary they need to describe the sounds accurately (*engine*, *cheer*, etc.). Encourage them to think laterally and use the words that they know to describe what they think is happening.

Possible answers

1 It sounds as if / like they've just had an argument.
2 It sounds as if / like a player has just missed a goal.
3 It sounds as if / like the plane has just landed.
4 It sounds as if / like they're opening a bag of crisps.
5 It sounds as if / like they're brushing their teeth.
6 It sounds like a lift.
7 It sounds as if / like they're cooking / cutting vegetables.
8 It sounds as if / like they're making tea.
9 It sounds as if / like they're turning on the computer.
10 It sounds like a dog eating its dinner.

7.13

(Sound effects for the following:)

1 *car pulling up, two people getting out and slamming the doors, opening front door, woman says, 'I'm going to bed.'*
2 *a football crowd reacting to a near miss*
3 *a plane's engines being turned off after the plane has landed*
4 *somebody opening a bag of crisps*
5 *someone cleaning their teeth with an electric toothbrush*
6 *a lift going up (or down)*
7 *somebody cutting vegetables*
8 *water boiling, mugs and spoons being taken out*
9 *somebody turning on a computer*
10 *a dog eating dry dog food*

j Put Sts in pairs, **A** and **B**, and tell them to go to **Communication Guess what it is**, **A** on *p.109*, **B** on *p.113*.

Go through the instructions, making sure Sts understand they mustn't say what the picture is, but they must say what type of things it is, e.g. *a vegetable*, *a kind of fruit*, etc., and describe it using *look / smell / feel / taste like* or *as if…*, etc. Point out the example, but do not read it aloud as it is the first one they need to tell their partner.

When Sts are ready, focus on the instructions in **b–d**.

Get feedback and find out who got the most correct answers.

Finally, deal with any new vocabulary, and elicit or model the pronunciation.

Tell Sts to go back to the main lesson **7B**.

2 READING & LISTENING understanding instructions

a Do this as a whole-class activity.

b Give Sts time to read the introduction to *How to improve your acting skills* and answer the question.

Check the answer.

EXTRA SUPPORT Before Sts read the article the first time, check whether you need to pre-teach any vocabulary.

In a group

c Focus on *Exercise 1 Developing your imagination* and give Sts time to read it. Check they have understood by eliciting exactly what you have to do in this exercise. Now focus on the photo and elicit what the emotion is (*surprise / shock*).

Put Sts in groups of four or five. Set a time limit for them to come up with as many reasons as possible as to why he might be feeling this emotion. One person in each group should be the secretary and make a note of their ideas.

Elicit some ideas from each group to see which has been the most imaginative.

d 7.14 Focus on the task and tell Sts they are now going to listen to a drama teacher explaining three more exercises. Play the audio for Sts to listen and match each exercise to what it is for.

Check answers.

EXTRA SUPPORT Read through the script and decide if you need to pre-teach any new lexis before Sts listen.

paying attention to details 3 (*What were they wearing?*)
showing emotions 4 (*The 'magic' image*)
using body language 2 (*Stroking an animal*)

7.14

(script in Student's Book on *p.128*)

Exercise two is called *Stroking an animal*.

This exercise is often used in drama classes for beginners, to help them to develop their body language. It should be done in a group. Each person must think of an animal they really like. It can be a wild or tame animal, big or small. Then imagine stroking it. Think about where it is: in your hand, in your arms, standing or sitting next to you. Now, one by one, mime the action to the rest of the group. They have to guess which animal it is.

***

OK, now, exercise three is called *What were they wearing?*

This exercise is aimed at developing attention. Attention is very important for an actor, as you have to be able to observe every detail of other people.

The exercise is done in a group, with one person acting as the host. In a group, sit in a circle and, for three minutes, try to focus on what everyone is wearing. It's important to remember as many details as you can: clothes, accessories, etc. After three minutes, close your eyes unless you are the host of the game, and the host asks questions, for example, 'Anna, tell me, please, what's Helen wearing?', 'John, what colour are Anna's shoes?', etc. At the end, everyone opens their eyes and checks the answers.

***

The last exercise we're going to do today is exercise four, *The 'magic' image*.

Showing emotions onstage or on camera can be very hard for some beginners. One trick, which this exercise helps with, is to develop a way of recalling the desired emotion.

The exercise can be done individually or in groups. Choose one emotion, for example 'anger', and then on a piece of paper, write down some situations that make you angry – for example, noisy neighbours, or bad drivers. If you are doing this in a group, show each other what you've written down – you may want to choose some ideas from another person's list to add to your own list. Choose no more than five situations in total. When you have your final list, think of an image for each situation. For example, for noisy neighbours, it could be a dog; for bad drivers, a car, and so on. Now the important part – you need to create one new image on the sheet of paper which combines your separate anger images, for example, a car with a dog in the back, etc. This is your 'magic image' of anger. Recalling this image will help you to show anger when you 're acting. You can do the same thing with other emotions, such as happiness, sorrow, and so on. So now let's actually do these exercises. We'll start with number two, stroking an animal. So if you can get into groups of five or six, we'll get going.

e Now focus on the instructions for how to do the three exercises.

Play the audio again, pausing after each exercise has been mentioned (see *** in script 7.14), to give Sts time to complete the gaps.

Get Sts to compare with a partner, and then play the audio again if necessary.

Check answers.

> **1** an animal   **2** imagine stroking it   **3** mime the action to the rest of the group   **4** is the host   **5** in a circle   **6** what everyone is wearing   **7** close your eyes   **8** you're the host   **9** asks questions   **10** one emotion   **11** anger   **12** situations that make you feel angry   **13** your list   **14** five situations   **15** your final list   **16** an image for each situation   **17** one new image   **18** your separate images

> **EXTRA SUPPORT**   If there's time, you could get Sts to listen again with the script on *p.128*, so they can see exactly what they understood / didn't understand. Translate / Explain any new words or phrases.

f Put Sts back in the groups of four or five they were in for *Exercise 1 Developing your imagination* in **c**. Give them time to do the three exercises.

Monitor and help if necessary.

Get some feedback. For *Exercise 2 Stroking an animal*, you could get a couple of Sts to mime in front of the class. For *Exercise 3 What were they wearing?*, you could find out which Sts were best at remembering the details. For *Exercise 4 The 'magic' image*, you could ask some Sts to share their images with the class.

3 VOCABULARY & SPEAKING the body

a Focus on the two photos and do the questions as a whole-class activity.

> The photos are 'mug shots' and would have been taken when the man was arrested by the police.

b Focus on the task and go through the words in the list to elicit the pronunciation of *forehead* /ˈfɔːhed/, *stubble* /ˈstʌbl/, and *wrinkles* (silent *w*). You could point out that *forehead* is also sometimes pronounced /ˈfɒrɪd/, but that /ˈfɔːhed/ is more common.

Point out that *chin* (8) has been done for them, and then get Sts, in pairs or individually, to match the words to the features in the photos.

> **EXTRA SUPPORT**   Before you start the exercise, you could revise the basic vocabulary of the face. Quickly sketch a face on the board with nose, ears, head, hair, and mouth, and check Sts can remember and pronounce these words.

c Get Sts, in pairs or individually, to answer the questions.
d ◉ **7.15** Play the audio for Sts to listen and check their answers to **b** and **c**.

Check answers. For **c**, you could point to the three words on yourself, or get Sts to show you on themselves, before checking where the features are in the photos.

> **b** see script 7.15   **c** eye

◉ **7.15**
b
1   eye
2   stubble
3   wrinkles
4   lips
5   neck
6   cheek
7   forehead
8   chin
c
eyebrow, eyelash, eyelid

Now either use the audio to drill the pronunciation of the words, or model and drill them yourself. Give further practice of any words your Sts find difficult to pronounce.

e Tell Sts to go to **Vocabulary Bank The body** on *p.159*.

> ### Vocabulary notes
> Sts should know all the basic parts of the body, and here they expand their knowledge and also learn the words for organs, some of which they may have already seen when doing the vocabulary for illnesses and injuries.
>
> The verbs related to parts of the body will probably all be new and will require extra practice.

Focus on **1 Parts of the body and organs** and get Sts to do **a** individually or in pairs.

◉ **7.16** Now do **b**. Play the audio for Sts to listen and check.

Check answers.

◉ **7.16**
The body
1 Parts of the body and organs
4   ankle
1   calf
2   heel
3   knee

7   elbow
6   fist
9   nails
5   palm
8   wrist

13   bottom
10   chest
14   hip
12   thigh
11   waist

15   brain
18   heart
17   kidneys
16   liver
19   lungs

Now either use the audio to drill the pronunciation of the words, or model and drill them yourself. Give further practice of any words your Sts find difficult to pronounce.

❗ Don't focus on silent consonants at this point, as Sts are going to practise this in the next section.

Now do **Activation** and get Sts to cover the words, look at the pictures, and try to remember the words.

Focus on **2 Verbs and verb phrases** and get Sts to do **a** individually or in pairs.

110   **7B**

7.17 Now do **b**. Play the audio for Sts to listen and check.

Check answers.

7.17

2 Verbs and verb phrases, b
1 bite your nails
2 blow your **nose**
3 brush your **hair** / brush your **teeth**
4 comb your **hair**
5 fold your **arms**
6 hold somebody's **hand**
7 touch your **toes**
8 suck your **thumb**
9 shake **hands** / shake your **head**
10 shrug your **shoulders**
11 raise your **eyebrows**

Now either use the audio to drill the pronunciation of the verb phrases, or model and drill them yourself. Give further practice of any words your Sts find difficult to pronounce.

EXTRA IDEA Pause the audio after each line and get Sts to mime the action.

Now focus on **c**. Explain that these verbs describe the movement of a part of the body, e.g. *wink* (demonstrate it). Then get Sts, individually or in pairs, to do the exercise.

7.18 Now do **d**. Play the audio for Sts to listen and check.

Check answers.

7.18

d
1 He winked at me to show that he was only joking. **eye**
2 The steak was tough and difficult to chew. **teeth**
3 When we met, we were so happy, we hugged each other. **arms**
4 Don't scratch the mosquito bite. You'll only make it worse. **nails**
5 She waved goodbye sadly to her boyfriend as the train left the station. **hand**
6 These days, men don't always kneel down when they propose marriage. **knee**
7 The teacher frowned when she saw all the mistakes I had made. **forehead**
8 The painting was so strange I stared at it for a long time. **eyes**
9 She got out of bed, and yawned and stretched. **mouth / arms**
10 If you don't know the word for something, just point at what you want. **finger**

Give further practice of any words your Sts find difficult to pronounce.

Now do **Activation** and put Sts in pairs, **A** and **B**. Sts **A** (book open) say a verb phrase to Sts **B**, who mime the action. Sts then swap roles.

Tell Sts to go back to the main lesson **7B**.

EXTRA SUPPORT If you think Sts need more practice, you may want to give them the **Vocabulary** photocopiable activity at this point.

EXTRA IDEA Tell Sts you are going to give them some instructions and they have to mime the action. Demonstrate by saying *Shake hands with the person next to you*, and check Sts are all doing the correct thing.

Read out some or all of the instructions, pausing after each imperative and checking that Sts are doing it correctly:
Fold your arms. Raise your hand. Scratch your head. Bite your nails. Wink. Wave goodbye. Stare at the person next to you. Point at the board. Stretch your arms. Shrug your shoulders. Touch your toes.

---

4 PRONUNCIATION silent consonants

Pronunciation notes

Many English words have a silent consonant which is not pronounced. Emphasize to your Sts that when they check the pronunciation of a new word in a dictionary, the phonetic transcript will help them to see when a consonant (or syllable) is not pronounced.

a Focus on the task. Remind Sts to say the words aloud to help them.

EXTRA CHALLENGE Elicit answers before playing the audio.

b **7.19** Play the audio for Sts to listen and check.

Check answers by getting Sts to write the words on the board and cross out the silent consonants (they are marked in orange in the key).

ca**l**f com**b** **k**neel pa**l**m thum**b** **w**rinkles **w**rist

---

7.19

See words in Student's Book on *p.72*

Then ask Sts the two questions.

At the beginning of a word, *kn* is pronounced /n/, and *wr* is pronounced /r/.
At the end of a word, *mb* is pronounced /m/.

EXTRA IDEA Elicit more words beginning with *kn* and *wr*, e.g. *know, knife, wrong, wrap, write*, and ending in *mb*, e.g. *bomb, lamb*, etc., but <u>not</u> the words in **c**.

c Focus on the task and give Sts time to do it in pairs. You could do the first two with the class (1 *honest*, 2 *fasten*). Tell Sts <u>not</u> to write the words.

d **7.20** Tell Sts to match the words A–L to the phonetics in **c**.

Play the audio for Sts to listen and check.

7.20

1 **H** honest
2 **F** fasten
3 **J** muscle
4 **K** whistle
5 **A** aisle
6 **E** doubt
7 **D** design
8 **G** half
9 **L** whole
10 **B** calm
11 **C** climb
12 **I** knock

Now play the audio again and tell Sts to cross out the silent consonant in each word.

Check answers (see the **bold** consonants in orange in the key) and make sure Sts can remember the meaning of all the words.

1 **h**onest 2 fas**t**en 3 mus**c**le 4 whis**t**le 5 ais**l**e
6 dou**b**t 7 desi**g**n 8 hal**f** 9 **w**hole 10 ca**l**m 11 clim**b**
12 **k**nock

EXTRA SUPPORT Give Sts time to practise saying the words. You could also play the audio again, pausing after each word for Sts to listen and repeat.

7B **111**

e Now focus on the phrases and get Sts to practise saying them in pairs.

Get some Sts to say the phrases to the class.

> **EXTRA SUPPORT** Read each phrase to the class, getting Sts to repeat it after you. Then put Sts in pairs and get them to practise saying them.

5 READING & SPEAKING understanding the principles of an experiment

a Focus on the title of the article, *The best way to spot a liar… or is it?*, and remind Sts what the verb *to spot* means (= to see or notice sth, especially suddenly).

Give Sts time to read the first paragraph and answer the questions.

Check answers.

> The accepted 'best way' is using body language clues such as avoiding eye contact, blushing, fidgeting, and laughing nervously.
> The purpose of Ormerod's experiment was to develop a more reliable method of lie detection which relied on people's words, not their body language.

b Focus on phrases A–E and make sure Sts understand all the lexis, e.g. *open questions*, *rapport*, *contradictions*, etc.

Give Sts time to read the rest of the article and complete the gaps.

Get Sts to compare with a partner, and then check answers.

> **EXTRA SUPPORT** Before Sts read the article the first time, check whether you need to pre-teach any vocabulary.

> **1** B **2** A **3** E **4** D **5** C

c Focus on statements 1–6 and make sure Sts understand all the lexis.

Give Sts time to read the article again and mark the statements *T* (true) or *F* (false). Remind them to correct the false ones.

Get Sts to compare with a partner, and then check answers.

> **1** T
> **2** F (They had to prepare their own cover story.)
> **3** F (The officers randomly selected passengers for questioning.)
> **4** T
> **5** F (Only if passengers suddenly began to give much shorter answers, or began to avoid answering directly.)
> **6** F (The experiment proved that verbal clues are far more effective than body language in helping to identify a liar.)

Deal with any other new vocabulary. Elicit or model the pronunciation of any tricky words.

d Put Sts in pairs, **A** and **B**. Go through the instructions and make sure Sts know what to do. Sts **A** start by asking Sts **B** the first question. Sts **B** must reply *Yes, I have* irrespective of whether it is true or not. Then Sts **A** must use some of the techniques mentioned in the article to get information and work out whether Sts **B** are telling the truth or not. When Sts **A** have finished, they should tell their partner whether they think they are lying or telling the truth. Sts **B** should then 'confess'.

Sts now swap roles and repeat the process for question 2. They then repeat the process for questions 3 and 4.

e Find out, with a show of hands, how many Sts guessed correctly for both situations in **d**.

Then ask if Sts think Thomas Ormerod's techniques helped them.

6 WRITING describing a photo

Tell Sts to go to **Writing Describing a photo** on *p.119*.

a Focus on the first photo and give Sts time to read the description. Tell them not to worry about the gaps.

Elicit some opinions.

b Focus on the task and the words and phrases in the list. Point out that the first one (*In the foreground*) has been done for them.

Get Sts to complete the gaps.

Check answers.

> **2** In the centre **3** in front of **4** On the left **5** outside
> **6** In the background **7** behind **8** opposite

c Go through the instructions. Put Sts in pairs to discuss what they think the people in photo 2 are thinking or feeling. Tell them also to discuss how they will divide the information into paragraphs.

Focus on the **Useful language: describing a photo or picture** box and go through it with Sts.

d Either get Sts to write the description in class (set a time limit of, e.g. 20 minutes), or get them to write at home for homework.

e Sts should check their description for mistakes before giving it in.

112 **7B**

6&7 Colloquial English Talking about... performances

Lesson plan

In The Interview, the person interviewed is Simon Callow, a British actor, stage director, and author.

In The Conversation, Sts watch three people discussing whether a live performance is always better than a recorded one. Sts then discuss this question as well as a couple of other questions related to the topic, focusing on phrases for giving yourself time to think, checking others agree with you, and phrases for apologizing for interrupting.

More materials
For teachers
Teacher's Resource Centre
Video Colloquial English 6&7
Quick Test 7
File 7 Test
For students
Workbook Colloquial English 6&7
Can you remember? 6&7
Online Practice Colloquial English 6&7
Check your progress

OPTIONAL LEAD-IN (BOOKS CLOSED)

Tell Sts that they are going to watch an interview with an actor who has worked in the theatre and in the cinema. Write on the board:

ACTING IN THE THEATRE / ACTING IN THE CINEMA

Give Sts two or three minutes, in pairs, to think of some of the differences between these two kinds of acting.

Get feedback from the class and write their ideas on the board.

1 ▶ THE INTERVIEW Part 1

a Books open. Focus on the biographical information about Simon Callow. Either read it out loud, or give Sts time to read it. You might want to point out that a CBE (Commander of the Order of the British Empire) is an award given by the Queen to someone who has made a distinguished contribution in their area of activity.

Focus on the question and do it as a whole-class activity.

b Focus on the task and give Sts time to read sentences 1–5. Remind Sts that they do not need to correct the false ones at this stage.

Go through the **Glossary** with the class.

Play the video (**Part 1**) once the whole way through for Sts to mark the sentences T (true) or F (false).

Get Sts to compare with a partner, and then check answers.

EXTRA SUPPORT Before playing the video, go through the listening scripts and decide if you need to pre-teach / check any lexis to help Sts when they watch.

1 F **2** T **3** T **4** T **5** F

I = interviewer, S = Simon Callow
Part 1
I How did you get into acting?
S I was about eighteen; it was my first real job, and it was a very unusual job because I was working in the box office of the Old Vic theatre. Then, not only did I get to see an awful lot of plays, but I also met the actors and I was able to sneak into rehearsals, in the theatre – quite illegally – and I became fascinated by the work of the theatre.
I What in particular fascinated you?
S The thing that fascinated me, as I said, was when I was in rehearsals, there was this…the work of the theatre, the sort of work it was. So, I'd stand at the back of the Old Vic theatre when the actors were rehearsing, but mostly it consisted of people sitting rather glumly about saying, 'Well, I don't know how to do this, I don't know how to do this, I don't know how to make this scene work, I don't understand my character,' and the director would try to help them to understand the character or suggest a move here or a move there, or maybe they'd try walking in a different way or putting on a different hat, and bit by bit it started to fall into place. And I thought, 'What a wonderful job, what a fantastically interesting job to wrestle with these kinds of problems, try to understand the characters, trying to find out how best to express them and show them off.' So I…I came to acting very much from that point of view.
I The role that first made you famous as a young actor was playing Mozart in the original theatre production of *Amadeus*, which later went on to become a film. What was the most challenging thing about playing the part of Mozart?
S What was a challenge was that Mozart was a person who'd actually lived and was indeed one of the greatest artistic geniuses of the whole of Western civilization, and I was a great lover and admirer of Mozart's music, so there was a tremendous…er… challenge to bridge the character that Peter Shaffer had written. Peter Shaffer knows all about Mozart; he could so that Mozart was…was…er…er…sort of a smutty…er…hysterical child, really…er…in a lot of the play. My job was to reconcile that with the fact that he wrote *The Marriage of Figaro*, and that was tremendously hard.
I Was Mozart one of your most satisfying roles?
S No, I wouldn't say that…that it was the most satisfying. It was the most exciting because its…its fame…er…almost from the moment it was announced was overwhelmingly greater than anything I had ever done, and to be honest, ever have done since. The fact that the play was very, very controversial when it opened proved to be…er…very, um, um, shocking for many people, only increased the excitement around it, and it was… er…er…astonishing to look out into the auditorium every night and to see Paul Red-Newman, or, or, or, or Robert Redford, or, or, or Ava Gardner, or Margaret Thatcher sitting out there, because everybody had to see that play.

---

c Before Sts watch again, put them in pairs to discuss why they think 1 and 5 are false.

Play the video again the whole way through, pausing as necessary.

Check answers.

1 His first job was in the box office of the Old Vic theatre.
5 It was the most exciting role he has had because it made him famous.

EXTRA SUPPORT If there's time, you could get Sts to watch again with subtitles, so they can see exactly what they understood / didn't understand. Translate / Explain any new words or phrases.

CE6&7 113

d Do the questions as a whole-class activity, or put Sts in pairs and then get some feedback.

▶ Part 2

a Focus on the task and **Glossary**.

Give Sts time to read 1–4, making sure they know the meaning of *crucial* and *utterly* in number 2.

Play the video (**Part 2**) once the whole way through. Then play again if necessary.

Get Sts to compare with a partner, and then check answers.

> 1 He loves them both.
> 2 There's an **audience**.
>   Every single performance is utterly **different**.
> 3 The director and editor because they can change the way the scene or the characters appear by the way they edit it (e.g. they can make a sad scene funny or an actor appear to be stupid).
> 4 No because when you act in film, you have the cameras right in front of you.

Part 2

I Over your career, you have acted in the theatre and you have also acted in many films. Which do you prefer?

S They're absolutely different media: they require different things from you as an actor – I love them both. But they are each of them completely different; you bring completely different things to them. Obviously, the crucial difference with the theatre is that there's an audience there, and that's such an important aspect of it in every way. It's important because you have to reach out to them – make sure that everybody can hear and see what you're doing. The beauty of the theatre is that every single performance is utterly different from every other one.

I How do you motivate yourself to play the same character again night after night?

S I think as you get older, you realize that, um, you never get it right. I…I mean, I've…I've probably about half a dozen times in my forty years of acting have thought, 'Well that was a really good performance,'…er…but it can always be better. And so, one goes to the theatre every day hoping that it'll be in some way better. Er…er…you know, there is always the possibility you might get it right. I mean, you never do; you never can.

I So what for you is the main difference with film acting?

S Er…in movies or…or television film – which is what almost all television is nowadays – um, a lot of those responsibilities are… lie with the director and the editor. And having directed a film myself, I know perfectly well that you can make a sad scene funny; you can make a slow scene fast…er…er…in the editing suite. It's…it's an astonishing…er…power that a director and editor have. Um…er…you can make a character seem stupid just by editing them a certain way, or make them seem brilliant by editing them in a different way. So in that sense, the actor is rather powerless.

I Anything else?

S The other thing that's very hard about acting on film is that, hilariously, it's regarded as a sort of naturalistic medium, but in no sense is it that for the actor, because you're…you're, you know, first of all, there are some, you know, little metal objects right in front of you, sort of, staring at you as you're doing your love scene or whatever else it might be.

b Focus on the task and give Sts time to read 1–4.

Play the video again the whole way through for Sts to complete the task.

Get Sts to compare with a partner, and then check answers.

EXTRA SUPPORT When you play the video the second time, pause after each question has been answered and get Sts to compare what they have understood.

> 1 He is referring to the audience in a theatre.
> 2 He is saying that you can never give the perfect performance as a theatre actor.
> 3 The film actor can't do anything, as the editor has all the power.
> 4 He is referring to the cameras.

EXTRA SUPPORT If there's time, you could get Sts to watch again with subtitles, so they can see exactly what they understood / didn't understand. Translate / Explain any new words or phrases.

c Do the questions as a whole-class activity.

▶ Part 3

a Focus on the photos and ask Sts if they know either of the actors.

Now focus on the **Glossary** and the task.

Play the video (**Part 3**) once the whole way through for Sts to do the task. Play again if necessary.

Get Sts to compare with a partner, and then check answers.

EXTRA SUPPORT When you play the video the second time, pause after each question has been answered and get Sts to compare what they have understood.

> 1 When they are good, he loves it. When they aren't good, it is painful.
> 2 He was very lucky to see them. Most people nowadays have forgotten them. They were wonderful onstage.
> 3 He is the only modern actor who approaches his roles as the great actors used to.
> 4 He hates wearing it. It's uncomfortable and sticky.
> 5 He doesn't get stage fright, but he becomes very self-conscious.

Part 3

I Do you enjoy watching other actors acting?

S I love watching other actors acting. I've been obsessed by acting since I was a child, and I'm a great connoisseur of it, and I think I'm quite a good judge of it, and so I adore watching other actors work when it's good. When it's not, it's a great pain to me.

I Who were the first great actors you saw?

S As a young man, and a boy, I was extraordinarily lucky to see that fabled generation of actors of…of Gielgud and Richardson, Olivier, Edith Evans, Peggy Ashcroft. People now almost all completely forgotten. Er…er…er…even if they made movies, it's unlikely that people of a younger generation know who they are, but…but…er…when…when they were alive and kicking, and…er…doing their extraordinary work onstage, it…it…it was something quite…quite remarkable. I mean, it was…it was the sort of thing that nobody attempts any more.

I Do any modern actors come close to that golden generation?

S In movies, not always, but…but sometimes Daniel Day-Lewis does…er…I think probably approach a role in the way that a lot of them might have approached it.

I Is there anything you don't like about acting?

S I don't much like wearing make-up. I sweat a lot, it comes off, it's uncomfortable, it's sticky, and I do everything I can to avoid wearing make-up.

I Do you still get stage fright?

S I don't get stage fright, but I do get self-conscious, and I hate that and I wish I didn't, particularly at events like first nights – because I don't know how it's impossible to ignore the fact that there are at least 100 people sitting out there, judging you. You know, I think almost all actors feel tremendous longing for the first night to be over, but it has to happen. It's like a sort of operation – it's, you know, it's got to happen, it's going to hurt, but you will feel better afterwards.

114 **CE6&7**

EXTRA SUPPORT If there's time, you could get Sts to watch again with subtitles, so they can see exactly what they understood / didn't understand. Translate / Explain any new words or phrases.

b Do the questions as a whole-class activity, or put Sts in pairs and then get some feedback. You could tell the class if you have any favourite actors, why you like them, and which of their characters you like best.

2 ▶ LOOKING AT LANGUAGE

This exercise looks at a feature of spoken English which is illustrated by the interviewer – using modifiers to make his language more expressive. Focus on the **Modifiers** box and go through it with the class.

Now focus on the task and give Sts time to read extracts 1–7.

Play the video, pausing after each extract to give Sts time to write.

Check answers.

> 1 fantastically 2 hard 3 greater 4 absolutely
> 5 completely 6 different 7 extraordinarily

1 …I thought, 'What a wonderful job, what a fantastically interesting job…'
2 My job was to reconcile that with the fact that he wrote *The Marriage of Figaro*, and that was tremendously hard.
3 …its fame, almost from the moment it was announced was overwhelmingly greater than anything I had ever done…
4 They're absolutely different media: they require different things from you as an actor…
5 …you bring completely different things to them.
6 The beauty of the theatre is that every single performance is utterly different from every other one.
7 As a young man, and a boy, I was extraordinarily lucky to see that fabled generation of actors of…of, of Gielgud and Richardson, Olivier,…

3 ▶ THE CONVERSATION

a Focus on the photo and tell Sts they are going to watch these three people answer a question, which they will see on the screen.

Focus on the task and make sure Sts understand what they have to do. Give Sts time to read the three options.

Play the video and pause after the question. Remind Sts of the pronunciation of *live* when it is an adjective.

Now play the video once the whole way through for Sts to listen and tick the correct option.

Check the answer.

EXTRA SUPPORT Before playing the video, go through the listening script and decide if you need to pre-teach / check any lexis to help Sts when they listen.

> 3 it's impossible to generalize because it depends on the event.

I = interviewer, D = Devika, J = John, M = Mark

I Do you think it's always true that a live performance is better than a recorded one?

D That's a really difficult question. I love going to the cinema. I will happily go to the cinema on a Saturday night and watch a big flashy superhero film where there's really good sound effects and music and visuals that obviously have already been made by you know, computer graphics and it's really fun, but I also have a really big soft spot in my heart for going to the theatre. Going to the theatre to watch some Shakespeare or any modern plays – um, live, onstage, maybe with a, a band or an orchestra underneath the stage you can see or you definitely hear. I think that has a certain magic to it that you can't replicate on, in the cinema. It's a very different experience.

J And is it true then that it is better for the, the audience to actually enjoy it more if it's a live performance rather than a pre-recorded or a, a film?

D That's the thing – for me personally as an audience member, I, it's really hard – I think it's difficult to say it's better or worse or which is the ultimate best experience because they're just very different.

J But if you go to a live one though you, then you participate don't you because you're part of it – there's the actors and everything that's happening…

D True.

J …and then you are part of it because they're bouncing off you and it's, so it is true.

M A lot will, a lot will depend on, on factors other than just what's happening in front of you on the stage or the pitch or whatever type of event it is. If you're sitting, let's say, high up or with a slightly obstructed view or the seats are uncomfortable or you don't have enough leg room – you know, there are other factors that could sway your enjoyment such that seeing a recorded version of the, the live event that you've been at would actually have been preferable. Um, I think a good example would be going to a major sporting event now because they're nearly always oversubscribed, you know, crowds of people everywhere. I was at a major rugby match recently and we were sitting way, way up in the gods at the very back of the stadium and they had giant screens which were kind of showing the match simultaneously and in fact, all around me I could see a whole sea of heads sort of turned to the screen because you got, you got a better view and you could better understand what was happening on the pitch by looking at the TV screen rather than peering down at what was going on several hundred metres down below you.

D True. Yeah. It'd say it's similar…

J As a live performance – excuse me, yeah – as a live performance though, you are involved if you are in the audience, obviously, because you're watching and seeing what happens and you're looking at the nuances and whatever, so I suppose it is true that it's um, that it is more – it's better, I suppose.

D I think it also really heavily depends on what the audience is like that you're with. So I've been – I love live music, and I've been to plenty of live music events – concerts and festivals and things, you know, around the country, and I love them. However, sometimes you'll be in a crowd of other people enjoying the music and they're talking and it's noisy and actually I couldn't hear anything in the first place – I couldn't actually hear the band or the singer or the musician I wanted to hear, so I could have just gone home and listened to a CD.

J That's intriguing isn't it, the difference between the two.

M At the end of the day, it's very subjective. So much depends on the person, the event, the arena, and so on.

---

b Focus on the task and give Sts time to read 1–5. Check they understand all the lexis, e.g. *flashy*, *sway*, etc.

Play the video again for Sts to answer the questions.

Get Sts to compare with a partner, and then play again if necessary.

Check answers.

CE6&7 115

1 Positive. She loves watching big flashy superhero films in the cinema on a Saturday night. She likes the sound effects and music and visuals.
2 Positive. She likes seeing Shakespeare and modern plays in the theatre. They are magical, a very different experience from the cinema.
3 Negative. Sitting too high up or having a bad view at the theatre, uncomfortable seats or not enough legroom.
4 Negative. He noticed that the crowd were watching the big screen because they had a better view rather than looking straight at the pitch.
5 Negative. They can be noisy, so she can't hear the music and would be better listening to a CD at home.

EXTRA SUPPORT If there's time, you could get Sts to watch again with subtitles, so they can see exactly what they understood / didn't understand. Translate / Explain any new words or phrases.

c Either do the questions as a whole-class activity, or put Sts in pairs and then get some feedback.

d Focus on the task and give Sts time to read the six extracts.
Play the video for Sts to listen and complete the missing words.
Get Sts to compare with a partner, and then play the video again if necessary.
Check answers.

1 really difficult question   2 it's difficult to say   3 don't you
4 let's say   5 you know   6 isn't it

1 That's a really difficult question. I love going to the cinema.
2 I think it's difficult to say it's better or worse…
3 But if you go to a live one though, then you participate, don't you, because you're part of it…
4 If you're sitting, let's say, high up or with a slightly obstructed view…
5 I've been to plenty of live music events – concerts and festivals and things, you know, around the country, and I love them.
6 That's intriguing isn't it, the difference between the two.

e Focus on the task and put Sts in pairs to answer the question.
Check answers.

give themselves time to think	1, 2, 4, 5
check the others agree	3, 6

EXTRA SUPPORT Do this as a whole-class activity.

EXTRA IDEA Dictate the following sentence stems:

1 *What's your favourite …?*
2 *Which do you prefer, … or …?*
3 *What the best … you have ever …?*

Put Sts in pairs and get them to ask and answer the questions, using phrases from **d** to give themselves time to think.

f Put Sts in small groups of three if possible. Focus on the questions, and check Sts understand them. Then set a time limit for Sts to discuss them.
Monitor and help, and encourage them to use phrases in **d** either to give themselves time to think or to check the others agree.

Get feedback from various groups. You could also tell the class what you think.

8A Cutting crime

G the passive (all forms); *have something done;*
it is said that…, he is thought to…, etc.
V crime and punishment
P the letter *u*

Lesson plan

The topic of this lesson is crime.

The lesson begins with a Metropolitan Police podcast, which gives practical tips on how to stay safe in city streets. This is followed by a vocabulary focus on crime and punishment, presented through a quiz based on information from an ex-burglar, and a pronunciation focus on the different pronunciations of the letter *u*. The first half of the lesson finishes with Sts talking about local crime in their area, witnessing crimes, and any experience they have of crimes such as theft and vandalism.

In the second half of the lesson, some light-hearted news stories about crimes which went wrong provide a natural context for the revision of passive forms, and Sts also learn how to use the causative *have* (*I had my bag stolen*), as well as the structure *it is said that… / he is said to…* They then read an article about a man who was a victim of the modern crime of identity theft, after he had posted photos online. Sts discuss whether they think certain activities should be illegal or not, and how perpetrators should be punished. The lesson ends with Sts writing a magazine article expressing their opinion on either the legality of downloading music or squatters' rights.

More materials

For teachers

Photocopiables

Grammar the passive (all forms); *have something done; it is said that…, he is thought to…,* etc. *p.176*
Communicative Good laws? *p.207* (instructions *p.187*)
Vocabulary Crime and punishment *p.226* (instructions *p.216*)

For students

Workbook 8A
Online Practice 8A

OPTIONAL LEAD-IN – THE QUOTE

Write the quote at the top of *p.76* on the board and the name of the person who said it, or get Sts to open their books and read it.

You could tell Sts that Val McDermid is also a feminist and socialist. Most of her writing is crime, but she has also written a children's book as well as non-fiction. Some of her novels have been adapted for TV.

Ask Sts what they think the quote means and whether they agree with it.

1 LISTENING using your knowledge of the world to help you understand formal advice

a Focus on the situation and do the questions as a whole-class activity. You could demonstrate by telling Sts how you would feel and what you might do to feel safer.

b Focus on the crime prevention website page and the task. You could ask Sts if similar websites exist in their country.

Either get Sts to read the introduction individually, or read it out loud.

EXTRA SUPPORT Ask Sts some comprehension questions to check they have understood the introduction, e.g. *What does 'make yourself less of a target' mean?* (Make yourself less obvious / visible) *Explain 'moving with purpose' in your own words.* (Walking with an aim, knowing where you are going) etc.

Now put Sts in pairs and set a time limit for them to look at each picture and decide what piece of advice they think they represent. They should also try to complete the gaps in the headings (highlight that there is just one word missing in each headline).

Elicit some ideas from various pairs, both for the advice and the headings, but <u>don't</u> tell Sts if they are correct or not.

c 🔊 **8.1** Tell Sts they are now going to listen to the police podcast. Play the audio, pausing after each piece of advice to give Sts time to complete the headings and listen to the advice.

Get Sts to compare with their partner, and then check answers. Make sure Sts understand each heading. Elicit or model any words your Sts find difficult to pronounce.

EXTRA SUPPORT Read through the script and decide if you need to pre-teach any new lexis before Sts listen.

---

1 prepared **2** assertive **3** aware **4** Hide **5** against
6 instincts **7** plan **8** trouble

🔊 **8.1**
(script in Student's Book on *pp.128–129*)
Stay safe
Street crime is often unplanned, so making yourself less of a target, moving with purpose, and being aware of your surroundings will go a long way to keeping you safe when you're out and about. Here are eight important pieces of advice.

One: Be prepared. Always plan your route in advance. Carry a fully charged mobile phone and some cash, and tell someone where you're going.

Two: Be assertive. From the moment you step out onto the street in the morning, you need to look assertive and act and walk with confidence. This will always make you appear in control and you will seem much less vulnerable.

Three: Be aware. Using a mobile phone, whether you're calling, messaging, or looking up information, reduces your awareness of your surroundings. So does listening to loud music on headphones, or wearing a hooded jacket or sweatshirt.

Four: Hide it. Keep your valuables hidden either in a bag or under your clothes. This includes your phone, other devices such as cameras or tablets, and jewellery. Remember – out of sight, out of mind.

8A 117

Five: Go against the flow. When you're walking on the pavement, always face towards the oncoming traffic. This will make it more difficult for thieves on two wheels to ride up from behind and snatch your bag. But don't forget to still be aware of anyone approaching from ahead of you.

Six: Trust your instincts. At night, try to avoid walking alone in places such as parks and quiet side streets, or in fact, in any area you don't know. If you do have to walk, keep to busy places where there is a lot of activity, good lighting, and CCTV. And if you're on public transport, it's much better to travel with people you know or stick to routes that other people are using.

Seven: Make a plan. Discuss with friends what to do if something were to go wrong on your night out together, for example, if you were to get separated. Agree on a backup plan and keep an eye on each other during the evening. And stick to what you've agreed.

Eight: Look out for trouble. Alcohol and drugs make it harder for you to assess risks and decide how to deal with them. So, be careful how much you drink, and never let your glass or bottle out of your sight, in case someone puts something into your drink.
Stay safe!

Now find out what advice Sts had predicted correctly in **b**.

d Tell Sts they are going to listen again and this time they must answer questions 1–8.

Give Sts time to read the questions, making sure they understand them.

Play the audio again, pausing after each piece of advice to give Sts time to answer the questions.

Get Sts to compare with their partner, and then play again if necessary.

Check answers.

> 1 Your route
> 2 It makes you appear in control and less vulnerable.
> 3 Call, message, look up information
> 4 Your phone, camera, iPod, jewellery
> 5 It makes it more difficult for thieves on bikes to ride up behind you and snatch your bag.
> 6 A lot of activity, good lighting, CCTV
> 7 Make a plan of what you would do if something went wrong, agree a backup plan, keep an eye on each other during the evening
> 8 Someone might put something into your drink

EXTRA SUPPORT If there's time, you could get Sts to listen again with the script on *pp.128–129*, so they can see exactly what they understood / didn't understand. Translate / Explain any new words or phrases.

e Either do this as a whole-class activity, or put Sts in pairs and then elicit some feedback for each question. You could also ask Sts if they know of any other advice to stay safe.

2 VOCABULARY crime and punishment

a Focus on the task and the title of the quiz, making sure Sts know what a *burglar* is. Elicit or model its pronunciation.

Give Sts time to do the quiz individually.

Get them to compare their choices with a partner. If they have chosen different options, get them to explain their choice.

EXTRA SUPPORT Quickly go through the quiz before Sts work individually, to make sure Sts understand all the lexis, but <u>not</u> the highlighted words or phrases.

b Put Sts in pairs, **A** and **B**, and tell them to go to **Communication Beat the burglar**, A on *p.109*, B on *p.113*.

Point out to Sts that the answers are from an ex-burglar. Give Sts time to read their answers.

Tell Sts to go back to the main lesson **8A**.

c In their pairs, Sts tell each other what they read in **Communication Beat the burglar**.

Then give Sts time to go through their quiz in **a** and check how many answers they got correct.

Find out with a show of hands how many Sts got all the answers correct. You could also ask Sts if they found any answers surprising.

Finally, deal with any new vocabulary, and elicit or model the pronunciation.

d Get Sts to match the highlighted words in the quiz to definitions 1–5.

Get them to compare with a partner.

e 🔊 **8.2** Play the audio for Sts to listen and check.

Check answers by writing the words onto the board. Elicit or model the pronunciation of *burgled*, *burglar*, and *burglary*.

🔊 **8.2**
1 burglar
2 be burgled
3 burglary
4 break into
5 steal

f Tell Sts to go to **Vocabulary Bank Crime and punishment** on *p.160*.

Vocabulary notes
Crimes and criminals
Point out that:

- the words for the criminal and the verb are usually another form of the word for the crime. The exceptions are *drug dealing*, where we tend to say *sell drugs*; *fraud*, where we use the verb *to commit fraud*; and *theft*, where the verb is *steal*. The verb *terrorize* also exists, but is normally used to mean 'to frighten and threaten people so that they will not oppose sth or will do as they are told', e.g. *Some local gangs are terrorizing the neighbourhood*. So, *terrorize* does not exactly equate with the crime of terrorism, which refers more to setting off bombs, etc.

- all the crime verbs are regular except for *set* (*set – set*), *steal*, and *sell*, which Sts should already know.

What happens to a criminal
Highlight:

- that *charged with sth* = formally accused of sth

- that *trial* is used for more serious offences, and *court case* for less serious cases.

- that *court* can refer to the building or to the institution, e.g. judge and jury. Common expressions with *court* are *to go to court* or *take sb to court*.

- the difference between *evidence* (= things which indicate that sb might be guilty) and *proof* (= things that show that sb is definitely guilty).

118 **8A**

Focus on **1 Crimes and criminals** and get Sts to do **a** individually or in pairs.

◗ 8.3 Now do **b**. Play the audio for Sts to listen and check.

Check answers.

◗ 8.3
Crime and punishment
1 Crimes and criminals
1 J blackmail, blackmailer, blackmail
2 M bribery, bribe
3 E burglary, burglar, break in / burgle
4 G drug dealing, drug dealer, sell drugs
5 L fraud, fraudster, commit fraud
6 F hacking, hacker, hack
7 C hijacking, hijacker, hijack
8 A kidnapping, kidnapper, kidnap
9 P mugging, mugger, mug
10 B murder, murderer, murder
11 D rape, rapist, rape
12 K robbery, robber, rob
13 H smuggling, smuggler, smuggle
14 Q stalking, stalker, stalk
15 N terrorism, terrorist, set off bombs
16 O theft, thief, steal
17 I vandalism, vandal, vandalize

Now either use the audio to drill the pronunciation of the words, or model and drill them yourself. Give further practice of any words your Sts find difficult to pronounce.

Focus on **Activation** and get Sts to cover the chart, look at situations A–Q, and say the crimes.

EXTRA CHALLENGE You may want to add other words for crimes, e.g. *arson*, *shoplifting*, *corruption*, etc.

Now focus on **2 What happens to a criminal** and get Sts to do **a** individually or in pairs.

◗ 8.4 Now do **b**. Play the audio for Sts to listen and check.

Check answers.

◗ 8.4
2 What happens to a criminal
The crime
1 Carl and Adam committed a crime. They robbed a large supermarket.
2 The police **investigated** the crime.
3 Carl and Adam were **caught** driving to the airport in a stolen car.
4 They were **arrested** and taken to a police station.
5 The police **questioned** them for ten hours.
6 Finally, they were **charged** with armed robbery.
The trial
7 Two months later, Carl and Adam appeared in **court**.
8 They were **accused** of armed robbery and car theft.
9 **Witnesses** told the court what they had seen or knew.
10 The **jury** looked at and heard all the **evidence**.
11 After two days, the jury reached their **verdict**.
12 There was no **proof** that Adam had committed the crime.
13 He was **acquitted** and allowed to go free.
14 Carl was found **guilty**. His fingerprints were on the gun used in the robbery.
15 The **judge** decided what Carl's **punishment** should be.
16 He **sentenced** him to ten years in prison.

Give further practice of any words your Sts find difficult to pronounce.

Get Sts to focus on the **bold** words under *The trial* and elicit their meaning.

EXTRA SUPPORT Get Sts to look at the words in the two lists and try to remember their meaning.

Tell Sts to go back to the main lesson **8A**.

EXTRA SUPPORT If you think Sts need more practice, you may want to give them the **Vocabulary** photocopiable activity at this point.

3 PRONUNCIATION & SPEAKING the letter *u*

Pronunciation notes

Like all vowels in English, the letter *u* can be pronounced in different ways, and crime vocabulary has several examples of the different pronunciations. Highlight to Sts that *ur*, unless followed by an *e*, is normally pronounced /ɜː/, and they should watch out for the 'hidden' /j/ in words like *accuse*, *music*, etc.

Remind Sts also that in *gu* + vowel, the *u* is silent, e.g. *guard*, *guess*, etc.

a Focus on the task and elicit the sound and picture word for each row: /ʌ/ *up*, /ʊə/ *tourist*, and /juː/.

Now get Sts, individually or in pairs, to put the words in the correct row. Encourage them to say the words out loud before deciding which row they go into.

b Now repeat the process and elicit the sound and picture word for each row: /ɪ/ *fish*, /ɜː/ *bird*, and /ɔː/ *horse*.

Give Sts time to put the words in the correct row.

c **◗ 8.5** Play the audio for Sts to listen and check their answers to **a** and **b**.

Check answers and then elicit answers to the questions.

See script 8.5
1 short **2** *caught* and *court* **3** /g/

◗ 8.5
a

up /ʌ/	drugs, judge, mugger, punishment, smuggling
tourist /ʊə/	jury
/juː/	accuse

b

fish /ɪ/	guilty
bird /ɜː/	burglar, murderer
horse /ɔː/	caught, court, fraud

Now play the audio again, pausing after each group of words for Sts to listen and repeat.

Then repeat the activity, eliciting responses from individual Sts.

EXTRA SUPPORT If these sounds are difficult for your Sts, it will help to show them the mouth position. You could model this yourself or use the Sound Bank videos on the *Teacher's Resource Centre.*

d **◗ 8.6** Tell Sts they must listen and write the five sentences they hear.

Play the audio, pausing after each sentence to give Sts time to write.

Get Sts to compare with a partner, and then play the audio again if necessary.

Check answers, eliciting the sentences onto the board.

8A 119

◀)) 8.6
1 Luke was accused of smuggling drugs.
2 'Murderers must be punished,' said the judge.
3 The burglar is doing community service.
4 The jury said he was guilty of fraud.
5 The mugger was caught and taken to court.

Give Sts time to practise saying the sentences.

EXTRA SUPPORT Play the audio again, pausing after each sentence for Sts to listen and repeat.

e Focus on the task and put Sts in small groups.

Give them time to ask and answer the questions. Encourage them to ask for and give as much information as possible.

Monitor and correct pronunciation where necessary.

Finally, get feedback from individual Sts and contribute opinions / experiences of your own if appropriate.

EXTRA SUPPORT You could do this as a whole-class activity, especially with a small class, eliciting answers from different Sts and contributing yourself.

EXTRA IDEA You could also ask Sts if they know of any famous or recent examples of the crimes below, and whether they can remember who was involved / what happened:
murder   kidnapping   stalking   blackmail
drug dealing   fraud   hijacking

4 GRAMMAR the passive (all forms); *have something done*; *it is said that…*, *he is thought to…*, etc.

a Give Sts time to read the three stories and answer the question. Tell them not to worry about options 1–9.

Check answers.

A Story 2   **B** Story 1   **C** Story 3

b This exercise revises different forms of the passive and Sts' ability to choose between the active and passive forms.

Get Sts to read the stories again and to circle the correct form of the verb.

Get them to compare with a partner, and then check answers.

1 being caught   **2** landed   **3** was spotted   **4** snatched
5 was demonstrating   **6** was caught   **7** had been broken
8 called   **9** has been charged

c Do this as a whole-class activity.

2

EXTRA CHALLENGE Get Sts, in pairs, to retell the three stories from memory. Or put Sts in groups of three and get each student to retell one of the stories.

d ◀)) 8.7 Tell Sts they are going to listen to another crime story.

Play the audio once the whole way through for Sts to listen and answer the question.

Get Sts to compare with a partner, and then check the answer.

He always says 'please' and 'thank you' when he orders people to give him money.

◀)) 8.7
(script in Student's Book on *p.129*)
N = newsreader, P = police officer
N Police in Stockport are looking for a man who is said to be Britain's most polite armed robber. The robber always says 'please' and 'thank you' when he orders shop staff to give him money from the till. It is believed that he is a tall man in his early forties and that he wears a mask and washing-up gloves during the robberies. It is thought that he has robbed at least four shops in Stockport in recent weeks. DI Anderson from Greater Manchester Police has given a warning to the public.
P He is reported to be polite to his victims, but there's nothing polite about armed robbery. Last week, this man used a knife to threaten shop staff and they were terrified. Saying 'please' and 'thank you' doesn't change that.

e Focus on the task and give Sts time to read the four extracts from the listening.

Play the audio again, pausing after each extract is said on the audio, for Sts to listen and complete the gaps.

Get Sts to compare with a partner, and then check answers.

1 to be   **2** that he is   **3** that he has robbed   **4** to be polite

Now ask Sts how the structure is different between 1 and 4, and 2 and 3.

After *is said* and *is reported…*, use *to* + infinitive.
After *it is believed…* and *it is thought…*, use *that* + subject + verb.

You might want to highlight that after *I / you / we / they*, you also use *to* + infinitive.

f Tell Sts to go to **Grammar Bank 8A** on *p.146*.

Grammar notes
The passive (all forms)

Sts at this level should be familiar with all the different forms of the passive, but it is likely that they will be more confident with the present and past forms that they have been using since Pre-intermediate level than with the more complex forms (e.g. past continuous, past perfect, gerund, and infinitive).

You may want to quickly revise the basic forms with a chart which shows that it is the verb *be* that keeps changing in each sentence, e.g.

A new car park	*is built every year.*
	was built last year.
	is being built at the moment.
	has just been built.

The use of *by* in passive sentences

Some Sts may tend to overuse *by* and want to include it every time they use the passive. One of the exercises here tries to correct this tendency.

have something done (causative *have*)

The most common use of this structure is to get somebody to do something for you, e.g. *I need to have my car serviced*. However, it can also be used to express something, usually bad, that has been done to you, e.g. *I had my wallet stolen*.

You may want to tell Sts that, especially in this first use, we sometimes use *get* instead of *have*, e.g. *I need to get my car serviced*.

120   **8A**

it is said that…, he is thought to…, etc.

These 'advanced' passive structures are included more for recognition than production, as they are low-frequency in spoken English. However, Sts will certainly come across them if they read news websites or watch TV in English.

Focus on the example sentences for **the passive (all forms)** and play audio 🔊 **8.8** for Sts to listen and repeat. Encourage them to copy the rhythm. Then go through the rules with the class.

Repeat for *have something done* (causative *have*) 🔊 **8.9** and *it is said that…, he is thought to…, etc.* 🔊 **8.10**.

Focus on the exercises and get Sts to do them individually or in pairs.

If they do them individually, get them to compare with a partner. Check answers, getting Sts to read the full sentences.

a
1 My phone **has been stolen.**
2 My house **is being painted.**
3 A meeting **will be held to discuss the problem.**
4 If the bomb **hadn't been found, it would have exploded.**
5 Miranda thinks she **was followed / was being followed last night.**
6 I hate **being woken up when I'm fast asleep.**
7 The local police station **is going to be closed.**

b
1 Tim **had his social media account hacked.**
2 Have you ever **had your bag snatched?**
3 They **need to have the CCTV checked to make sure that it's working.**
4 We **had our photo taken in front of the Colosseum.**
5 As a result of the burglary, they**'re going to have a safe put in.**

c
1 The burglar is believed to be a local man.
2 It is said that the muggers are very dangerous.
3 The robbers are thought to have entered through an open window.
4 It is said that the murderer has disappeared.
5 The trial is expected to last three weeks.

Tell Sts to go back to the main lesson **8A**.

EXTRA SUPPORT If you think Sts need more practice, you may want to give them the **Grammar** photocopiable activity at this point.

5 READING understanding truth and lies

a Put Sts in pairs and give them time to discuss questions 1–3. You could demonstrate the activity by answering the questions yourself.

Get some feedback from various pairs.

b Focus on the photos and article, and questions 1–3, making sure Sts know the meaning of the adjective *suspicious* /səˈspɪʃəs/ (= feeling that sb has done something wrong, illegal, or dishonest, without having any proof) and the noun *scammer* /ˈskæmə/ (= a person who illegally tricks sb, usually with the purpose of getting money from them). Elicit or model their pronunciation. If necessary, elicit / explain that the *black market* is an illegal form of trade in which things that are difficult to obtain are bought or sold.

Set a time limit for Sts to read the article once and answer the questions.

Get Sts to compare with a partner, and then check answers.

EXTRA SUPPORT Before Sts read the article the first time, check whether you need to pre-teach any vocabulary, but <u>not</u> the highlighted words or phrases.

1 Steve and his sister; Martin said it was him and his dead wife.
2 Because one showed Steve (having breakfast in a hotel) with long hair, and one that was supposed to have been taken later the same day showed Steve (in a pool) with shorter, darker hair.
3 Steve had scratched his face; the scammer used it to claim he (Martin) had been in a car accident.

c Give Sts time to read questions 1–5 and their three options.

Get Sts to read the article again and answer the questions.

EXTRA IDEA You could get Sts to underline the parts of the text that give them the answers.

Check answers.

1 c 2 b 3 b 4 a 5 b

d Focus on the highlighted words and phrases related to scams. Get Sts, in pairs or individually, to guess their meaning. Tell them to read the whole sentence, as the context will help them guess. Then they should match them to a synonym in the list.

Check answers, either explaining in English, translating into Sts' L1, or getting Sts to check in their dictionaries.

1 thought that 2 trick (vb) 3 said that (even though it wasn't true) 4 fraud 5 make use of (in a dishonest way) 6 give 7 chosen 8 careful

Deal with any other new vocabulary. Elicit or model the pronunciation of any tricky words.

6 SPEAKING

a Do this as a whole-class activity.

b Focus on the instructions and go through each question, eliciting the meaning of any words you think your Sts don't know, e.g. *threatening*, *breed*, etc.

Give Sts time to decide whether they think each 'situation' is illegal or not, why (not), and if illegal, what they think the punishment should be.

c Put Sts in small groups of three or four. They should choose a secretary who will make notes of their decisions. You may want to set a time limit, but extend it if they need more time.

Get feedback. Start with the first question and ask each secretary what their group concluded.

If there's time, do the same with the other ones.

Deal with any general vocabulary problems that arose.

EXTRA SUPPORT Remind Sts of the language they can use for saying what they think, by writing the following examples on the board:

I THINK / DON'T THINK IT SHOULD BE ILLEGAL / AGAINST THE LAW BECAUSE…

I THINK PEOPLE WHO…SHOULD BE FINED / SENT TO PRISON / BANNED FROM… / MADE TO…

8A 121

EXTRA IDEA You may want to give Sts some more crime-related topics to discuss that you think are relevant to them, e.g. *Do you think that…?*

trial by jury is a good system

parents should be held responsible for the crimes of children under 18, etc.

7 WRITING expressing your opinion

Tell Sts to go to **Writing Expressing your opinion** on *p.120*.

a Focus on the task and read the title of the post out loud to the class. Elicit / Explain what a *minor offence* means (= a not very serious crime). Then ask Sts if they agree or disagree.

Give Sts time to quickly read the post to find out what the writer's opinion of community service is. Tell them not to worry about the gaps.

Elicit the writer's opinion.

> The writer thinks that, in general, community service is a good thing.

b Tell Sts to read the post again and this time to complete the gaps with words and phrases from the list.

Get Sts to compare with a partner, and then check answers.

> **2** In most cases   **3** Firstly   **4** For instance   **5** whereas
> **6** Secondly   **7** so   **8** Finally   **9** In addition   **10** In conclusion

c Focus on the task and the two titles.

Give Sts a little time, in pairs, to think about which title they want to write about.

d Focus on the instructions and go through points 1–3 with the class.

Now give Sts time to think of the reasons they are going to write about in the main paragraphs.

EXTRA SUPPORT Sts could discuss the reasons they are going to write about with their partner from **c**.

e Focus on the **Useful language: ways of giving your opinion**, **Ways of giving examples**, and **Sequencing words** box and go through it with the class.

Go through the instructions. Then either get Sts to do the writing in class (set a time limit of, e.g. 20 minutes), or get them to write at home for homework.

f Sts should check their article for mistakes before giving it in.

122 **8A**

8B Fake news

G reporting verbs
V the media
P word stress

Lesson plan

The topic of this lesson is the media, and in particular the very current issue of fake news.

The first half starts with Sts talking about the different media they use to get the news and which sections of news they are interested in. They then listen to two stories from the press and read two more stories which provide a context to revise the basic rules of reported speech. Sts then decide which story is in fact fake, i.e. invented. Extracts from the four stories introduce reporting verbs, such as *offer*, *convince*, *admit*, *deny*, etc., which are followed by gerund or infinitive constructions. After Sts have been to the Grammar Bank and learned more reporting verbs, there is a pronunciation focus on word stress in two-syllable verbs.

In the second half of the lesson, the vocabulary of the media is developed in the Vocabulary Bank and a speaking activity about the media. Sts then read an article about how to spot fake news. Finally, they watch a short documentary about the history of journalism.

More materials
For teachers
Photocopiables
Grammar reporting verbs *p.177*
Communicative TV political debate *p.208*
(instructions *p.188*)
Vocabulary The media *p.227* (instructions *p.216*)
Teacher's Resource Centre
Video The speed of news
For students
Workbook 8B
Online Practice 8B

OPTIONAL LEAD-IN – THE QUOTE

Write the quote at the top of *p.80* on the board and the name of the person who said it, or get Sts to open their books and read it.

Ask Sts what they think the quote means and whether they agree with it.

1 LISTENING & SPEAKING identifying the main events in news stories

a Focus on the title of the lesson, *Fake news*, and ask Sts where they have seen this phrase (on TV news programmes and websites). Elicit the meaning (*false reports of events, written and read on websites*).

Now focus on questions 1–4 and get Sts to discuss them in pairs.

Get some feedback. You could do question 4 as a whole-class activity.

b Focus on the task and either do it as a whole-class activity, or put Sts in pairs and then elicit some ideas, but <u>don't</u> tell Sts if they are correct or not.

c 🔊 **8.11** Play the audio once the whole way through for Sts to listen and check their guesses in **b**.

Elicit what each story is about (without going into any detail) and find out if any Sts had guessed correctly.

EXTRA SUPPORT Read through the script and decide if you need to pre-teach any new lexis before Sts listen.

🔊 **8.11**
(script in Student's Book on *p.129*)
Story 1
And now, some news for wine drinkers. It seems that 'red' and 'white' are no longer the only options. France finally has a wine to match all three of the colours on its national flag, as a new blue variety hits the shelves. Vindigo is a chardonnay that gets its distinctive blue colour by being passed through red grape skins. The grape skins contain a natural dye found in blackcurrants, red cabbage, and raspberries. The new wine is the responsibility of French entrepreneur René Le Bail. He persuaded a company in Almeria in Spain, to produce the wine, after he was unable to convince anyone in France to become involved. Around thirty-five thousand bottles of Vindigo are now on sale in the south of France – in the port city of Sète – for about twelve euros a bottle. In an interview with a French newspaper, *Monsieur* Le Bail describes the wine as 'ideal for the summer'. He says that it has aromas of cherry, blackberry, and passionfruit, and recommends drinking it on the beach, or around the swimming pool.
Story 2
And now for our last story today – a zoo in Egypt has denied painting a donkey with black stripes in order to make it look like a zebra. Egyptian student Mahmoud Sarhan, eighteen, was visiting the zoo in Cairo when he noticed the animal, which had strange-looking black stripes. Mr Sarhan was suspicious and took a photo of the animal, which appeared to have strange black marks on its face, and posted it online. He later told the media, 'I knew that it was a donkey as soon as I saw it. I'm an artist. I know the different shape of a donkey and a zebra, so it was easy to tell the difference.' After the image was shared on social media, it went viral. Egyptian news site Extranews.tv approached a local vet, who agreed to examine the photo. He pointed out that zebras usually have a black nose and mouth, whereas the animal in Mr Sarhan's photo appears to be pale in this area. The vet added that authentic zebra stripes are usually straighter and clearer than those on the animal in Mr Sarhan's photo. The local radio station contacted the zoo's director, Mohamed Sultan. However, he refused to admit that the animal was a donkey.

---

d Now focus on sentence stems 1–8, and give Sts time to think about how they might be completed.

Play the audio again, pausing after the first story for Sts to listen and complete 1–4.

Get Sts to compare with a partner, and then play again if necessary. Repeat the same process for the second story. Check answers.

1 red grape skins
2 Spain (Almeria), he couldn't get anyone in France to become involved
3 about €12
4 the summer / drinking on the beach or by a swimming pool
5 an animal with strange stripes
6 he's an artist and he knows what the two animals look like
7 zebras usually have a black nose and mouth, and this animal didn't
8 the animal was a donkey

8B 123

EXTRA SUPPORT If there's time, you could get Sts to listen again with the script on *p.129*, so they can see exactly what they understood / didn't understand. Translate / Explain any new words or phrases.

e Now focus on the two news headlines and put Sts in pairs to discuss them and predict what each story is about.

Elicit some ideas from various pairs, but <u>don't</u> tell them if they are correct or not.

f Put Sts in pairs, **A** and **B**, and tell them to go to **Communication Strange, but true**, **A** on *p.109*, **B** on *p.113*.

Sts **A** will read the first story and Sts **B** the second. Go through the instructions, making sure Sts understand they must highlight ten key pieces of information to help them retell the story to their partner.

EXTRA SUPPORT You could put Sts **A** and Sts **B** together to do **a** first. Then get them to check they have got the key elements of the story before putting them in their pairs, **A** and **B**.

When Sts are ready, focus on the instructions in **b** and **c**.

Get some Sts to tell the stories to the class, making sure they mention the main points.

EXTRA CHALLENGE As feedback to the class, get Sts **A** to retell the story of *Shark baby drama* and Sts **B** to retell *Football fan gets Word Cup fever*.

Find out if any Sts had made correct guesses in **e**. Finally, deal with any new vocabulary, and elicit or model the pronunciation.

Tell Sts to go back to the main lesson **8B**.

g Elicit ideas from the class, e.g. with a show of hands, as to which story is invented, getting them to say why they don't think it is true.

Then tell Sts that the fake story (which was published on a satirical website) is *Football fan gets Word Cup fever*, and find out how many Sts guessed correctly.

2 GRAMMAR reporting verbs

a Focus on the task and give Sts time to match sentences 1–6 to the direct speech in A–F.

Check answers.

1 E	2 B	3 F	4 A	5 D	6 C

b Tell Sts to go to **Grammar Bank 8B** on *p.147*.

Grammar notes

Sts should be familiar with normal reported speech with *say / tell / ask*, e.g.

Direct speech: *'I'm sorry.'*

Reported (or indirect) speech: *He said he was sorry.*

In this lesson, Sts are introduced to a number of specific reporting verbs which are followed by either the infinitive or gerund. Some of these verbs and the structure following them have already been studied in **6A**.

Highlight that using these reporting verbs is an alternative and more exact way of reporting what someone says, e.g.

Direct speech: *'I'm sorry I stole your recipe.'*

Reported speech: *He said he was sorry he had stolen the recipe.*

Reporting verb: *He apologized for stealing the recipe.*

Emphasize the use of the negative infinitive (*not to go*) and the negative gerund (*not going*) after these reporting verbs. Some of these verbs can also be used with *that* + clause, e.g. *He admitted that he had stolen the recipe.*

Focus on the example sentences and play audio 🔊 **8.12** for Sts to listen and repeat. Encourage them to copy the rhythm. Then go through the rules with the class.

Now focus on the **Verbs that use a *that* clause** box and go through it with the class.

Focus on the exercises and get Sts to do them individually or in pairs. If they do them individually, get them to compare with a partner. Check answers, getting Sts to read the full sentences.

a
1 Jamie insisted on **paying** for the meal.
2 Lauren has agreed **to work** late next week.
3 I warned Jane **not to wear** those shoes to the park.
4 The man admitted **stealing** the woman's handbag.
5 The doctor advised Lily **to give up** drinking coffee.
6 The boss persuaded Megan **not to leave** the company.
7 Freya accused me of **trying / having tried** to steal her phone.
8 I apologized to Evie for **not remembering** her birthday.
9 Did you manage to convince your parents **to come** tonight instead of tomorrow?
10 My neighbour denies **damaging** my car, but…

b
1 Ryan **suggested going** for a walk.
2 The teacher **accused Simon of copying** Anna's exam.
3 Sam's neighbour **threatened to call** the police if he had any more parties.
4 The children **refused to go** to bed.
5 Peter **invited me to have** dinner with him.
6 Molly **reminded Jack to phone** the electrician.
7 Ricky **promised to never do / never to do** it again.
8 Sarah **recommended trying** Giacobazzi's.

Tell Sts to go back to the main lesson **8B**.

EXTRA SUPPORT If you think Sts need more practice, you may want to give them the **Grammar** photocopiable activity at this point.

3 PRONUNCIATION word stress

Pronunciation notes

Sts have, by now, built up an instinct for how words in English are pronounced and will know that many English two-syllable nouns are stressed on the first syllable. However, many two-syllable verbs are stressed on the second syllable (e.g. *depend*). In fact, almost all the reporting verbs which Sts learn in this lesson are stressed on the second syllable.

Highlight the difference between the /s/ sound in *convince*, *persuade*, *promise*, and *suggest*, and the /z/ sound in *accuse*, *advise*, and *refuse*.

You may also want to point out that when a two-syllable verb has the stress on the second syllable and ends in consonant–vowel–consonant, the final consonant is doubled in the gerund and past simple, e.g. *admit–admitting–admitted*, *regret–regretting–regretted*. If the stress is on the first syllable, it is not doubled, e.g. *threaten–threatening–threatened*. However, *travel* is an exception (*travelling*, *travelled*).

124 **8B**

a Focus on the task and give Sts time, individually or in pairs, to underline the stressed syllable in each verb and to circle the four exceptions.

b ◗) **8.13** Play the audio for Sts to listen and check.

Check answers.

> Sts should have circled *offer*, *order*, *promise*, and *threaten*.

◗) **8.13**

a<u>ccuse</u>, ad<u>mit</u>, ad<u>vise</u>, a<u>gree</u>, con<u>vince</u>, de<u>ny</u>, in<u>sist</u>, in<u>vite</u>, <u>offer</u>, <u>order</u>, per<u>suade</u>, <u>promise</u>, re<u>fuse</u>, re<u>gret</u>, re<u>mind</u>, su<u>ggest</u>, <u>threaten</u>

Focus on the **Spelling of two-syllable verbs** box and go through it with the class.

c Focus on the task and give Sts time to complete the sentences with the correct reporting verb. Point out that the first one (*offered*) has been done for them.

Get them to compare with a partner.

d ◗) **8.14** Play the audio for Sts to listen and check.

Check answers.

◗) **8.14**
1 He **offered** to make some coffee.
2 He **refused** to go.
3 He **agreed** to help me.
4 He **promised** to call me.
5 He **reminded** me to lock the door.
6 He **advised** me to buy a new car.
7 He **invited** me to have dinner.
8 He **denied** breaking the window.
9 He **admitted** stealing the money.
10 He **regretted** marrying Susan.
11 He **suggested** going to a club.
12 The police **accused** him of killing his boss.

e Focus on the **Linking** box and go through it with Sts.

Now focus on the task and make sure Sts understand what they have to do. Highlight that Sts should use the pronoun *He* each time, except with the verb *accuse* in the last one, when they should begin *The police…*

Demonstrate by modelling and drilling the first sentence (*He offered to make some coffee*).

EXTRA SUPPORT Before Sts work individually, tell them to cover the right-hand column in **c**. Get them to look at 1, elicit the corresponding reported sentence from the class or individual Sts, and then play the audio for Sts to listen and check.

EXTRA IDEA Put Sts in pairs, **A** and **B**. Sts **A** (book open) read in any order a direct sentence in **c** to their partner. Sts **B** (book closed) respond with the corresponding reported sentence, but this time if their partner is female, they should use *She*. Then they swap roles.

f ◗) **8.15** Focus on the instructions and example.

Play the audio, pausing after each sentence for Sts to listen and form the corresponding reported speech sentence using the verb they hear.

◗) **8.15**
1 I didn't steal the wallet! – deny (*pause*)
   He denied stealing the wallet.
2 I wish I hadn't bought a second-hand car. – regret (*pause*)
   She regretted buying a second-hand car.
3 Of course I'll come with you. – agree (*pause*)
   He agreed to come with me.

4 Why don't we go out for dinner? – suggest (*pause*)
   She suggested going out for dinner.
5 Shall I open the window? – offer (*pause*)
   He offered to open the window.
6 You should ask the teacher. – advise (*pause*)
   She advised me to ask the teacher.

Then repeat the activity, eliciting responses from individual Sts.

4 VOCABULARY & SPEAKING the media

a Do this as a whole-class activity, or put Sts in pairs and then check answers.

> **1** sport **2** politics **3** celebrity gossip **4** business

EXTRA SUPPORT If Sts can't remember the different categories of news, tell them to look back at **1a** on *p.80*.

b Put Sts in pairs and get them to try to guess the meaning of the **bold** verbs in **a**. Then they should match each verb to a word or phrase in the list.

Check answers.

> **1** leaves **2** is predicted **3** is going to marry **4** separate

Deal with any vocabulary problems that arose.

EXTRA CHALLENGE Look at the headlines again and ask Sts to think how they would say them in normal English. Ask Sts *What kind of words get left out in headlines?* (Elicit that articles and auxiliary verbs are often left out, e.g. *A man was run over by a bus* becomes *Man run over by bus*.) *What form or tense is used for a) the future b) the passive (all tenses)?* (The future is expressed by an infinitive, e.g. *Becks to go*, and passives by a past participle, e.g. *Man stabbed on Tube*.)

c Tell Sts to go to **Vocabulary Bank** The media on *p.161*.

> **Vocabulary notes**
> **The language of headlines**
> Highlight that many of the 'headline' verbs are not commonly used in conversation, especially *wed*, *vow*, *quiz*, and *axe*.
>
> **Journalists and people in the media**
> Highlight the difference between a *critic* (the person) and a *review* (the article a critic writes), as these may be false friends in your Sts' L1.

Focus on **1 The language of headlines** and go through the information box with the class.

Get Sts to do **a** individually or in pairs.

◗) **8.16** Now do **b**. Play the audio for Sts to listen and check.

Check answers.

◗) **8.16**
The media
1 The language of headlines
1 **D** Prime Minister backs his Chancellor in latest scandal
2 **A** Thousands of jobs axed by UK firms
3 **F** Stock market hit by oil fears
4 **C** Astronaut bids to be first man on Mars
5 **E** Ministers clash over new car tax proposal
6 **H** Bayern Munich boss vows to avenge defeat
7 **B** Police quiz witness in murder trial
8 **G** Actress rows with co-star over unfair pay

8B 125

Give further practice of any words your Sts find difficult to pronounce.

Now do **Activation** and get Sts to cover definitions A–H, read the headlines, and try to remember what the highlighted verbs mean.

Focus on **2 Journalists and people in the media** and get Sts to do **a** individually or in pairs.

🔊 **8.17** Now do **b**. Play the audio for Sts to listen and check. Check answers.

🔊 **8.17**

2 Journalists and people in the media

1	critic	6	freelance journalist
2	commentator	7	newsreader
3	reporter	8	paparazzi
4	editor	9	agony aunt
5	presenter		

Now either use the audio to drill the pronunciation of the words, or model and drill them yourself. Give further practice of any words your Sts find difficult to pronounce.

Do **Activation** as a whole-class activity.

EXTRA SUPPORT Get Sts to cover the words in the left-hand column, look at the definitions, and try to remember the words.

Focus on **3 Adjectives to describe the media** and get Sts to do **a** individually or in pairs.

🔊 **8.18** Now do **b**. Play the audio for Sts to listen and check.

Check answers.

🔊 **8.18**

3 Adjectives to describe the media

1 D The reporting in the paper was very sensational.
2 E The news on Channel 12 is really biased.
3 B I think *The Observer* is the most objective of the Sunday papers.
4 A The film review was quite accurate.
5 C I think the report was censored.

Then get Sts to look at the adjectives and try to guess their exact meaning. In a monolingual class, and if you know the L1, elicit the meaning in your Sts' language or get them to check with a dictionary. Give further practice of any words your Sts find difficult to pronounce.

Do **Activation** as a whole-class activity.

EXTRA SUPPORT Get Sts to cover sentences 1–5, look at sentences A–E, and try to remember the **bold** adjectives.

Tell Sts to go back to the main lesson **8B**.

EXTRA SUPPORT If you think Sts need more practice, you may want to give them the **Vocabulary** photocopiable activity at this point.

d The new vocabulary is recycled in this speaking activity. Focus on the five questions and the sentence stems.

Give Sts time to read them and think about how they are going to answer.

EXTRA IDEA Before Sts do the speaking activity in groups, you could elicit / remind Sts of some useful language for saying what you think and agreeing / disagreeing. Write the phrases on the board for Sts to use as a reference:

IN MY OPINION / VIEW…,
IF YOU ASK ME…
PERSONALLY, I THINK…
I COMPLETELY AGREE / I DON'T AGREE AT ALL.
I THINK / DON'T THINK YOU'RE RIGHT.

e Put Sts in small groups of three or four. Tell Sts to take turns to ask one of the questions in **d** and then say what they think, giving their reasons. Then the other Sts in the group should agree or disagree.

Set a time limit for the groups to discuss each question.

Monitor and help if necessary.

Get some feedback, finding out what the majority opinion was on each topic. Deal with any general vocabulary problems that arose.

5 READING using headings to understand the main point of a paragraph

a Focus on the task and find out if Sts know what the *Tour de France* is (*It is an annual multiple-stage bike race for men, held mainly in France*).

Give Sts time to read the news report and answer the question.

Check the answer.

EXTRA SUPPORT Before Sts read the article the first time, check whether you need to pre-teach any vocabulary.

Because he isn't experiencing the real France.

Deal with any vocabulary problems that arose.

b Focus on the questions and then get Sts to read the article again. Elicit any aspects of the article that made Sts think it was fake, and ask them at what point they realized this.

EXTRA IDEA You could find some more stories on The Daily Mash website and give Sts just the headlines or the beginning of the article, and ask them to guess the story; then look at the stories on The Daily Mash.

c Focus on the title of the article and check Sts can remember the meaning of the verb *to spot*.

Give Sts time to read the article and complete the eight headings with the words in the list.

Check answers. Elicit or model pronunciation if necessary.

EXTRA SUPPORT Before Sts read the article the first time, check whether you need to pre-teach any vocabulary, but not the adjectives in **e**.

1 sense 2 name 3 addresses 4 date 5 spellings
6 fake 7 images 8 trust

d Give Sts time to read the article again and answer the questions about each section.

Get Sts to compare with a partner, and then check answers.

126 **8B**

Introduction For political or personal gain

1 Because they don't exist.
2 There is no such newspaper.
3 It isn't the correct URL for ABC news, just deliberately similar.
4 They were actually of another attack in Russia five years earlier.
5 Because authentic news sites use editors to check the text is accurate.
6 Because the surname is spelled wrong.
7 Because these types of images are often used in order to make a fake story more likely to go viral.
8 Check that the information appears on other, reputable news sites.

e Focus on the task and either get Sts to do it individually or in pairs.

Check answers, making sure Sts know what the adjectives mean. Elicit or model pronunciation.

1 exaggerated, misleading, improbable, doctored
2 legitimate, reliable, trustworthy

Deal with any other new vocabulary. Elicit or model the pronunciation of any tricky words.

f Do this as a whole-class activity, or put Sts in pairs and then get some feedback.

6 ▶ VIDEO LISTENING

a Tell Sts they are going to watch a documentary about the history of journalism. Focus on the instructions and then give Sts time to read the different ways of delivering news.

Play the video once the whole way through for Sts to listen and number the ways of delivering the news in the order they are mentioned.

Check answers.

EXTRA SUPPORT Read through the script and decide if you need to pre-teach any new lexis before Sts watch the video.

1 live Twitter feeds 2 Facebook 3 the Boston newsletter
4 the telegraph line 5 radio and television 6 cable TV

The speed of news

Hi, my name's Matt Wilder. I'm a freelance journalist based in Washington, D.C. At the moment, I'm trying to find a good story. I have a six o'clock deadline…but nothing's going on. I know, I'll see what topics are trending on Twitter.

Today we live in the era of new media. People can access the news at any time, from any place on all kinds of digital devices.

The internet and social media sites such as Twitter and Facebook allow these news consumers to become news producers.

If you want to be a journalist, all you have to do is post an article online, and it can be read instantly by anyone anywhere in the world.

Journalism has changed a lot during the first days of the newspaper, and most of these changes have been driven by technology. There's no better place to discover this than Washington, DC – home of the Newseum.

There are over thirty thousand newspapers here, covering over five hundred years of news. This is the *Boston News-Letter*, thought to be the first continuously published newspaper in North America.

This edition, from seventeen eighteen, reports on the sensational killing of Edward Teach – better known as Blackbeard – believed to be one of the most dangerous pirates at the time.

Reporting in the early days of journalism must have been very difficult. Journalists would ride their horses to the nearest town that had a printing press. Their reports were then published in a newspaper, which was often just a single sheet of paper, and distributed on horseback.

The roads were bad, so it was very difficult to send news over long distances. By the time most people read these newspapers, the news was often very out-of-date.

This all changed when the first telegraph line was built in eighteen forty-four. Suddenly, journalists could send stories quickly. The telegraph is said to have revolutionized news reporting. This new style of journalism came just in time for the American Civil War. For the first time, news could be sent at the same time as battles were being fought. War correspondents, and the stories they sent, became very popular. But there were still problems. These war reports were very biased because journalists represented their own side in the war. There was no objectivity, and reports were usually censored by the army or the government. So, stories were often inaccurate and sometimes completely wrong!

It wasn't until the invention of radio and television that news could be broadcast live. This completely transformed news and created the age of the mass media, where news could be communicated to a huge audience.

Throughout the twentieth century, demand for news stories increased and news technology continued to advance. By the end of the century, there were hundreds of cable TV channels, lots of twenty-four-hour news channels, and the internet had been invented. Suddenly we were in the information age.

This is the HP New Media Gallery. It shows the news as it is today. Visitors to this exhibit are placed right at the centre of the digital news revolution.

They are instantly connected to the day's news by live Twitter feeds showing the day's trending news stories. They can also check out major news stories which were first reported on social media. These pictures of a plane landing on New York's Hudson River were taken on a smartphone and uploaded to Twitter seconds after the incident had occurred.

Speaking of smartphones…

Ah, fantastic! A tweet from The White House. Oh! There's a big announcement in twenty-five minutes. I'd better go! Bye!

b Tell Sts they are going to watch the documentary again, and give them time to read questions 1–7.

Play the video again, pausing occasionally to give Sts time to answer the questions.

Get Sts to compare with a partner, and then play the video again if necessary.

Check answers.

EXTRA SUPPORT You could get Sts to compare their answers between the first and second playing of the documentary.

1 In Washington, DC; 30,000
2 He was believed to be one of the most dangerous pirates at the time; 1718
3 On horseback; the roads were bad, so it was very difficult to send news over long distances.
4 By telegraph line
5 They were very biased because journalists represented their own side in the war and reports were usually censored by the army or the government.
6 The inventions of radio and television
7 The plane landing on New York's Hudson River

EXTRA SUPPORT You could get Sts to watch the video again with subtitles, so they can see exactly what they understood / didn't understand. Translate / Explain any new words or phrases.

c Do this as a whole-class activity. If you don't come from the same country as your Sts, tell them about any newspapers or magazines that have existed there for a long time. You could also tell them about their reputation nowadays and whether or not you read them.

8B 127

7&8 Revise and Check

For instructions on how to use these pages, see *p.41*.

More materials
For teachers
Teacher's Resource Centre
Video Can you understand these people? 7&8
Quick Test 8
File 8 Test
For students
Online Practice Check your progress

GRAMMAR

1 must have left   2 should have told   3 might have got
4 can't have been   5 as if   6 tastes like   7 smells awful
8 was being repaired   9 never be found   10 to be   11 is said
12 the shower fixed   13 to talk   14 killing her husband
15 apologized for being

VOCABULARY

a
1 remind   2 matter   3 stole   4 raise   5 argue   6 refuses
b
1 calf (the others relate to hands)
2 hip (the others are organs)
3 wink (the others are things you do with your hand)
4 vandal (the others are all kinds of thieves)
5 smuggler (the others are crimes)
6 evidence (the others are people)
c
1 chew   2 scratch   3 stare   4 frown   5 hack   6 blackmail
7 bribe   8 quit
d
1 critic   2 biased   3 censored   4 newsreader   5 accurate

PRONUNCIATION

a
1 elb**ow** /əʊ/   2 **h**onest (the h is silent)   3 j**our**nalist /ɜː/
4 sh**ou**lder /əʊ/   5 j**u**ry /ʊə/
b
1 <u>r</u>ealize   2 <u>black</u>mail   3 <u>van</u>dalism   4 <u>c</u>ommentator
5 obj<u>ec</u>tive

CAN YOU understand this text?

a
A web sleuth is a citizen-detective who investigates crimes by going online.
b
1 B   2 F   3 D   4 E   5 A   6 C

▶ CAN YOU understand these people?

1 a   2 c   3 b   4 a

◑ 8.19

1
I = interviewer, M = Melanie
I   Is there anyone you often have arguments with?
M   I suppose I often have arguments with my sister, and that is mostly about, you know, who's going to clean the dishes, whose turn is it to bring out the trash, who's going to get the toilet paper next, things like that.
I   Who usually wins the argument? Why?
M   Depends on who's more awake at the time, they usually win the arguments. Yeah, they're more, hey just do it, and the other person just kind of is like, oh OK fine.

2
I = interviewer, E = Erica
I   Have you ever acted in a play or a film?
E   I have acted in both plays and films actually. I, that's my profession, I'm an actor, yeah.
I   What was your most recent play?
E   Hmm, OK, so my most recent play was called *A Woman's Worth*, where I played Jayda who is a wedding planner, whose fiancé just refuses to make the commitment and actually get married to her.
I   Did you enjoy the experience?
E   I did enjoy the experience. I got a chance to perform in front of my friends and my family and my boyfriend, so that was really cool.

3
I = interviewer, H = Hugo
I   Have you ever witnessed a crime?
H   I've witnessed someone being sort of mugged in the street. So, having their, yeah, threatened unless they didn't hand over their mobile phone and wallet.
I   What happened?
H   In the end, the, um, culprit ran off with what he'd sort of taken and left the individual just shocked and, yeah, a bit helpless. And then I think by the time the police did come it was, it was sort of too late.

4
I = interviewer, D = Diarmuid
I   Where do you get your news from?
D   Er, I read most of my news online or on my phone. Um, and I do use newspaper apps, um, but I'm ashamed to say that a lot of my news does also come through social media.
I   What kind of news are you most interested in?
D   Er, I'm interested in politics, er, sports, um, and really most news. I studied journalism, so I have an interest in it.
I   Do you mostly believe what you hear or read in the news?
D   Er, no, I don't believe anything I read in the news. And I, I think, um, you have to filter everything you read through the organization that it comes from, because every, er, media outlet has some kind of bias.

128 **Revise and Check**

9A Good business?

G clauses of contrast and purpose
V advertising, business
P changing stress on nouns and verbs

Lesson plan

The topic and lexical area of this lesson is business and advertising.

In the first half, the focus is on honesty (or dishonesty) in advertising. Sts look at words and phrases related to advertising and then discuss famous misleading advertisements. This is followed by a speaking activity in which Sts discuss various aspects of advertising in general, and cover language such as *viral adverts*, *logos*, and *pop-ups*. Sts then listen to a radio programme about how companies try to trick us through the use of misleading advertisements. This leads to the grammar, which is on clauses of contrast after expressions like *Even though…*, *In spite of…*, etc., and clauses of purpose after expressions like *so that…*, *in order to…*, etc.

The advertising and business topic is continued in the second half of the lesson, where Sts read a chapter from a book about the razor-and-blades business model, which was developed after King Camp Gillette invented the disposable razor blade. In Vocabulary, Sts look at words and phrases related to business, after which there is a pronunciation focus on how stress changes in words that can be used both as nouns and verbs, like *export*, *increase*, etc. Sts round off by talking about aspects of business in their country / region.

More materials

For teachers

Photocopiables
Grammar clauses of contrast and purpose *p.178*
Communicative Tell me about… *p.209*
(instructions *p.188*)
Vocabulary Business *p.228* (instructions *p.216*)

For students
Workbook 9A

Online Practice 9A

OPTIONAL LEAD-IN – THE QUOTE

Write the quote at the top of *p.86* on the board and the name of the person who said it, or get Sts to open their books and read it.

You could tell Sts that Mark Twain (1835–1910) is best known for writing the classic American novels *The Adventures of Tom Sawyer* and *Adventures of Huckleberry Finn*. He was also a riverboat pilot, journalist, lecturer, entrepreneur, and inventor.

Ask Sts what they think the quote means and if they agree with it.

1 VOCABULARY & SPEAKING

a Focus on the advert and ask Sts if they have ever tried the drink or know what kind of drink it is (a non-alcoholic, high-caffeine energy drink).

Then do the questions as a whole-class activity.

b Now tell Sts to read the article, check their answers to **a**, and to answer why Benjamin Careathers did what he did.

Check answers. You could ask Sts if they think this is an example of deliberately misleading advertising, or whether the company just miscalculated. Ask them also if they think the reaction would have been the same in their culture.

EXTRA SUPPORT Before Sts read the article the first time, check whether you need to pre-teach any vocabulary, but not the highlighted words and phrases.

Because Red Bull doesn't actually give you real wings.
Possibly for the money, or the publicity, or he was really naive.

c Focus on the highlighted words and phrases, and give Sts time, in pairs, to try and work out what they mean. Remind them to read the whole sentence or paragraph.

Then point out that the first one (*advertisements*) has been done for them and get Sts to match the highlighted words and phrases to definitions 2–9.

Check answers and elicit or model pronunciation. You could write ADVERTISEMENT and ADVERT on the board and elicit which syllables are stressed in each (*advertisement*, *advert*). You could also highlight the difference between *consumer* (a marketing / business term), *customer* (a more general word for sb who buys sth from a shop or a business), and *client* (sb who uses the services or advice of a professional person or organization).

| 2 claims | 3 brands | 4 was sued | 5 misleading |
| 6 consumers | 7 advertising campaigns | 8 publicity |
| 9 slogan |

Deal with any other new vocabulary. Elicit or model the pronunciation of any tricky words.

d Put Sts in small groups of three, **A**, **B**, and **C**. Get them to look at the three adverts and discuss the question.

Elicit some ideas for each brand, but don't tell Sts if they are correct.

e In their groups, tell Sts to go to **Communication Misleading ads**, **A** on *p.110*, **B** on *p.112*, and **C** on *p.114*.

Sts **A** read about the Volkswagen ad, Sts **B** read about Danone, and Sts **C** about Olay. Go through the instructions, making sure Sts understand they must find the key information for 1–3 in their advert, to help them tell their partners about the ad.

EXTRA SUPPORT You could put Sts **A**, Sts **B**, and Sts **C** together to do **a** first. Then get them to check they have got the key elements before putting them in their small groups.

9A 129

When Sts are ready, focus on the instructions in **b** and give Sts time to tell each other about their ads.

You could do **c** as a whole-class activity.

Finally, deal with any new vocabulary, and elicit or model the pronunciation.

Tell Sts to go back to the main lesson **9A**.

f Focus on questions 1–6 and quickly go through them to make sure Sts understand them. If they ask you what a *viral advert* is (in number 2), you can give the example of a video clip advertising a product which is produced by a company, but is then spread like a virus from person to person via the internet and other social networks. Elicit or model the pronunciation of *viral* /ˈvaɪrəl/.

Put Sts in small groups of three and give them time to discuss the questions.

Monitor and help if necessary.

Deal with any general vocabulary problems that arose.

Get some feedback from various groups. You could find out if Sts disagreed whilst discussing any questions, and then open the discussion to the class.

2 LISTENING understanding explanations

a 🔊 **9.1** Focus on the task and give Sts time to read messages 1–6.

Play the audio once the whole way through for Sts to listen and complete the gaps. You could pause the audio after each marketing technique has been discussed, to give Sts time to write.

Get Sts to compare with a partner, and then check answers.

> **EXTRA SUPPORT** Read through the script and decide if you need to pre-teach any new lexis before Sts listen.

> 1 free Bluetooth speaker 2 only a few 3 Everybody's using 4 You too 5 independent study 6 Trust me

🔊 **9.1**
(script in Student's Book on *p.129*)
The first point to bear in mind is that nothing, but nothing, is ever free. How often have you seen adverts saying things like 'Get a free Bluetooth speaker when you subscribe to our magazine for six months?' There's something about the word 'free' that immediately attracts us – I want it! It makes us feel clever, as if we are going to get something for nothing. But, of course, that Bluetooth speaker (which, incidentally, will probably break the second time you use it) wasn't free at all. In spite of what the advert said, its price was really included in the magazine subscription. So don't trust any advert which offers something for free.

A second trick which advertisers use is when they tell us 'There are only a few left! Buy now while stocks last!' What happens to us when we read or hear these words? Even though we don't really need the products, and maybe don't even like them, we immediately want to be among the lucky few who have them. But – let's be clear about this – companies just don't run out of products. Do you really think the manufacturers couldn't produce a few more if they thought they could sell them? Of course they could.

When it comes to new products, we, the consumers, are like sheep and we follow each other. So, another way advertisers have of getting us to use something is to tell us 'Everybody's using it'. And of course, we think everybody can't be wrong, so the product must be fantastic. So as to make us believe it, they use expressions like 'It's a must-have' or 'It's the in-thing', and they combine this with a photograph of a large group of people, so that we can't fail to get

the message. But don't be fooled. Even if everybody is using it (and they may not be), everybody can be wrong.

Another favourite message is 'You too can look like this', accompanied by a photo of a fabulous-looking man or woman. But the problem is: you can't look like this, because actually the woman or man in the photo is a model, and also because he or she doesn't really look like that, either. The photo has been airbrushed in order to make the model look even slimmer, with perfect skin, and even more attractive than they are in real life.

Finally, what most annoys me is 'Trust me, I'm a doctor' or 'Trust me, I'm a celebrity.' The idea is that if a celebrity is using the product, it must be fantastic, or if a doctor recommends it, it must really work. But be careful. Although the actress is holding the product in the photo, do you really think she colours her hair with it at home? And the doctor in the advert – is he really a doctor, or just an actor wearing a white coat? Adverts also often mention a particular organization which recommends their product, for example, things like 'Our dog biscuits are recommended by the International Association of Dog Nutritionists' – well, that's probably an organization which the company set up themselves. Or 'A recent independent study found that our toothpaste cleans your teeth better than any other brand'. What study was it? Who commissioned the study? It was probably produced for the company itself, and paid for by them, too.

b Focus on the task and the two questions.

In pairs, Sts see if they can remember any of the information.

Now play the audio again, pausing after each marketing technique is mentioned to give Sts time to make notes.

Get Sts to compare with their partner, and then play again if necessary.

Check answers.

> 1 The word *free* makes us want it.
>   Its price is really included in the magazine subscription.
> 2 We want to be among the lucky few who have the products.
>   It's not really true that there are only a few remaining; companies can always produce more.
> 3 We think everybody can't be wrong.
>   Not everybody is using it, and even if they are, everybody can be wrong.
> 4 We want to look fabulous.
>   We can't look like the person in the photo, because he / she is a model and the photo has been airbrushed.
> 5 It sounds like an official recommendation.
>   The company probably paid for the study.
> 6 It must be fantastic / really work if a doctor or celebrity recommends it.
>   It's probably not true. The 'doctor' may be an actor.

> **EXTRA SUPPORT** If there's time, you could get Sts to listen again with the script on *p.129*, so they can see exactly what they understood / didn't understand. Translate / Explain any new words or phrases.

> **EXTRA CHALLENGE** You could get Sts to listen again with the script, and notice how the speaker gives extra stress to certain words in order to make her point, e.g. *The first point to bear in mind is that nothing, but nothing, is ever free.*

c Focus on the task and check Sts understand *keep falling for* (= continue to be tricked into believing sth that isn't true).

Do the questions as a whole-class activity, or put Sts in pairs and then get some feedback.

130 **9A**

3 GRAMMAR clauses of contrast and purpose

a Focus on the task and on phrases A–G, which Sts have to match to the extracts. Although this grammar is being focused on for the first time, Sts should have seen most of the highlighted expressions before, and the context will help them to complete the gaps even if they are unsure of the exact meaning of some of the highlighted phrases.

Get Sts to compare their answers with a partner.

EXTRA SUPPORT You could do the first one with the class as an example (1F).

b 🔊 **9.2** Play the audio for Sts to listen and check.

Check answers. Sts might find it helpful if you write the completed phrases on the board, in order to be able to focus easily on the examples of contrast and purpose. Alternatively, you could refer them to the complete sentences in the script.

> **1** F **2** E **3** D **4** C **5** G **6** A **7** B

🔊 **9.2**
1 In spite of what the advert said, its price was really included in the magazine subscription.
2 Even though we don't really need the products, and maybe don't even like them, we immediately want to be among the lucky few who have them.
3 So as to make us believe it, they use expressions like 'It's a must-have'…
4 …and they combine this with a photograph of a large group of people, so that we can't fail to get the message.
5 The photo has been airbrushed in order to make the model look even slimmer, with perfect skin, and even more attractive than they are in real life.
6 It was probably produced for the company itself, and paid for by them, too.
7 Although the actress is holding the product in the photo, do you really think she colours her hair with it at home?

Now focus Sts' attention on the seven highlighted phrases and ask them, in pairs, to decide which express a purpose (= the aim or function of sth).

Check answers, and elicit that all the others express a contrast.

> **3** So as to **4** so that **5** in order to **6** for

c Tell Sts to go to **Grammar Bank 9A** on *p.148*.

Grammar notes

Clauses of contrast

- **Rule 1:** Sts should be familiar with the meaning and use of *although*. Here they are introduced to *even though* and *though*, and the differences between the three in terms of level of formality and sentence position.
- **Rule 2:** Sts will have seen *in spite of* or *despite*, e.g. in reading texts, but in this lesson, they learn how to use them.

Clauses of purpose

Sts have previously learned to use *to* + infinitive to express purpose. Here they learn other ways of expressing the same idea.

- **Rule 1:** *In order to* and *so as to* are more formal than *to*. Make sure Sts don't use *for* + infinitive here. NOT *I went to the bank ~~for~~ to talk to my bank manager.*

- **Rule 2:** Stress that *for* + gerund is used to describe the purpose of a thing (often in answer to the question *What's it for?*). *For* can also be used to express the purpose of an action if that purpose is expressed with a noun, e.g. *We went to Venezuela for a holiday*, but not when it is expressed with a verb phrase, e.g. NOT *I come to this school ~~for learning~~ English.* Another typical mistake is using the infinitive after *for* instead of simply *to*, e.g. NOT *I come here ~~for to learn~~ English.*
- **Rule 3:** Point out that when there is a new subject in a clause of purpose, we <u>must</u> use *so that* (and not *to*, *in order to*, or *so as to*), e.g. *We bought a big car so that the children would have more space.* NOT *…~~in order to~~ the children have more space.*
- **Rule 4:** The main point to stress here is that the most common way of expressing purpose in spoken English (*to* + infinitive) <u>can't</u> be used to express negative purpose; you have to use *so as not to…* or *in order not to…*

Focus on the example sentences for **clauses of contrast** and play audio 🔊 **9.3** for Sts to listen and repeat. Encourage them to copy the rhythm. Then go through the rules with the class.

Repeat for **clauses of purpose** 🔊 **9.4**.

Focus on the exercises and get Sts to do them individually or in pairs.

If they do them individually, get them to compare with a partner. Check answers, getting Sts to read the full sentences.

> **a**
> **1** despite **2** even **3** to **4** as **5** order **6** spite **7** that **8** although / though **9** for **10** though
> **b**
> **1** …we wouldn't / didn't have to spend too much money on accommodation.
> **2** …she earns a fortune, she drives a very old car.
> **3** …the sad ending. / the ending being sad. / the fact that the ending was sad.
> **4** …the weather conditions were terrible.
> **5** …not to offend her.
> **6** …to allow the president's car through safely.

Tell Sts to go back to the main lesson **9A**.

EXTRA SUPPORT If you think Sts need more practice, you may want to give them the **Grammar** photocopiable activity at this point.

d Sentence race: Put Sts in pairs. Focus on the task and make sure Sts know what they have to do. They are competing against other pairs to try to be the first to complete the eight sentence stems in a way that makes sense and is grammatically correct. Set the time limit.

Monitor while pairs are writing and point out any incorrect sentences you see, but <u>don't</u> correct them.

When the time limit is up, elicit several possible answers for each sentence and write them on the board.

9A 131

Some possible answers
1 …children don't see them.
2 …the new product didn't sell very well.
3 …young people still buy them.
4 …experience life in a big city.
5 …not being very good at his job.
6 …it wasn't true.
7 …get a refund.
8 …a meeting.

4 READING dealing with an authentic text

a Do this as a whole-class activity, or put Sts in pairs and then elicit some ideas, but <u>don't</u> tell them if they are correct or not.

b Start by explaining to Sts that when they are reading authentic texts, they can use some simple strategies to find the correct meaning quickly for words and phrases they don't understand.

Firstly, they should check they know what part of speech a word is. Sometimes the meaning in the article won't be the most common, e.g. in the article they're going to read, *fleece* is more common as a noun (= the wool of a sheep), but here they need to know its meaning as a verb.

Secondly, if they need to look up a phrase, they will need to know the key word, as this is where they will find it listed in the dictionary or glossary. In a verb phrase, the key word is usually the verb, not the noun, e.g. in the phrase *suck people in*, the key word is *suck*.

Now focus on the instructions. Make sure Sts know that the chapter is not simplified – it is taken directly from a real economics book, so they should find it motivating to be able to understand it. You could tell them that the book is based on a series of radio programmes of the same name (available as podcasts), and is aimed at a general audience, not just people who study or work in economics.

Set Sts a time limit to read the first part of the article to find the answer to **a**, using the techniques they've just read about to deal with any unknown words and phrases.

Check the answer.

❗ Don't pre-teach any vocabulary before Sts read the chapter, as the focus of this activity is to work out the meaning of unknown words from context or to look them up.

They are all things where the main product, e.g. the machine, is quite cheap, but the things you buy to use with them, e.g. games, coffee pods, printer ink, blades, are very expensive.

c Tell Sts to read **Part 1** of the chapter again and then mark sentences 1–6 *T* (true) or *F* (false). Remind them to underline the information in the article that helped them find the answer.

Get Sts to compare with a partner, and then check answers.

1 T (*The United Company will make all of life's necessities as cost-effectively as possible*)
2 F (*The book's author had a vision that has ended up shaping the economy. But…it wasn't this particular vision. No, it was another idea, which he had a year later.*)
3 T (*If you've ever bought replacement cartridges for an inkjet printer, you are likely to have been annoyed…that they cost almost as much as you paid for the printer itself…But how can it possibly cost almost as much to supply a bit of ink in tiny plastic pots? The answer, of course, is that it doesn't.*)
4 T (*It's also known as the razor-and-blades model…suck people in with an attractively priced razor, then repeatedly fleece them for extortionately priced replacement blades.*)
5 F (*…initially, he made both parts expensive.*)
6 F (*Consider the PlayStation 4. Whenever Sony sells one, it loses money…But that's okay, because Sony coins it in whenever a PlayStation 4 owner buys a game.*)

Deal with any other new vocabulary. Elicit or model the pronunciation of any tricky words.

EXTRA CHALLENGE You may want to focus on the example from the article *Whenever Sony sells one, it loses money*. Elicit / Explain the meaning of *whenever* (= every time or at any time; it doesn't matter when). Explain that we can also use *whatever*, *whichever*, *whoever*, *however*, and *wherever* in the same way.

d Focus on the questions and make sure Sts know the meaning of *disposable* (= made to be thrown away after use).

Point out the **Glossary**, but <u>don't</u> go through it as a class, as Sts should now refer to it only if necessary while they read.

Tell Sts to read **Part 2** of the chapter and not to worry about the gaps.

Put Sts in pairs and get them to discuss the questions.

Check answers.

1 They are patent-protecting them or changing the technology so that other company's disposable products don't work with them.
2 Because, especially with digital products, it costs a lot to change to another platform, and takes time to learn how to use it. People also stay because of brand loyalty.
3 King Camp Gillette might have thought that the razor-and-blades model is not at all like his original business vision of 1894.

e Tell Sts to read the second part again and this time to complete each gap with a word or phrase from 1–7.

Check answers.

1 c 2 a 3 c 4 b 5 a 6 a 7 c

Deal with any other new vocabulary. Elicit or model the pronunciation of any tricky words.

f Focus on the questions and elicit answers from the class, making sure they understand the difference between *generic* (= a product that doesn't show the name of the company that made it) and *branded* (= made by a well-known company and having that company's name on it). You could tell the class if you own any products which use the two-part pricing system, and if so, why you bought them. You could also tell Sts if you generally use generic or branded products, and why.

132 **9A**

EXTRA IDEA Ask Sts if they think two-part pricing is an acceptable business practice, or whether they think it should be illegal.

5 VOCABULARY business

a Do this as a whole-class activity, or put Sts in pairs and then check the answer. Tell Sts that *manufacture* (= make things in large quantities, usually in a factory, e.g. cars) and *produce* (= make things either in a factory or by growing sth, e.g. wine).

manufacture

b Tell Sts to go to **Vocabulary Bank Business** on *p.162*.

Vocabulary notes
Verbs and expressions
Highlight:

- the difference between *merge* (= when two companies join together to make one bigger one) and *take over* (= when one company takes control of another company, especially by buying shares).

- *make sb redundant* = to take sb's job away from him / her because he / she isn't needed any more or because, for example, the company is losing money and needs to cut down on staff. Compare this with *sack sb*, which Sts learned in *English File* Intermediate, which means take someone's job away from them because they have done something wrong.

Focus on **1 Verbs and expressions** and get Sts to do **a** individually or in pairs.

🔊 **9.5** Now do **b**. Play the audio for Sts to listen and check.

Check answers.

🔊 **9.5**
Business
1 Verbs and expressions, b
1 Apple products are easy to market because people are immediately attracted to the stylish designs.
2 In nineteen eighty-nine, Pepsi-Cola **launched** a new product called Pepsi A.M., which was aimed at the 'breakfast cola drinker'. It was an immediate flop.
3 The Spanish airline Iberia **merged** with British Airways in twenty eleven and became one of the world's biggest airline groups.
4 Although GAP stands for Genuine American Product, most of its clothes are **manufactured** in Asia.
5 Prosciutto is a kind of Italian ham. Two of the best-known kinds are San Daniele and Parma, which are **produced** in the Friuli and Emilia regions of Italy, and are **exported** all over the world.
6 When BMW **took over** Mini, the smaller company became part of the larger organization.
7 The supermarket chain Tesco **became** the market leader in nineteen ninety-five and is still the UK's biggest-selling chain.
8 The first Zara store was opened in La Coruña in Spain in nineteen seventy-five, where its head office still is today. The company started to **expand** into new markets in nineteen eighty-eight, and it now has branches in ninety-six countries.
9 Many banks are now offering loans to people who want to **set up** a new small business.
10 The cost of living in Iceland is so high because so many food products have to be **imported**.
11 During a boom period, the economy **grows** quickly and living standards improve.
12 During a recession, many companies **close down** and living standards **drop**.

Give further practice of any words your Sts find difficult to pronounce.

Put Sts in pairs and get them to try to work out the meaning of the **bold** words and phrases.

Check answers.

a new product /ə ˌnjuː ˈprɒdʌkt/ = a thing that is grown or produced, usually for sale, for the first time
flop /flɒp/ = sth that is not successful
the market leader /ðə ˌmɑːkɪt ˈliːdə/ = the company that sells the largest quantity of a particular kind of product
chain /tʃeɪn/ = a group of shops, hotels, etc. owned by the same person or company
head office /hed ˈɒfɪs/ = the main office of a company
branches /brɑːntʃɪz/ = offices or shops that are part of a larger organization, e.g. a bank
a small business /ə ˌsmɔːl ˈbɪznəs/ = not doing business on a very large scale
a boom /ə buːm/ = a sudden increase in trade and economic activity; a period of wealth and success
a recession /ə rɪˈseʃn/ = a difficult time for the economy of a country, when there is less trade and industrial activity than usual and more people are unemployed

Now focus on **c** and give Sts time to put the words into the correct column.

🔊 **9.6** Now do **d**. Play the audio for Sts to listen and check.

Check answers. You might want to tell Sts that you can also say *do a deal*, but *make a deal* is more frequent.

🔊 **9.6**
d
do business, do a job, do market research, do well, do badly
make a deal, make a decision, make a loss, make money, make somebody redundant

Give further practice of any words your Sts find difficult to pronounce.

Do **Activation** and get Sts to cover the columns in **c**, look at the words in the list, and remember if they go with *do* or *make*.

Now look at **2 Idioms with *business***. Focus on the ***business*** box and go through it with the class.

Get Sts to do **a** individually or in pairs. Make sure they can remember what an *idiom* is.

🔊 **9.7** Now do **b**. Play the audio for Sts to listen and check.

Check answers.

🔊 **9.7**
2 Idioms with *business*
1 F I think we've been through everything on today's agenda. Now, is there any other business?
2 D Now that so many people book their holidays and travel online, many travel agencies have gone out of business.
3 C Let's get down to business right away – we'll have a break after an hour or so.
4 E She looks very determined – like a woman who means business.
5 B A What are you doing?
     B I'm sorry, but it's none of your business.
6 H A Is he your new boyfriend?
     B Mind your own business!
7 A He arranged to meet his ex-girlfriend because they had some unfinished business.
8 G Why are you taking your tennis racket on a work trip? It's never a good idea to mix business with pleasure.

9A 133

Give further practice of any words your Sts find difficult to pronounce.

Do **Activation** and get Sts to cover 1–8, look at A–H, and see if they can remember the idioms.

EXTRA SUPPORT Put Sts in pairs, **A** and **B**. Sts **A** (book open) say the highlighted phrases in random order to Sts **B**. Sts **B** (book open), looking only at definitions A–H, read the letter and definition. Then they swap roles.

Tell Sts to go back to the main lesson **9A**.

EXTRA SUPPORT If you think Sts need more practice, you may want to give them the **Vocabulary** photocopiable activity at this point.

EXTRA CHALLENGE Put Sts in pairs and get them to explain, in their own words, the difference between the following pairs of phrases:

1 *export a product* and *import a product*
2 *launch a product* and *market a product*
3 *take over a company* and *merge two companies*
4 *a boom* and *a recession*
5 *do business with sb* and *do a deal with sb*
6 *a consumer* and *a client*
7 *a manager* and *an owner*

6 PRONUNCIATION & SPEAKING changing stress on nouns and verbs

Pronunciation notes

Some words change their stress depending on whether they are verbs or nouns. The nouns are usually stressed on the first syllable, e.g. *an export*, *a record*, and the verbs on the second syllable, e.g. *to export*, *to record*. This section covers: *increase, decrease, import, progress, permit, produce, refund,* and *transport.*

Other words which behave in the same way include: *conduct, conflict, contract, impact, insult, object, permit, present, project, rebel, reject, repeat, subject, suspect.*

a 🔊 **9.8** Play the audio for Sts to listen and underline the stress in the **bold** words. You could pause the audio after each sentence and elicit the correct stress as you go, or check answers after you have played the audio.

Check answers.

1 ex<u>port</u> 2 <u>ex</u>port 3 in<u>crea</u>sed 4 <u>in</u>crease 5 pro<u>gre</u>ssing
6 <u>pro</u>gress 7 pro<u>du</u>ced 8 <u>pro</u>duce

🔊 **9.8**
1 We export to customers all over the world.
2 Our main export is wine.
3 Sales have increased by ten per cent this month.
4 There has been a large increase in profits this year.
5 The new building is progressing well.
6 We're making good progress with the report.
7 Most toys nowadays are produced in China.
8 The demand for organic produce has grown enormously.

EXTRA CHALLENGE Get Sts to underline the stress on the words in **bold** before playing the audio.

Now ask Sts which syllable is stressed when the word is a verb, and then when it is a noun.

a) verb – the second syllable is stressed
b) noun – the first syllable is stressed

EXTRA IDEA Get Sts to practise saying the sentences. They could do this individually or in pairs. You could get them to listen and repeat after the audio.

b Focus on the task and get Sts to practise saying the six words both ways, first as a verb, then as a noun, e.g. verb *decrease*, noun: *decrease*.

EXTRA SUPPORT Write the rule from **a** on the board for reference. Then say each word, first as a verb and then as a noun, getting Sts to listen and repeat after you.

Get Sts to practise in pairs.

Finally, get individual Sts to say the words.

EXTRA CHALLENGE Put Sts in pairs, **A** and **B**. Sts **A** say one of the words and Sts **B** have to say whether it is the verb or the noun. Sts then swap roles.

c Focus on the task. Then put Sts in pairs or small groups and get them to discuss each statement, giving as much information as possible.

Monitor and help Sts with any vocabulary they need.

Get some feedback for each statement.

EXTRA IDEA You could give Sts more statements to discuss, e.g.:

- *There has been a big increase in the price of food during the last year.*
- *Big companies rarely refund customers quickly for faulty goods or poor service.*
- *People prefer to use their own cars rather than public transport.*

9B Super cities

G uncountable and plural nouns
V word building: prefixes and suffixes
P word stress with prefixes and suffixes

Lesson plan

The context of this lesson is cities.

In the first half of the lesson, Sts read about author and philosopher Alain de Botton's vision on how to make a modern city attractive to live in. Sts then listen to five people who talk about the most beautiful city they have ever been to. Sts talk about which of the places mentioned they would like to visit, and their favourite and least favourite cities. This is followed by the grammar focus, where Sts extend their knowledge of uncountable nouns (e.g. *luggage*, *furniture*, etc.) and plural nouns (e.g. *news*, *politics*). They round off the first half with a speaking game to practise the grammar.

In the second half, Sts read an article about a city in South Korea, which was designed as a showpiece of modern urban design. This is followed by a speaking activity on modern cities and the changes population growth might have on a city. There is then a vocabulary focus on word building with prefixes and suffixes, followed by a pronunciation focus on word stress. Sts then practise the vocabulary by discussing different aspects of cities and regions they know. The lesson ends with Sts writing a report on the features of a city they know well.

More materials
For teachers
Photocopiables
Grammar uncountable and plural nouns *p.179*
Communicative Give your opinion *p.210*
(instructions *p.188*)
Vocabulary Word building *p.229* (instructions *p.216*)
For students
Workbook 9B
Online Practice 9B

OPTIONAL LEAD-IN – THE QUOTE

Write the quote at the top of *p.90* on the board and the name of the person who said it, or get Sts to open their books and read it.

You could tell Sts that Desmond Morris is an English zoologist and author on human sociobiology.

Ask Sts what they think the quote means and if they agree with it.

1 READING

a Focus on the questions. Elicit the difference between a *city* and a *town* (a city is larger and more important than a town).

Then put Sts in pairs and get them to answer the question and give their city a score.

Get some feedback. If all your Sts live in the same city (or near the same city), then do the questions as a whole-class activity.

EXTRA SUPPORT You could demonstrate the activity by talking about the city you come from if it isn't the same as your Sts.

b Focus on the task and make sure Sts know the meaning of *criteria* /kraɪˈtɪəriə/ (= standard or principle by which sth is judged). Point out that the 'criteria' being referred to are the six headings in the article. You could tell Sts that Alain de Botton is a Swiss-born British philosopher and author who has written on travel, architecture, love, and literature. His books have been bestsellers in 30 countries.

Put Sts in pairs and give them time to read the article.

When they have finished, they should explain the six criteria in their own words and then discuss the questions with their partner.

Check answers and elicit opinions on the two questions from various pairs.

EXTRA SUPPORT Before Sts read the article the first time, check whether you need to pre-teach any vocabulary.

1 *Order and variety* = well-organized, but not all the same
2 *Visible life* = seeing people in the streets
3 *Compactness* = limited size
4 *Orientation and mystery* = easy to find your way around, but with areas where you can wander and get a bit lost
5 *Scale* = relative size of buildings should be five floors
6 *Local colour* = having its own personality and using local materials

Deal with any other new vocabulary. Elicit or model the pronunciation of any tricky words.

c Focus on the task and example.

Give Sts time individually to think of some ideas. If Sts have problems thinking of more ideas, you could write some prompts on the board, e.g. WATER, GREEN SPACES, TREES, etc. Monitor and help with vocabulary if necessary.

Now put Sts in small groups of four or five. Get them to assign a 'secretary' to make the group list.

When all the groups have finished, elicit their ideas onto the board and have a class discussion.

2 LISTENING & SPEAKING understanding place names

a 🔊 **9.9** Focus on the task and elicit some cities for each country in 1–5. <u>Don't</u> tell Sts if they are correct or not.

Play the audio once for Sts to find out what the cities are.

Check answers by writing the names on the board.

9B 135

❗ Don't ask Sts if they have been to any of these cities, as they will be doing this later in the lesson.

EXTRA SUPPORT You could write the jumbled city names on the board to help Sts.

1 Venice 2 Curitiba 3 Bruges 4 Edinburgh 5 Kyoto

🔊 **9.9**
1 I think I'd have to say Venice in Italy.
2 The most beautiful city I've been to recently is probably Curitiba, which is in southern Brazil.
3 The most beautiful city I've ever been to is Bruges in Belgium.
4 I know lots of beautiful cities and…er…I wouldn't choose one above all the others, but one I always love going back to is Edinburgh in Scotland.
5 The most beautiful city I've been to is Kyoto in Japan.

b 🔊 **9.10** Focus on the task and make sure Sts understand what they have to do. Tell Sts that they are going to hear a list of places and they are going to complete the names – they are not going to hear sentences or the speakers talking about these places. Tell Sts to write what they hear and not to worry too much about the correct spelling.

Play the audio, pausing after each place to give Sts time to write.

Get Sts to compare with a partner, and then play the audio again if necessary.

Check answers by eliciting the places onto the board, and correct any spelling as necessary. Elicit / Explain the meaning of *wire* (= thin metal cable) and that *Alemão* = *German* in Portuguese.

🔊 **9.10**
Piazza **San Marco**
the **Rialto** Bridge
the **Grand** Canal
the **Wire** Opera House
the Bosque **Alemão**
the **Scotsman** Steps
the River **Leith**
the **Kinkaku-ji** Temple

c 🔊 **9.11** Tell Sts they are now going to listen to each speaker talking about the city they mentioned in **a**. They must identify the place the speaker mentions in each photo (in fact, they all show one of the places named in **b**). Sts then decide if it is something to see or do. They should also make a note of any other information they hear about it.

Play the audio, pausing after each speaker to give Sts time to make notes.

Get Sts to compare with a partner, and then play the audio again.

Check answers.

EXTRA SUPPORT Read through the script and decide if you need to pre-teach any new lexis before Sts listen.

1 A *vaporetto* on the Grand Canal in Venice. It's something to do. It's cheaper than going on a gondola.
2 The Wire Opera House. It's something to see. It's in the middle of an artificial lake in a park. It's made from steel tubes.
3 Having coffee and chocolates in the market square in Bruges. It's something to do. Most of the shops there sell chocolate. It's really beautiful.

4 The Scotsman Steps in Edinburgh. It's something to see. It's an artwork called *1059*. It's a marble staircase, and each step is a different colour.
5 A *ryokan* in Kyoto. It's something to do. It's a traditional Japanese guesthouse. You sleep on tatami matting and have rice, eggs, fish, and seaweed for breakfast.

🔊 **9.11**
(script in Student's Book on *pp.129–130*)
1
I think I'd have to say Venice in Italy. In spite of all the tourists, all the clichés, I still think it's the most beautiful city I know. I always remember the first time I went. I arrived by train, and we stepped out of the station, and suddenly it was all there – the canals, the wonderful old buildings. What makes it beautiful for me is the light, the combination of the reflections of the churches and palaces in the water, the wonderful winding streets alongside canals, which are all different but also all similar – it's an incredibly easy city to get lost in. And of course, the fact that there are no cars, no traffic. I fell totally in love with it that first time, and I've been back since then and loved it just as much. It's difficult to think of just one thing to see. I mean, Piazza San Marco is beautiful, the Rialto Bridge, but I wouldn't say they were the things I remember most. I would actually say just wander, without a map or a goal, and get lost. Everything is beautiful. The one thing I'd say to do is go on a *vaporetto* – a water bus – down the Grand Canal. I don't think gondolas are worth it – they're ridiculously expensive – and you can enjoy everything just as much on a *vaporetto*.

2
The most beautiful city I've been to recently is probably Curitiba, which is in southern Brazil. I think one of the things I liked about it most was it's described as the greenest city on Earth, and they've really focused on creating a quality public transportation system. There's a huge number of parks in Curitiba – in fact, there's so much grass that the local authority use sheep to cut the grass, not lawnmowers. And I just think that what I like about it is their commitment to trying to make the city an environmentally-friendly place to live. One place you need to see there is the Wire Opera House, which, it's built in the middle of an artificial lake, in the middle of a park, and it's built out of steel tubes, it's really extraordinary, and beautiful, I think. And if I had to recommend one thing to do, I'd say go for a walk in the Bosque Alemão – it's one of the wonderful parks in Curitiba – and visit the free environmental university which is built up in the trees just nearby. Its mission is to educate people about the environment, and I just think that's a wonderful goal to have.

3
The most beautiful city I've ever been to is Bruges in Belgium – well, I'm not absolutely sure if it's a city or a town, but anyway, it's my all-time favourite place. What makes it beautiful for me is the fact that it just looks as if it came out of a fairytale – it's…er…there are very old buildings that aren't too tall, and it's very traditional, and the whole place is like that. There's nothing super-modern, like skyscrapers, that breaks that illusion of being somewhere magical. There are lots of things to see – there are two really beautiful churches, but I think that the whole of the old city is just amazing to look at. And also there are hardly any cars, so you can just cycle or walk round. There are lots of canals with swans, I just sat there staring at everything and feeding the swans – it was so peaceful and beautiful. Something everyone who visits Bruges needs to do is go to the market, which is like a square with lots of shops. And most of the shops sell chocolate, which is one of the main things they sell in Bruges – and it's absolutely delicious, so I think you need to sit down and have a tea or a coffee and a couple of chocolates, just looking out on this really beautiful square.

4
I know lots of beautiful cities, and, er, I wouldn't choose one above all the others, but one I always love going back to is Edinburgh in Scotland. And something I really love about Edinburgh is that

136 **9B**

because it's quite compact, more or less wherever you are in the city, you can see outside the city – so you can see the sea, you can see the hills around – so you always have a sense of the city and the landscape, and I really like that. And one place, one thing I would recommend people to see in Edinburgh is something called the Scotsman Steps, which is a staircase that goes from the wall that joins the old town to the new town. And it's actually an artwork – it's called work number one oh five nine, by an artist called Martin Creed, and it's basically a staircase made of marble steps. Each one is a different colour marble, so you really have a feel of going somewhere – you're going from one colour to the next – and I love that place. And something I would do in Edinburgh would be to walk along the river Leith either way – either from the port of Leith up into the city, or the other way, because it's like a secret bit of Edinburgh, and you see Edinburgh from a different perspective.

5

The most beautiful city I've been to is Kyoto in Japan. It's a really lovely place because it's a mix of well, like, many Japanese cities: very, very modern buildings, and a lot of traditional…er…temple areas as well, and you can walk down any Japanese shopping street and find a big supermarket or a modern office block next to a little temple where you step back in time many centuries. The one place that I would recommend you see is the Kinkaku-ji temple, which is a very, very famous tourist site. It has a golden pavilion in the middle, and it's the most wonderful place. It gets very, very busy, but I was lucky enough to visit it when I lived in Japan, and I was able to stay with a friend and go there very early in the morning to avoid the crowds. One thing you need to do if you go to Kyoto is to try to stay not in a modern hotel, but in a ryokan, which is a traditional Japanese guest house where you can sleep on tatami matting and have…um…Japanese breakfast, which is rice, eggs, fish, and seaweed.

d Play the audio again for Sts to listen and write any other recommendations the speakers make. You could pause the audio after each speaker and elicit the recommendations.

Check answers.

1 Piazza San Marco, the Rialto Bridge, just wander without a map
2 Go for a walk in the Bosque Alemão, visit the environmental university
3 Two beautiful churches, just walk or cycle around the city, feed the swans in the canal
4 Walk along the River Leith, from the port to the city, or the other direction
5 Visit the Kinkaku-ji temple, with its golden pavilion

Now give Sts time, in pairs or individually, to look back at Alain de Botton's criteria in **1b** and decide if any of the speakers mentioned them.

Check answers.

Speaker 1   Orientation and mystery
Speaker 2   Scale
Speaker 3   Compactness

EXTRA SUPPORT If there's time, you could get Sts to listen again with the script on *pp.129–130*, so they can see exactly what they understood / didn't understand. Translate / Explain any new words or phrases.

e Finally, give Sts time, in pairs or individually, to look back at their own group list in **1c** and decide if any of the speakers mentioned their criteria.

Elicit any criteria from the group lists that were mentioned.

f Put Sts in small groups of three or four and get them to discuss the questions.

Monitor and help while Sts do the task.

Get feedback from various groups. You could do the first question as a whole-class activity. You could also tell the class your answers for questions 2 and 3.

3 GRAMMAR uncountable and plural nouns

a Focus on the task. Encourage Sts to use their instinct if they are not sure.

Get Sts to compare with a partner, and then check answers. Elicit why the other form is wrong and that these nouns (i.e. *advice*, *weather*, etc.) are uncountable, and so can't be used with *a* or in the plural in English, although this may be different in Sts' L1.

1 advice   2 some bad weather   3 accommodation is
4 too much luggage   5 the outskirts are   6 the staff were

b Tell Sts to go to **Grammar Bank 9B** on *p.149*.

Grammar notes

Uncountable nouns

- **Rules 1 and 2:** Sts will be familiar with the concept of countable (C) and uncountable (U) nouns, especially in the context of food, e.g. *an orange* (C), *some water* (U), etc. However, there are many non-food nouns which are uncountable in English, though they may be countable in Sts' L1, e.g. *information*, *advice*, *furniture*. Other uncountable nouns can be confusing because they end in *s* and so would seem to be plural, e.g. *politics*, *news*, but are uncountable. Here Sts are introduced to the most common nouns of these types and shown how to use some of them with *a piece of* to talk about individual items, e.g. *Do you want a piece of toast? I've just heard a very interesting piece of news. Some* can also be used with these words to mean an unspecified amount, e.g. *Do you want some toast? I've had some news from my parents about their new house.*

  As the list of nouns here is not very long, encourage Sts to learn them by heart.

- **Rule 3:** Sts probably already know the different uses of these words passively. Words like this include many materials, and also abstract nouns like *light* and *space*, which are uncountable but have a different meaning when they are countable. Check that Sts know the difference in meaning between the two forms, e.g.:

  business (= general word to describe commercial activity), *a business* (= a company)

  iron (= a metal), *an iron* (= a household tool used to make clothes smooth)

  light (= the energy from the sun), *a light* (= a lamp)

  paper (= the material), *a paper* (= a newspaper)

  space (= where the planets are), *a space* (= an area that is empty)

  time (= what is measured in minutes, hours, etc.), *a time* (= an occasion).

9B 137

Plural and collective nouns

- **Rule 1:** Make sure Sts know the meaning of these words, e.g. *belongings* = things that are yours. Remind Sts that words that can be used with *a pair of* can also be used with *some*. Other words in this group are *jeans*, *pyjamas*, *pants / knickers*, *tights*, *(sun)glasse*
- **Rule 2:** These nouns, though singular (*the crew*, *the family*, etc.), are often used with a plural verb, as they refer to a group of people. In some contexts, you can use *either*. However, *police* is an exception and is always used with a plural verb. Other similar words are *army*, *choir*, *class*, *firm*, *government*, *orchestra*, *(political) party*, *public*, and *school*.

Focus on the example sentences for **uncountable nouns** and play audio 🔊 **9.12** for Sts to listen and repeat. Encourage them to copy the rhythm. Then go through the rules with the class.

Repeat for **plural and collective nouns** 🔊 **9.13**.

Focus on the exercises and get Sts to do them individually or in pairs.

If they do them individually, get them to compare with a partner. Check answers, getting Sts to read the full sentences.

---

a
1 is **2** ✓ **3** look **4** ✓ (depending on whether you're thinking of them as individuals or as a team) **5** ✓
6 a piece of paper **7** some **8** some **9** progress **10** an

b
1 ✗ We had beautiful weather
2 ✗ some lovely furniture
3 ✓
4 ✗ a pair of scissors
5 ✓
6 ✗ some new trousers / a new pair of trousers
7 ✓
8 ✗ The homework was
9 ✓
10 ✗ The police are sure

Tell Sts to go back to the main lesson **9B**.

EXTRA SUPPORT If you think Sts need more practice, you may want to give them the **Grammar** photocopiable activity at this point.

c This is an oral grammar practice activity. You could tell Sts that *Just a minute* is a very popular radio programme on BBC Radio 4 and has been running since 1967.

Focus on the task and go through the rules with the class. Stress that Sts have to try and keep going for one minute and not 'dry up'. If a student hesitates for too long, then he or she is 'out', the time is paused, and the next student must continue speaking on the same topic until the minute is up. However, he / she mustn't just repeat things that the previous person said. Tell Sts to appoint one person in each group to be the timekeeper.

Give Sts a minute to look at all the topics.

Now put Sts in small groups of three or four and get them to decide which order they will go in.

Tell Sts to start, and the timekeeper to start the clock. After a minute is up, the next student in the group takes the next topic. Stop the activity either when Sts have been through all the topics, or each student has spoken at least twice. Monitor and help with the scoring.

Find out who got the most points.

4 READING & SPEAKING identifying advantages and disadvantages

a Focus on the task and then give Sts time to look at the photo.

Put Sts in pairs and get them to discuss the advantages and disadvantages of living in Songdo.

Elicit ideas from the class.

b Tell Sts that they are now going to read an article about Songdo. Before they start, tell them that Songdo is a new, smart city 65 kilometres south-west of Seoul. It now has approximately 100,000 inhabitants. Conceived in 2001, it was planned to be finished in 2015, but the city is still a work in progress. It is connected to Incheon International Airport by a 12.3-kilometre road bridge.

Put Sts in pairs and tell them to answer the questions with their partner when they have finished reading.

Check answers. You could also elicit the noun used meaning the same as *city* (*megacity*), and then tell Sts the definition of each word:

- *city* = a large and important town; in the UK, it is also a town that has a cathedral
- *megacity* = a very large city, usually one with a population of over ten million people

EXTRA SUPPORT Before Sts read the article the first time, check whether you need to pre-teach any vocabulary, but <u>not</u> the highlighted words or phrases.

---

1 Hi-tech services, e.g. the recycling of rubbish; many parks; eco-friendly, e.g. state of the art water recycling
2 It isn't a vibrant community. It isn't yet car-free.
3 Too wide roads, spread out across a wide area, not enough public transport, not enough residents to bring the city alive

---

c Tell Sts to read the article again. As they read, they should stop and focus on the highlighted words and phrases 1–8 and use the context to help them choose the best meaning, *a* or *b*.

Get Sts to compare with a partner, and then check answers.

---

1 a **2** b **3** b **4** a **5** a **6** b **7** b **8** b

Deal with any other new vocabulary. Elicit or model the pronunciation of any tricky words.

d Focus on the task and put Sts in pairs to discuss the questions.

Get some feedback for each question from various pairs. For question 3, you could have a class vote with a show of hands. You could also tell Sts which you would choose and why. If all your Sts are from the same city, you could do question 4 as a whole-class activity.

138 **9B**

5 VOCABULARY word building: prefixes and suffixes

a Focus on the **Prefixes and suffixes** box and go through it with the class. Note that in the example *pre-war*, the form changes as well as the meaning (i.e. from noun *war* to adjective *pre-war*).

EXTRA CHALLENGE Before reading the **Prefixes and suffixes** box, ask the class what prefixes and suffixes are and elicit some examples.

Give Sts time to answer the questions individually or in pairs.

Check answers, making sure Sts know the meaning of all the words. Elicit or model pronunciation.

---

1 a) mega   b) eco

2 abund**ance**   cold**ness**   connec**tion**   conveni**ence** develop**ment**   expecta**tion**   modern**ism** neighbour**hood**   pollu**tion**   sil**ence**

---

b Tell Sts to go to **Vocabulary Bank** Word building on *p.163*.

Vocabulary notes

Learning prefixes and suffixes which add meaning, and suffixes which change the form of a word, is one of the best ways to help Sts to expand their vocabulary.

You could remind Sts that a prefix is something that you add to the beginning of a word, usually to change its meaning, e.g. *pre* = before (e.g. *pre-war*). Note that, in the example given, the form changes as well from a noun (*before the war*) to an adjective.

Prefixes and suffixes which add meaning

Sts should already be familiar with some of these, e.g. *over-* and *under-*, and *-less* and *-ful*, but the others will probably be new to them, although some may exist in Sts' L1.

Nouns formed with suffixes

Sts will have seen several of these before, but here they are brought together and Sts are given clear rules for which type of words take which suffixes.

Focus on **1 Prefixes and suffixes which add meaning** and get Sts to do **a** individually or in pairs.

🔊 **9.14**   Now do **b**. Play the audio for Sts to listen and check.

Check answers.

🔊 9.14
Word building

1 Prefixes and suffixes which add meaning, b
1 G Mumbai is a very overcrowded city.
2 C Tokyo was one of the first megacities.
3 D This part of the city is very poor and underdeveloped.
4 B London is a very multicultural city, with many different races and religions.
5 J The quickest way to get around New York is on the subway.
6 H Many people in Montreal, Canada, are bilingual – they speak English and French.
7 E If you want to avoid the traffic jams in Bangkok, get the monorail.
8 F The autopilot was switched on after the plane had taken off.
9 A Vandalism, especially breaking public property, is very antisocial behaviour.

---

10 K I misunderstood the directions that man gave me, and now I'm completely lost.
11 I He's doing a postgraduate degree in aeronautical engineering.

Give further practice of any words your Sts find difficult to pronounce.

Get Sts to do **c** individually or in pairs.

🔊 **9.15**   Now do **d**. Play the audio for Sts to listen and check.

Check answers.

🔊 9.15
d
1 D There are a lot of homeless people in this city. The situation is hopeless.
2 A Be careful how you drive! The instructions were very useful.
3 C The police usually wear bullet-proof vests. My watch is waterproof.
4 B Their new laptops are completely unbreakable. I don't think the tap water here is drinkable.

Give further practice of any words your Sts find difficult to pronounce.

Now do **Activation** and get Sts to cover sentences 1–11 in **a**, look at meanings A–K, and say the prefixes.

EXTRA CHALLENGE Get Sts to cover meanings A–D in **c**, look at sentences 1–4, and remember the **bold** suffixes.

Now focus on **2 Nouns formed with suffixes** and go through the **Common noun suffixes** box with the class.

Get Sts to do **a** individually or in pairs.

🔊 **9.16**   Now do **b**. Play the audio for Sts to listen and check.

Elicit the answers onto the board, getting Sts to spell the words.

🔊 9.16
2 Nouns formed with suffixes
accommodation, intention, reduction
employment, entertainment, excitement, government, improvement
friendliness, loneliness, ugliness, weakness
absence, distance, ignorance, violence
alcoholism, racism, vandalism
brotherhood, childhood

Now either use the audio to drill the pronunciation of the words, or model and drill them yourself. Give further practice of any words your Sts find difficult to pronounce.

Focus on **Activation** and get Sts to cover the chart, look at the nouns in the list, and say them with the correct suffix.

Now focus on **3 Nouns which are different words** and go through the **Noun formation with spelling or word change** box with the class.

Get Sts to do **a** individually or in pairs.

🔊 **9.17**   Now do **b**. Play the audio for Sts to listen and check.

Check answers.

9B **139**

◆) 9.17

3 Nouns which are different words
1 **lose**, loss
2 **die**, death
3 **succeed**, success
4 **think**, thought
5 **believe**, belief
6 **hot**, heat
7 **strong**, strength
8 **hungry**, hunger
9 **high**, height
10 **wide**, width

Now either use the audio to drill the pronunciation of the words, or model and drill them yourself. Give further practice of any words your Sts find difficult to pronounce.

Finally, focus on **Activation** and get Sts to cover the column on the right, look at the verbs and adjectives on the left, and say the nouns.

Tell Sts to go back to the main lesson **9B**.

EXTRA SUPPORT If you think Sts need more practice, you may want to give them the **Vocabulary** photocopiable activity at this point.

6 PRONUNCIATION & SPEAKING word stress
with prefixes and suffixes

a Focus on the **Word stress on words with prefixes and suffixes** box and go through it with the class.

Now give Sts time to underline the main stressed syllable in the multi-syllable nouns and adjectives in the list. Encourage them to say the words out loud.

Get Sts to compare with a partner.

EXTRA SUPPORT Get Sts to do **a** in pairs.

b ◆) 9.18 Play the audio for Sts to listen and check. Check answers.

◆) 9.18

accommo<u>da</u>tion
anti<u>so</u>cial
bi<u>lin</u>gual
enter<u>tain</u>ment
<u>go</u>vernment
<u>home</u>less
<u>lone</u>liness
multi<u>cul</u>tural
<u>neigh</u>bourhood
over<u>crow</u>ded
<u>po</u>verty
underde<u>ve</u>loped
unem<u>ploy</u>ment
<u>van</u>dalism

Now give Sts time to practise saying the words.

EXTRA SUPPORT You could play the audio again, pausing after each word for Sts to listen and repeat.

c Put Sts in small groups of three or four and get them to discuss the questions, giving as much information as possible.

Monitor and help if necessary.

Get some feedback.

EXTRA SUPPORT Do some as whole-class questions.

7 WRITING a report

Tell Sts to go to **Writing A report** on *p.121*.

a Focus on the introduction to the report, and either read it out loud, or give Sts time to read it.

Focus on the question and do it as a whole-class activity.

Information about Milton Keynes, including history, features, facilities, and what it's like to live there

b Focus on the main paragraphs in the report and the task. Put Sts in pairs to match the headings to paragraphs 1–4.

Check answers.

1 History   **2** Present day   **3** Activities   **4** Culture

c Focus on the list of information, making sure Sts understand all the lexis, e.g. *layout*, etc.

Now tell Sts to tick all the items that are mentioned in the main paragraphs (1–4) of the report.

Check answers.

Sts should tick:
what the town planners wanted to achieve
the size of the town
the layout of the town
transport connections
things to do

d Tell Sts to read the conclusion of the report and complete the gap with the best option.

Check the answer.

the new town of Milton Keynes has been a success

e Focus on the instructions and then give Sts time, in pairs, to plan the content of their report of a city of their choice. You could tell Sts that they don't have to write about the same city as their partner – they are brainstorming ideas together at the moment.

f Focus on the **Useful language: Signposting** box and go through it with the class.

Now go through the instructions. Then either get Sts to write the report in class (set a time limit of, e.g. 20 minutes), or get them to write at home for homework.

g Sts should check their report for mistakes before giving it in.

8 & 9 Colloquial English Talking about... advertising

Lesson plan

In The Interview, the person interviewed is George Tannenbaum, an ad executive, who owns his own ad agency and is the director of an international one.

In The Conversation, Sts watch three people discussing whether people are influenced by advertising campaigns. Sts then discuss this question as well as a couple of other questions related to the topic, focusing on correcting something someone has said and phrases to make something clearer.

More materials
For teachers
Teacher's Resource Centre
Video Colloquial English 8&9
Quick Test 9
File 9 Test
For students
Workbook Colloquial English 8&9
........................Can you remember? 8&9
Online Practice Colloquial English 8&9
........................Check your progress

OPTIONAL LEAD-IN (BOOKS CLOSED)
Tell Sts that they are going to watch an interview with a man who makes adverts. Write the word JINGLE on the board and elicit / explain that it is a short song or tune which is used in advertising and is easy to remember.

Elicit from the class any jingles which are being used in their country now.

! Don't ask Sts if they remember any jingles from the past, as they will be doing this later in the lesson.

1 ▶ THE INTERVIEW Part 1

a Books open. Focus on the photo and the biographical information about George Tannenbaum. Either read it out loud or give Sts time to read it.

Focus on the question and do it as a whole-class activity.

b Focus on the **Glossary** and go through it with the class.

Now focus on the task and give Sts time to read questions 1–6.

Play the video (**Part 1**) once the whole way through for Sts to watch and answer the questions. Then play it again, pausing as necessary to give Sts time to write.

Get Sts to compare with a partner, and then check answers.

EXTRA SUPPORT Before playing the video, go through the listening scripts and decide if you need to pre-teach / check any lexis to help Sts when they listen.

1 His father's brother / His uncle and his father
2 In 1984
3 Talk when the commercials were on
4 Because they get into your head and you can't get them out, and you sometimes hear them several times a day.
5 Animated cartoons advertising cereal for children
6 Willie trips over a rock every day, so one day Wilhelmina tells him to move it. When he says he can't, as it is too big, she says she will do it. Willie says she isn't strong enough, but he is wrong – Wilhelmina eats H.O. Farina, so she is strong.

I = interviewer, G = George Tannenbaum

Part 1
I What first drew you to advertising as a career choice?
G What drew me to advertising was, actually, in a weird way, I had no choice – I'm a third-generation advertising guy. My father's brother – my uncle – who was fifteen years older than he, was in advertising, believe it or not, in the nineteen forties in Philadelphia. My father kind of took the baton from him, was in advertising, and I grew up with it, so I've been making a living in the business since nineteen eighty-four. It's a long time. It's thirty years.
I Do you still remember any commercials from your childhood?
G So I remember a lot of commercials. You know, growing up in an advertising household as we did, TV was more of a social event in those days – there wasn't a TV in every room, like, the family would gather to watch television. And, we were told not to talk, you know, during the commercials. We could talk during the shows, so I grew up kind of watching commercials. I remember a lot of commercials. I bet you most people of my… er…generation would remember a lot of…I feel kind of guilty saying this, because they are usually decried as not very creative, but you remember a lot of jingles.
I What do you think makes jingles memorable?
G Among purists in the field, jingles are, you know, laughed at – scoffed at – but God, you remember them. You know they – what do they call them, ear worms? They get into your head and you can't get them out sometimes, and you add that to, you know, almost everyday exposure six times a day – it's going to get in there. I can do…There was a, you know, there was a…there was a…I could sing one for you; there was a kids' hot cereal, a hot cereal for children called H.O. Farina, and it was an animated cartoon. It was very rudimentary. If you saw it today, you wouldn't believe it was a national-broadcast cartoon. And it was a little story of Willie and Wilhelmina, and Willie trips on a rock and he goes, 'Every day I trip over that rock, Wilhelmina.' And she says, 'Move it, Willie.' And he says, 'Can't, too big.' And I bet you I'm getting this word for word if you could find it. And she says, 'I will.' And he says, 'Huh, you're a girl.' And she picks it up and then the jingle comes up and it goes 'Strong Wilhelmina eats her Farina.' Like I said, I probably heard that five hundred times, maybe more, when I was growing up, because it was…it was every weekend for about eight years.

c Do the questions as a whole-class activity.

CE8&9 141

⏵ Part 2

a Focus on the **Glossary** and go through it with the class.

Give Sts time to read notes 1–4 and make sure they know what an *acronym* is (= a word formed from the first letters of the words that make up the name of something, for example, *NATO* is an acronym for *North Atlantic Treaty Organization*). Remind them to only write one or two words in each gap.

Now play the video (**Part 2**) once the whole way through. Then play it again, pausing as necessary to give Sts time to complete the task.

Get Sts to compare with a partner, and then check answers.

EXTRA SUPPORT When you play the video the second time, pause after each question has been answered and get Sts to compare what they have understood.

1	1 impact 2 communication 3 persuasion
2	**A**ttention, **I**nterest, **D**esire, **A**ction
3	getting impact, (giant) fan
4	incredibly important

Part 2

I What elements of a commercial are the most important?

G To me, a commercial basically is built in three parts. If you think of it as a pyramid, the top part of the pyramid I would say is impact. I have to intrude upon your life because you are probably working on your computer while you're watching TV or you're doing something, and when I'm talking about a TV commercial, it's the same for a web ad or an app. So, you have to get impact, you have to intrude, you have to kind of knock on the door. The second thing is communication – what do you want the person to know? And…and that needs to be clear and precise. And the third thing is the hardest: it's persuasion, because ultimately, you're running a commercial to get people to do something, so it's that amalgamation. Another way of talking about it – and this is old school – but there's an acronym, that probably comes from *Mad Men* era, that is called AIDA – you know, like the opera: Attention, Interest, Desire, Action.

I How do you feel about using celebrities to sell things?

G Sometimes it's a short…using a celebrity is a shortcut to…er… intrusion, because people pay attention to celebrities. Hopefully, it's a celebrity that has some bearing on the brand. I don't think if I was working on a depilatory, I'd want to use Tommy Lee Jones, but, um, that would just be gross. But, you know, if you find the right person, they can have special, um, special meaning, I think, and we do live in a celebrity culture, and people, you know, their ears perk up when they see a celebrity. So, if you go back to that pyramid I drew, it's a way of getting impact. I'm not a giant fan of it, but sometimes you do things you're not a giant fan of.

I On your website you say *I can make people laugh*. How important is humour in advertising?

G I tend not to be funny in TV commercials – I'm just…partly because I am a kind of cerebral guy, and I wind up having to use that more than humour, but I think humour is incredibly important in the business, and a lot of the commercials that really resonate with people, I think are funny – a lot of the movies, a lot of everything, you know.

b Do the questions as a whole-class activity.

⏵ Part 3

a Focus on the task and give Sts time to read the **Glossary** and sentences 1–5, making sure they understand all the lexis.

Now play the video (**Part 3**) once the whole way through for Sts to watch and complete the task.

Give Sts time to discuss what they understood with a partner. Then play the video again if necessary.

Check answers.

EXTRA SUPPORT When you play the video the second time, pause after each question has been answered and get Sts to compare what they have understood.

1	remain important
2	only well-made adverts
3	because they make people feel good about themselves
4	innovative
5	honest and clear

Part 3

I With all the technology, viral advertising, etc., do you think billboards and TV commercials have had their day?

G Have billboards and TV commercials had their day? You know what, I don't think so. I mean, I can tell you empirically and I can tell you rationally that seventy-five per cent of all media dollars is spent on broadcast, and I know it's, like, current to say, 'I don't have a TV' or 'I never watch TV', but people do. The fact is, TV viewership is at an all-time high. So I don't think TV is dead and I don't think billboards will be – you know, something as kind of passé as a billboard will be dead as long as, like, the highways are crowded, because you've got a captive audience. And until we can kind of pixelize ourselves and beam ourselves to work, I think there will be billboards. I mean, they can be effective.

I As a consumer, and obviously as an advertiser, does advertising influence the decisions you make?

G Yeah, you know, I'm very…I'm very susceptible to advertising. I think 'cause I tend to notice it. You know, I think I am very sensitive…er…to, um, I think I'm very sensitive to, um, stuff that isn't true. But when I see something that's well-crafted and appeals, I think, to both my head and my heart, you know, I think…I think I register those things.

I Is there an existing advertising campaign you wish you'd come up with, and why do you think it is so effective?

G Um. Is there an existing advertising campaign? Yeah, that I wish I did? There's a few. Um, I think the stuff that is being done for Nike, just in general for thirty years, has been exemplary, you know. They tapped into a mindset, and they made everyone feel like they were athletic, and they became kind of the gold standard, and they rarely hit a false note. Same thing with Apple, though people are just stressed in the industry about the latest direction Apple has been taking, which seems less sincere.

I Why do you think the Apple campaign is so effective?

G You know, Apple took…I think Apple is effective because they looked at an industry and they said, 'Here's what's wrong with the industry, and everything that that industry does, we're going to do differently.' So that industry, for years and years and years and years, was talking about speeds and feeds, and they were talking about six hundred and ninety-seven megahertz and four megabytes of RAM or gigabytes of RAM, whatever it is, and Apple just said, 'It works.' And they…what they did was say is that, 'You want to be creative? This machine makes you creative.' And they simplified…they simplified, and they were compelling, um, and they never lied, yeah.

b Do the questions as a whole-class activity. You could tell the class what you think, too.

142 **CE8&9**

2 ▶ LOOKING AT LANGUAGE

a This exercise focuses on a feature of spoken English which the interviewer illustrates – in this case using idiomatic language. Focus on the **Metaphors and idiomatic expressions** box and go through it with the class.

Now focus on the task and give Sts time to read extracts 1–7.

Play the video, pausing after each extract to give Sts time to write.

Check answers. You could tell Sts that the expression *perk up your ears* is American English, and in British English it is *prick up your ears*.

> **EXTRA CHALLENGE** Ask Sts if they can remember any of the missing words before they listen to the extracts.

> **1** ear **2** head **3** word **4** perk **5** day **6** audience
> **7** false

---

1 You know they, what do they call them, ear worms?
2 They get into your head and you can't get them out sometimes…
3 And I bet you I'm getting this word for word if you could find it.
4 …we do live in a celebrity culture, and people, you know, their ears perk up when they see a celebrity.
5 Have billboards and TV commercials had their day?
6 …because you've got a captive audience.
7 …they became kind of the gold standard, and they rarely hit a false note.

---

b Put Sts in pairs and give them time to discuss the meaning of each **bold** expression.

Elicit the meaning of each expression.

Deal with any vocabulary problems that arose, and get feedback from Sts on what parts they found hard to understand and why, e.g. speed of speech, etc.

> **EXTRA SUPPORT** If there's time, you could get Sts to watch again with subtitles, so they can see exactly what they understood / didn't understand. Translate / Explain any new words or phrases.

3 ▶ THE CONVERSATION

a Focus on the photo and tell Sts they are going to watch the three people answer a question, which they will see on the screen. Focus on the task and make sure Sts understand what they have to do.

Play the video and pause after the question. Remind Sts of the meaning of *advertising campaigns*.

Then play the video once the whole way through for Sts to watch and answer the question.

Check the answer.

> **EXTRA SUPPORT** Before playing the video, go through the listening script and decide if you need to pre-teach / check any lexis to help Sts when they listen.

> They conclude that everybody is influenced by advertising campaigns whether they want to be or not.

I = interviewer, Sy = Syinat, J = Joanne, S = Simon
I Do you think everybody is influenced by advertising campaigns?
Sy I think it is impossible to not be influenced by advertising these days because it's everywhere – it's on the buses, it's on the taxis, it's just on buildings…
S Yep.
Sy …so just by going outside you are seeing these advertisements and you're being influenced, so, for example, we, we, we all know certain brands just because they're everywhere around us. It doesn't mean that we're going to buy from them…
S No.
Sy …but you know them and you can recognize them, which is kind of the point of advertisements.
J It is.
S Indeed, yeah.
J I mean it's, it's, you know, exposure, over and over again, and gradually that sinks in. You know, we barely, we really don't really watch TV and we have a TV, we just don't watch it very much, I thought, 'Well actually that's some advertising out of the way of my children', but inevitably the radio's on, you hear jingles…
S Mhmm. Yep.
J …and that sound gets into your brain and they recognize things. And like you say, they see films on buses and they know 'That's the film I want to go see' because it's everywhere.
S And sometimes I find that you, you go to a supermarket and you buy a product and you think, 'I haven't bought that before, where, why am I suddenly buying this product?'…
J Yeah.
S …and it's because you've either seen it somewhere, someone's talked about it, it's been in a magazine and it's just in your head, and that's super subtle advertising. I mean, um, I never thought I was being influenced, but I think I am. I'm, I'm normally quite specific about what I buy – but suddenly, suddenly buying, I don't know, a different brand of blueberries or something for no reason, well, it's like, well, why did I do that? You know, so, there's definitely, you're definitely being influenced.
J It is, it's that recognition, isn't it? And subliminally, I think, if we recognize something, particularly if you're in a rush, you think, 'Yeah, I know that one', and you might buy that one.
S Yeah.
J I actually try to – because I have young children – I try to actually teach them a little bit so that they become more aware of what the advertisers are trying to do, um, because…
Sy Wow.
J Which is hard actually, you know, but you see pictures in magazines and they're starting to be – my eleven-year-old, is starting to become a little bit more cynical about what he sees, so he'll look at things and say, 'Mummy, that's not very good, they're just trying to get me to spend my money, and I don't like the way they're doing that'…
S And I know…
J …and I think, 'Yes, well done!'
S …apparently in Sweden they're not allowed to advertise to children under eleven at Christmas, so they're not allowed to target children after a certain time of day, which is a great idea because remember in the UK they just target you all the time with the latest toy and so forth, so that sort of advertising is blatant.
Sy Yeah, especially for children, I mean I, I have, I have younger siblings and it's kind of like 'Ooh, all of my friends have this toy, so I must have it as well', …
J Yes.
Sy …and actually I think if, if we were to remove that in England, that would be very good to kind of to teach them that actually self-worth comes from something else rather than from material possessions.
J That's right, it's part of this whole consumerist society that, that we live in, really.
S Yeah. So, I think, um, I think definitely I think that the answer to the question is yes, we are all influenced in different ways by advertising, I suppose. Yeah. What do you think?
J I agree. Whether we want to be or not.
S Yeah, sure.
J Sadly.

CE8&9 143

b Focus on the task and give Sts time to read sentences 1–6.

EXTRA CHALLENGE Put Sts in pairs to see if they can remember any of the information in 1–6.

Play the video again for Sts to mark the sentences *T* (true) or *F* (false).

Get Sts to compare with a partner, and then play again if necessary.

Check answers.

1 T **2** F **3** T **4** F **5** T **6** F

EXTRA SUPPORT If there's time, you could get Sts to watch again with subtitles, so they can see exactly what they understood / didn't understand. Translate / Explain any new words or phrases.

c Either do the questions as a whole-class activity, or put Sts in pairs and then get some feedback.

d Highlight that the focus here is on understanding and helping them unpick the kind of language they are likely to hear in unplanned conversations, rather than teaching them useful phrases.

Focus on the task and give Sts time to read 1–5.

Play the video for Sts to watch and focus on the highlighted phrases. Pause after each one to give them time to complete the phrase.

Get Sts to compare with a partner, and then play again if necessary.

Check answers.

1 we all know **2** really don't really **3** starting to become
4 I have, I have **5** I think
a) give themselves time to think 4, 5
b) make something clearer 1, 2, 3

---

1 …and you're being influenced, so, for example, we, we all know certain brands just because they're everywhere around us.
2 You know, we barely, we really don't really watch TV and we have a TV, we just don't watch very much…
3 …but you see pictures in magazines and they're starting to be – my eleven-year-old, is starting to become a little bit more cynical about what he sees…
4 Yeah, especially for children, I mean I, I, I have, I have younger siblings and it's kind of like 'Ooh, all of my friends have this toy, so I must have it as well'
5 So, I think, um, I think definitely I think that the answer to the question is yes…

Highlight that in 1–3 the speaker stops and then starts again in a slightly different way, because she wants to be clearer or more exact. In 4 and 5 the speaker simply repeats something while he / she is organizing his / her ideas.

e Put Sts in small groups of three if possible. Focus on the questions, and check Sts understand what they mean. Then set a time limit for Sts to discuss them.

Monitor and help, and remind them them to simply start a phrase again if they think they could express themselves better, or to repeat a word or phrase if they need to give themselves time to think.

Get feedback from various groups. You could also tell the class what you think.

144 **CE8&9**

10A Science fact, science-fiction

G quantifiers: *all, every, both*, etc.
V science
P stress in word families

Lesson plan

The topic of this lesson is science.

In the first half, Sts begin by revising science-related vocabulary through doing a quiz of questions commonly asked by children that parents struggle to answer, and then listening to an expert answering each question. The vocabulary focus is on more words related to science, and Pronunciation deals with changing stress in word families (e.g. *science, scientist, scientific*). The first half ends with Sts interviewing each other about science-related issues.

In the second half of the lesson, Sts read about the plausibility of some of the ideas in science-fiction, and whether they might actually become reality. Then the grammar – revision and extension of the use of a variety of quantifiers – is presented through sentences from the article, and finally practised in another science quiz.

More materials
For teachers
Photocopiables
Grammar quantifiers: *all, every, both*, etc. *p.180*
Communicative Science quiz *p.211* (instructions *p.188*)
For students
Workbook 10A
Online Practice 10A

OPTIONAL LEAD-IN – THE QUOTE

Write the quote at the top of *p.96* on the board and the name of the person who said it, or get Sts to open their books and read it.

You could elicit from Sts any other information they know about Marie Curie (1867–1934), e.g. she was both a physicist and a chemist. In 1903, Pierre Curie (Marie's husband), Marie Curie, and Henri Becquerel were awarded the Nobel Prize in physics. Marie Curie was the first woman to win a Nobel Prize, and the only woman to have won two Nobel Prizes, as in 1911, she won the Nobel Prize in chemistry.

Ask Sts what they think the quote means and if they agree with it.

1 SPEAKING & LISTENING understanding scientific explanations

a Focus on the cartoon and give Sts time to read it. If they are having trouble with the handwriting font, you could read it to them: *Well, rain is liquid water in the form of droplets that have condensed from atmospheric water vapour and then become heavy enough to fall under gravity. The major cause of rain production is moisture moving along three-dimensional zones of temperature…*

Now elicit opinions from the class.

Elicit that the answer is probably too detailed and boring for the child to understand. Ask Sts if they know parents or children like this, or have had a similar experience.

b Put Sts in pairs and get them to read the article. Then with their partner, they should try to explain the meaning of the highlighted words, which are all related to science. Remind them to use the context to help them guess. Tell them <u>not</u> to answer the questions yet.

Check answers. Elicit or model pronunciation.

> **reflect** /rɪˈflekt/ = throw back light (or heat, sound, etc.) from a surface
> **scatter** /ˈskætə/ = throw or drop things in different directions so that they cover an area of ground
> **dissolve** /dɪˈzɒlv/ = mix with a liquid and become part of it
> **rotate** /rəʊˈteɪt/ = move or turn around a central fixed point
> **moist** /mɔɪst/ = slightly wet
> **gas** /gæs/ = any substance like air that is neither a solid nor a liquid, for example hydrogen and oxygen
> **particle** /ˈpɑːtɪkl/ = a very small piece of sth
> **water vapour** /ˈwɔːtə ˈveɪpə/ = a mass of very small drops of water in the air
> **gravity** /ˈgrævəti/ = the force that attracts objects in space towards each other, and that on the Earth pulls them towards the centre of the planet, so that things fall to the ground when they are dropped

c Now give Sts time, individually or in pairs, to answer questions 1–8.

Deal with any other new vocabulary. Elicit or model the pronunciation of any tricky words.

d 🔊 **10.1** Tell Sts they are now going to listen to a scientist answer each question.

Play the audio, pausing after each fact has been mentioned, and elicit the answer.

Finally, find out with a show of hands if any Sts got all the answers correct. Ask how many questions Sts already knew the answer to, and which information was new to them.

EXTRA SUPPORT Read through the script and decide if you need to pre-teach any new lexis before Sts listen.

1 B	2 B	3 A	4 B	5 A	6 A	7 B	8 A

10A 145

◆) 10.1
(script in Student's Book on *p.130*)
C = child, S = scientist

1
C Why is the sky blue?
S To understand why the sky is blue, we first need to understand a little about light. Although light from the Sun looks white, it's really made up of many different colours, as we see when they are spread out in a rainbow. Light is like a wave of energy, and each colour has a different wavelength. Red is the longest, and blue and violet are the shortest. When the Sun's light reaches the Earth's atmosphere, it's scattered by tiny molecules of gas in the air. Shorter wavelengths – violet and blue – are scattered the most widely, and our eyes are much more sensitive to blue than violet, so we see more of the blue light than the other colours. So that's why we see the sky as blue.

2
C Why is the sea salty?
S Most of our planet's surface is covered in salt water. But where does the salt come from? Well, some of it comes from rocks on the bottom of the sea, but most of it actually comes from the land around us. Every time it rains, tiny amounts of mineral salts dissolve into rivers, and these eventually get to the sea. Rivers aren't very salty, because they flow continually, but the Sun's heat causes the seawater to evaporate, so the salt in the sea becomes more concentrated.

3
C Why can we sometimes see the moon during the day?
S We all know that the Sun produces a lot of strong light. So, when it's in the sky, we can't see the stars or the other planets. The moon doesn't produce light – it reflects the light of the Sun. The moon is visible for about twelve out of every twenty-four hours because of the way it rotates around the Earth. This means it's visible for some time during daylight nearly every day.

4
C Why do we have a leap year?
S The one about leap years. A year is the amount of time it takes the Earth to go around the Sun, and we've divided our calendar year into three hundred and sixty-five days. However, it actually takes the Earth three hundred and sixty-five days, five hours, forty-eight minutes and forty-five seconds to go round the Sun. To deal with this difference, we add one day (twenty-four hours) to our calendar every four years. This adjustment is not exactly correct, because it effectively adds six hours per year rather than the exact amount of the difference.

5
C Why do we blink?
S A 'blink of an eye' lasts only a tenth of a second. Every time you blink, your eyelids spread fluid across the surface of your eyes, to keep them moist, and also to stop them getting dirty. Blinking also keeps eyes safe from things that might damage them, such as bright light and, sometimes, bigger objects coming into our eyes, like a small stone. Blinking stops the activity in your brain that detects changes, so you never notice that you actually stop seeing for a very short time when you blink.

6
C Why does cutting onions make us cry?
S For a vegetable, onions have very complicated chemistry. When you cut them, a chemical reaction changes molecules in the onion into a gas. When this gas reaches the cornea – the transparent layer that covers and protects the outer part of your eye – the cornea senses it as an irritant. It acts to protect your eyes by making you cry, and the tears clean your eyes.

7
C What is a cloud?
S We all enjoy looking at clouds and seeing their different shapes, but what's the science behind them? Well, the sky is full of drops of water. But most of the time, you can't see them, because they are too small; the drops have turned into water vapour. As the water vapour goes higher in the sky, the air gets cooler. The cooler air causes the drops to start to stick to things, like bits of dust, ice, or sea salt, which make them visible. So that's what we see when we see clouds.

8
C What is a black hole?
S This is another physics question. A black hole is caused by gravity. There are places in space where gravity pulls so hard that even light cannot get out. The reason that gravity is so strong in a black hole is that a lot of matter – that's physical 'stuff' – has been compressed into a tiny space. A lot of matter has a high mass, and this creates a strong gravitational pull. Inside a black hole, space is falling faster than light, which is why light can't escape.

e Focus on the task and then get Sts, in pairs, to discuss what extra information they can remember about each statement.

Then play the audio again, pausing after each statement to give Sts time to write.

Get Sts to compare with their partner, and then play again if necessary.

Check answers.

1 Our eyes are more sensitive to blue than to violet.
2 It causes it to evaporate.
3 12
4 The adjustment adds six hours rather than the exact difference.
5 It stops the activity that detects changes.
6 It protects the outer part of your eye.
7 It makes the drops of water start to stick to things like dust.
8 It creates a strong gravitational pull.

EXTRA SUPPORT If there's time, you could get Sts to listen again with the script on *p.130*, so they can see exactly what they understood / didn't understand. Translate / Explain any new words or phrases.

f Do this as a whole-class activity. You could elicit a simple explanation for each question in **b** from different Sts.

2 VOCABULARY & PRONUNCIATION
science; stress in word families

Pronunciation notes
In some 'word families', i.e. groups of words from the same root, the stress is always on the same syllable, e.g. in all the words related to *physics* (*physical*, *physicist*), the stress is on the first syllable. In others, however, the stress shifts, e.g. *scientist*, *scientific*, and these groups are often problematic.

a Focus on the task and the first column of the chart. Explain that the answers to questions 1–8 are the names of the subjects Sts need to complete in the chart. Point out that the first one (*science*) has been done for them.

Give Sts time to do the task individually or in pairs. Make sure they <u>only</u> complete the first column.

b ◆) **10.2** Play the audio for Sts to listen and check.

Check answers.

◆) 10.2
1 science
2 physics
3 chemistry
4 biology
5 astronomy
6 genetics
7 botany
8 zoology

146 10A

Now focus on the other two columns in the chart and the examples. Give Sts time, individually or in pairs, to complete the rest of the chart.

c ◉ **10.3** Play the audio for Sts to listen and check.
Check answers.

❗ Some Sts may come up with the word *physician*. If they do, explain that this is also related to physics, but does not mean a scientist who studies physics. It is another (old-fashioned) word for a doctor.

> See words in script 10.3

Now focus on the **Stress in word families** box and go through it with the class.

Play the audio again, pausing after each word or group of words for Sts to underline the stressed syllables.

Check answers by writing the words on the board and underlining the stressed syllables.

> <u>phy</u>sics, <u>phy</u>sicist, <u>phy</u>sical
> <u>chem</u>istry, <u>chem</u>ist, <u>chem</u>ical
> bi<u>o</u>logy, bi<u>o</u>logist, bio<u>log</u>ical
> a<u>stron</u>omy, a<u>stron</u>omer, astro<u>nom</u>ical
> <u>gen</u>etics, ge<u>net</u>icist, ge<u>net</u>ic
> <u>bot</u>any, <u>bot</u>anist, bo<u>tan</u>ical
> zo<u>o</u>logy, zo<u>o</u>logist, zoo<u>log</u>ical

◉ **10.3**
1 science, scientist, scientific
2 physics, physicist, physical
3 chemistry, chemist, chemical
4 biology, biologist, biological
5 astronomy, astronomer, astronomical
6 genetics, geneticist, genetic
7 botany, botanist, botanical
8 zoology, zoologist, zoological

Now elicit in which groups the stress changes on the adjective.

> The adjectives from *science*, *biology*, *astronomy*, *botany*, and *zoology* have the stress on a different syllable from the base word.

EXTRA CHALLENGE Get Sts to underline the stressed syllables in the words before they listen to the audio for the second time. Get feedback, and then play the audio for Sts to listen and check.

d Give Sts time to practise saying the word groups. They could do this individually or in pairs.

EXTRA SUPPORT Drill the pronunciation with the whole class first, and then get them to practise in pairs. You could use the audio to do this.

EXTRA CHALLENGE Ask Sts if they can think of any more scientific word families, e.g. *oceanography*, *geology*, *anthropology*, *psychology*, *sociology*, etc.

e ◉ **10.4** Focus on the task and make sure Sts understand that they are only going to hear phrases, not sentences.
Play the audio, pausing after each phrase to give Sts time to write.

Check answers, by eliciting the phrases onto the board. Explain / Elicit the meaning of each phrase.

> **genetically modified** = having had its genetic structure changed artificially, so that it will produce more fruit or not be affected by disease
> **botanical gardens** = a park where plants, trees, and flowers are grown for scientific study
> **chemical reaction** = a chemical change produced by two or more substances acting on each other
> **human biology** = the scientific study of man
> **physical energy** = the ability to put effort and enthusiasm into an activity, work, etc.
> **astronomically expensive** = extremely expensive

◉ **10.4**
1 genetically modified
2 botanical gardens
3 chemical reaction
4 human biology
5 physical energy
6 astronomically expensive

f Focus on the task and go through the words in the list. Elicit / Explain *guinea pigs* /ˈgɪni pɪgz/, *laboratory* /ləˈbɒrətri/, and *theory* /ˈθɪəri/.

Give Sts time to complete the sentences. Point out that the first one (*experiments*) has been done for them.

Get them to compare with a partner.

g ◉ **10.5** Play the audio for Sts to listen and check.

Check answers. As Sts have previously seen the word *trial* in relation to crime, you might want to explain / elicit the meaning of the phrase *clinical trial* in 6 (= the process of testing the ability, quality or performance of sb / sth, especially before you make a final decision about them).

> 1 laboratory   2 discovery   3 theory   4 drugs, tests
> 5 research, side effects   6 guinea pigs   7 clone

◉ **10.5**
1 Scientists carry out experiments in a laboratory.
2 Archimedes made an important discovery in his bath.
3 Isaac Newton's experiments proved his theory that gravity existed.
4 Before a pharmaceutical company can sell new drugs, they have to do tests to make sure they are safe.
5 Scientists have to do a lot of research into the possible side effects of new drugs.
6 People can volunteer to be guinea pigs in clinical trials.
7 In nineteen ninety-six, scientists were able for the first time to clone a sheep, which they named Dolly.

Now get Sts to underline the stress on the **bold** multi-syllable words in 1–6.

Play the audio again, pausing after each sentence.

Check answers.

> 1 <u>car</u>ry   4 pharma<u>ceu</u>tical <u>com</u>pany   6 vol<u>un</u>teer, <u>clin</u>ical <u>tri</u>als

Give Sts time to practise saying the sentences.

10A 147

3 SPEAKING

The vocabulary from **2** is now put into practice in this speaking activity.

Focus on the instructions and make sure Sts understand what they have to do.

Put Sts in pairs, **A** and **B**, and give them time to read the questions. Check Sts understand the word *cosmetics* (= a substance that you put on your face or body to make it more attractive).

Then get Sts **A** to ask Sts **B** the questions in the green circles. Encourage Sts **B** to answer each question in as much detail as possible and Sts **A** to ask follow-up questions to extend the conversation. Sts **B** then ask Sts **A** the questions in the blue circles. Alternatively, you could do this activity as a small-group discussion.

Monitor and help, correcting any mispronunciation of the new lexis.

Get feedback from the whole class on some of the questions.

EXTRA CHALLENGE Sts could return the questions they answer by saying *What about you?*, or if they finish quickly, ask each other the questions which they previously answered.

EXTRA IDEA Get Sts to choose two or three questions to ask you after they have done the activity.

4 READING   understanding the language of speculation

a Focus on the task. Go through the questions, making sure Sts understand all the lexis, e.g. *teleport*, *invisible*, etc. Try to exploit the information that Sts already know.

Put Sts in pairs and give them time to discuss the questions.

Get some feedback.

b Focus on the instructions and make sure Sts understand what they have to do. Make sure Sts know who Harry Potter is (*a boy wizard who has an invisibility cloak, in the books by J.K. Rowling*). Sts don't need to know exactly what quantum information is; if they ask, then you could tell them that it's a tiny amount of electromagnetic energy. Quantum theory is a complex concept in physics, but it essentially refers to information about the physical world at an atomic and subatomic level, where the traditional laws of physics no longer apply.

Give Sts time to read the article individually and score each concept in **a** from 1 (= very unlikely) to 5 (= very likely).

Get Sts to compare with a partner, and then elicit opinions.

EXTRA SUPPORT Before Sts read the article the first time, check whether you need to pre-teach any vocabulary, but not the highlighted words and phrases.

c Focus on the task and make sure Sts understand what they have to do. Put Sts in pairs, and tell them to look at the context and check what the highlighted words and phrases refer to in the text. You could do the first one (*plausible*) with the class, and then get Sts to continue in pairs.

Check answers.

a) quite likely	b) not very likely, but possible	c) extremely unlikely
plausible	could in theory	a long way from
a real possibility	might be possible	faces extreme obstacles
	quite a way off	only speculative
	might be achievable	far-fetched
	not totally implausible	

Deal with any other new vocabulary. Elicit or model the pronunciation of any tricky words.

EXTRA SUPPORT You could do up to half of the phrases as a whole-class activity, and then get Sts to complete the rest in pairs.

d Focus on the task and go through the **Talking about future possibilities** box with the class.

Put Sts in small groups or pairs to discuss which ideas in the article they think might happen in the next 50 years, which they would like to happen, and which will never happen. Encourage them to give reasons for their answers.

Get some feedback from various groups or pairs.

e Focus on the phrases in the list and make sure Sts know what they mean.

Now put Sts in small groups of three or four and get them to discuss how likely each one is to happen and whether it would be a good thing or not.

Get some feedback from various groups for each item. Find out if there were any disagreements in any groups.

5 GRAMMAR   quantifiers: *all, every, both*, etc.

a Focus on the instructions. Point out to Sts that they are going to be looking at quantifiers – all of which they probably will have seen before. However, the rules of use will probably be new, although they may instinctively know what sounds correct.

Give Sts time to circle the correct form, and then check answers. If Sts ask why, say that they are now going to the **Grammar Bank** to find out.

1 all   **2** All the   **3** everything   **4** No   **5** Both   **6** Neither

b Tell Sts to go to **Grammar Bank 10A** on *p.150*.

Grammar notes

Sts will have frequently seen and heard all the quantifiers they learn here and should know what they mean.

The rules here have been simplified (i.e. there are some other uses or positions which we haven't referred to). If Sts find the rules a little overwhelming, focus particularly on the examples and encourage them to use their instinct when they do the exercises and are not sure which form to choose. For example, a phrase like *every animals* should sound wrong, even if they can't remember why.

all, every, most

You might want to point out that *all* can sometimes be used without a noun when it is followed by a relative clause, e.g. *I've forgotten all (that) I learned at school / everything (that) I learned at school.*

- **Rule 4:** You could also point out that the verb agrees with the object pronoun, e.g. *all of them are, most of it is,* etc.

no, none, any

Sts should know the difference between *no* and *none*, but the use of *none of* + pronoun / noun, and *any* meaning it doesn't matter what / who, etc., may be new. They may still be making mistakes with double negatives (NOT ~~we haven't got no time~~), or using *any* on its own to mean *none*. In **rule 1**, remind Sts that *any* can also be used without a noun, e.g. *Would you like some tea? No thanks, I don't feel like any right now.*

both, neither, either

You may also want to point out that you can use *not* + *either* instead of *neither…nor*, e.g. *Neither Tim nor Andrew can come. Tim can't come and Andrew can't (come), either.* This is also more informal than *neither…nor*, which can sound quite formal in spoken English.

Focus on the example sentences for **all, every, most** and play audio 🔊 **10.6** for Sts to listen and repeat. Encourage them to copy the rhythm. Then go through the rules with the class.

Go through the **every and all + time expressions** box with the class.

Repeat for **no, none, any** 🔊 **10.7** and **both, neither, either** 🔊 **10.8**.

Focus on the exercises and get Sts to do them individually or in pairs.

If they do them individually, get them to compare with a partner. Check answers, getting Sts to read the full sentences.

a
1 Most of   2 Everything   3 Most   4 every   5 any   6 None
7 Anybody   8 neither   9 no

b
1 ✗ Both the kitchen and the bathroom need cleaning.
2 ✗ The food wasn't cheap or tasty. / The food was neither cheap nor tasty.
3 ✓
4 ✗ My sister and I were both late for school.
5 ✗ It's either Jane's or Karen's birthday today.
6 ✓
7 ✗ Neither of my best friends called to see how I was.
8 ✗ We can either walk or take the bus.
9 ✓
10 ✓

Tell Sts to go back to the main lesson **10A**.

EXTRA SUPPORT   If you think Sts need more practice, you may want to give them the **Grammar** photocopiable activity at this point.

c This is an oral grammar practice activity. Focus on the quiz and give Sts time to do it in pairs. You might want to check Sts know the meaning of some of the words, e.g. *a current*, *intense*, and *a circuit*. Tell Sts to write the number and correct option *a*, *b*, or *c* on a separate piece of paper.

Elicit some ideas from Sts, but <u>don't</u> tell them if they are correct or not.

d 🔊 **10.9**   Play the audio for Sts to listen and check.

Check answers. Find out which pair got the most correct answers.

1 a   **2** c   **3** b   **4** a   **5** b   **6** c   **7** b   **8** c   **9** c   **10** a

🔊 **10.9**
1 In direct current, the electrons move in only one direction.
2 Helium gas can be found in both liquid and solid form.
3 Adult giraffes remain standing all day.
4 Of all the water on our planet, hardly any of it is found underground.
5 Snakes eat either other animals or eggs.
6 A diamond can be destroyed only by intense heat.
7 The human brain can continue to live without oxygen for nearly six minutes.
8 In our solar system, Pluto is no longer considered to be a planet.
9 When we breathe out, some of that air is oxygen.
10 An individual blood cell makes a whole circuit of the body in nearly sixty seconds.

10A

10B Free speech

G articles
V collocation: word pairs
P pausing and sentence stress

Lesson plan

The topic of this final lesson is public speaking.

In the first half, Sts begin by listening to a programme about the controversy surrounding Neil Armstrong's famous words when he stepped on the moon (Did he make a mistake by omitting an indefinite article?). This leads into the Grammar, where Sts revise and extend their knowledge of use and non-use of the definite and indefinite articles. Sts then read a short text about what makes a good speech according to Cicero, before focusing on eight sound bites from famous speeches. Then they read about the circumstances in which four of the speeches were written. Sts discuss which speech they would most like to have heard, great speakers they know of, and past or present politicians who are either good or bad speakers.

In the second half of the lesson, Sts listen to a radio programme in which an expert gives tips for giving a good presentation and a young woman talks about an international public speaking competition she took part in. The vocabulary focus is on word pairs joined with *and* and *or*, e.g. *sick and tired*, *all or nothing*. Then in Pronunciation, Sts learn how pausing in the correct places and stressing sentences correctly will make them much easier to understand if they are giving a presentation in English. They then have the opportunity to give a short presentation to the class. The lesson ends with a documentary on speaking in public.

More materials

For teachers

Photocopiables
Grammar articles *p.181*
            Revision Grammar Auction *p.182*
Communicative General knowledge quiz *p.212*
(instructions *p.189*)
            Revision *p.213* (instructions *p.189*)
Vocabulary Revision *p.230* (instructions *p.217*)

Teacher's Resource Centre
Video Giving presentations: a voice coach

For students

Workbook 10B

Online Practice 10B

OPTIONAL LEAD-IN – THE QUOTE

Write the quote at the top of *p.100* on the board and the name of the person who said it, or get Sts to open their books and read it.

You could tell Sts that Dale Carnegie (1888–1955) was an American writer and lecturer, and the developer of famous courses in self-improvement, salesmanship, corporate training, public speaking, and interpersonal skills. He wrote

How to Win Friends and Influence People in 1936, which is still a bestseller today.
Ask Sts if they agree with him.

1 GRAMMAR articles

a Do this as a whole-class activity.

Neil Armstrong was the first man to walk on the moon in 1969 (on 20 July).

b 🔊 **10.10** Tell Sts that they are going to hear the original recording of Neil Armstrong speaking from the moon. Warn them that, understandably, the recording is quite crackly.

Play the audio for Sts just to listen.

Now play it again and get Sts to complete the gaps.

Get Sts to compare with a partner, and then check answers.

small, man, mankind

🔊 **10.10**
(Neil Armstrong original recording)
That's one small step for man, one giant leap for mankind.

Put Sts in pairs and get them to answer questions 1 and 2. Check answers.

1 *a step* = the act of lifting your foot and putting it down in order to walk or move somewhere
a leap = a long or high jump; a sudden large change or increase in sth
2 *mankind* = all humans, thought about as one large group; the human race

c 🔊 **10.11** Tell Sts they are going to listen to an interview about the moon landing. Focus on the three questions they need to answer and make sure they know the meaning of *controversy*.

Play the audio once the whole way through for Sts to listen and answer the questions.

Get Sts to compare with a partner, and then if necessary, play the audio again.

Check answers.

The controversy is whether he said 'one small step for man' or 'one small step for a man'. The version without *a* doesn't really make sense.
'One small step for a man' means one small step for an individual human being.
'One small step for man' means one small step for all men, i.e. the human race (which is the same as *mankind*).
New technology proved him right.

🔊 **10.11**
(script in Student's Book on *p.130*)
P = presenter, J = James
P When Neil Armstrong became the first man to walk on the moon on July the twentieth nineteen sixty-nine, a global audience of five hundred million people were watching and listening. As he climbed down the steps from the spacecraft and stepped onto

150 **10B**

the moon, they heard him say, 'That's one small step for man, one giant leap for mankind.' It seemed like the perfect quote for such a momentous occasion. But from the moment he said it, people have argued about whether Armstrong got his lines wrong and made a mistake. James, tell us about it.

J Well, Armstrong always said that he wrote those words himself, which became some of the most famous and memorable words in history, during the time between landing on the moon and actually stepping out of the capsule onto the moon. That was nearly seven hours.

P And so what is the controversy about what Armstrong said when he stepped down the ladder, onto the moon?

J The question is: did he say, 'one small step for *man*' or 'one small step for *a* man'? That's to say: did he use the indefinite article or not? It's just a little word, but there's a big difference in meaning. Armstrong always insisted that he wrote *one small step for a man, one giant leap for mankind*. Of course, this would have been a meaningful sentence. If you say *a man*, then it clearly means that this was one small step for an individual man, i.e. himself, but one giant leap for mankind – that's to say men and women in general. But what everybody actually heard was, 'one small step for man, one giant leap for mankind', with no indefinite article, and that sentence means, 'one small step for people in general, one giant leap for people in general.' And that doesn't really make sense.

P So did he just get the line wrong when he said it?

J Well, Armstrong himself was never sure if he actually said what he wrote. In his biography, *First Man*, he told the author James Hansen, 'I must admit that it doesn't sound like the word *a* is there. On the other hand, certainly the *a* was intended, because that's the only way it makes sense.' He always regretted that there had been so much confusion about it.
But almost four decades later, Armstrong was proved to be right. Peter Shann Ford, an Australian computer expert, used very hi-tech sound techniques to analyse his sentence, and he discovered that the *a* was said by Armstrong. It's just that he said it so quickly that you couldn't hear it on the recording, which was broadcast to the world on the twentieth of July nineteen sixty-nine.

P Was Armstrong relieved to hear this?

J Yes, he was. I think it meant a lot to him to know that he didn't make a mistake.

d Tell Sts they are going to listen to the interview again and this time they need to answer questions 1–6. Give Sts time to read the questions.

Play the audio again once the whole way through for Sts to listen and answer the questions.

Get Sts to compare with a partner, and then, if necessary, play the audio again.

Check answers.

1 During the time (nearly seven hours) between landing on the moon and actually stepping out of the capsule onto the moon
2 He says he wrote *That's one small step for a man*…
3 Because that sentence means 'one small step for people in general, one giant leap for people in general'.
4 He thought he said, 'one small step for a man…'.
5 He is an Australian computer expert who used very hi-tech sound techniques to analyse Armstrong's sentence.
He discovered that, in fact, Armstrong *did* say **a** *man*, but he said it so quickly that you can only hear it with special sound equipment.
6 He felt relieved.

e Focus on the facts about Neil Armstrong and make it clear to Sts that the mistakes are all to do with using or not using the indefinite article *a / an* or the definite article *the*.

Give Sts time to do the task.

Get Sts to compare with a partner, and then check answers.

1 the USA ✓
2 a shy boy ✓, ~~the~~ books and ~~the~~ music
3 at ~~the~~ university
4 the first man ✓, on **the** moon
5 by people all over the world ✓
6 **an** astronaut, the US navy ✓
7 ~~the~~ autographs
8 ~~the~~ Armstrong's hair

f Tell Sts to go to **Grammar Bank 10B** on *p.151*.

Grammar notes

Sts should be familiar with the basic rules for using articles, but this is an area that can be very difficult for some nationalities who don't have articles in their L1. The basic rules are revised here, as well as introducing Sts to new areas, such as the use of articles with institutions, e.g. *hospital*, and with geographical and other place names, e.g. *streets, hotels*, etc.

Basic rules: *a / an / the*, no article

• **Rule 2:** (non-use of the definite article when generalizing) is an area where Sts often make mistakes, e.g. *Men are better at parking*… NOT ~~*The men are better at parking*…~~

Institutions

The use and non-use of *the* with *church, hospital*, and *school* is a tricky little point, but with a clear rule. It will help to give Sts other examples, e.g.:

I'm studying at university. (= I am a student there) NOT …*at the university*.

The university is in the centre of town. (= we are talking about the buildings of a particular university).

Other words which are used like this are *college* and *mosque / synagogue* (and other places of worship).

More rules: geographical names

The number of rules here, most of which are new for Sts, may seem overwhelming. Emphasize, however, that Sts should already have a good instinct for whether they need to use *the* or not, and also that the easiest way to internalize the rules is by learning and remembering a clear example, e.g. *Fifth Avenue*, **the** *River Nile*, **the** *Mediterranean Sea*, (*Mount*) *Everest*, **the** *Andes*, etc.

If their L1 has articles, Sts should also focus especially on any rules that are different.

Focus on the example sentences for **basic rules: *a / an / the*, no article** and play audio 🔊 **10.12** for Sts to listen and repeat. Encourage them to copy the rhythm. Then go through the rules with the class.

Repeat for **institutions** 🔊 **10.13** and **more rules: geographical names** 🔊 **10.14**.

Focus on the exercises and get Sts to do them individually or in pairs.

If they do them individually, get them to compare with a partner. Check answers, getting Sts to read the full sentences.

10B 151

a
1 (–) 2 The 3 (–) 4 (–) 5 The 6 (–) 7 the 8 (–)
9 a 10 the

b
1 (–) Sicily is the largest island in **the** Mediterranean.
2 Cairo is on **the** River Nile.
3 We didn't have time to visit **the** Louvre when we were in Paris.
4 (–) South-west England is famous for its beautiful countryside and beaches.
5 (–) Mount Everest is in **the** Himalayas.
6 The largest inland lake is **the** Caspian Sea.
7 We stayed at **the** Palace Hotel while we were in Madrid.
8 *Romeo and Juliet* is on at **the** Globe Theatre.
9 Pico d'Aneto is the highest mountain in **the** Pyrenees.
10 I've always wanted to visit (–) India.

Tell Sts to go back to the main lesson **10B**.

EXTRA SUPPORT If you think Sts need more practice, you may want to give them the **Grammar** photocopiable activity at this point.

g Put Sts in pairs, **A** and **B**, preferably face-to-face. Tell them to go to **Communication True or false**, **A** on *p.110*, **B** on *p.114*.

Go through the instructions and make sure Sts know what they have to do.

When Sts have completed their sentences in **a**, check answers using the key below. <u>Don't</u> read out the sentences: just elicit where articles are necessary, and which ones.

Sts A	Sts B
1 The, the, the	1 The, the, –
2 –, the	2 The, the, the
3 The, the, –	3 The, the, the
4 –, the	4 The, the, –
5 The, the, –	5 The, –
6 –, –	6 The, the, –, –
7 –, –	7 –, the, the
8 –, –, –	8 –, –

Now give Sts time to take turns to read their sentences to each other and to guess whether they are true or false.

When the activity has finished, you could ask who got the most correct answers in each pair.

Tell Sts to go back to the main lesson **10B**.

2 READING understanding context

a Tell Sts they are going to read about some famous speeches through the ages. Focus on the task and give Sts time to read the introduction and try to work out the meaning of the highlighted words and phrases.

Get Sts to compare with a partner, and then check answers.

1 a short phrase or sentence taken from a longer speech, especially a speech made by a politician, that is considered to be particularly effective or appropriate
2 the ability to speak easily and to persuade other people with your words

3 a person who makes formal speeches in public or is good at public speaking
4 the ability to say or write things that are both clever and amusing

EXTRA CHALLENGE Ask Sts what they think are the elements of a good speech.

Deal with any vocabulary problems that arose.

b Tell Sts to focus on the eight images, and find out if they know any information about the people. Don't worry if they don't.

Now give Sts time to match the sound bites to the images of the people. They could do this individually or in pairs. Tell them to guess if they don't know.

If Sts worked individually, get them to compare with a partner.

The speeches can be found online, in original and acted versions.

c 🔊 **10.15** You might want to tell Sts that the recording they are going to listen to is a mix of actors and authentic clips. Play the audio for Sts to listen and check.

Check answers.

A Elizabeth I **B** Abraham Lincoln **C** Emmeline Pankhurst
D Winston Churchill **E** John F Kennedy **F** Martin Luther King
G Nelson Mandela **H** Barack Obama

🔊 **10.15**
(script in Student's Book on *pp.130–131*)
(*actor*) – **Elizabeth the First A**
I know I have the body of a weak and feeble woman, but I have the heart and stomach of a king, and a king of England, too.
(*actor*) – **Abraham Lincoln B**
It is rather for us to be here dedicated to the great task remaining before us – that from these honored dead we take increased devotion to that cause for which they gave the last full measure of devotion – that we here highly resolve that these dead shall not have died in vain – that this nation, under God, shall have a new birth of freedom – and that government of the people, by the people, for the people, shall not perish from the Earth.
(*actor*) – **Emmeline Pankhurst C**
The title of my speech today is *The laws that men have made*. Men politicians are in the habit of talking to women as if there were no laws that affect women. 'The fact is,' they say, 'the home is the place for women. Their interests are the rearing and training of children. These are the things that interest women. Politics have nothing to do with these things, and therefore politics do not concern women.'
(*original recording*) – **Winston Churchill D**
We shall fight on the beaches, we shall fight on the landing grounds, we shall fight in the fields and in the streets, we shall fight in the hills; we shall never surrender.
(*original recording*) – **John F Kennedy E**
And so, my fellow Americans, ask not what your country can do for you; ask what you can do for your country. My fellow citizens of the world, ask not what America will do for you, but what together we can do for the freedom of man.
(*original recording*) – **Martin Luther King F**
I have a dream that my four little children will one day live in a nation where they will not be judged by the color of their skin but by the content of their character. I have a dream today!
(*original recording*) – **Nelson Mandela G**
I have cherished the ideal of a democratic and free society in which all persons live together in harmony, and with equal opportunities. It is an ideal which I hope to live for and to achieve. But, if needs be, it is an ideal for which I am prepared to die.

152 **10B**

(*original recording*) – **Barack Obama H**
For when we have faced down impossible odds, when we've been told we're not ready, or that we shouldn't try, or that we can't, generations of Americans have responded with a simple creed that sums up the spirit of a people. Yes, we can! Yes, we can! Yes, we can!

d Tell Sts they are now going to read a little more information about four of the speeches in **b**. They must complete each one with the name of the person who made it, and the correct sound bite from **b**.

Check answers.

EXTRA SUPPORT Before Sts read the four speeches the first time, check whether you need to pre-teach any vocabulary.

1	Elizabeth I, A	**3**	Emmeline Pankhurst, C
2	Abraham Lincoln, B	**4**	Nelson Mandela, G

Deal with any other new vocabulary. Elicit or model the pronunciation of any tricky words.

Now ask Sts if they know in what context the other four people made their speeches.

H	Barack Obama during his presidential campaign in 2008
D	Winston Churchill after the D-Day landings in 1941
E	John F Kennedy at his inaugural address in 1961
F	Martin Luther King at the end of a march against racial discrimination in 1963

e Focus on the task and questions 1–8, making sure Sts understand all the lexis, e.g. *convey*, *applauded*, etc.

Give Sts time to answer each question with the speaker's initials. Get Sts to compare with a partner, and then check answers.

1	AL	**2**	NM	**3**	QE	**4**	AL	**5**	QE	**6**	EP	**7**	NM	**8**	EP

f Put Sts in pairs and get them to discuss the three questions.

Get some feedback from various pairs. If your Sts come from the same country, you could do question 3 as a whole-class activity.

3 LISTENING & SPEAKING identifying dos and don'ts

a Either get Sts to answer the questions in pairs and get feedback, or do them as a whole-class activity and elicit Sts' experiences. If you have a story of your own, tell it to the class.

b Do this as a whole-class activity.

That you shouldn't use too many slides when doing a PowerPoint presentation.

c ◑ **10.16** Focus on the task. Tell Sts that Lynne Parker is the founder of an organization which helps women perform, write, and do business. In particular, she provides coaching for women who want to improve their public speaking skills.

Give Sts time to read tips 1–6. Play the audio once the whole way through for Sts to listen and complete the gaps.

Get Sts to compare with a partner, and then check answers.

EXTRA SUPPORT Read through the script and decide if you need to pre-teach any new lexis before Sts listen.

1	yourself	**2**	type out your talk	**3**	eye contact	**4** Rehearse,
rehearse, rehearse	**5**	sound bites	**6**	other speakers		

◑ **10.16**
(script in Student's Book on *p.131*)

P = presenter, L = Lynne Parker, A = Anya Edwards

P Welcome to today's programme. Our topic today is public speaking. Public speaking is right up there at the top of what most people say they're most afraid of. There is even a name for it – *glossophobia*. But hopefully after this programme, you will feel a lot more confident if you do have to make a speech or give a presentation.
First, we have Lynne Parker, an expert in the art of public speaking, who's going to tell us some of her dos and don'ts. Then after that, we're going to talk to Anya Edwards from Chile. Anya was a finalist in last year's English Speaking Union International public speaking competition. Lynne, I believe you have six key tips for us, is that right?

L Yes, that's right. My first tip, and maybe the most important one, is be yourself. This applies both to how you speak, and to what you actually do on the stage, whether that's standing up, sitting down, or moving about. Do what you feel comfortable with. The only don't as regards how you are onstage, I'd say, is try not to continually walk up and down, because this tends to distract people from what you're saying.

P Yes, I do find that distracting.

L Secondly, if you're using PowerPoint, don't just type out your talk. You want people to listen to what you're saying, not to read ahead. Slides are best for illustrating your talk or for drawing attention to a point. Pictures are often better than words, but if you use words, do keep it short. And do remember the ten-twenty-thirty rule. Do you know what that is?

P Er…no, do tell us.

L The ten-twenty-thirty rule is that the ideal presentation should have ten slides, last twenty minutes, and never have a font size on the slides that's less than thirty points.

P Ah, great, that's an easy one to remember. And tip number three?

L Maintain eye contact with your audience, whether it's to five hundred people in a room, or twenty people in a classroom or round a table. Don't spend the whole talk looking at your notes or slides.

P How can you maintain eye contact with five hundred people?

L Well, you can't with all of them, of course, but a good technique is to scan the audience occasionally from side to side and front to back, to give the impression you're talking to everyone.

P Number four?

L Rehearse, rehearse, rehearse. In front of a mirror, or even better, video yourself. It will make you aware of how you use your hands and body, and even what clothes look right.

P Number five?

L Include a couple of good sound bites. Whenever you hear something good, write it down, as you might be able to use it later.

P So, sound bites rather than stories or examples?

L Well, no, not instead of – a good story or example can also help to illustrate a situation, or help people to remember the point you were making. Just don't make it too long, and if you're telling a little story, remember – good stories have a beginning, a middle, and an end.

P And your last point?

L Listen to other speakers. There are lots of good resources online, such as TED talks and The Moth, which is a great storytelling website. Also, listen to people talking when you're out and about, for example traveling on public transport or queuing up in the supermarket. You never know what witty remarks or good stories you might pick up along the way.

P Thank you very much, Lynne.

d Focus on the chart and tell Sts that they are going to listen to Lynne again and this time, for each tip, they must write any more information that she mentions. Point out to Sts that tips 2, 4, and 6 don't have any more information for *Don'ts*.

10B 153

Play the audio, pausing after each tip to give Sts time to write.

Get Sts to compare with a partner, and then check answers.

	Dos	Don'ts
Tip 1	Do what you feel comfortable with.	Don't continually walk up and down.
Tip 2	Do keep it short. Do remember the 10–20–30 rule.	–
Tip 3	Do occasionally scan from side to side and front to back.	Don't spend the whole time looking at your slides or notes.
Tip 4	Do use a mirror or video yourself.	–
Tip 5	Do write down anything you hear. Do make sure a story has a beginning, middle, and end.	Don't make it too long.
Tip 6	Do use online resources. Do listen to people when you're out and about.	–

EXTRA SUPPORT If there's time, you could get Sts to listen again with the script on *p.131*, so they can see exactly what they understood / didn't understand. Translate / Explain any new words or phrases.

e 🔊 **10.17** Tell Sts that they are now going to listen to **Part 2** of the interview. Remind Sts that the presenter introduced Anya at the beginning of **Part 1**.

Play the audio once the whole way through for Sts to listen and answer the question.

Check the answer.

EXTRA SUPPORT Read through the script and decide if you need to pre-teach any new lexis before Sts listen.

She agrees with Lynne's Tip 1, 'Be yourself'.

🔊 **10.17**
(script in Student's Book on *p.131*)
P   And now we have Anya on the line, from Chile.
A   Hello.
P   Anya, you took part in the competition last year, is that right?
A   Yes.
P   Can you tell us a bit about it?
A   Well, it's open to people from any country between the ages of sixteen and eighteen. First, you compete at home – so for me, in Chile – and then the international finals take place in London.
P   What exactly did you have to do there?
A   So you have to give two speeches. The first one is a prepared speech, which is a maximum of five minutes on a subject that they give you – that year for me it was on the role of education. And then after your speech, you have to answer questions for three to four minutes. And then the second speech, and this was definitely the scariest, was the impromptu speech. You are given three subjects to choose from which you've never seen before, and then fifteen minutes to choose one and prepare a speech of three minutes.
P   What did you choose?
A   I chose the title *To be grown up is a state of mind*.
P   Were you nervous?

A   I was nervous – very nervous. But then I've never not been nervous before speaking in front of an audience. I've done a lot of drama, of acting, and that's taught me that nerves are good because you can learn to channel them into a better performance.
P   How is public speaking different from acting?
A   Well, in many ways they're similar, because you need many of the same qualities: to be able to stand in front of an audience confidently and speak clearly, to be convincing. But I'd say that public speaking is harder because you can't rely on anyone else. If you miss a line, there won't be someone next to you to give you your cue, and you're the main focus of attention one hundred per cent of the time.
P   And what did you learn from the experience?
A   I think it was one of the most useful skills I've ever learnt, and that any person can have because if you've learnt to do it well, and practised, it means that you'll never, ever have to worry about standing up and speaking in front of other people.
P   What tips would you give to someone about writing a speech?
A   Well, for writing a speech, I'd say to start by talking about the topic out loud and record whatever comes into your head on your phone. Then listen back to it, and start by ordering your ideas on paper. And if you think the subject you have to talk about is a bit dry, try to come up with some anecdotes to illustrate it. Also, use plain, simple language. Vocabulary that's too complicated puts people off.
P   And to deliver it?
A   I agree entirely with Lynne about being authentic, about being yourself. If you want your speech to be effective, people need to believe what you say, and in order to convince them, you need to be convinced yourself.

f Tell Sts they are going to listen to the audio again and this time they need to answer multiple-choice questions 1–6.

Give Sts time to read the questions and options.

Play the audio again, pausing after Anya has answered a question, to give Sts time to choose the best option.

Check answers.

1 b   **2** a   **3** b   **4** c   **5** b   **6** a

EXTRA SUPPORT If there's time, you could get Sts to listen again with the script on *p.131*, so they can see exactly what they understood / didn't understand. Translate / Explain any new words or phrases.

g Do this as a whole-class activity, or put Sts in pairs and then get some feedback.

4 VOCABULARY collocation: word pairs

a Focus on the **Word pairs** box and go through it with the class.

Focus on the questions and elicit the equivalent expressions in the Sts' L1, and ask them which order the words come in.

b Focus on the instructions. Do one with the class. Ask Sts which word (from box B) often goes with *backwards* (in box A), and elicit *forwards*. Then ask Sts if we say *backwards and forwards* or *forwards and backwards*, and elicit that it is the former. Elicit / Explain that in these word pairs *and* is usually pronounced /ən/.

Sts then continue matching the pairs. Don't check answers yet.

EXTRA SUPPORT Get Sts to do **b** and then **c** in pairs.

c Focus on the task and get Sts to do it individually or in pairs. Sts should know most of these or be able to guess them.

154 **10B**

d 🔊 **10.18** Play the audio for Sts to listen and check their answers to **b** and **c**. Check answers.

🔊 **10.18**

b
backwards and forwards, cause and effect, forgive and forget, health and safety, live and learn, thunder and lightning, pros and cons, peace and quiet, supply and demand, short and sweet

c
right or wrong, now or never, more or less, sooner or later, all or nothing, once or twice, dead or alive, rain or shine

---

EXTRA SUPPORT Get Sts to practise saying the phrases. You could use the audio to do this.

EXTRA IDEA Put Sts in pairs and get them to test each other by saying the first word from each pair for their partner to complete the expression, e.g.:

A (book open) *Backwards…*
B (book closed) *…and forwards.*

Make sure they swap roles.

e Tell Sts that they are now going to look at some more word pairs which are idioms. Focus on the task and give Sts time to match the idioms to their meanings.

Check answers and make sure Sts are clear about the meaning of these idioms.

---

1 C **2** G **3** E **4** H **5** A **6** B **7** D **8** F

---

f This exercise recycles some of the expressions Sts have just learned. Focus on the sentences and give Sts time to complete them.

Check answers. You might want to point out that *now and then* and *on and off* are close synonyms for *now and again* (item 2).

---

1 bits and pieces **2** now and again **3** wait and see
4 safe and sound **5** by and large **6** law and order
7 sick and tired **8** touch and go

EXTRA IDEA This activity could be done in pairs or small groups as a timed race.

EXTRA CHALLENGE Tell Sts to cover sentences 1–8 in **e**, and call out in random order the phrases in A–H, to prompt the highlighted idiom. Alternatively, Sts could do this in pairs.

5 PRONUNCIATION & SPEAKING pausing and sentence stress

a 🔊 **10.19** Focus on the instructions and elicit / explain that a *chunk* is a reasonable amount of something, e.g. *a chunk of cheese*. In this case, it refers to a section / a few sentences of a speech. Highlight that there will always be a pause after full stops and commas, but that there are sometimes more pauses, which help the listener to follow what is being said. Point out the first pause, which has already been marked.

Play the audio once the whole way through for Sts just to listen. Then play it again and get Sts to mark the pauses.

Get Sts to compare with a partner, and then play the audio again. Check answers.

Good afternoon everyone / and thank you for coming. / I'm going to talk to you today about one of my hobbies, / baking. / I've loved baking since I was a child. / My grandmother taught me to make simple biscuits and cakes / and later, / when I was a teenager, / I watched a lot of TV programmes and online videos / to learn how to make more complicated ones. / What I like about baking / is that it's very creative / and it makes other people happy.

🔊 **10.19**
See text in Student's Book on *p.103*

---

b Get Sts in pairs to practise reading the speech in **a**, making the correct pauses and trying to get a good rhythm. You might want to explain that the content of this example talk is relatively easy, and on a familiar topic, because the focus of this activity is less about what you say and more about improving the way you deliver a talk.

EXTRA SUPPORT Play the audio again and get Sts to listen and repeat at the same time. Then put them in pairs to practise again.

EXTRA CHALLENGE After doing the activity, elicit what else this speaker might go on to say in her speech.

c Focus on the instructions. You could elicit / suggest some other topics, e.g. a famous person you admire, the good or bad side of your job / course, a sport you play, etc. Set a time limit for Sts to prepare their presentation, and monitor and help with vocabulary. Encourage Sts to make a plan and write notes, rather than writing the presentation out in full. Remind them to think about some of the tips they listened to earlier in the lesson.

❗ If you know that some of your Sts will be nervous about giving a presentation, tell them now that they won't be doing it in front of the whole class, but in small groups.

EXTRA SUPPORT Less confident / proficient Sts might want to write up their presentation at home and practise it before doing the presentation in the following class.

EXTRA CHALLENGE Get Sts to look back through Files 1–9 and choose a topic for their presentation which relates to one of the topics they have covered in the course.

d Now put Sts in small groups of three or four to give the presentations to each other. Remind them of the question-and-answer session after each presentation; while they are listening, they should write down at least one question to ask the speaker after the presentation is over.

Try to listen to as many Sts as possible and to give positive feedback to the whole class, as this may be one of the most challenging speaking activities that they have done.

EXTRA IDEA If you have a video camera, you could film some or all of the presentations to show later, provided Sts feel comfortable with this.

6 ▶ VIDEO LISTENING

a Tell Sts they are going to watch a short film about public speaking. Give Sts time to read the three questions.
Play the video once the whole way through for Sts to listen.

10B 155

Check answers.

EXTRA SUPPORT Read through the script and decide if you need to pre-teach any new lexis before Sts watch the video.

Sandie criticised Louise for playing with her feet and crossing her legs.
Sandie said Louise should slow down, be confident, relax, and use her voice.
Sandie said Louise had slowed down, was clear, and an effective communicator.

Giving presentations: a voice coach

P = presenter, S = Sandie, L = Louise

P *Hi, I'm Louise, and I work for a local newspaper here in London. I love writing and I enjoy interviewing, but there's one part of my job I really hate – and that's public speaking.*
The problem is that no matter what work you do, speaking in public is almost impossible to avoid. These days, most roles require communication skills. From small presentations to big conference speeches, you need to be able to deliver a message clearly and confidently. But for people like me, this isn't easy. I find speaking in public terrifying. I become tense and nervous and find it very difficult to relax. That's why I've come here – to the Royal Academy of Dramatic Art.
RADA first opened in the Haymarket in London in nineteen oh four. It offers training for theatre specialists, including actors, stage managers, directors, and designers. It has become one of the most famous acting schools in the world, and some of the entertainment industry's biggest names have studied here.
But what am I doing here? Well, it's about time I overcame my fear of public speaking, and to do this, I need to become a good actor. After all, actors and public speakers use a lot of the same skills. Both should tell a story, and both should engage an audience. Because of this, RADA run several public speaking courses.
S …into a series of individuals and of course, individuals are never as scary as the mass. Does that make sense?
P *I've come here to develop an actor's approach to speaking effectively, and Sandie – an actor for over thirty years – is going to show me the way.*
S but nothing weird or spooky, but…
P *The RADA approach to public speaking can be summarized in three words – think, breathe, speak.*
S Tell me if anything doesn't make sense.
L No, it does, and I've always wanted a really grown-up…
P *First, we're going to focus on the 'think' part.*
S First of all, I hope you don't mind me asking, but why are you here?
L Um, well, I tend to do a lot of one-to-one work with people when I'm interviewing them…
P *At this stage, you talk through your concerns and set an objective for the session.*
L … there's a big group of people and they're not behind a microphone or TV camera. I get so nervous – even when I'm meeting new people at parties or dinner parties, so it would just be good to learn a few techniques to feel more confident.
S OK, so…
P *Then you give a presentation in your usual style, and get some interesting feedback from Sandie.*
L … So, that's about it.
S Very, very well done. Thank you very much indeed. Really well done, Lou. How was that for you? So, I think you're absolutely charming, Lou. You come across with a really positive energy. You've got a lovely open face. You very clearly are naturally engaging, which means I, as your audience, am naturally engaged. You're friendly, you're affable, and you've got a great smile, which is wonderful. Things – small things – that I think you might be able to do differently: so, you were playing with your feet. You were playing with your feet like a five-year-old. So, if I say that you were doing that on your heels…
L Right. Oh, yeah.
S Do you know what I mean?
L Yeah, yeah, yeah.
S And then you crossed your legs.

L Right.
S Probably the most significant thing that I noticed that you could do differently is to slow down.
…see yourself and feel yourself confident and sure…
P *If you can get your body language right, it will help your breathing, and controlling your breath is central to good public speaking. You learn to relax and find the power behind the voice through warm-up and breathing exercises.*
S … trust, Lou, that you are aware of that amazing range you in fact have. Yes?
L Yeah.
S So, you're breathing in, sighing in, pushing out. Pushing all the air right out. Waiting…
P *Once you have mastered the thought and the breath, you can finally speak. But this isn't as easy as it sounds.*
L Good afternoon.
S Brilliant, you've done that really, really well. You've got the hang of that. So now we're going to get a bit of oomph into our voice by doing it like an opera singer. Good afternoon.
L Good afternoon.
P *It isn't always easy to speak naturally, but finally – after a lot of practice – the words start to flow. Now I can try a full paragraph.*
L I'll share some very embarrassing stories and I'll explain the impact that our work has on very lonely people.
P *You have to make an impact from the beginning, and Sandie gives you the A, B, C, D of the perfect opening. And it's just as important to end on a positive note.*
S …and language and anticipate finishing by four p.m.
P *Speaking and communicating are two very different things, and communicating effectively takes skill, perseverance, and lots of hard work. Unfortunately, it isn't as easy as just reading the right words; you need to tell the story, too. But if you can do this, you will draw in your audience, and as they relax, you'll relax, too.*
S Yeah, I thought your pace was excellent: it was really measured, it was clear. I would have understood exactly what you were about to do, who you were, and why you were doing that. So, as far as I'm concerned, that was really effective communication.
L Thank you.
S Pleasure.
P *I still feel nervous about speaking in front of people, but at RADA I enjoyed public speaking for the first time, and the more I enjoyed it, the better I became. And that's what the RADA technique is all about. It gives you the skills to grow in confidence so…so like an actor, you can face your audience with assurance rather than fear.*

b Focus on the task and give Sts time to read sentences 1–10. Point out that the acronym RADA is explained in the film.

Play the video again for Sts to watch and complete the gaps.

Get Sts to compare with a partner, and then play the video again if necessary.

Check answers.

EXTRA SUPPORT You could get Sts to compare their answers with a partner before the second playing of the video.

1 public speaking   2 clearly, confidently   3 London, 1904
4 same skills   5 think, breathe, speak   6 interesting feedback
7 body language   8 make, impact   9 positive note
10 grow, confidence

EXTRA SUPPORT You could get Sts to watch the video again with subtitles, so they can see exactly what they understood / didn't understand. Translate / Explain any new words or phrases.

c Do this as a whole-class activity.

EXTRA IDEA After doing the **Revise and Check** lesson, you could give Sts one or all of the final three photocopiable activities (**Grammar**, **Communicative**, and **Vocabulary**), which include questions to revise all the grammar points and lexis they studied in this level.

156 **10B**

Revise and Check

For instructions on how to use these pages, see *p.41*.

More materials

For teachers

Teacher's Resource Centre
Video Can you understand these people? 9&10
Quick Test 10
File 10 Test
Progress Test Files 6–10
End-of-course Test

For students

Online Practice Check your progress

GRAMMAR

1 b 2 c 3 a 4 c 5 b 6 a 7 c 8 a 9 c 10 c
11 b 12 b 13 a 14 b 15 a

VOCABULARY

a 1 genetic 2 scientific 3 neighbourhood 4 loneliness
5 death
b 1 overpopulated 2 mispronounced 3 multinational
4 autobiography 5 underpaid
c 1 loss 2 set up 3 leader 4 launch 5 branches
6 business 7 rise 8 side 9 carry 10 guinea
d 1 quiet 2 sound 3 later 4 order 5 never

PRONUNCIATION

a
1 br**a**nch /ɑː/ 2 g**o**vernment /ʌ/ 3 res**ear**ch /ɜː/
4 deci**si**on /ʒ/ 5 th**ough** /ð/
b
1 bio**lo**gical 2 **phy**sicist 3 multi**cul**tural 4 in**crease**
5 manu**fac**ture

CAN YOU understand this text?

a Because he considered it the best he'd ever heard and because it became iconic and recognizably his own.
b 1 a 2 c 3 b 4 c

🔊 CAN YOU understand these people?

1 c 2 b 3 c 4 b

🔊 10.20
1
I = interviewer, T = Thomas
I   Are there any brands which you think have a really good logo or slogan?
T   I think, you know, one, the one that sticks out to me the most is the Nike swoosh. Er, you know the, I've sort of been fascinated by that and the whole progression of the company over the years. I, I find them to be one of the strongest brands. I think American, er, icons like Coca-Cola – that's a great brand name. Disney, that's a great brand.

I   Does it make you want to buy the products?
T   You know, I will say I am loyal to those products. I think each one brings a little different thing to it. When I think of, you know, Disney, I think about customer service. When I think about Coca-Cola, I think about the quality of their product. Nike, Nike, I think about their, sort of, um, cutting edge marketing campaigns, and they've got a product that is, sort of, backs it up, too.
I   Are there any advertisements that make you not want to buy the product?
T   I tend to dislike, er, car ads that are on the radio. I don't mind them on television, but on ads, I, er, I tend to want to turn them off. I don't think I'm not going to buy a car, but I don't like listening to the ads, that's for sure.

2
I = interviewer, D = Devika
I   What's your favourite city?
D   My favourite city would have to be Rome. I love Italy and I've spent a lot of time there. And Rome doesn't bore me, even if I go there several times.
I   Why do you like it?
D   I love the food in Rome, I love the sights. The people are so friendly and no matter what time of year, in winter or summer, there's lots going on.
I   Do you think cities will be different in the future?
D   Ooh, that's a difficult question. I think some cities which are already quite wealthy and have a lot of modern aspects to them, such as New York or London, might become more efficient. I hope they do. But I can imagine lots of cities around the world that aren't so wealthy, or have, um, more kind of commercial centres to not be too different. Even in maybe twenty years' time.

3
I = interviewer, N = Noel
I   Do you think it's more important to study science than arts at school or university?
N   Er, well, from, for the economy's point of view I think studying science is important. But from a, a kind of creativity, learning and educational point of view, possibly art because it, it's about imagination, and, you know, we don't know what skills we're going to need in twenty or thirty years' time. So, something to do with creativity. I'm sure scientists can be creative, but arts tend to promote that a bit more.
I   Which scientific subjects do you think have taught you something useful?
N   Oh, I've never been very good at sciences, I, to be quite honest with you. So, um, I quite like maths. Um, I, I was a bit late coming to maths, but I quite like the kind of logic to it, and the, kind of, the thinking process that goes alongside it.
I   What would you most like scientists to discover in the future?
N   Oh, er, definitely how to, um, respond to global warming. Um, and, er, anything that gets us away from carbon-based heating or fuel. Um, I mean, obviously there's the medical sciences which are quite important. Um, I, I suppose anything to do with the neurosciences and how we cope with, um, er, learning or mental health problems, that type of thing

4
I = interviewer, S = Sophie
I   Have you ever had to make a speech, or give a talk or presentation, in front of a lot of people?
S   Yes, it was at my university. It was part of an exam, we had to give a PowerPoint presentation to a group of people and some examiners.
I   How did you feel?
S   Not great. It was not enjoyable.
I   Was it a success?
S   I passed. Success in some way, yeah.

Revise and Check 157

Photocopiable activities

Overview

- There is a **Grammar activity** for each main (A and B) lesson of the Student's Book.
- There is a **Communicative activity** for each main (A and B) lesson of the Student's Book.
- There is a **Vocabulary activity** for each section of the Vocabulary Bank in the Student's Book.

The photocopiable material is also available on the **Teacher's Resource Centre** (TRC) and the **Classroom Presentation Tool** (CPT), allowing you to display the worksheets on an interactive whiteboard or projector. This will make it easier to set up and demonstrate the activities, and show answers.

Using extra activities in mixed ability classes

Some teachers have classes with a very wide range of levels, and where some Sts finish Student's Book activities much more quickly than others. You could give these fast finishers a photocopiable activity (Grammar, Vocabulary, or Communicative) while you help the slower Sts. Alternatively, some teachers might want to give faster Sts extra oral practice with a communicative activity while slower Sts consolidate their knowledge with an extra grammar activity.

Tips for using Grammar activities

- Use the Grammar Introduction worksheet as diagnostic tests for your class.
- The grammar activities are designed to give Sts extra practice in the main grammar points from each lesson. How you use these activities depends on the needs of your Sts and the time available. They can be used in the lesson if you think all of your class would benefit from the extra practice or you could set them as homework for some or all of your Sts.
- Before using the worksheets in class, check for any vocabulary that may be either new or difficult for your Sts.
- All of the activities start with a writing stage. If you use the activities in class, get Sts to work individually or in pairs. Allow Sts to compare before checking answers.
- If Sts are having trouble with any of the activities, make sure they refer to the relevant Grammar Bank in the Student's Book.
- All of the activities have an **Activation** section. Some of them have a task that gets Sts to cover the sentences and test their memory. If you are using the activities in class, Sts can work in pairs and test their partner. If you set them for homework, encourage Sts to use this stage to test themselves. Alternatively, you could set the main activity for homework and then get Sts to do the **Activation** at the start of the next class.
- Make sure that Sts keep their worksheets and that they review any difficult areas regularly. Encourage them to go back to activities and cover and test themselves.

Tips for using Communicative activities

- Before using the worksheets in class, check for any vocabulary that may be either new or difficult for your Sts.
- We have suggested the ideal number of copies for each activity. However, you can often manage with fewer, e.g. one worksheet per pair instead of one per student.
- When Sts are working in pairs, if possible get them to sit face-to-face. This will encourage them to really talk to each other and also means they can't see each other's worksheet.
- If your class doesn't divide into pairs or groups, take part yourself, get two Sts to share one role, or get one student to monitor, help, and correct.
- If some Sts finish early, they can swap roles and do the activity again, or you could get them to write some of the sentences from the activity.

Tips for using Vocabulary activities

- These worksheets are intended to recycle and consolidate Sts' understanding of the vocabulary in the Student's Book Vocabulary Banks. As such, we suggest not using them directly after doing these exercises. Instead, get Sts to do them in a subsequent lesson.
- If Sts are having trouble with any of the activities, make sure they refer to the relevant Vocabulary Bank page.
- You could ask Sts to check their answers by referring to the relevant Student's Book Vocabulary Bank.
- All the activities are suitable for use in class. However, you may wish to set some of the tasks for homework.
- Most of the Vocabulary worksheets have an **Activation** task and this can be treated in a similar way to the Grammar ones.
- Make sure that Sts keep their and that they review any difficult areas regularly. Encourage them to go back to activities and cover and test themselves.

Customisable worksheets

There are customisable versions of some of the Grammar, Communicative, and Vocabulary activities on the **Teacher's Resource Centre**. These allow you to adapt the material to make it more applicable and/or relevant to your Sts. For instance, you could:

- change some of the names to the names of Sts in your class.
- change place names to ones that are more relevant and/or familiar to your Sts.
- change items of grammar or vocabulary to focus on the needs and interests of your Sts and/or adapt the level of challenge.
- reduce the number of items if you are short of time.

Grammar activity answers

Introduction What do you remember?

2 decided to move **3** is five / five years old **4** who are
5 the oldest / eldest child **6** He used to be **7** in charge of
8 to meet / in order to meet **9** I've been learning **10** went to
11 as a waitress **12** very hard work / a very hard job
13 had improved **14** to be able to speak **15** good at reading
16 is good enough **17** have very little **18** I'd learn

1A question formation

a 1 paid for **2** who that woman is **3** are they going, long are they (going) for **4** did, did she leave **5** Have you seen, who made, What happened
b 2 it's going to rain this afternoon **3** if / whether Thomas has arrived yet **4** how much it'll cost to repair the roof
5 if / whether I have to pay to park here **6** why you left your last job **7** what time the library closes **8** if / whether Susan's flight took off on time

1B auxiliary verbs

a 2 do **3** isn't **4** Have **5** aren't **6** do **7** Is **8** will
b 2 am **3** are **4** do / did **5** Did **6** did **7** Couldn't
8 do **9** can't

2A present perfect simple and continuous

a 2 've been **3** haven't I seen **4** 've come
5 Have you forgotten **6** 've been drinking
7 haven't been talking **8** has your throat been hurting
9 's been **10** haven't been able **11** 've had
12 've been taking **13** haven't made **14** 've just bought
b 2 Have you ever been injured **3** have you been coming
4 have you missed **5** have you been living / have you lived
6 Have you ever studied

2B adjectives as nouns, adjective order

a 2 The French **3** homeless people **4** Japanese girl **5** ✓
6 The Spanish **7** the poor **8** ✓ **9** The Chinese
10 The young
b 2 blue denim **3** awful loud **4** big dark **5** long black silk
6 beautiful old wooden **7** small black leather
8 delicious Thai **9** short curly brown **10** new striped

3A narrative tenses: past simple, past continuous, past perfect, past perfect continuous

a 2 hadn't noticed, had stopped **2** had been (carefully) saving, had been concentrating, had been watching, had (only) been looking **3** was leaving, was happening, were looking
b 2 asked **3** mentioned **4** had been looking
5 had accused / accused **6** had searched / searched **7** made
8 had said **9** jumped up **10** made **11** had never seen
12 drove **13** parked **14** had taken place **15** came
16 started **17** had never stolen **18** made **19** found
20 had stopped **21** were watching

3B the position of adverbs and adverbial phrases

a 2 do you **really** mean that; were **absolutely** awful
3 England played **well**
4 **Unfortunately**, England **never** play **well**
5 were **incredibly** lucky
6 do you **ever** have
7 **To be honest**, they were **quite** lucky

8 were **extremely** lucky
9 **Personally**, I thought both teams played **badly**; England were **a bit** better, **especially** in the second half
10 in Munich **next**, so let's see how they do **there**
b 2 slowly **3** quickly **4** earlier that day **5** obviously
6 actually **7** angrily **8** a little **9** badly **10** incredibly
11 here **12** always **13** well **14** naturally
15 in (a) quarter of an hour

4A future perfect and future continuous

a 1 won't be thinking
2 'll (still) be working; 'll have been promoted
3 will have left
4 won't be using
5 won't have gone; 'll (still) be watching
6 'll have graduated; 'll be looking for
7 won't have had
8 Will (you) be coming
9 Will (you) be picking me up
10 will (they) have visited
11 'll have finished; 'll be celebrating
12 won't have saved

4B zero and first conditionals, future time clauses

2 a and b **3** a **4** b **5** b and c **6** c **7** a and c **8** a and b
9 a **10** c **11** b **12** a and c **13** b and c **14** a and b **15** c

5A unreal conditionals

a 2 'd put; would have tasted / would taste
3 found; be
4 wouldn't have got; 'd taken
5 were; wouldn't swim
6 wouldn't have left; hadn't fallen
7 hadn't used; wouldn't have found
8 'd buy; could
9 would have gone; hadn't been
10 didn't spend; could
11 would have bought; 'd known
12 wouldn't be; practised

5B *wish* for present / future, *wish* for past regrets

a 2 was / were **3** could **4** didn't have to **5** wouldn't sing
6 would stop **7** wouldn't make **8** would call
b 2 They wish they'd put on **3** He wishes he hadn't broken up
4 We wish we'd bought **5** I wish I hadn't eaten
6 She wishes she hadn't dyed **7** We wish we hadn't thrown away
8 I wish I hadn't had

6A *used to, be used to, get used to*

a 2 get used to **3** usually **4** was used to being able
5 used to be **6** usually go
b 2 'm used to **3** get used to **4** used to **5** usually
6 get used to **7** 'm used to **8** get used to **9** get used to
10 used to
c 2 being **3** seeing **4** get up **5** eating

159

6B gerunds and infinitives

2 seeing **3** go out **4** to have **5** not stay **6** working
7 to wear **8** live **9** laughing **10** to finish **11** going
12 not to tell **13** work **14** to study **15** to help **16** waiting
17 to park **18** speaking **19** getting up / to get up
20 not come **21** spending **22** to give **24** not to be
25 changing **26** meeting **27** arriving **28** to revise
29 to tell **30** turning

7A past modals

a **2** might have broken **3** must have left **4** must have put
5 can't have drunk **6** might not have seen **7** must have
worked **8** can't have finished **9** might not have been able
to get / might not have got **10** must have switched off

b **2** shouldn't have used **3** shouldn't have broken up
4 should have come **5** should have waited **6** should have
kept **7** should have told **8** shouldn't have bought

7B verbs of the senses

a **2** smells **3** smells as if (like) **4** smells like **5** feels
6 feels like **7** feels as if (like) **8** feels **9** tastes
10 tastes like **11** tastes as if (like) **12** tastes **13** look as if (like)
14 look **15** look as if (like) **16** look **17** look like **18** look
19 sounds **20** sounds **21** sounds as if (like) **22** sound like

8A the passive (all forms); *have something done*; *it is said that…*, *he is thought to…*, etc.

a **2** is thought that **3** is said to **4** are understood to
5 is expected that **6** are thought to

b **2** to have my wallet stolen **3** 'm having / 'm going to have a
tooth filled **4** had your heart broken **5** have your eyes tested
6 do you have your car serviced **7** are having a swimming
pool built **8** haven't had my hair cut **9** having my photo taken
10 had our house burgled **11** has his shopping delivered
12 've had our car broken into

8B reporting verbs

a **1** to give **2** to come **3** having / having had
4 not going / not having gone **5** to tell; breaking
6 going **7** not to leave **8** making

b **2** promised to tidy **3** apologized (for) forgetting **4** advised
(me) to keep **5** suggested trying **6** admitted eating
7 invited (me) to come **8** blamed (me for) losing

9A clauses of contrast and purpose

a **2** j **3** h **4** i **5** f **6** e **7** a **8** c **9** d **10** b

b **2** A lot of companies have reduced staff numbers in order to
save money.
3 Despite the long flight / Despite the fact the flight was long,
she felt great when she arrived in New York.
4 Nick didn't tell Louisa the truth so as not to hurt her feelings.
5 I bought the shoes even though they were ridiculously
expensive.
6 The company has a big market share in spite of doing very
little advertising / in spite of the fact that they do very little
advertising.
7 They had to leave the hotel early so that they wouldn't miss
their train.
8 She didn't get the job, though she was a strong candidate. /
She didn't get the job. She was a strong candidate, though.

9B uncountable and plural nouns

2 look **3** is **4** shorts **5** a piece of **6** is
7 some belongings **8** isn't **9** behaviour **10** staff
11 some **12** advice **13** some **14** some **15** the
16 those **17** homework **18** rubbish

10A quantifiers: *all, every, both*, etc.

a **1** every
2 all of the research; all of it
3 everything
4 all day; any
5 They all passed.
6 Most of
7 either of them; both
8 nor; Both; neither of them

b **2** Neither **3** Every **4** All **5** Most of **6** no **7** anyone
8 Most **9** all **10** both **11** every **12** None of

10B articles

2 the **3** – **4** an **5** – **6** The **7** the **8** – **9** The **10** –
11 – **12** an **13** The **14** the **15** the **16** a **17** The
18 – **19** the **20** – **21** – **22** the **23** the **24** – **25** the
26 the **27** – **28** a **29** – **30** the **31** the **32** the **33** –
34 the **35** – **36** the **37** the

Revision Grammar auction

Instructions

Sts revise the main grammar points of the book by playing
a game where, in pairs, they have to bid to try to 'buy'
correct sentences. Copy one sheet per pair.

- Put Sts in pairs. Give each pair the list of 20 sentences.
Elicit what an auction is = a public sale where things are
sold to the person who offers the most money. Explain
that Sts have 1,000 euros (or dollars, depending on
which currency they are most familiar with). They have
a list of sentences, some of which are correct and some
incorrect. They bid to 'buy' as many correct sentences as
they can. Bids start at 50, the next bid is 100, then 150,
etc. Sts must record on their sheet how much they have
spent on a sentence, in order to calculate how much
money they have left. The pair which buys the most
correct sentences is the winner.
- Start with the first sentence and invite bids. Make
the activity more fun by using typical language of an
auctioneer, e.g. *How much am I offered for this fantastic
sentence: 50 euros, 100? Do I hear 150? Going, going, gone
to Marc and Andrea for 150 euros.*
- When you have 'sold' all the sentences, go through each
one eliciting whether it is correct or not, and what the
mistake is. Then find out who bought the most correct
sentences.

1 ✓
2 ✗ Her name's Hannah, isn't **it**?
3 ✓
4 ✗ She has **beautiful** long dark hair.
5 ✓
6 ✗ I like classical music **very much**.
7 ✓
8 ✓
9 ✗ I would have enjoyed the film more if it **hadn't** had subtitles.
10 ✗ I wish I **had** more free time! / I wish I **could** have more
free time!
11 ✓
12 ✓
13 ✗ He **can't** have seen you or he would have said hello.
14 ✗ It looks **like / as if** it's going to rain.
15 ✗ The missing man is thought **to be** from Manchester.
16 ✓
17 ✗ Lily is going to hospital this afternoon **to** visit her husband.
18 ✗ I need to buy some new **furniture** for my living room.
19 ✓
20 ✗ The man was sent **to prison** for ten years.

160

INTRODUCTION GRAMMAR   What do you remember?

● Read about Beata. Then correct the **bold** phrases 1–18.

My name's Beata and I'm from Poznań in Poland. I was born there and ¹**I have lived there** until I was 14. Then my family ²**decided move** to Warsaw, and that's where I live now.

I'm divorced and I have a son called Filip, who ³**is five years**. He spends weekdays with me and weekends with his father. I have two brothers, ⁴**which are** both studying at university. I am ⁵**the older child** in the family. My mother works in a bank and my father is retired. ⁶**He use to be** a business consultant.

I work for a big clothing company. I am ⁷**on charge of** foreign suppliers, which means that I have to use English when I talk to them on the phone, and sometimes I travel to other countries such as Morocco and Turkey ⁸**for to meet** suppliers.

⁹**I am learning** English for about nine years. I studied it at school, and then after I left school, I spent eight weeks in Ireland. During the day I ¹⁰**was going to** English classes, and in the evening I worked ¹¹**like a waitress** in a restaurant. It was ¹²**a very hard work**. When I came home, my English ¹³**has improved** a lot, but that was a few years ago and I've forgotten a lot since then. My main aim this year is ¹⁴**to be able speak** more fluently and to improve my writing. I think I'm quite ¹⁵**good at read** in English. As soon as my level of English ¹⁶**will be good enough**, I'll take the IELTS exam.

I ¹⁷**have very few** free time, but when I can, I go horse riding. If I had more time, ¹⁸**I'll learn** another language, maybe French or German.

1 *I lived there*
2 _____
3 _____
4 _____
5 _____
6 _____
7 _____
8 _____
9 _____
10 _____
11 _____
12 _____
13 _____
14 _____
15 _____
16 _____
17 _____
18 _____

ACTIVATION

Write a similar text about yourself, in five paragraphs. Include the following information:

- where you live
- your family
- what you do
- how long you've been learning English and why
- what you do in your free time

1A GRAMMAR question formation

a Complete the questions.

1. **A** I don't like her dress.
   B What *don't you like* about it?
   A The style. I think it's awful.
   B It must have cost a fortune though.
   A Yes. Who _____ _____ it?
   B Her grandparents paid for it. It was a wedding present.

2. **A** Do you know _____ _____ _____ _____ over there?
   B That woman there? I think she's Claire's cousin.
   A Her hairstyle is very old-fashioned!

3. **A** Where _____ _____ _____ on their honeymoon?
   B On an African safari, I think.
   A How _____ _____ _____ going _____?
   B Three weeks!

4. **A** Who _____ Tony come with?
   B Nobody. He came on his own. His girlfriend left him last month.
   A Why _____ _____ _____ him?
   B I think she met someone else.

5. **A** _____ _____ _____ the wedding cake yet?
   B Yes, I have. It looks fantastic! Do you know _____ _____ it?
   A Matt's aunt. Apparently, that's the second cake she made.
   B Oh, really? _____ _____ to the first one?
   A She dropped it!
   B Oh, no! What a shame!

b Change the direct questions to indirect questions.

1. 'What's the wi-fi password?' 'Do you remember *what the wi-fi password is*?'
2. 'Is it going to rain this afternoon?' 'Do you think _____?'
3. 'Has Thomas arrived yet?' 'Do you know _____?'
4. 'How much will it cost to repair the roof?' 'Can you tell me _____?'
5. 'Do I have to pay to park here?' 'Could you tell me _____?'
6. 'Why did you leave your last job?' 'Would you mind telling me _____?'
7. 'What time does the library close?' 'Do you know _____?'
8. 'Did Susan's flight take off on time?' 'Do you have any idea _____?'

ACTIVATION

Work with a partner. Write two direct and two indirect questions to find out something you don't know about your partner. Ask for more information.

1B GRAMMAR auxiliary verbs

a Circle the correct answer.

Andreas Hello.

Beatriz Good morning. Are you here for an interview, too?

Andreas Yes. They say it's a good company to work for, ¹**don't** / **doesn't** / **do** they?

Beatriz Yes, they ²**do** / **are** / **don't** say that.

Andreas By the way, I'm Andreas Kourkoulos.

Beatriz That's a Greek name, ³**is** / **does** / **isn't** it?

Andreas Yes. I'm from Athens, but I've been living in New York for the past two years.

Beatriz ⁴**Do** / **Are** / **Have** you? I've got a friend who lives there. Anyway, I'm Beatriz Flores, from Buenos Aires, in Argentina.

Andreas Nice to meet you.

Beatriz You're a bit nervous, ⁵**are** / **don't** / **aren't** you?

Andreas A little. Don't you get nervous before interviews?

Beatriz Not really. I ⁶**am** / **will** / **do** get nervous before exams, but not before interviews. What's the time now?

Andreas 2.15. My interview's at 3.00.

Beatriz ⁷**Is** / **Has** / **Does** it? Mine's at 2.30. We won't have to wait much longer, ⁸**have** / **will** / **do** we?

b Complete the next part of the conversation with auxiliary verbs.

Andreas So, do you live here in Boston?

Beatriz No, I actually live in Dallas. I flew here yesterday afternoon.

Andreas ¹*Did* you? I arrived yesterday, too.

Beatriz Oh, right. Where are you staying?

Andreas At the Hotel Europe.

Beatriz Ah, so ²_____ I. The rooms aren't very nice, ³_____ they?

Andreas No, they aren't. But I ⁴_____ like the restaurant. I had a good meal there last night.

Beatriz ⁵_____ you? Are you working at the moment?

Andreas No, I resigned last week.

Beatriz Why? Didn't you like your job?

Andreas Well, I ⁶_____ like the job, but to be honest, I couldn't stand my boss!

Beatriz ⁷_____ you? I get on with my boss, but I think I need a new challenge.

Andreas So ⁸_____ I. Ah, it's your turn now. Good luck, Beatriz.

Beatriz Thanks. Shall we meet at the coffee bar later?

Andreas OK. And we can compare notes, ⁹_____ we?

ACTIVATION

Practise the conversations in **a** and **b** with a partner. Try to use the correct rhythm and intonation.

2A GRAMMAR present perfect simple and continuous

a Complete the conversation with the verbs in brackets in the present perfect simple or continuous.

Doctor Mrs Jones! Would you like to come through now, please?

Patient Oh, thank goodness! I ¹ _'ve been waiting_ (**wait**) for ages.

Doctor Yes, sorry about that. We ² _____ (**be**) extremely busy all morning. Now then, ³ _____ (**I / not see**) you this week already, Mrs Jones?

Patient Yes, doctor. Actually, this is the third time I ⁴ _____ (**come**) to see you this week. I was last here on Wednesday. ⁵ _____ (**you / forget**)? I had a terrible sore throat. Anyway, I took your advice and I ⁶ _____ (**drink**) plenty of water and I ⁷ _____ (**not talk**) too much.

Doctor Right, and ⁸ _____ (**your throat / hurt**) less since then?

Patient Oh, yes. It feels much better now.

Doctor Ah, that's great news. So, …

Patient Well, yes, it is, but now I've got a more serious problem with my foot. It ⁹ _____ (**be**) swollen since yesterday and I ¹⁰ _____ (**not be able**) to walk on it properly.

Doctor OK. If you could just lie down here on the…

Patient I think maybe I ¹¹ _____ (**have**) an allergic reaction to something. I ¹² _____ (**take**) antihistamine tablets every four hours, but they ¹³ _____ (**not make**) any difference.

Doctor Right, Mrs Jones. If you would please lie down here on the couch, I'll take a look…hmm. Well, there really is absolutely nothing to worry about. It's just a blister.

Patient Really? Hmm. Well, I ¹⁴ _____ (**just / buy**) these new shoes, so maybe they caused the problem.

Doctor Yes, I'd say that's very likely. Now, I'll put a plaster on it and I'm sure it'll be fine in a few days.

Patient Alright then. Thank you, doctor.

b Complete the questions with the verbs in brackets in the present perfect simple or continuous.

1 How long _have_ you _had_ your phone? (**have**)
2 _____ you ever _____ in an accident? (**be injured**)
3 How long _____ you _____ to this school? (**come**)
4 How many classes _____ you _____ this year? (**miss**)
5 How long _____ you _____ in your current home? (**live**)
6 _____ you ever _____ abroad? (**study**)

ACTIVATION

Work with a partner. Ask and answer the questions in **b**. Ask your partner for more information.

2B GRAMMAR adjectives as nouns, adjective order

a (Circle) the correct form. Tick (✓) if both forms are correct.

1 *The unemployed / Unemployed people* can apply to do these training courses free of charge. ✓
2 *The French / Frenchs* are very proud of their language and culture.
3 There are a lot of *homeless people / homeless* sleeping on the streets at night.
4 I met a very nice *Japanese girl / Japanese* in Manchester. She was really friendly.
5 *Rich people / The rich* always live in the best part of a city.
6 *The Spanish / Spanish* love being outside on warm, summer evenings.
7 Prime Minister, a lot of people say that your government just doesn't care about *poor / the poor*.
8 Don't talk like that – you should show more respect for *elderly people / the elderly*.
9 *The Chinese / The Chineses* invented paper.
10 *The young / Young* are finding it very difficult to buy their first flat or house.

b Complete the sentences with the adjectives in brackets in the correct order. Use your instinct if you are not sure.

1 **A** Can I help you?
   B Yes, I'm looking for some <u>smart, high-heeled</u> sandals. (**high-heeled / smart**)
2 **A** Did you see either of the robbers?
   B It all happened so fast. I saw a young man wearing a _____ jacket running out of the restaurant. (**denim / blue**)
3 **A** Your granddaughter's boyfriend is a rock musician, isn't he, Mrs Smith?
   B Yes, he is, but I can't stand the _____ music he plays! (**loud / awful**)
4 **A** Your son looks really like you – he has your _____ eyes. (**dark / big**)
   B Do you think so? I think he looks more like my husband.
5 **A** Are you looking for something?
   B Yes. I've lost a _____ scarf. Have you seen it? (**silk / long / black**)
6 **A** We used to live in a _____ house near the river. (**wooden / beautiful / old**)
   B How lovely. It must have been really peaceful.
7 **A** I've just arrived on the flight from Athens, but my suitcase hasn't arrived.
   B Can you describe it?
   A It's a _____ case. (**black / leather / small**)
8 **A** Ever since Simon came back from Bangkok, he's been cooking me _____ curries. (**delicious / Thai**)
   B Lucky you! I love curries.
8 **A** What does Adam's wife look like?
   B She's quite slim and she has _____ hair. (**brown / curly / short**)
10 **A** I'm going to wear my _____ shirt to the party. (**new / striped**)
   B Good idea. It really suits you.

ACTIVATION

Describe three items that you own, e.g. clothes, a car, a guitar, etc., using two or three adjectives in the correct order. Use the chart to help you.

item	adjectives	description
bag	*leather, brown, lovely*	*I have a lovely, brown leather bag that I bought in Italy last summer.*

English File fourth edition Teacher's Guide Upper-intermediate   Photocopiable © Oxford University Press 2020

3A GRAMMAR narrative tenses: past simple, past continuous, past perfect, past perfect continuous

a) Read Part 1 of Richard's story and find examples of each tense below.

1 the past perfect   *had finished*   _____   _____
2 the past perfect continuous _____   _____   _____   _____
3 the past continuous   _____   _____   _____   _____

The most embarrassing moment of my life (Richard, Sussex)

Part 1

When I was about nine years old, I used to go to the cinema every Saturday morning – in those days it was very popular. After the film *had finished*, I would go to a toy shop and look at model planes and trains, and sometimes I bought them with the pocket money that I had been carefully saving. One day after the film, I went to a big department store to have a look at the model planes they had. I didn't buy anything, but as I was leaving, a very large man grabbed my arm quite violently and accused me of shoplifting. The man said that he was a store detective. As I had been concentrating on the toys, I hadn't noticed that he had been watching me. He made me empty my pockets and he went through my coat, searching for stolen goods, even though I told him very clearly that I had only been looking. Of course, he didn't find anything, but by this time several people had stopped to see what was happening. I felt very embarrassed and humiliated that so many people were looking at me, and I was very glad to leave the shop when it was all over.

b) Complete Part 2 of the story with the correct form of the verbs in brackets: past simple, past continuous, past perfect, or past perfect continuous.

Part 2

An hour or so later, when I ¹*was having* (have) lunch with my family at home, my father ² _____ (ask) me about the film. I then ³ _____ (mention) that I ⁴ _____ (look) at toys in a department store when a store detective ⁵ _____ (accuse) me of shoplifting and ⁶ _____ (search) me in the middle of the shop. My father ⁷ _____ (make) me repeat what I ⁸ _____ (say), and then immediately ⁹ _____ (jump up) from the table. Without either of us having finished our lunch, he ¹⁰ _____ (make) me get into the car. I ¹¹ _____ (never see) my father look so angry! He ¹² _____ (drive) quickly to the store, ¹³ _____ (park) outside, and took me to where the incident ¹⁴ _____ (take place). He then

demanded to see the manager and the store detective. When the manager ¹⁵ _____ (come), my father ¹⁶ _____ (start) shouting at him and he told him that I ¹⁷ _____ (never steal) anything in my life. He ¹⁸ _____ (make) the manager and store detective apologize to me for having accused me of shoplifting and for embarrassing me. But the thing is, I ¹⁹ _____ (find) this scene even more embarrassing than the first one, especially as I could see that a lot of customers ²⁰ _____ (stop) and ²¹ _____ (watch) us!

ACTIVATION

Work with a partner.

Student A: Cover the text. Try to remember what happened to Richard in Part 1.

Student B: Cover the text. Try to remember what happened to Richard in Part 2.

3B GRAMMAR the position of adverbs and adverbial phrases

a Put the adverbs in brackets in the best place in the conversation.

Gary So, what did you think of the match?

Craig ¹Even though they lost, I think Scotland played ~~brilliantly~~ again. (*brilliantly* / *tonight*)

John ²Craig, do you mean that? (**really**) I thought they were awful. (**absolutely**)

Craig ³I suppose you think England played. (**well**)

John ⁴No, I don't. England play these days. (**unfortunately** / **never** / **well**) But they deserved to win.

Craig ⁵But you must admit that they were lucky. (**incredibly**)

Gary ⁶Craig, do you have anything good to say about England? (**ever**)

John ⁷They were lucky with their second goal. (**to be honest** / **quite**)

Craig ⁸Come on, John, England were lucky with both the first and second goals! (**extremely**)

Gary ⁹I thought both teams played (**personally** / **badly**), but at the end of the day, Craig, I'd say England were better in the second half. (**a bit** / **especially**)

John ¹⁰Well, they are playing Germany in Munich, so let's see how they do. (**next** / **there**)

b Complete the conversation with the correct adverbs from the list.

~~absolutely~~ actually always angrily a little badly earlier that day here in quarter of an hour incredibly naturally obviously quickly slowly well

Director Jason, that was ¹*absolutely* marvellous, but you've got to get to the centre of the stage.

Jason But I have to wait for Tanya to finish her line and she's doing it too ²_____ .

Tanya Well, I could try saying it more ³_____ if you want me to.

Director Yes, could you? Now, Jason, remember, when Tanya tells you she's going to marry Henry, you know about it, because you heard them talking in the garden ⁴_____ , so you aren't at all surprised.

Jason Well, ⁵_____ I know about it, but I thought maybe I should pretend at first that I didn't know.

Director No, we want to see your emotion! You reacted very calmly, but ⁶_____ you're not a calm person at all. I want you to react ⁷_____ , OK? Now the next scene. Sally, you were great. But, when you've finished reading Tanya's letter, when you're on the last couple of lines, pause ⁸_____ and look up at the audience. Let them feel how ⁹_____ you've been treated by her.

Sally Do you want me to cry? I am ¹⁰_____ good at crying.

Director Not ¹¹_____ , not in this scene. Look out at the audience.

Tanya Can I just ask why you ¹²_____ ask me to play horrible characters?

Director Because you do it so ¹³_____ , darling. It just comes ¹⁴_____ to you. Right everyone, take a break and come back ¹⁵_____ .

ACTIVATION

Write five sentences using the adverbs. Then compare your ideas with a partner.

brilliantly fortunately gradually incredibly sadly

English File fourth edition Teacher's Guide Upper-intermediate Photocopiable © Oxford University Press 2020

4A GRAMMAR future perfect and future continuous

● Complete the conversations with the verbs in brackets in the future perfect or future continuous.

1 A I'm really looking forward to our trip to Paris on Friday.

B Me, too! This time tomorrow we_'ll be getting on_ (**get on**) the plane, and we _____ (**not think**) about work!

2 A Do you think you _____ still _____ (**work**) here in ten years' time?

B Probably. But I hope I _____ (**be promoted**) to Head of Department by then.

3 A Why are you walking so fast?

B If we don't hurry, by the time we get to the station, the train _____ (**leave**).

4 A Oh no! My car won't start and I need to pick up a friend at the airport.

B You can borrow mine. I _____ (**not use**) it today.

5 A Do you think it's too late to phone Hilary?

B No, it's only eleven o'clock. Knowing her, she _____ (**not go**) to bed yet. She _____ still _____ (**watch**) TV.

6 A Is this your son's final year at university?

B Yes, by this time next year, he _____ (**graduate**), and he _____ (**look for**) for a job.

7 A Shall I make some soup or something for your parents when they arrive?

B Good idea! They'll be starving, as they _____ (**not have**) time for lunch.

8 A _____ you _____ (**come**) with us to see the new Marvel film tonight?

B Sorry, I won't – I still have lots of work to do.

9 A What time does your plane land?

B At seven in the morning. _____ you _____ (**pick me up**) from the airport?

A Of course. I always do!

10 A Mark and Paul are travelling around Asia. They've already been to China and Thailand.

B Wow! How many countries _____ they _____ (**visit**) by the time they get back home?

11 A I'm fed up with all these exams.

B Yes, but just think – we _____ (**finish**) them all by Friday, and we _____ (**celebrate**)!

12 A Tim's going to South Africa next month, isn't he?

B No, he's decided to wait. He _____ (**not save**) enough money until at least July.

ACTIVATION

Write one thing that you'll…

1 be doing at midday tomorrow.

2 have done by the end of next week.

3 have done a year from now.

Work with a partner. Compare your sentences. Ask for more information.

168   **English File fourth edition Teacher's Guide Upper-intermediate**   Photocopiable © Oxford University Press 2020

4B GRAMMAR zero and first conditionals, future time clauses

● Circle the correct answer. Sometimes two answers are possible.

1 I'll have my mobile phone with me _____.
a in case you need to call me
b in case you'll need to call me
c in case you've needed to call me

2 Phone him as soon as _____ that report.
a you finish
b you've finished
c you'll finish

3 I'll play football with you when _____.
a I've had my dinner
b I'll have my dinner
c I have my dinner

4 I'm not going to go to the party unless _____.
a you'll go too
b you go too
c you've gone too

5 Could you get me some milk if _____?
a you'll go to the shop
b you go to the shop
c you're going to the shop

6 If the weather _____, we'll go for a walk.
a will have improved
b will improve
c improves

7 I won't tell my boss I'm leaving _____.
a until I find a new job
b until I'm finding a new job
c until I've found a new job

8 If I don't have breakfast, _____.
a I'll be hungry all morning
b I'm hungry all morning
c I'll be being hungry all morning

9 Please come in quietly because _____.
a the children will be sleeping when you arrive
b the children will sleep when you arrive
c the children are sleeping when you arrive

10 Take a jacket in case _____ later.
a it'll have got cold
b it's getting cold
c it gets cold

11 Their flight was delayed, so they _____ back until after midnight.
a 'll be
b won't be
c 'll have been

12 We're going to have a picnic at the beach tomorrow unless _____.
a it rains
b it will be raining
c it's raining

13 I _____ book our flights until we've found a hotel.
a don't
b 'm not going to
c won't

14 If you want to improve your English, _____.
a you'll have to practise
b you have to practise
c you've had to practise

15 Come and say goodbye tomorrow _____.
a before you'll leave
b before you've left
c before you leave

| 15 |

11–15 Excellent. You can use conditionals and future time clauses very well.

8–10 Good. But check the rules in the Grammar Bank (Student's Book p.139) for any questions that you got wrong.

0–7 This is difficult for you. Read the rules in the Grammar Bank again (Student's Book p.139). Then ask your teacher for another photocopy and do the exercise again at home.

ACTIVATION

Complete the sentences with your own ideas. Then compare your ideas with a partner.

1 As soon as I get home, I _____.

2 If I don't have time for breakfast, _____.

3 When I retire, _____.

4 You won't get a good job unless _____.

5 Don't forget to take _____ in case _____.

6 I'm not going to _____ until _____.

English File fourth edition Teacher's Guide Upper-intermediate   Photocopiable © Oxford University Press 2020

5A GRAMMAR unreal conditionals

● Complete the sentences with the correct form of the verbs in brackets, using second or third conditionals.

1 They met in Paris at a conference.
If they _hadn't gone_ to the conference in Paris, they _wouldn't have met_. (**not go / not meet**)

2 The curry doesn't taste great. I should have put more spices in it.
If I _____ more spices in it, it _____ better. (**put / taste**)

3 I'm not very happy in my present job. Maybe I should quit and look for another.
If I _____ another job, I might _____ happier. (**find / be**)

4 We got wet because you wouldn't take the bus. You wanted to walk.
We _____ wet if we _____ the bus. (**not get / take**)

5 Don't swim in that river; there might be crocodiles.
If I _____ you, I _____ in that river, there might be crocodiles. (**be / not swim**)

6 Laura fell in love with Tom. She left Liam.
Laura _____ Liam if she _____ in love with Tom. (**not leave / not fall**)

7 He used the stolen credit card at a hotel, so the police found him.
If he _____ the stolen credit card at a hotel, the police _____ him. (**not use / not find**)

8 They don't have enough money to buy a new car.
They _____ a new car if they _____ afford one. (**buy / can**)

9 We didn't go on the London Eye because the queue was too long.
We _____ on the London Eye, if the queue _____ so long. (**go / not be**)

10 They spend all their money on designer clothes. They can't afford to go on holiday.
If they _____ all their money on designer clothes, they _____ afford to go on holiday. (**not spend / can**)

11 I didn't know you wanted to go to the concert. I didn't buy you a ticket.
I _____ you a ticket if I _____ that you wanted to go to the concert. (**buy / know**)

12 Nicola isn't very good at the piano because she doesn't practise.
Nicola _____ so bad at the piano if she _____. (**not be / practise**)

ACTIVATION

Cover the sentences. Look at the pictures and try to remember the sentences.

170

English File fourth edition Teacher's Guide Upper-intermediate   Photocopiable © Oxford University Press 2020

5B GRAMMAR *wish* for present / future, *wish* for past regrets

a Complete the sentences with a verb from the list. For sentences 1–4, use the past simple. For sentences 5–8, use would / wouldn't + infinitive.

be   call   can   ~~live~~   not have to   not make   not sing   stop

1 I wish we *lived* in a bigger house.
2 I wish my husband _____ better at cooking.
3 I wish we _____ afford to buy a new car.
4 I wish I _____ wear a suit to work.

5 I wish my mum _____ all the time. Her voice is awful!
6 I wish the dog _____ chasing the cat.
7 I wish my parents _____ me practise the piano every day.
8 I wish my boyfriend _____ me more often.

b Complete the sentences using *wish* + past perfect

1 I didn't apply for the job and now I regret it.
   I wish I'd applied for the job.
2 They didn't put on sunscreen and now they're burnt.
   _____ sunscreen.
3 He broke up with his girlfriend and now he misses her.
   _____ with his girlfriend.
4 We didn't buy concert tickets yesterday and now they're sold out.
   _____ concert tickets yesterday.
5 I ate too much chocolate and now I feel sick.
   _____ so much chocolate.
6 She dyed her hair and now she hates the colour.
   _____ her hair.
7 We threw away some old books and now they're worth a lot of money.
   _____ the old books.
8 I had an argument with Sophie and now she isn't talking to me.
   _____ an argument with Sophie.

ACTIVATION

Write three sentences beginning *I wish*: one with the past simple, one with person + *would*, and one with the past perfect. Then compare your ideas with a partner.

6A GRAMMAR used to, be used to, get used to

a Circle the correct form.

Inge
Madrid, Spain

I come from Germany. I ¹**used to live** / **would live** in the north, in Hamburg, but then I moved to Madrid about five years ago. I love the weather in Spain – there are more sunny days and it's a lot warmer. But I had to ²**be used to** / **get used to** having lunch quite late, at about 2.00 p.m., and dinner as late as 9.00 or 10.00 p.m. In Germany, things ³**usually** / **use to** happen exactly on time, but here things are much more relaxed. I like that, too. The only thing I really miss is the bread! I ⁴**was used to being able** / **was used to be able** to choose from between 20 or 30 different kinds of bread, but here it's more like two or three. And sometimes I have problems with noisy neighbours, especially at night. That never ⁵**used to be** / **was used to being** a problem in Hamburg. People there ⁶**usually go** / **are used to going** to bed earlier.

b Complete the blog with *used to*, *be used to*, *get used to*, or *usually*.

Lennart
Parma, Italy

I ¹ *used to* live in Sweden, but I married an Italian woman and now I live in Parma, Italy. I've been here for six years now, so I ² _____ the lifestyle. Life is more hectic here than in Sweden. Italian people socialize more than Swedish people, and I really enjoy that. I had to ³ _____ eating lots of pasta, particularly tortellini, which is Parma's local speciality. In Sweden I ⁴ _____ eat pasta once or twice a month, and now I ⁵ _____ have it once or twice a week! I also had to ⁶ _____ the different mentality. For example, people here are very family-orientated. This was new to me and hard to understand at first. But now I ⁷ _____ having lunch every Sunday with my in-laws! It was also quite hard for me to ⁸ _____ the dialect they speak in Parma. I still sometimes have to ask people to repeat things. The only thing I can't ⁹ _____ is the coffee. I know espresso is supposed to be the best coffee in the world, but it's just too strong for me. In Sweden I ¹⁰ _____ drink a lot of coffee, but it was much weaker. Still, I do love the smell of espresso!

c Complete the blog with a verb from the list in the correct form.

Neil and Shirley
Queensland, Australia

be   eat   get up   ~~live~~   see

We used to ¹ *live* in England, but we've been living in Queensland, Australia, since 2010. We're used to ² _____ here now, but at first it was quite hard. We live in the country, and when we first moved into the house, I just couldn't get used to ³ _____ snakes in the garden, but now it's not a problem. We just leave them alone. Although we speak the same language, there are still some things here that are strange. People here usually ⁴ _____ really early, at about 5.00 a.m., which we still haven't got used to. Christmas doesn't feel right either – I haven't got used to ⁵ _____ roast turkey when the temperature is 40°C!

ACTIVATION

Complete the sentences with information about your life. Compare your answers with a partner.

1 I usually _____.
2 I used to _____.
3 I'm used to _____.
4 I'm not used to _____.
5 It's difficult to get used to _____.
6 I didn't use to _____.
7 When I was younger, I would _____.

6B GRAMMAR gerunds and infinitives

● Complete the sentences with the verbs in brackets in the infinitive (with or without *to*) or the gerund (*-ing*).

1 I learnt *to speak* French when I was at school. (**speak**)
2 Do you fancy _____ a film tonight? (**see**)
3 Laura's mother lets her _____ when she wants. (**go out**)
4 I can't afford _____ a holiday this year. (**have**)
5 It's getting late. We'd better _____ much longer. (**not stay**)
6 I'm going to carry on _____ until 8.00 p.m. tonight. (**work**)
7 What are you planning _____ to the party? (**wear**)
8 Would you rather _____ in the country or in a town? (**live**)
9 I couldn't help _____ when my brother fell off his bicycle. (**laugh**)
10 Did you manage _____ the report before the meeting? (**finish**)
11 The satnav died and we ended up _____ completely the wrong way. (**go**)
12 If I tell you a secret, do you promise _____ anybody? (**not tell**)
13 My boss made me _____ late last night. (**work**)
14 At school, I was made _____ really hard. (**study**)
15 Would you like me _____ you with the dinner? (**help**)
16 I don't mind _____. I'm not in a hurry. (**wait**)
17 Sorry, you aren't allowed _____ here. (**park**)
18 We need to practise _____ before the oral exam. (**speak**)
19 I like _____ early in the morning in the summer. (**get up**)
20 Monica might _____ tomorrow. She's ill. (**not come**)
21 I love _____ time with my grandparents. (**spend**)
22 Will you be able _____ me a lift to work tomorrow? (**give**)

● Complete the sentences with the verbs in brackets in the gerund or the infinitive with *to*.

23 You forgot *to buy* the milk. (**buy**)
24 Could you try _____ late tomorrow? (**not be**)
25 The sheets on this bed are dirty. They need _____. (**change**)
26 Don't you remember _____ his wife at the Christmas party? (**meet**)
27 I'll never forget _____ in New York for the first time. (**arrive**)
28 I think you need _____ the irregular verbs. (**revise**)
29 Did you remember _____ James about the meeting tomorrow? (**tell**)
30 If the computer doesn't work, try _____ it off and on again. (**turn**)

25–30 **Excellent.** You can use gerunds and infinitives very well.

16–24 **Quite good.** But check the rules in the Grammar Bank (Student's Book p.143) for any questions that you got wrong.

0–15 **This is difficult for you.** Read the rules in the Grammar Bank again (Student's Book p.143). Then ask your teacher for another photocopy and do the exercise again at home.

ACTIVATION

Write sentences that are true for you, using the prompts. Compare your ideas with a partner. Ask him / her for more details.

- something you learnt to do when you were a child
- something your parents didn't let you do when you were younger
- a place you remember visiting
- a person you enjoy spending time with
- something you often forget to do
- something that you try not to do

English File fourth edition Teacher's Guide Upper-intermediate   Photocopiable © Oxford University Press 2020

7A GRAMMAR past modals

a Read the conversations and the sentences in brackets. Then complete the conversations with *might (not) have*, *must have*, or *can't have* + past participle.

1 A Why is there so much traffic today?

B I don't know. There <u>*might have been*</u> an accident. (maybe there was)

2 A Can you move your leg?

B No, it hurts too much. I think I _____ it. (perhaps I have broken it)

3 A Look! The gate's open and the dog has gone.

B Oh no! We _____ it open when we went out. (I'm sure we left it open)

4 A Oh no, the cake's burning!

B You _____ the oven on too high. (you definitely put the oven on)

5 A I can't find the milk. We _____ it all. (I'm sure we didn't drink it)

B Yes, you're right. It must be in there somewhere.

6 A Where's Jeremy? He should be here.

B He _____ the email about the meeting. (perhaps he didn't see)

7 A Ellen passed all her exams with top marks!

B Wow! She _____ really hard. (I'm sure she worked)

8 A I've done my homework, Mum. I'm going out.

B What? You _____ all of it. Let me see it. (it's impossible you've finished)

9 A We didn't see Dan and Sarah at the concert.

B They _____ tickets. I think the concert was sold out. (perhaps they weren't able to get)

10 A I called you earlier, but I got your voicemail.

B Sorry. I _____ my phone by mistake. (I'm sure I switched off)

b Complete the sentences with *should / shouldn't have* and the past participle of a verb from the list.

break up   buy   come   keep   ~~take~~   tell   use   wait

1 We're lost. I knew we <u>*should have taken*</u> the second exit at the roundabout!

2 This tastes too spicy. You _____ so much chilli.

3 You _____ with James. He was perfect for you.

4 The concert was amazing. You _____ with us.

5 Jim's already gone? I don't believe it – he _____ for us.

6 I'm afraid we can't exchange the jacket now. You _____ the receipt.

7 You _____ us that you were in hospital. We would have visited you.

8 I _____ these jeans. They really don't suit me.

ACTIVATION

Write **four** conversations of two lines using *must have*, *might have*, *can't have*, and *should(n't) have*.

174

English File fourth edition Teacher's Guide Upper-intermediate   Photocopiable © Oxford University Press 2020

7B GRAMMAR verbs of the senses

● Complete the conversations with the phrases in each list. Sometimes two forms are possible.

---

1 smells   smells like   smells as if

Customer I'm looking for a perfume for my wife that [1] _smells_ nice and fresh.
Assistant What about this one? It [2] _____ very flowery.
Customer No, I don't like it. It [3] _____ it's for an older woman.
Assistant Try this one then – it's called 'Paris'.
Customer That's very nice. It [4] _____ roses.

---

2 feels   feels like   feels as if

Assistant It's very good quality and it [5] _____ very smooth. Touch it and see.
Tourist Hmm, yes. It [6] _____ silk. Is it silk?
Assistant No, it's cotton, but it [7] _____ it's made of silk.
Tourist The material [8] _____ very soft. I like it.

---

3 tastes   tastes like   tastes as if

Woman 1 Try a piece of this. It [9] _____ delicious.
Woman 2 Mmm. This one [10] _____ the cakes my grandma used to make.
Woman 1 It's very nice. It [11] _____ there's a little bit of orange in there.
Woman 2 That's right! And it [12] _____ much better than the ones you get in the shops.

---

4 look   look like   look as if

Woman You shouldn't have said you wanted to come if you didn't.
Man Why do you say that?
Woman You [13] _____ you are totally bored.
Man I did want to come. It's just that they all [14] _____ fine to me.
Woman Even the ones that make me [15] _____ I'm 60 years old?
Man OK, those ones do [16] _____ a bit old-fashioned.
Woman And these ones that [17] _____ something a 13-year-old would wear?
Man They [18] _____ OK to me.
Woman Oh, you're so helpful.

---

5 sound(s)   sound(s) like   sound(s) as if

Engineer Wait! You're coming in too soon. It [19] _____ wrong.
Guitarist It [20] _____ fine to me.
Engineer No, it [21] _____ you're rushing in.
Guitarist Well, how should it sound?
Engineer It should [22] _____ an early 80s rock band, remember?

ACTIVATION

Practise the conversations with a partner. Then cover the conversations and try to act one of them out from memory.

English File fourth edition Teacher's Guide Upper-intermediate   Photocopiable © Oxford University Press 2020

8A GRAMMAR   the passive (all forms); *have something done*; *it is said that...*, *he is thought to...*, etc.

a Complete the newspaper report with the verbs in brackets in the passive. Add any other necessary words, e.g. *to* or *that*.

Investigation after seaside incident

Police have begun an enquiry after a fight broke out between several people in Lindhurst Road, Poole.

The fight [1] *is believed to* (**believe**) have started in the early hours of Friday morning at an address near the corner of Lindhurst Road. It [2] _____ (**think**) the fight started after a car was damaged by one of the men.

At least one of the men involved [3] _____ (**say**) have been armed. Three men remain in hospital and are being treated for injuries, which [4] _____ (**understand**) be the result of the fight. It [5] _____ (**expect**) one man will be released from hospital later today. Five men, who [6] _____ (**think**) be

from the Brighton area, and are aged between 21 and 32, have been arrested. The police are asking anyone who witnessed the incident to contact them urgently. All information will be treated confidentially.

b Complete the sentences with the correct form of *have*, the past participle, and the words in brackets.

1 She *had her wedding dress made* by a famous designer. It cost a fortune! (**wedding dress / make**)
2 I thought this was a safe city. I didn't expect _____. (**my wallet / steal**)
3 I _____ at the dentist tomorrow. I'm terrified! (**a tooth / fill**)
4 Have you ever _____? (**your heart / break**)
5 You should _____ if you can't see the board clearly. (**your eyes / test**)
6 How often _____? (**your car / service**)
7 Our neighbours _____ at the moment. (**a swimming pool / build**)
8 I really need to go to the hairdresser's. I _____ for ages. (**my hair / cut**)
9 I don't mind _____, but I hate being videoed. (**my photo / take**)
10 Unfortunately, we _____ last night. (**our house / burgle**)
11 My grandfather _____ every Friday. (**his shopping / deliver**)
12 It's the second time this year that we _____. (**our car / break into**)

ACTIVATION

Work with a partner. Ask and answer the questions. If your partner says yes, ask for more information.
Have you ever had your...?
- portrait painted
- hair cut by a friend
- fortune told
- photo taken by a professional photographer
- house or car broken into

8B GRAMMAR reporting verbs

a Complete each sentence with the correct form of the verb in brackets.

1 A Remind me _to book_ a taxi to the airport. (**book**)

   B We don't need one; Andy's offered _____ us a lift. (**give**)

2 A Hi, Tom. I'm surprised to see you here. I didn't think you liked opera.

   B I don't, but Delia persuaded me _____ tonight. (**come**)

3 A Have the police found the men that robbed the supermarket?

   B Apparently, they've arrested one man, but he denies _____ anything to do with it. (**have**)

4 A I've always regretted _____ to university. (**not go**)

   B Well it's never too late. Why don't you apply?

5 A Have the kids been fighting again? Oliver's really upset, but he refuses _____ me why. (**tell**)

   B Oh, Harry accused Oliver of _____ one of his toys, and now they aren't speaking to each other. (**break**)

6 A Where are you going on holiday this year?

   B We haven't decided yet. Molly suggested _____ camping in Scotland, but I'm not very keen. I'd rather go somewhere warmer. (**go**)

7 A Someone broke into the car and stole my laptop while I was in the supermarket.

   B I warned you _____ it in the car. Have you reported it to the police? (**not leave**)

8 A There's a funny smell in the kitchen.

   B That's because your dad insisted on _____ curry for dinner and he burnt it. (**make**)

b Complete the sentences using the reporting verb in brackets and a verb from the list.

come ~~cook~~ eat forget keep lose tidy try

1 Adam _offered to cook_ dinner for everyone. (**offer**)

2 Pablo _____ his room at the weekend. (**promise**)

3 Roger _____ for _____ my birthday. (**apologize**)

4 Bill _____ me _____ all my money in the bank. (**advise**)

5 Sofia _____ the new pizza place. (**suggest**)

6 Ruby _____ all the chocolates. (**admit**)

7 Mike _____ me _____ to the theatre with him. (**invite**)

8 Jamie _____ me for _____ the tickets, but I think he had them. (**blame**)

ACTIVATION

Think of a time when you…

- received some good advice.
- apologized to someone for something.
- offered to help someone.
- advised somebody to do (or not to do) something.
- were blamed for something you didn't do.
- regretted something you did / didn't do.

Make sentences using reported speech. Then compare your sentences with your partner.

My sister advised me to do a course to improve my computer skills.

English File fourth edition Teacher's Guide Upper-intermediate   Photocopiable © Oxford University Press 2020

9A GRAMMAR clauses of contrast and purpose

a Match 1–10 with a–j to make complete sentences.

1 They went to London for… `g`
2 She flew to São Paulo to…
3 Although Josh played really well, …
4 We downloaded a travel app so that…
5 Despite losing the first set, …
6 Even though I wasn't feeling very well, …
7 I took a taxi so as not to…
8 He went for a walk in spite of…
9 We left early in order to…
10 The men went out fishing in spite of…

a be late.
b the rough sea.
c the fact that it was raining.
d avoid the traffic.
e I still went to work.
f she won the match.
g ~~a weekend break.~~
h he lost in the end.
i we would know the best things to see.
j visit her brother.

b Rewrite the sentences using the words in brackets so that both sentences mean the same.

1 In spite of the cold weather, the barbecue was a success. (**although**)
Although the weather was cold, the barbecue was a success.

2 A lot of companies have reduced staff numbers so that they can save money. (**in order to**)
_____ .

3 Even though the flight was long, she felt great when she arrived in New York. (**despite**)
_____ .

4 Nick didn't tell Louisa the truth because he didn't want to hurt her feelings. (**so as**)
_____ .

5 I bought the shoes in spite of the fact that they were ridiculously expensive. (**even though**)
_____ .

6 The company has a big market share even though they do very little advertising. (**in spite of**)
_____ .

7 They had to leave the hotel early. If they hadn't, they would have missed their train. (**so that**)
_____ .

8 She didn't get the job in spite of being a strong candidate. (**though**)
_____ .

ACTIVATION

Complete the sentences with your own ideas. Then compare with a partner.

1 Sara is learning English in order to _____ .
2 My husband isn't making very good progress in English, even though _____ .
3 Nicola watches films in English to _____ .
4 Jan passed his English exam despite _____ .
5 Our English teacher took us to London for the weekend so that _____ .

Write **two** true sentences about yourself and learning English. Use expressions of contrast and purpose.
Then compare your ideas with a partner.

178

English File fourth edition Teacher's Guide Upper-intermediate Photocopiable © Oxford University Press 2020

9B GRAMMAR uncountable and plural nouns

● Circle the correct option.

Hurry up, kids! You don't have [1]**a time** / **time** to watch videos! Daniel, your trousers [2]**look** / **looks** dirty. Go and put on a clean pair. Bertha, don't forget athletics [3]**is** / **are** after school today. Have you remembered your [4]**short** / **shorts** and a T-shirt? OK, good. And have you both had breakfast? No, Bertha? Well, you'll have to have [5]**a** / **a piece of** toast because there isn't any cereal. And hurry up!

I'm sorry, but your hand luggage [6]**is** / **are** too heavy, Madam. You'll need to put [7]**a belonging** / **some belongings** into your suitcase. Oh, right. There [8]**isn't** / **aren't** any space in your suitcase? Well then, I'm afraid we'll have to charge you extra.

Now then, Brian. I've talked to you before about your [9]**behaviour** / **behaviours** with customers. I know they can sometimes be rude, but we expect our [10]**staff** / **staffs** to be polite at all times. Do you understand? Good. Then I hope to see [11]**a** / **some** progress from you very soon.

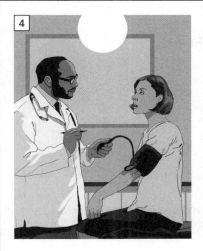

I know what you're going to say, doctor. You're going to give me some [12]**advices** / **advice** about reducing stress, and give me [13]**a** / **some** medicine to help me sleep at night. But I read [14]**an** / **some** information on a website which said that sleeping tablets aren't good for you.

Be careful you don't scratch [15]**a** / **the** furniture with [16]**that** / **those** scissors, Bertha! And have you finished your [17]**homework** / **homeworks**? Good, then come and help me take out the [18]**rubbish** / **rubbishes**.

ACTIVATION

Choose **four** nouns from the list and write a sentence using each one. Compare your sentences with a partner.

accommodation   equipment   manners   news   police   politics   research   team

10A GRAMMAR quantifiers: *all*, *every*, *both*, etc.

a Circle the correct form.

1. **A** We don't do **any** / **no** experiments in our chemistry class.
   B Don't you? We do something practical in **every** / **all** class.
2. **A** Did you do **all research** / **all of the research** yourself?
   B Yes, I did **all** / **all of it** myself.
3. **A** How often do you use the library?
   B Hardly ever. I can find **everything** / **all** on the internet.
4. **A** When can I see you to discuss my science project?
   B I'll be in my office **all day** / **every day** today. Come **any** / **all** time.
5. **A** How did your students do in the biology exam?
   B Not too badly. **They passed all.** / **They all passed**.
6. **A** How did the trip to the science museum go?
   B It was fine. **Most** / **Most of** the students enjoyed it.
7. **A** What subject do you like best – physics or chemistry?
   B I don't like **either of them** / **both of them**. They're **either** / **both** boring!
8. **A** Neither my mother **or** / **nor** father went to university.
   B Really? **Both** / **Either** my parents studied law, but **either of them** / **neither of them** work as lawyers.

b Complete the column on the right with quantifiers from the list.

| ~~all~~ all all anyone both every every |
| most most of neither no none of |

quantifiers

1. Not ▬▬ birds can fly. — *all*
2. ▬▬ kiwis nor penguins can fly. _____
3. ▬▬ country in South America, except Bolivia and Paraguay, has a coastline. _____
4. ▬▬ cars nowadays are fitted with seatbelts at the front and the back. _____
5. ▬▬ the students in my class, about 80%, live very near the school. _____
6. There are ▬▬ wild tigers in Africa. However, some can still be found in parts of Asia. _____
7. In Ireland, ▬▬ who is aged 18 or over can vote in an election. _____
8. ▬▬ Canadians speak English as their first language (77%), but some speak French. _____
9. Nocturnal animals are animals that sleep ▬▬ day and hunt for food at night. _____
10. Alexander Graham Bell and Elisha Gray ▬▬ invented the telephone at the same time. _____
11. Trains in France run ▬▬ day of the year, including Christmas Day. _____
12. ▬▬ the people who survived the sinking of the Titanic are still alive today. The last survivor, Millvina Dean, died in 2009. _____

ACTIVATION

Cover the **quantifiers** column in **b**. Work with a partner and take turns to say the sentences using the correct quantifier.

10B GRAMMAR articles

● Complete the sentences with *a*, *an*, *the*, or – (no article).

A [1] *The* Kremlin is probably [2] _____ most famous building in [3] _____ Moscow.

B James had [4] _____ accident while he was skiing in Austria and now he's in [5] _____ hospital.

C [6] _____ first state in [7] _____ USA where [8] _____ women could vote was Wyoming.

D [9] _____ population of [10] _____ South Africa is approximately 52 million.

E I took a year off before I went to [11] _____ university. First, I worked as [12] _____ au-pair in Italy for six months.

F [13] _____ River Ebro in Spain flows into [14] _____ Mediterranean Sea.

G We couldn't visit [15] _____ village church yesterday because there was [16] _____ wedding taking place.

H [17] _____ quickest way to get from London to Oxford by [18] _____ car is to take [19] _____ M40 motorway.

I [20] _____ Lake Superior, in [21] _____ Canada, is [22] _____ biggest lake in [23] _____ world.

J I'm not usually frightened of [24] _____ spiders, but [25] _____ spiders in [26] _____ zoo were enormous!

K The man was sent to [27] _____ prison for eight years for robbing [28] _____ bank in Zürich.

L I love eating at [29] _____ Mario's. I think it's the best pizza restaurant in the city.

M Whenever I'm in London, I take [30] _____ bus to [31] _____ Science Museum and spend the morning looking around.

N We spent our honeymoon in Morocco and camped in [32] _____ Sahara desert for two nights.

O My sister doesn't normally like [33] _____ heights, but she managed to get to the top of [34] _____ Eiffel Tower.

P [35] _____ Mont Blanc is [36] _____ highest mountain in [37] _____ Alps.

> 28–37 **Excellent.** You can use articles very well.
>
> 10–27 **Good.** But check the rules in the Grammar Bank (Student's Book p.151) for any questions that you got wrong.
>
> 0–9 **This is difficult for you.** Read the rules in the Grammar Bank (Student's Book p.151). Then ask your teacher for another photocopy and do the exercise again at home.

ACTIVATION

Write two paragraphs about your country and city or town. Include the following information:

Your country:
- Where is it?
- What are the most important geographical features, e.g. mountains, lakes, rivers, etc.?

Your city or town:
- Where is it?
- What are the most important buildings, tourist sites, shops, etc.?

Revision GRAMMAR Auction

Sentences   **Price**

1 Can you tell me what the time is?   _____
2 Her name's Hannah, isn't she?   _____
3 How long have you been having driving lessons?   _____
4 She has long beautiful dark hair.   _____
5 The accident happened because the driver had been drinking.   _____
6 I like very much classical music.   _____
7 This time tomorrow we'll have finished all our exams.   _____
8 I can't wait to tell my dad the news when he comes home.   _____
9 I would have enjoyed the film more if it wouldn't have had subtitles.   _____
10 I wish I have more free time!   _____
11 It's getting late. We'd better go now.   _____
12 I'm not used to getting up so early.   _____
13 He mustn't have seen you or he would have said hello.   _____
14 It looks like if it's going to rain.   _____
15 The missing man is thought that he is from Manchester.   _____
16 Nick insisted on paying for the meal.   _____
17 Lily is going to hospital this afternoon for to visit her husband.   _____
18 I need to buy some new furnitures for my living room.   _____
19 You can have either the chocolate or the vanilla ice cream. Not both.   _____
20 The man was sent to the prison for ten years.   _____

Communicative activity instructions

Tell me about it

A pairwork activity

Sts write information about themselves in a chart. They then swap charts with a partner and ask each other to explain the information. **This is a two-page activity.** Copy one page (**A** and **B**) per student.

> **LANGUAGE**
>
> general revision of Intermediate grammar and vocabulary

- Put Sts in pairs, **A** and **B**, and give out the worksheets.
- Focus on the instructions for **a** and give Sts five minutes to write their answers in the correct spaces. Point out that they each have different instructions for what to write. When Sts have finished, tell them to fold the worksheet in half (or tear off the instructions).
- Now get Sts to swap worksheets with their partner. Demonstrate the activity by taking a worksheet from a student, looking at the answers in the chart, and asking him / her *Why did you write…?* Ask follow-up questions to continue the conversation.
- Sts now do the activity in their pairs. Tell them they had different instructions in **a**, and encourage them ask about the information in any order. Monitor and help where necessary. Stop the activity when most Sts have asked about all their partner's information.

1A Ask me a question

A semi-controlled speaking activity

Sts practise question formation. Copy one worksheet per student.

> **LANGUAGE**
>
> question formation

- Give out the worksheets and focus on **a**. Tell Sts they have five minutes, in pairs, to decide what the missing words are for each question. They must <u>not</u> write anything.
- Check answers.

> **Your home**
> 1 do you   2 have you   3 do you, with   4 do you
> 5 there, don't
> **Getting around**
> 1 do you, to   2 does it   3 Do you, What, do you drive / have   4 How, do, use   5 What's, to, around
> **Free time**
> 1 do you   2 What kind / type, do you, to
> 3 often do you   4 What, do you   5 How much
> **Lifestyle**
> 1 much, do you, a   2 How many, do you   3 do you, to
> 4 you, to   5 was, to
> **Travel**
> 1 the most, 've / have ever   2 are, to go   3 Do you, to, or
> 4 Do you, in   5 you ever, to
> **Family**
> 1 How many, are   2 Who, do you, to
> 3 Who do you, with, or   4 do you, about   5 was the, your

> **Childhood and school**
> 1 were you   2 did / do you, to   3 was / is your
> 4 Have you, Did you   5 did you, to
> **A male or female relative**
> 1 What's his / her   2 is he / she   3 What does he / she
> 4 What does he / she, like   5 What's / is he / she

- Now focus on **b** and put Sts in pairs. Tell them to choose a topic and ask and answer the questions.
- When you feel the activity has gone on for long enough, get feedback from a few pairs.
- If a pair finishes early, get them to try another topic.

1B What's in a signature?

An interpretation and free-speaking activity

Sts use information to interpret famous people's signatures and also their own. Copy one worksheet per student.

> **LANGUAGE**
>
> present simple (narrative), *the…the* + comparatives, personality vocabulary
>
> *This person uses their full name and the initial of their surname. That means their private life is more important.*
>
> *The more illegible the signature is, the less assertive that person is.*

- Give out the worksheets. Focus on **a** and get Sts to write *Yours sincerely* on a piece of paper, and then their signature underneath. Then get them to exchange their pieces of paper with a partner. Tell them to put their partner's piece of paper somewhere safe as they will be using it later on in the lesson.
- Focus on the signatures in **b**. In their pairs, get Sts to match the names to the signatures, and say what they know about the people's personalities.
- Check answers and elicit what Sts know about the people's personalities.

> 1 **Charles Schultz** (1922–2000) was an American cartoonist. He created Charlie Brown and Snoopy.
> 2 **Paul McCartney** (1942–) is an English musician, singer and songwriter. He was a member of The Beatles.
> 3 **Leo Tolstoy** (1828–1910) was a Russian writer. He wrote *War and Peace* and *Anna Karenina*.
> 4 **Charles Dickens** (1812–1870) was an English writer. He wrote *Oliver Twist*, *A Christmas Carol*, and *David Copperfield*.
> 5 **Barack Obama** (1961–) was elected the 44th president of the USA on 4 November 2008.
> 6 **Paris Hilton** (1981–) is an American heiress and socialite.
> 7 **Sean Connery** (1930–) is a Scottish actor. He is best known for his roles as James Bond and Dr Henry Jones (father of Indiana Jones).
> 8 **Elijah Wood** (1981–) is an American actor. He is most famous for his role as Frodo in *The Lord of the Rings* and *The Hobbit* sagas.

183

9 **Usain Bolt** (1986–) is a Jamaican former sprinter who won several Olympic gold medals.
10 **Damien Hirst** (1965–) is an English artist, entrepreneur and art collector.

- Focus on **c** and tell Sts they are going to read some information about how to interpret signatures. Check Sts know the meaning of *legibility* /ˌledʒəˈbɪləti/ (and its derivatives *legible* and *illegible*). Model and drill its pronunciation.
- In their pairs, Sts read the information and use it to interpret each of the famous people's signatures. Do their interpretations match what they previously thought about these famous people?
- Get some feedback on each signature.
- Now focus on **d** and get Sts to look at the pieces of paper with their partner's signature. Tell them to interpret their partner's signature according to the information they read.
- Get some quick feedback to find out if Sts agree with the interpretation of their personality.

EXTRA IDEA Before Sts do **d**, you could sign your name on the board and get Sts to tell you what they can find out about you from it, according to what they read.

2A Ask the doctor
Two pairwork role-play activities

Sts role-play different situations, using the grammar and vocabulary of the lesson. Copy one worksheet per pair and cut into **A** and **B**.

LANGUAGE

present perfect, illness and medicine vocabulary
How long have you been feeling like this?

- Put Sts in pairs, **A** and **B**, and give out the worksheets. If you have odd numbers, make one pair a three and have two Sts **A** (or take part in the role-play yourself).

EXTRA SUPPORT You could pre-teach / check the meaning and pronunciation of *alternative medicine* = non-traditional medicine; *acupuncture* = a way of treating illness or stopping pain by inserting thin needles into the body; *diagnosis* = what a doctor thinks is wrong with a patient; *homeopathy* = a system of treating diseases or conditions using very small amounts of the substance that causes the disease or condition.

- Tell Sts they are going to role-play two situations. Tell them to read the first situation and prepare the information they will need. Encourage the patients and doctors to be as imaginative and inventive as possible in their questions and answers. Tell the patients they can invent a new persona (age, job, etc.). Give Sts time to do this and encourage them to write notes if they need to.
- Sts then role-play the first situation. Monitor to make sure Sts are doing the activity properly.
- When they have finished the first role-play, tell them to repeat the process for the second situation.
- Finally, get feedback from some pairs on the outcome of the patient / doctor conversation.

2B You're only as old as you feel
A groupwork speaking activity

Sts compare their opinions on age and fashion. Copy one sheet per student.

LANGUAGE

managing discussions, agreeing and disagreeing, clothes and fashion

- Give out the worksheets and give Sts enough time to read through the statements. Explain that they have to put a cross on the line below each statement, showing to what extent they agree or disagree with each one.
- Put Sts in small groups of three or four. Tell them to compare their answers and explain the reasons for their choices. Encourage Sts to use the language for managing discussions and politely disagreeing in the Student's Book on p.23. You might like to write the target language on the board for easy reference. Monitor and help where necessary.
- Get feedback from the groups.

3A Talk about it
A groupwork activity

Sts are dealt cards with prompts for anecdotes. They plan what they are going to say. Copy and cut up one set of cards per group of three.

LANGUAGE

narrative tenses: past simple, past continuous, past perfect simple and past perfect continuous

- Put Sts in groups of three and give each group a set of cards. Tell them to each choose two that they can talk about. Set a time limit, e.g. two minutes, for Sts to think about what they are going to say. Help with vocabulary if necessary.

EXTRA SUPPORT Sts may want to make notes to help them tell their anecdotes.

- You could suggest that each student starts with *I'm going to tell you about a time when*…. Then Sts take turns to tell their first anecdote. Monitor, help, and make a note of any misuse of narrative tenses to focus on at the end.
- If there's time, let each student tell two anecdotes.
- Get feedback to find out if there were any unusual / interesting stories.

NON-CUT ALTERNATIVE Make one copy per pair. Put Sts in pairs and give them some time to read through the cards. Tell them to choose two anecdotes each to tell each other. Then continue as above.

EXTRA IDEA Play *Truth or Lie*. For each anecdote, Sts first decide if they are going to tell the truth or lie. They then tell their anecdotes and the group decides whether it's the truth or a lie.

184

3B Tell the story
A groupwork activity

Sts describe pictures to each other and then put them in the correct order to make a story. Copy and cut up one worksheet per group of four.

> **LANGUAGE**
> adverbs, narrative tenses revision, linkers

- Cut up the worksheet into four strips with two pictures on each. Put Sts in small groups of four. Shuffle the strips and give Sts one each.

! If you have a group of three or a pair, give one or both Sts two strips.

- Tell Sts that the pictures tell one story, so they have to describe their two pictures to the rest of the group (without letting them see them), and decide which order all the strips go in. Tell Sts not to worry about the adverbs on the picture.
- Monitor while Sts describe their pictures. When they have finished, tell them to look at the four strips and decide if their order is correct.
- Check Sts have the strips in the correct order. Now tell Sts to tell the story using narrative tenses and the adverbs on each picture.
- Finally, get feedback by getting students from different groups to tell the story picture by picture.

> 1 She wanted to go on a dream holiday, but she **obviously** didn't have the money.
> 2 She stayed up **all night** reading about how to make more money.
> 3 **Unfortunately**, the bank refused to help her.
> 4 It was raining **incredibly** hard one day when she met a sad little dog.
> 5 She **suddenly** had a great idea when she was drying the dog.
> 6 **Two weeks later** she'd started a successful (dog-walking) business.
> 7 She was walking in the park when she met a man with his dog. They **immediately** liked each other.
> 8 **In the end**, she did have her dream holiday.

EXTRA IDEA As a follow-up activity, get Sts to write the story in pairs.

NON-CUT ALTERNATIVE Make one copy per group. Sts work together to tell the story, using all the adverbs and narrative tenses. Ask one / two groups to tell their story during feedback.

4A In 20 years' time
A group discussion

Sts revise the two new future tenses by discussing predictions. Copy one worksheet per group of three or four Sts.

> **LANGUAGE**
> *will be* + gerund, *will have* + past participle, *will probably / definitely happen*
> *It's already happening*
> *I think it's very unlikely*

- Put Sts in small groups of three or four and give out the worksheets. Focus on the title of the worksheet and the predictions, making sure Sts understand them all. Sts then discuss each one in turn and decide if they think it will happen, and if they think it will be a good thing. They then take a group vote before making a decision and moving onto the next prediction.

EXTRA SUPPORT Discuss the first prediction with the whole class, eliciting opinions and giving your own opinion.

- Stop the activity when Sts have discussed all the predictions or when you think it has gone on for long enough.
- Get feedback from various groups, and find out which prediction Sts think is the most positive and which is the most negative.

4B Finish the sentences
A group activity

Sts race to complete sentences. Copy and cut up one worksheet per group of four or five Sts.

> **LANGUAGE**
> future time clauses

- Put Sts in groups of four or five and give each group a set of cards, either face down or in an envelope. Make one person the 'secretary'.
- Each group picks up a card, and together Sts decide on a way to correctly finish the sentence. Tell Sts that they should use a verb phrase and <u>not</u> just a noun to complete the sentences. Then, the 'secretary' writes down the sentence and takes it to the teacher, who checks if it is correct. If it's correct, their group scores a point. If not, they must re-write it.
- Set a time limit, e.g. ten minutes. Sts continue until they run out of cards or the time is up. The group with the most points when you stop the activity wins.

NON-CUT ALTERNATIVE Copy one worksheet per pair. Set a time limit for the pair to write continuations of the sentences. When the time is up check answers. The pair with the most correct continuations wins.

185

5A Would you survive?

A survival test and free-speaking activity

Sts read six extreme situations and discuss how to survive each one. Copy one worksheet per student and cut in half.

> **LANGUAGE**
>
> second conditional: *What would you do?*

- Tell Sts that they are going to look at some survival questions and at the end of the activity, they'll find out whether they'd survive or not.
- Put Sts in groups of four and give out one worksheet to each group – only the *Would you survive?* part, not the bottom half with the answers.
- Tell Sts to take turns reading one of the situations to their group. They should then discuss what would be the best thing to do in each situation. Encourage them to give as much information as possible.
- When Sts have read each situation, give each student a copy of the bottom half of the worksheet with the answers. Sts read through the answers and see if they knew any of the answers.
- Get some quick feedback from the groups to find out which Sts might have survived in each situation.

5B Wishes

A pairwork activity

Sts write their wishes in circles. They then swap circles with a partner, and ask each other to explain the information. **This is a two-page activity.** Copy one page (**A** and a **B**) per student.

> **LANGUAGE**
>
> *wish* for present / future
> *wish* for past regrets

- Put Sts in pairs, **A** and **B**, and give out the worksheets.
- Focus on **a** and instructions 1–10 for the circles. Point out that they each have different instructions for what to write. Make it clear that Sts should just write words in the circles, not sentences with *wish*, e.g. in **A**'s circle 1 he / she should write a celebrity's name – not *I wish I could meet George Clooney*.
- Give Sts five minutes to write answers in at least seven circles. When they have finished, focus on **b** and **c**, and tell them to fold their worksheet in half (or tear off the instructions).
- Now get Sts to swap worksheets with their partner. Demonstrate the activity by taking a copy from one student and asking him / her *Why did you write…?* And elicit: *Because I wish….* Ask follow-up questions to continue the conversation.
- Tell Sts that they can ask about the information in any order. Monitor and help where necessary, correcting any errors Sts make using *wish* during feedback. Sts now do the activity in pairs.
- Get some feedback. Find out if there were any interesting / unusual answers.

6A *usually, used to, get used to*

A pairwork activity

Sts practise asking and talking about things people usually do, used to do, or could / couldn't get used to doing. Copy one worksheet per pair and cut into **A** and **B**.

> **LANGUAGE**
>
> *Do you usually…?*
> *Did you use to…?*
> *Do you think you could get used to…?*

- Put Sts in pairs, **A** and **B**, and give out the worksheets. Focus on the instruction for **a** and on the three question forms. Highlight that for each verb phrase from the list Sts must use the most appropriate question form. Tell an **A** student to ask the first question: *Do you usually read everything on a tablet?* Then elicit **B**'s first question: *Did you use to have a favourite toy?*
- Remind Sts that after *get used to* they will need to use the gerund and highlight that the *get used to* questions need to be about something their partner doesn't already do.

EXTRA SUPPORT You could elicit all the possible questions for each category before moving to the next stage.

- In their pairs, Sts take turns to ask and answer the questions. Remind them that the 'questioner' should show interest and ask follow-up questions wherever possible.
- Get some feedback from various pairs.

6B Gerund or infinitive?

A pairwork activity

Sts complete questions with gerunds or infinitives and then ask each other the questions. Copy one worksheet per pair and cut into **A** and **B**.

> **LANGUAGE**
>
> verbs + gerund or infinitive (with or without *to*)

- Put Sts in pairs, **A** and **B**, and give out the worksheets. Focus on **a** and explain that Sts should write in the **VERB** column on the right (not in the sentences). Give Sts time to work individually, and then check answers by eliciting the verbs only – first Sts **A**s and then Sts **B**s.

> **A** 1 to live 2 speaking 3 to like 4 doing 5 eating
> 6 doing 7 to worry 8 play 9 to do 10 visiting
> 11 getting 12 to spend
> **B** 1 having 2 doing 3 to assemble / assembling
> 4 emigrating 5 read 6 doing 7 meeting 8 eating
> 9 learn 10 studying 11 seeing 12 watching

- Focus on instruction **b**. Tell Sts to fold their sheet on the fold line, so they can't see the verbs in the **VERB** column, and to try to remember the correct form of the **bold** verb in brackets. Sts **A** ask Sts **B** their questions, and then they swap roles. Encourage Sts to react to what their partner says, and ask for more information when they can.
- Monitor and correct any mistakes with gerunds and infinitives.
- Finally, get feedback on some of the more interesting answers.

7A Guess my verb

A pairwork activity

Sts practise using past modals by trying to guess their partner's sentences. Copy one worksheet per pair and cut into **A** and **B**.

> **LANGUAGE**
>
> past modals
> *He may have got lost, He can't have seen you, He shouldn't have done it*, etc.

- Put Sts in pairs, **A** and **B**, and give out the worksheets. If possible, sit Sts face to face, so they can't see each other's worksheet.

- Demonstrate the activity by writing on a piece of paper in big letters: JACK DIDN'T COME TO MY PARTY LAST NIGHT. HE MUST HAVE FORGOTTEN. Then write the same sentences on the board like this: JACK DIDN'T COME TO MY PARTY LAST NIGHT. HE MUST HAVE _____ . Elicit ways of finishing the sentence. Highlight that there are often several possibilities, but Sts have to guess the exact ending you have on the piece of paper. If they say a correct sentence but not your original ending, say *Try again*. When they guess correctly, say *That's right*. Finally, show them the sentence you wrote on the piece of paper.

- Focus on the instructions for **a** and tell Sts to look at their sentences. Explain that their **bold** sentences have gaps, and that the missing words are a verb phrase. Where Sts **A** have a gapped sentence, Sts **B** have the completed sentence, and vice versa. The aim of the activity is for Sts to try and guess the missing verbs. Give Sts time to complete the gaps either by writing their answers down or by thinking what the missing words might be.

- Now focus on **b** and **c**, and tell Sts to try guessing until they say the exact phrase their partner has. Stress that they have a maximum of three guesses. Sts **A** should begin by trying to guess the missing verbs in their first sentence. Emphasize that, when Sts make their guesses, they should say the whole sentence. When **A** guesses the missing verbs correctly, he / she writes it in the gap.

- Then Sts **B** try to guess their first verbs, and Sts continue taking turns.

EXTRA CHALLENGE At the end of the activity, you could get Sts to turn over the sheets and try to recall the verbs by reading out the sentences one by one. Say 'blank' or make a noise where the missing verbs are, and let the class call them out.

7B Two photos

A pairwork describing activity

Sts describe their photos to each other. Copy one worksheet per pair and cut into **A** and **B**.

> **LANGUAGE**
>
> present continuous, verbs describing body language, feelings adjectives, describing photos
> *This photo looks as if it was taken in the family's living room.*
> *In the foreground…*
> *In the centre (of the photo), there is / there are…*
> *In the background…*

- Before Sts start the activity, you might like to elicit or write on the board the phrases from Language.

- Put Sts in pairs, **A** and **B**, ideally face to face, and give out the worksheets. Make sure Sts can't see each other's worksheets.

- Explain that they both have different photos and have to describe them to each other. Tell Sts that they should focus on the people and their body language, and say who they think they are, what they think they're doing, and how they might be feeling. Demonstrate if you can with a photo from the Student's Book, or one you have looked up online. Give Sts a minute to look at their photo 1 and think about how they are going to describe it. Sts **A** start with their photo 1. Then Sts swap roles and Sts **B** describe their photo 1. Sts then repeat for photos 2.

- Monitor and help if necessary.

- Sts then look at their partner's photos to see if they agree with each other's interpretations of the photos.

- Get some feedback from various pairs.

8A Good laws?

A group speaking activity

Sts read about laws in different countries and discuss whether they think they are good or not. They then invent some new laws they would like to see introduced in their own countries. Copy one worksheet per student or per group of three or four Sts.

> **LANGUAGE**
>
> passive (all forms), crime and punishment vocabulary

- Put Sts in pairs or small groups of three or four and give out the worksheets.

- Focus on the instructions and emphasize that all these laws are real laws. Tell Sts to look at the *Animals* section and read the two laws. Then set a time limit for Sts to discuss them (you can adjust the time limit as necessary if Sts have a lot to say). When the time is up, elicit some feedback to find out Sts' opinions.

- Now tell Sts to think of one new law related to animals. Monitor while Sts are talking, helping with vocabulary.

- Finally, get each group to explain their new law to the class. Get the class to vote if they think it is a good law.

- Repeat the process for the other topics.

8B TV political debate
A role-play activity

Sts discuss political ideas. Copy one worksheet per group of four Sts and cut into **A** & **B** and **C** & **D**.

> **LANGUAGE**
> reporting verbs, media vocabulary
> *We promise to give free meals to all homeless people.*

- Put Sts in groups of four and then put them in two pairs. Give out the worksheets. Ideally, Sts **A** and **B** should sit opposite **C** and **D**. If you have an odd number, you could have two Sts representing one political party and only one strong student representing the other.
- Go through the instructions. Highlight that Sts have to first decide how to defend their own policies, and then how to attack the opposition's policies. Stress that Sts are playing the role of politicians and it doesn't matter if they don't personally agree with the policies they have to defend.
- Set the scene by reminding Sts that it's a live TV debate the day before elections, and it's the politicians' last chance to convince viewers to vote for them.
- Set a time limit for Sts to prepare for the debate. Monitor and help with vocabulary if necessary.
- Sts now have their debate. Sts **A** and **B** begin by introducing their first policy and giving their reasons. Sts **C** and **D** then try to attack the policy, giving reasons. Next, Sts **C** and **D** introduce their first policy.
- When Sts have debated all the policies, ask Sts which ones they think would be a good idea in their country and why.

9A Tell me about…
A pairwork speaking activity

Sts complete circles and then use the information to explain their answers. Copy one worksheet per pair and cut into **A** and **B**.

> **LANGUAGE**
> vocabulary: clauses of contrast and purpose, e.g. *in spite of*, *in order to*, etc.

- Put Sts in pairs, **A** and **B**, and give out the worksheets. If possible, sit Sts face to face, so they can't see each other's worksheet.
- Focus on **a** and give Sts time to complete at least six circles. Point out that they each have different instructions for what to write.
- Now focus on **b** and tell Sts to take turns to ask each other what they wrote in each circle and why. Encourage Sts to ask follow-up questions to get a conversation going. You could demonstrate the activity by asking a student about circle 1.
- When Sts have finished asking about what they have written in all the circles get some feedback.

9B Give your opinion!
A group board game

Sts revise countable and uncountable nouns by moving around the board and trying to talk for a minute about their opinion on different statements. Copy one worksheet per group of three or four Sts. You also need one dice per group and one counter per student.

The emphasis of the activity is fluency, but the teacher and Sts should also watch out for mistakes with the target language.

> **LANGUAGE**
> countable and plural nouns

- Put Sts in groups of three or four. Give each group the worksheet, a dice, and enough counters.

! If you don't have enough dice, give each group a coin. Sts toss the coin for their go and move 1 for heads and 2 for tails.

- Each player puts a counter on **START**.
- Explain the rules of the game: Sts take turns to throw the dice and move their counter. If Sts land on a square with a statement, they must then talk for one minute about the topic on that square. They should first read out the statement, and then say what they think. Ask someone in each group to monitor the time. If Sts successfully speak for one minute about the subject, they can keep their counter where it is. If they 'dry up' before the minute is up, they must move their counter back to the last square it was on. If they land on a blank square, their turn is over and the next person plays.
- Before Sts start, remind them that the main emphasis of the activity is fluency.
- The first student to reach **FINISH** wins.
- When everyone has finished, highlight any common or important errors with the target language and get Sts to provide the correct answers.

10A Science quiz
A quiz about natural sciences

Sts revise quantifiers by doing a true / false science quiz. Copy one worksheet per pair and cut into **A** and **B**.

> **LANGUAGE**
> quantifiers, animal vocabulary
> *each*, *all*, *neither*, etc.

- Put Sts in pairs, **A** and **B**, and give out the worksheets.
- Focus on **a** and give Sts time, e.g. five minutes, to circle the correct quantifier in each sentence.
- Check answers, by eliciting the quantifiers only.

> **A 1** Most **2** All the **3** anything **4** either **5** None **6** all **7** any
> **B 1** both **2** no **3** Every **4** Most **5** Both **6** any **7** nor

- Tell Sts to read the information again and to remember the explanation for each sentence.
- Now focus on **b** and tell Sts **A** to read all their sentences to Sts **B**, who have to guess whether they are true or false.

- Encourage them to try and give an explanation for their answers and to use their own words when giving the explanation for a wrong answer.
- Make sure Sts swap roles.
- At the end of the activity, find out who got the most answers correct.

10B General knowledge quiz

A quiz on a range of subjects

Sts revise articles by completing quiz questions and try to answer them in pairs. Copy one worksheet per student.

LANGUAGE

definite and indefinite articles

- Put Sts in pairs and give out the worksheets.
- Focus on **a** and set a time limit for Sts to complete the questions. They can do this individually or in their pairs.
- Check answers.

1 – 2 the, the 3 a 4 the 5 the, the 6 – 7 – 8 the, the 9 the, – 10 –, – 11 the 12 –, – 13 the 14 a 15 a 16 the, the 17 –, the 18 the, the 19 a, – 20 the 21 – 22 a, an 23 the, a 24 the 25 –, –

- Focus on **b** and set a time limit, e.g. five minutes, for Sts to try to answer as many questions as possible.
- When time is up, check answers, making sure Sts use the article correctly in their answers. Find out which pair had the most correct answers.

1 Peru and Bolivia
2 Buzz Aldrin
3 4
4 The Indian Ocean
5 Mont Blanc
6 25
7 Blue for Caucasian babies, grey or brown for babies of African or Asian descent.
8 The Bald Eagle
9 'P' on both 'QWERTY' and 'AZERTY' keyboards. NB: You may wish to check the keyboard type used in your country, as there are sometimes national differences.
10 Dogs
11 Neptune
12 The most common answer amongst researchers in this area is that there are slightly more men than women.
13 4: England, Scotland, Wales, Northern Ireland
14 Apple
15 5
16 Aries
17 New Zealand
18 Yuri Gagarin
19 Switzerland
20 The Great Wall of China
21 Potatoes
22 No, it's an arachnid
23 Orange
24 Russia
25 light

Revision

Questions to revise vocabulary, verb forms, and tenses

Sts ask each other questions about key vocabulary areas, using a range of tenses and verb forms from the Student's Book. This could either be used as a final 'pre-test' revision or as an oral exam. Copy and cut up one set of cards per pair.

LANGUAGE

grammar and vocabulary of the book

- Put Sts in pairs. Give each pair a set of cards face down. Sts take turns to pick up the top card and talk to their partner about the topic on the card, using the prompts.
- Tell Sts to keep their cards and then if there is time, to swap cards with their partner.
- Encourage Sts to ask follow-up questions.
- Monitor, help, and correct if necessary.

NON-CUT ALTERNATIVE Give one worksheet per pair. Give Sts time to read through the cards. They take it in turns to ask their partner questions on one topic. They continue until they have used up all their topics.

COMMUNICATIVE Tell me about it

Student A Instructions

a Read the instructions and write your answers in the correct place in the chart.

In number 1, write your first name.
In number 2, write the name of a café or bar you often go to.
In number 3, write the name of the last film you really enjoyed.
In number 4, write the place you went to on your last holiday.
In number 5, write the name of an app you use a lot.
In number 6, write the number of years you've been living in this town / city.
In number 7, write your favourite day of the week.
In number 8, write a date that is important for you.
In number 9, write the name of the person in your family you get on with best.
In number 10, write two things you like doing in your free time.

b Swap charts with **B**. Ask **B** to explain his / her answers. Ask for more information.

Why did you write '4'?
   Because I've been learning English for 4 years.
Where did you study before?

c Now answer **B**'s questions.

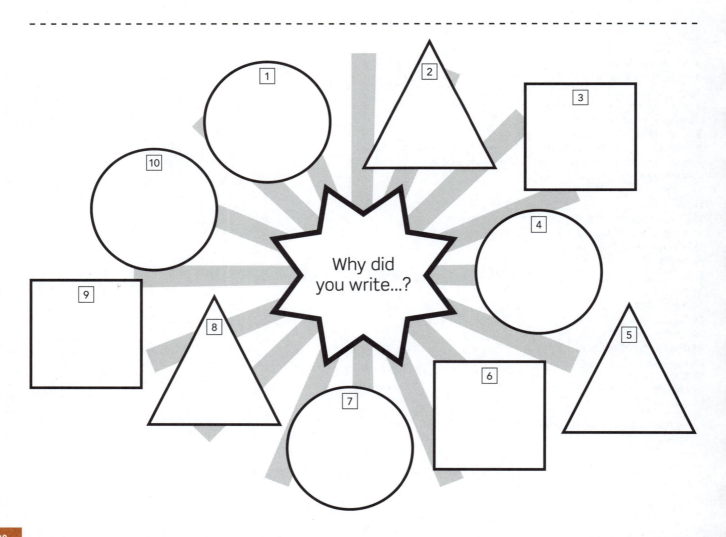

COMMUNICATIVE Tell me about it

Student B Instructions

a Read the instructions and write your answers in the correct place in the chart.

In number 1, write your first name.
In number 2, write the number of years you've been learning English.
In number 3, write your favourite food or drink.
In number 4, write the name of a website you've used to improve your English.
In number 5, write the last gadget you bought.
In number 6, write the name of a TV series you've been watching recently.
In number 7, write the name of a game you play a lot, e.g. on your phone.
In number 8, write a number that is important to you in some way.
In number 9, write the name of a sport you like watching or doing.
In number 10, write the name of your oldest friend.

b Swap charts with **A**. Answer **A**'s questions.

c Ask **A** to explain his / her answers. Ask for more information.

Why did you write 'Starbucks'?
    Because I often go there for coffee.
Why do you like it?

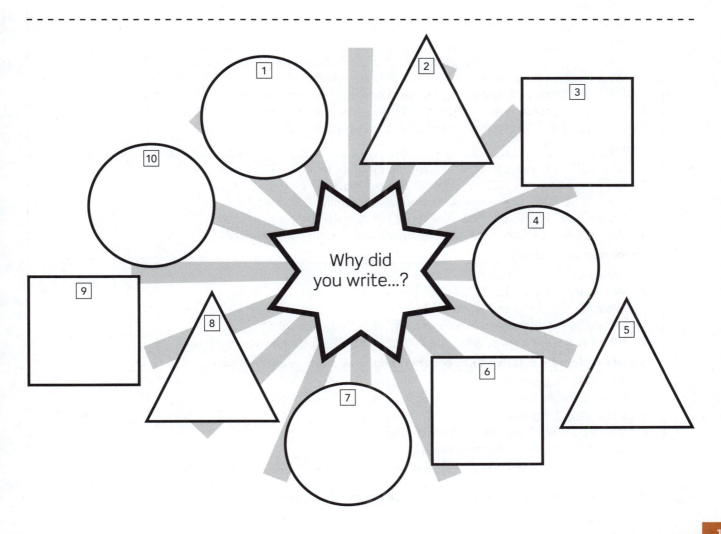

1A COMMUNICATIVE Ask me a question

a In pairs, read the questions and think about what the missing words are. <u>Don't</u> write them in.

Your home

1 Where ▓▓▓ ▓▓▓ live?
2 How long ▓▓▓ ▓▓▓ lived there?
3 Who ▓▓▓ ▓▓▓ live ▓▓▓?
4 What ▓▓▓ ▓▓▓ like most about your home?
5 Is ▓▓▓ anything you ▓▓▓ like about your neighbourhood? Why not?

Getting around

1 How ▓▓▓ ▓▓▓ usually get ▓▓▓ work (or school / university)?
2 How long ▓▓▓ ▓▓▓ take?
3 ▓▓▓ ▓▓▓ drive? ▓▓▓ car ▓▓▓ ▓▓▓ ▓▓▓?
4 ▓▓▓ often ▓▓▓ you ▓▓▓ public transport?
5 ▓▓▓ the best way ▓▓▓ get ▓▓▓ your town / city?

Free time

1 What ▓▓▓ ▓▓▓ enjoy doing in your free time?
2 ▓▓▓ ▓▓▓ of music ▓▓▓ ▓▓▓ listen ▓▓▓?
3 How ▓▓▓ ▓▓▓ ▓▓▓ go out during the week?
4 ▓▓▓ sport(s) ▓▓▓ ▓▓▓ like doing?
5 ▓▓▓ ▓▓▓ time do you spend on social media every day?

Lifestyle

1 How ▓▓▓ tea or coffee ▓▓▓ ▓▓▓ drink ▓▓▓ day?
2 ▓▓▓ ▓▓▓ hours ▓▓▓ ▓▓▓ sleep at night?
3 What ▓▓▓ ▓▓▓ do ▓▓▓ relax?
4 What do ▓▓▓ do ▓▓▓ keep healthy?
5 What ▓▓▓ the last live event you went ▓▓▓?

Travel

1 What's ▓▓▓ ▓▓▓ beautiful place you ▓▓▓ ▓▓▓ been to?
2 Where ▓▓▓ you going ▓▓▓ ▓▓▓ for your next holiday?
3 ▓▓▓ ▓▓▓ think it's better ▓▓▓ travel alone ▓▓▓ with other people?
4 ▓▓▓ ▓▓▓ prefer having holidays ▓▓▓ your country or abroad?
5 Have ▓▓▓ ▓▓▓ been ▓▓▓ an English-speaking country?

Family

1 ▓▓▓ ▓▓▓ people ▓▓▓ there in your immediate family?
2 ▓▓▓ in your family ▓▓▓ ▓▓▓ most like talking ▓▓▓?
3 ▓▓▓ ▓▓▓ prefer spending time ▓▓▓, family ▓▓▓ friends?
4 How much ▓▓▓ ▓▓▓ know ▓▓▓ your family tree?
5 When ▓▓▓ ▓▓▓ last time all ▓▓▓ family did something together?

Childhood and school

1 Where ▓▓▓ ▓▓▓ born?
2 Which secondary school ▓▓▓ ▓▓▓ go ▓▓▓?
3 What ▓▓▓ ▓▓▓ best / worst subject?
4 ▓▓▓ ▓▓▓ ever cheated in an exam? ▓▓▓ ▓▓▓ get caught?
5 When you were a child, what ▓▓▓ ▓▓▓ want ▓▓▓ be when you grew up?

A male or female relative (e.g. brother, nephew, aunt, grandmother)

1 ▓▓▓ ▓▓▓ name?
2 How old ▓▓▓ ▓▓▓?
3 ▓▓▓ ▓▓▓ ▓▓▓ do?
4 ▓▓▓ ▓▓▓ ▓▓▓ look ▓▓▓? (appearance)
5 ▓▓▓ ▓▓▓ ▓▓▓ like? (personality)

---

b Choose a topic. Interview your partner. Ask for more information.

English File fourth edition Teacher's Guide Upper-intermediate Photocopiable © Oxford University Press 2020

1B COMMUNICATIVE What's in a signature?

a On a piece of paper, write *Yours sincerely* and your signature underneath.

b Look at the signatures of some famous people. Match the names to the signatures. Do you know anything about these people's personalities?

Leo Tolstoy [3]   Barack Obama [ ]   Paris Hilton [ ]   Usain Bolt [ ]   Charles Schultz [ ]

Charles Dickens [ ]   Elijah Wood [ ]   Damien Hirst [ ]   Paul McCartney [ ]   Sean Connery [ ]

c Read the information about interpreting someone's personality from their signature. With your partner, look at the signatures above again and interpret them.

1 How you write your name

Your first name represents your private self, and your surname represents your public self. If you use only initials for your first name or surname, it means you are more secretive and protective about that part of your personality. Is there a space between the first name and surname? The bigger the space, the more you want to keep those two parts of your personality separate.

2 Size

The part of the signature (first name or surname) that is bigger is the most important part of your personality. So, if it's the first name, for example, you care more about your private self. If both are big, you are very confident. Capital letters suggest that you are arrogant or big-headed. If you have very small writing, you may be insecure or have low self-esteem.

What your signature says about you

3 Legibility

If the signature is easy to read, you have clear ideas and objectives, but if it's difficult to read, it may mean you're disorganized or indecisive and maybe also quite secretive. The more illegible the signature is, the less assertive you are.

4 Angle

If the signature goes up, it means you work hard to overcome problems. You are determined, optimistic, and ambitious. If the signature goes down, it means that you get depressed when you have problems, and you aren't very self-confident. A horizontal signature, one which goes straight, means that you are well-balanced, emotionally stable, and generally satisfied with life.

d Now look at your partner's signature and try to interpret it. Do you both agree with the interpretation of your signatures?

English File fourth edition Teacher's Guide Upper-intermediate   Photocopiable © Oxford University Press 2020

2A COMMUNICATIVE Ask the doctor

A Role-play 1

You're a family doctor. B is your patient.

You've just finished medical school, and today is your first day in this surgery. You feel very enthusiastic! At medical school, they taught you to find out as much as you can about a patient when you first meet them. You're a great believer in alternative medicine like homeopathy and acupuncture. You really believe that some conditions can be better treated using alternative remedies, e.g. hypnotherapy for people with phobias or weight problems.

- Find out as much information as you can about the patient, e.g. age, job, family life, previous illnesses, operations, etc.
- Ask the reason for today's visit. Find out how long he / she has had this problem.
- You don't like the medicine the patient usually takes, Calmozone. You prefer a natural, homeopathic one called Tranquilium.

B will start.

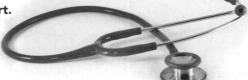

Role-play 2

You're a patient. B is your family doctor.

You know your doctor very well because you make an appointment to see him / her at least once a week. You're a favourite patient! You think of him / her as a friend and that's why you call him / her by his / her first name (Chris) and not Dr Jones.

- Today, you've made an appointment with the doctor because you've got some very strange symptoms (decide what they are), and you're convinced that you have a problem with your heart. You want the doctor to take you seriously and agree with what you think is the problem.
- Explain all your symptoms to the doctor.
- Ask the doctor to check your blood pressure and take your pulse.
- Tell him / her that you'd like to see a specialist. Be prepared to argue with him / her if necessary.

You start the conversation.

Hi Chris. How are you?

B Role-play 1

You're a patient. A is your family doctor.

You haven't been to the doctor's for about a year, so you're really surprised to see that you have a new family doctor. He / she's very young! What experience does he / she have? You'd known your previous doctor all your life. He knew all about your fear of flying and was very sympathetic to the problem. You're going on holiday next week – by plane. Your old doctor always prescribed Calmozone, a tablet which relaxes you when you fly.

If you take two before the plane takes off, you don't feel nervous. You know what you want – Calmozone!

If you don't get it, you can't go on holiday. You aren't very convinced by alternative remedies, especially hypnotherapy and homeopathy!

- Answer any questions the doctor asks you. Explain the reason for today's visit.
- Ask the doctor to prescribe Calmozone and explain why you need it.
- Only accept an alternative remedy you feel completely happy with.

You start the conversation.

Good morning doctor. You're new, aren't you?

Role-play 2

You're a family doctor. A is your patient.

You're fed up and exhausted! The government spending cuts mean that today you've worked for eight hours on your own in the surgery and there's still paperwork to do. You want to go home! Unfortunately, you have one more patient to see and he / she is a nightmare! He / She comes to see you at least once a week, always with a different problem. You think he / she is a hypochondriac.
For some reason, this patient always calls you by your first name. You hate that!

- Ask him / her not to call you by your first name. Ask him / her to call you Dr Jones.
- Ask him / her what his / her symptoms are (this week!) and how long he / she has had them.
- Give your diagnosis (decide what you think) and decide what medication (if any) to prescribe. You don't think he / she needs to see a specialist.

A will start.

English File fourth edition Teacher's Guide Upper-intermediate   Photocopiable © Oxford University Press 2020

2B COMMUNICATIVE You're only as old as you feel

a Read the statements. Put a cross on the line, showing to what extent you agree or disagree with each one.

1 The older people become, the less productive they are.
Disagree — Agree

2 The cultural gap between young and old people has widened considerably, and consequently they have much less in common nowadays than in the past.
Disagree — Agree

3 Older people should be paid more than younger people, because they have more experience.
Disagree — Agree

4 My culture values the young more than the elderly.
Disagree — Agree

5 Men tend to age better than women.
Disagree — Agree

6 'Age and size are only numbers. It's the attitude you bring to clothes that make the difference.' (*Donna Karan, fashion designer*)
Disagree — Agree

7 The older people are, the less adventurous they are about what they wear.
Disagree — Agree

8 Fashion designers design for the young, but the young often can't afford them.
Disagree — Agree

9 Young people don't care about being warm or comfortable, they only want to look good.
Disagree — Agree

10 It is a fact that women can wear any clothes that are designed for men, but men can't wear most clothes that are designed for women.
Disagree — Agree

b Work in small groups. Discuss each of the statements.

3A COMMUNICATIVE Talk about it

something you wanted that you recently bought
- What exactly did you buy?
- Why had you wanted it for so long?
- Did you do any research before you bought it? How?
- Where did you buy it?
- Have you been using it much since you bought it?

a time you went for an interview for a job or course
- What job / course was it for?
- Where had you found out about the job / course?
- How did you feel before the interview?
- Were there any questions you found hard to answer? What were they?
- Did you get the job / place on the course?

a time you had a really bad restaurant meal
- When / Where did you have it? Who with?
- Why had you decided to go to this particular restaurant?
- Why was the meal so bad?
- Were you or any of the other people ill afterwards?
- Did you complain? If not, why not?

a time when someone stole something from you (or someone you know)
- What was taken?
- What had you been doing just before it was stolen?
- How did you feel after you realized it had been stolen?
- Did you call the police? Were they helpful?
- Did you ever get it back?

a time when you overslept and missed something important
- What important thing were you going to do that day?
- Had you gone to bed very late the night before? Why?
- Had you set an alarm?
- How late did you wake up? What did you do?
- What happened in the end?

a time when your parents were very angry with you about something
- How old were you?
- Why did they get angry? What had you done / been doing?
- How did your parents find out?
- Did they punish you? How?
- Have you parents forgotten about it?

a time you met or were very close to a celebrity
- When did it happen?
- Where were you?
- What were you doing?
- Which celebrity did you see?
- What was he / she doing there?
- Did you speak to him / her? What about?
- Did you take a photo of him / her?

a time you won something
- What was it?
- When? Where? How old were you?
- Were you expecting to win?
- How did you feel when you realized you'd won?
- Did you celebrate? What did you do?

a holiday you didn't enjoy
- Where / When was it?
- Who went?
- Had you been there before?
- What did you do there?
- Why didn't you enjoy it? Did you ever go there again?

3B COMMUNICATIVE Tell the story

obviously

all night

unfortunately

incredibly

suddenly

two weeks later

immediately

in the end

4A COMMUNICATIVE In 20 years' time

• Discuss each prediction with your group. Decide:
  a if you think it will happen.
  b if you think it will be a good thing.

1 People will be mostly reading print books and e-readers will have declined in popularity.

2 The number of people learning foreign languages will have fallen because apps will translate everything simultaneously.

3 There will be no retirement age. People will be working until 70 and even beyond.

4 We will have established a colony on Mars.

5 The bicycle will have replaced the car as the main form of private transport in towns and cities.

6 People will have stopped using social media sites like Facebook and Twitter and returned to face-to-face communication.

7 An increasing number of jobs will have been replaced by robots.

8 We will be mainly watching films with computer-animated actors who will have replaced human actors.

9 Families will be getting smaller and the birth rate will have dropped even further.

10 We will be seeing much more women's sport on TV as it will have greatly increased in popularity.

11 Life expectancy will have gone down in the developed world because of unhealthy eating habits.

12 It won't be necessary for anyone to learn to drive because we'll be using self-driving cars.

4B COMMUNICATIVE Finish the sentences

As soon as we've arrived at the hotel…	Carry on taking the antibiotics **until**…
What are you going to do **when**…	Don't disturb the boss **unless**…
I'll give you a call **after**…	Let's take the satnav **in case**…
I'll do the washing up **if**…	I'm going to buy a motorbike **as soon as**…
I'm sure your husband will understand **if**…	We'll be having a barbecue tomorrow **unless**…
Shh! Don't make a noise **in case**…	**Unless** you hurry up…
We could go for a walk **after**…	**If** his wife has told him to do it…
We must say goodbye to Louise **before**…	We need to book the holiday soon **in case**…
If you're not feeling better tomorrow, …	We're going to open a bottle of champagne **when**…
You might get an electric shock **if**…	I won't be able to start cooking dinner **until**…

English File fourth edition Teacher's Guide Upper-intermediate   Photocopiable © Oxford University Press 2020

199

5A COMMUNICATIVE Would you survive?

1. You're walking on a beach on your own. You walk on some sand and you begin to sink very quickly. It's quicksand! What would you do?

2. You're in a tall building. Suddenly, you can smell smoke and everything feels quite hot. The building's on fire! What would you do?

3. You're walking in a forest when suddenly you feel a terrible pain in your leg. You've been bitten by a snake that you think is poisonous. What would you do?

4. You're camping in a forest, and decide to go for a walk. Suddenly, you come face-to-face with a black bear. It looks ready to attack you! What would you do?

5. You're in a city street and suddenly shooting starts between two rival gangs. What would you do?

6. You're swimming in the sea when you see the dark fin of a shark approaching you. What would you do?

The answers

1. The good news is, you can't sink all the way down because, like in water, your body floats. Take off anything heavy, though, like a backpack or a camera. You need to try and create space between your legs and the sand by moving them slowly but continuously, and move slowly up until you can get out.

2. Don't try to put the fire out! Leave the building and pull a fire alarm on your way out if you can. Touch every door before you open it. If it's hot, it means there's fire on the other side and you should find a different way. If there's too much smoke, get closer to the floor. Once you're out of the building and in a safe place, call the emergency services.

3. Wash the bite with soap and water as soon as you can. Keep the area where the bite is lower than your heart. Wrap a bandage tightly around your leg above the bite to help slow the poison until you can get medical help. Don't suck out the poison and don't tie the bandage too tight.

4. Lie still and quiet. An attack by a mother bear often ends when the person stops fighting. Don't run or climb a tree as a bear can run much faster than you, and is an expert at climbing trees. If you lie still and the bear still attacks you, try to scare it away by hitting it with anything you can find. Try to aim for the eyes or nose if possible.

5. Get down on the ground and stay there. Lie flat on your stomach. If there are cars, lie down behind one of the wheels. If there are no cars, lie in the road right next to the pavement. Don't run away because that will only draw attention to you and you could be shot by mistake.

6. Your only hope if the shark attacks you is to try to hit the shark in the eyes, which is the area most sensitive to pain.

5B COMMUNICATIVE Wishes

Student A Instructions

a Write something in at least seven of your circles.

Circle 1: a well-known person you wish you could meet or could have met

Circle 2: a new gadget you wish you had

Circle 3: a name you wish your parents had called you (instead of the one they gave you)

Circle 4: something you wish the local government would do to improve your town / city

Circle 5: a concert or sporting event you wish you'd been able to go to

Circle 6: something you wish people wouldn't do in the cinema

Circle 7: an activity you wish you didn't have to do every day

Circle 8: a language (other than English) you wish you could speak

Circle 9: something you wish you had learned to do when you were younger

Circle 10: something you wish you hadn't spent money on

b Give your sheet to **B**. He / She will ask you to explain what you have written.

c Ask **B** to explain what he / she has written.

Why did you write 'Breaking Bad' in circle 1?

Because I wish they had made more series of it. I love it.

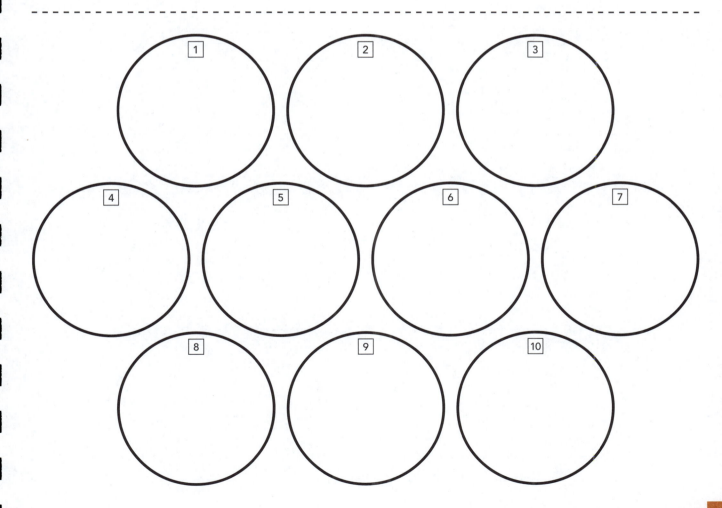

English File fourth edition Teacher's Guide Upper-intermediate   Photocopiable © Oxford University Press 2020

5B COMMUNICATIVE Wishes

Student B Instructions

a Write something in at least seven of your circles.

Circle 1: a TV drama or comedy you wish they had made more series of

Circle 2: something you wish drivers or cyclists would or wouldn't do

Circle 3: somebody you wish you could see more often

Circle 4: somewhere you wish you had a house or flat

Circle 5: a free-time activity you wish you had more time to do

Circle 6: a group or singer you wish would come and play in your city

Circle 7: something you wish hadn't been invented

Circle 8: something you wish people wouldn't do on social media

Circle 9: something annoying you wish someone in your family wouldn't do

Circle 10: something you wish you hadn't done when you were younger

b Give your sheet to **A**. He / She will ask you to explain what you have written.

c Ask **A** to explain what he / she has written.

Why did you write 'Salvador Dali' in circle 1?

Because I wish I could have met him. He was a great artist.

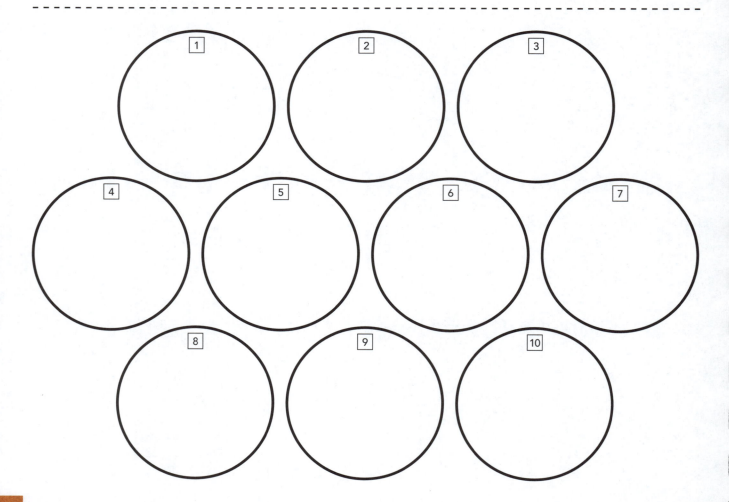

6A COMMUNICATIVE *usually, used to, get used to*

Student A

a Complete the questions with an appropriate verb phrase from the box in the correct form. You don't need to use all the phrases.

Do you usually _____?
_____?
_____?

Did you use to _____?
_____?
_____?

Do you think you could get used to _____?
_____?
_____?

b Ask **B** your questions.

c Answer **B**'s questions.

(read) everything on a tablet

(study) in the evenings or at night

(share) a bedroom with a brother or sister

(eat) a lot of sweets when you were a child

(cook) for yourself

(watch) cartoons on TV when you were young

(buy) books and music online

(live) in the UK or the USA

(cheat) in exams at school

(go) to bed before midnight

(not eat) meat

(have) only two weeks holiday a year

Student B

a Complete the questions with an appropriate verb phrase from the box in the correct form. You don't need to use all the phrases.

Do you usually _____?
_____?
_____?

Did you use to _____?
_____?
_____?

Do you think you could get used to _____?
_____?
_____?

b Answer **A**'s questions.

c Ask **A** your questions.

(have) a favourite toy

(cycle) to work or school

(get up) at 5.30 every morning

(listen) to music in the car

(celebrate) your birthday

(live) on your own

(read) a lot when you were a child

(drive) on the left

(live) without having access to the internet

(watch) TV in the morning

(hate) a particular food or drink when you were a child

(go) to the hairdresser's more than twice a month

English File fourth edition Teacher's Guide Upper-intermediate Photocopiable © Oxford University Press 2020

203

6B COMMUNICATIVE Gerund or infinitive?

Student A

a Complete the **VERB** column with the correct form of the verbs in brackets.

VERB

1 Could you manage ▮▮▮ for a week without your phone? (**live**) _____

2 Do you ever get the chance to practise ▮▮▮ English outside class? (**speak**) _____

3 If you really hated your friend's partner, would you pretend ▮▮▮ him / her? (**like**) _____

4 Is there any kind of housework you can't stand ▮▮▮? (**do**) _____

5 Would you ever risk ▮▮▮ something which was past its sell-by date? (**eat**) _____

6 Is there anything that you think you ought to give up ▮▮▮? (**do**) _____

7 What kind of things do you tend ▮▮▮ about? (**worry**) _____

8 Did your parents let you ▮▮▮ in the street when you were a child? (**play**) _____

9 Do you have a good memory, or do you sometimes forget ▮▮▮ things? (**do**) _____

10 Is there a city or country that you really fancy ▮▮▮? (**visit**) _____

11 Are there any apps you'd recommend ▮▮▮? (**get**) _____

12 Would you prefer ▮▮▮ a week on the beach or a week in the country? (**spend**) _____

FOLD

b Ask your partner the questions in **a**.

c Answer **B**'s questions.

Student B

a Complete the **VERB** column with the correct form of the verbs in brackets.

VERB

1 Do you think it's worth ▮▮▮ a medical check-up every year? (**have**) _____

2 Is there anything that really needs ▮▮▮ to your house or flat? (**do**) _____

3 Have you ever tried ▮▮▮ flat pack furniture? (**assemble**) _____

4 Can you imagine ▮▮▮ to another country? (**emigrate**) _____

5 Would you rather ▮▮▮ an e-book or a printed book? (**read**) _____

6 Are there any jobs in the house that you don't mind ▮▮▮? (**do**) _____

7 Do you remember ▮▮▮ your best friend for the first time? (**meet**) _____

8 Have you ever had to stop ▮▮▮ a type of food because you were allergic to it? (**eat**) _____

9 Did your parents ever make you ▮▮▮ something you really didn't enjoy? (**learn**) _____

10 Do you think that you'll carry on ▮▮▮ English next year? (**study**) _____

11 Is there a film you're looking forward to ▮▮▮ at the cinema? (**see**) _____

12 Is there a TV programme you can't help ▮▮▮ even though you don't think it's very good? (**watch**) _____

FOLD

b Answer **A**'s questions.

c Ask your partner the questions in **a**.

English File fourth edition Teacher's Guide Upper-intermediate Photocopiable © Oxford University Press 2020

7A COMMUNICATIVE Guess my verb

Student A

a Complete the **bold** sentences in a natural way using a verb phrase.

1 **Greg's really late. He may have _____ .**
2 You can't have finished that book. You only started it yesterday and it's got over 600 pages!
3 **Maria looks so tired. She can't have _____ last night.**
4 You should have come with us last night. We had a great time!
5 **Ellie usually rings me on my birthday, but this year she didn't. She must have _____ .**
6 I don't have my wallet with me! I must have left it at home.
7 **My neighbour's just bought a really expensive new car. She might have _____ !**
8 It's your own fault you got sunburnt! You ought to have put on sunscreen.
9 **Have you seen Kathy's huge engagement ring? It must have _____ !**
10 They can't have gone out. Their car's outside.
11 **I've got a stomach ache. I shouldn't have _____ .**
12 Michelle isn't in her office. She may have gone home. She wasn't feeling very well.

b Read sentence 1 to **B**, who has the completed sentence. If you say what **B** has, he / she will say *'That's right'*, if not, he / she will say *'Try again'*. You can have another two tries. If none of your endings are what **B** has, **B** will tell you his / her ending.

c Now listen to **B** invent an ending for sentence 2. If it is the same as what you have, say *'That's right'*, if not, say *'Try again'*. **B** can have another two tries. If none of **B**'s endings are what you have, tell **B** your ending.

- -

Student B

a Complete the **bold** sentences in a natural way using a verb phrase.

1 Greg's really late. He may have got lost.
2 **You can't have _____ . You only started it yesterday and it's got over 600 pages!**
3 Maria looks so tired. She can't have slept very well last night.
4 **You should have _____ last night. We had a great time!**
5 Ellie usually rings me on my birthday, but this year she didn't. She must have forgotten.
6 **I don't have my wallet with me! I must have _____ .**
7 My neighbour's just bought a really expensive new car. She might have won the lottery!
8 **It's your own fault you got sunburnt! You ought to have _____ .**
9 Have you seen Kathy's huge engagement ring? It must have cost a fortune!
10 **They can't have _____ . Their car's outside.**
11 I've got a stomach ache. I shouldn't have eaten so much.
12 **Michelle isn't in her office. She may have _____ . She wasn't feeling very well.**

b Now listen to **A** invent an ending for sentence 1. If it is the same as what you have, say *'That's right'*, if not, say *'Try again'*. **A** can have another two tries. If none of **A**'s endings are what you have, tell **A** your ending.

c Read sentence 2 to **A**, who has the completed sentence. If you say what **A** has, he / she will say *'That's right'*, if not, he / she will say *'Try again'*. You can have another two tries. If none of your endings are what **A** has, **A** will tell you his / her ending.

English File fourth edition Teacher's Guide Upper-intermediate   Photocopiable © Oxford University Press 2020

7B COMMUNICATIVE Two photos

Student A

a Look carefully at your photo 1. Then describe it in detail to **B**, focusing on the people and their body language. Say who you think they are, what you think they're doing, and how they might be feeling.

b Listen to **B** describe his / her photo. Try to visualize it.

c Repeat with your second photos.

d Show your photos to **B** and see if he / she agrees with your interpretation of the photos.

Student B

a Listen to **A** describe his / her photo 1. Try to visualize it.

b Now describe your photo 1 in detail to **A**, focusing on the people and their body language. Say who you think they are, what you think they're doing, and how they might be feeling.

c Repeat with your second photos.

d Show your photos to **A** and see if he / she agrees with your interpretation of the photos.

8A COMMUNICATIVE Good laws?

a Read about some existing laws in different countries. In pairs or small groups, discuss whether you think each law is a good one, and whether you would like to have it in your country.

b For each section write one new law that you would like to see introduced in your country.

Animals

1 **Poland**
If you have a dog, it must always wear a muzzle and be kept on a lead when you take it for walks.

2 **Sweden**
All animals which are kept inside a house / flat must have access to natural light.

3 **New law**
_____
_____ .

The environment

1 **Norway**
When you buy a bottle or a can of drink you have to pay a deposit. When the bottle or can is empty, you take it back to a recycling centre where your deposit is refunded.

2 **Mexico**
There is a complete ban on free plastic bags in Mexico City. Customers are charged if they want them, and the bags must be biodegradable.

3 **New law**
_____
_____ .

On the road

1 **Germany**
People who want to get a driving licence have to do a first-aid training course. They must also carry a first-aid kit in their cars.

2 **Spain**
Car drivers are not allowed to wear flip-flops while driving.

3 **New law**
_____
_____ .

Food and health

1 **Brazil**
All Brazilian state-school children are given one free meal at school every day. 70% of this food has to be fresh, and the other 30% must come from local family farmers.

2 **Japan**
There is a special tax on food or drink which the government considers to be unhealthy. People who want to buy these things have to pay a lot more than they would for healthier options.

3 **New law**
_____
_____ .

In the street

1 **Iceland**
Teenagers aged between 13 and 16 are not allowed to be outdoors after 10.00 at night unless they are on their way home from a recognized event organized by a school, sports organization, or youth club. During the summer months, they can be outdoors for two hours longer.

2 **Italy**
In Genoa, people are not allowed to walk around with a bottle of wine or a can of beer in their hand.

3 **New law**
_____
_____ .

8B COMMUNICATIVE TV political debate

Students A & B

You're the leader and deputy leader of a local political party. Tonight, you're going to appear 'live' on TV in a face-to-face debate with the leader and deputy leader of the opposition party.

a Prepare some ideas to <u>defend</u> your party's five policies before the interview. Think of reasons why your policies are good ideas. Make notes. Add one new policy of your own.

b Now prepare some other ideas to <u>attack</u> your opponent's policies. Think of reasons which explain why the other party's policies aren't good ideas. Make notes.

c Sit opposite **C & D** and take turns to present and debate your policies.

Your party's policies
- To ban all dogs from the town centre
- To close the town centre to traffic on Saturday mornings from 9.00 a.m. – 1.00 p.m.
- To promote tourism in the town by organizing a big sporting event (decide what)
- To introduce strict fines for people who download music or films from the internet without paying
- To ban fast food restaurants near all schools and universities
- _____

Your opponent's policies
- To ban cyclists from using all main roads
- To make it compulsory for everyone to vote in local elections
- To make tourists pay a tax when they come into the country
- To make bars and restaurants in the town centre close before 11 p.m. during the week
- To give free internet access to all homes and mobile devices
- _____

- -

Students C & D

You're the leader and deputy leader of a local political party. Tonight, you're going to appear 'live' on TV in a face-to-face debate with the leader and deputy leader of the opposition party.

a Prepare some ideas to <u>defend</u> your party's five policies before the interview. Think of reasons why your policies are good ideas. Make notes. Add a new policy of your own.

b Now prepare some other ideas to <u>attack</u> your opponent's policies. Think of reasons which explain why the other party's policies aren't good ideas. Make notes.

c Sit opposite **A & B** and take turns to present and debate your policies.

Your party's policies
- To ban cyclists from using all main roads
- To make it compulsory for everyone to vote in local elections
- To make tourists pay a tax when they come into the country
- To make bars and restaurants in the town centre close before 11.00 p.m. during the week
- To give free internet access to all homes and mobile devices
- _____

Your opponent's policies
- To ban all dogs from the town centre
- To close the town centre to traffic on Saturday mornings from 9.00 a.m. – 1.00 p.m.
- To promote tourism in the town by organizing a big sporting event
- To introduce large fines for people who download music or films from the internet without paying
- To ban fast food restaurants near all schools and universities
- _____

9A COMMUNICATIVE Tell me about…

Student A

a Look at the circles. Try and write something in at least six of them.

1. a country you'd like to visit **in order to** try the local food
2. something you aren't very good at **in spite of** trying hard to get better at it
3. something you never do **although** you know it would be good for you
4. an app or YouTube channel you use **for** practising your English
5. something you do **to** relax at weekends
6. a technique you use **so as to** remember vocabulary in English
7. something you would like to buy **even though** you don't really need it
8. something (apart from English) that you'd like to study **so that** you can get a good job

b Ask **B** what he / she wrote in circle 1, and why. Continue with the other circles.

Student B

a Look at the circles. Try and write something in at least six of them.

1. a place where you had a great holiday **in spite of** having bad weather (or other problems)
2. a job you wouldn't mind having **even though** the pay isn't very good
3. a 'white lie' you've told **so as not to** offend a friend
4. something you do **to** improve your understanding of spoken English
5. a restaurant you'd recommend **for** a great night out with friends
6. something you wear from time to time **although** it's not very comfortable
7. something you used to do when you were younger **so that** you would look older
8. things you do **to** keep reasonably fit and healthy

b Ask **A** what he / she wrote in circle 1, and why. Continue with the other circles.

9B COMMUNICATIVE Give your opinion

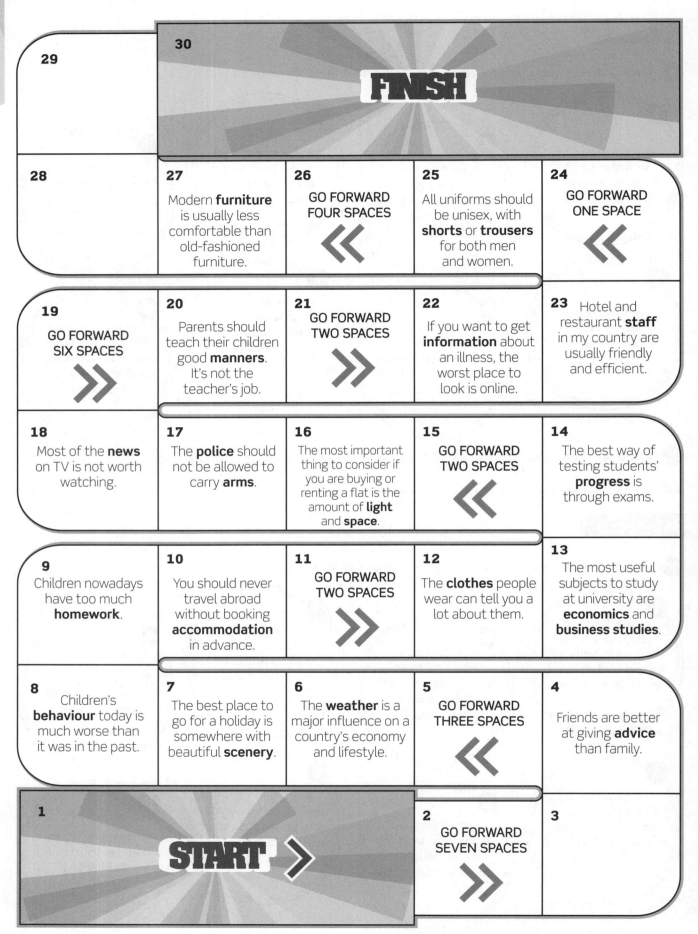

10A COMMUNICATIVE Science quiz

Student A

a Read the sentences. Circle the correct quantifier, and read the answers so that you can re-tell them from memory.

1 *Most / Most of* thunderstorms happen at night.
(False. Most happen late afternoon, as the ground and air are warmest at that time of day. This heat fuels the storms. But thunderstorms can happen any time of the day if the conditions are right.)

2 *All the / All* bones in our body continue to grow until we are 16 and then they stop growing.
(False. Our bones continue growing until we are around 20.)

3 A snake can't see *anything / nothing* if both its eyes are closed.
(False. It can see through its eyelids.)

4 A new-born shark doesn't swim close to *either / neither* of its parents.
(True. As soon as it's born it swims away so that the mother doesn't eat it.)

5 *No / None* of the footprints or tyre marks made on the moon are still visible today.
(False. Footprints from the astronauts who landed on the moon in 1969 could be there forever as there is no wind to blow them away.)

6 Twelve per cent of *every / all* humans that have ever been born are alive at this very moment.
(True. The total human population today is around 7 billion. Scientist estimate that 57 billion people have existed since humans first evolved 200,000 years ago.)

7 Whales don't have *any / no* teeth.
(False. The whole family is divided into two types: toothed whales such as dolphins, and baleen whales which have a 'filter feeder' instead of teeth, e.g. blue whales.)

b Read your sentences to **B**, and ask if they are *True* or *False*. If **B** is wrong, tell him / her the answer, and give the explanation.

c Listen to **B**'s sentences and say whether they are *True* or *False*. If you can, say why.

- -

Student B

a Read the sentences. Circle the correct quantifier, and read the answers so that you can re-tell them from memory.

1 If a child's parents *the both / both* have blue eyes, it is impossible for the child to have brown eyes.
(False. It is not common, but it is possible for the child to have brown eyes if both parents carry the brown-eye gene.)

2 Almost *no / none* wild birds sing during the summer.
(True. Birds usually sing during spring and early summer to establish a territory and attract a mate. By the middle of summer most birds have already mated, so there is no need for them to sing.)

3 *Every / All the* time we sneeze, our heart stops for one second.
(False. Although it feels as if our heart stops for a very short period, it doesn't, it's just a change in pressure in our chests.)

4 *Most / Most of* fruit and vegetables (but not all) contain vitamin C.
(False. All fruit and vegetables contain some vitamin C. Among those containing the highest amounts are citrus fruits, kiwi fruit, broccoli, and green and red peppers.)

5 *Both / Both of* men and women who are left-handed live longer than people who are right-handed.
(False. Although some studies showed that right-handed people live for longer, the figures were in fact misinterpreted. There is no connection between being right- or left-handed and life span.)

6 Children grow more quickly in the summer than in *any / no* other season.
(False. In most children, there will be weeks or months of slow growth. This will alternate with mini 'growth spurts' when they grow more quickly and suddenly. Children tend to grow a bit faster in the spring than during other times of the year.)

7 Neither dogs *or / nor* cats should be given cow's milk to drink.
(True. Neither of them have systems that can break down lactose, a chemical found in some types of milk. They should only be given water to drink.)

b Listen to **A**'s sentences and say whether they are *True* or *False*. If you can, say why.

c Read your sentences to **A**, and ask if they are *True* or *False*. If **A** is wrong, tell him / her the answer and give the explanation.

English File fourth edition Teacher's Guide Upper-intermediate   Photocopiable © Oxford University Press 2020

10B COMMUNICATIVE   General knowledge quiz

a Complete the questions with *a*, *an*, *the*, or – (nothing) where necessary.

1 What two countries is _____ Lake Titicaca between?
2 Who was _____ second person to walk on _____ moon?
3 How many strings does _____ bass guitar have?
4 In which ocean can you find _____ Seychelles?
5 What's _____ highest mountain in _____ Alps?
6 What is _____ 50% of 50?
7 What colour are _____ babies' eyes at birth?
8 Which bird is _____ symbol of _____ USA?
9 What letter is on _____ right of _____ 'O' on a keyboard?
10 Which animals were domesticated first: _____ cats or _____ dogs?
11 Which planet in our solar system is furthest from _____ sun?
12 Who are more numerous in the world, _____ men or _____ women?
13 How many countries are there in _____ UK?
14 What type of fruit is _____ Granny Smith?
15 How many players can be on court in _____ basketball team?
16 What is _____ first sign of _____ zodiac?
17 Which nation first gave _____ women _____ right to vote?
18 What was _____ name of _____ first man to be sent into space?
19 Which European country hasn't fought in _____ war since _____ 1815?
20 What is _____ largest man-made structure on Earth?
21 What vegetable is _____ vodka often made from?
22 Is _____ spider _____ insect?
23 What colour is _____ 'black box' flight recorder on _____ plane?
24 What country does _____ Volga river flow through?
25 Which travels faster: _____ light or _____ sound?

b In pairs, see how many questions you can answer.

COMMUNICATIVE Revision

1 Personalities

Tell your partner about somebody you know who is...
- very bad-tempered.
- incredibly absent-minded.
- extremely big-headed.
- rather tight-fisted.
- a bit two-faced.

2 Your style

- Do you have a lot of clothes that you never wear?
- Do you prefer wearing plain or patterned clothes?
- Do you consider yourself to be quite trendy?
- What's your favourite item of clothing?
- Where do you tend to buy most of your clothes?
- Do you ever buy clothes online?

3 Your town

- In which part of your town / city do you live? (in the centre, on the outskirts, etc.)
- What do you like best / least about your neighbourhood?
- Are there any famous landmarks or sights in your town?
- Are there any problems with...?
  a homelessness   b pollution   c crime
- If you had to choose one adjective to describe your town, what would it be?
- Are you happy living in your town, or would you like to move?

4 Your health

Tell your partner about a time when you, or someone you know,...
- needed stitches.
- fainted.
- had food poisoning.
- choked on something.
- had an allergic reaction to something.
- twisted their ankle.

5 Music

- When and where do you normally listen to music?
- What kind of music do you listen to?
- Did your parents listen to a lot of music when you were growing up? What kind?
- Is your taste in music similar in any way to your parents'?
- Do you tend to have friends who share your musical tastes?
- If you could be a world-class musician, what instrument would you choose to play?

6 The media

- How up-to-date are you with what's going on in the world?
- Where do you usually get the news from?
- Do you think news reporting in your country is objective or biased?
- What's the biggest story in the news at the moment?
- What kind of reviews do you usually read? Are you influenced by them?

7 Feelings

Tell your partner about a time you felt...
- really disappointed about something.
- a bit homesick.
- very grateful for something someone did for you.
- proud because of something a friend or family member did.
- scared stiff before you had to do something.

8 The weather

Tell your partner about...
- the kind of weather you enjoy.
- the kind of weather you hate.
- the most extreme weather you have ever experienced.
- a holiday, trip, or excursion that was a disaster because of the weather.

9 Crime and punishment

- What are common crimes in your town / city?
- Have you, or someone you know, ever been the victim of a crime?
- What would you do to reduce crime?
- Have you or someone you know ever been on a jury?
- Do you enjoy...?
  a reading detective novels
  b watching TV crime series

10 Advertising

Talk about...
- an advert (or TV commercial) you love.
- an advert which really irritates you.
- a brand that has a memorable logo or slogan.
- an advert which made you buy something.

English File fourth edition Teacher's Guide Upper-intermediate   Photocopiable © Oxford University Press 2020

Vocabulary activity instructions

2A Illnesses and injuries

A pairwork vocabulary race

Sts race to think of answers to questions. Copy one worksheet per pair.

LANGUAGE
illnesses and injuries

- Put Sts in pairs and give out the worksheets. Tell Sts that they have to read the questions or definitions and write down as many answers as they can in three minutes. You could give Sts more time if you see that they need it.
- Check answers. Model and drill the pronunciation of any words your Sts find difficult to pronounce. The first pair to complete all the answers correctly wins, or the pair with the most correct answers at the end of the time limit wins.

> **2** blood pressure **3** sunburn **4** painkillers **5** get over
> **6** sniff / sneeze, cough **7** allergic reaction **8** lie down
> **9** faint, pass out, come round **10** flu **11** bleed
> **12** sprained **13** burn **14** plaster **15** food poisoning
> **16** choke **17** swollen **18** vomit, throw up

- Now focus on **Activation**. Put Sts in pairs and get them to discuss the questions.
- Get feedback.

2B Clothes and fashion

A crossword puzzle activity

Sts read clues and complete the crossword. Copy one worksheet per student or one worksheet per pair.

LANGUAGE
clothes and fashion

- Explain to Sts that they are going to complete a crossword. Make sure they understand the difference between *across* and *down*.
- Either give each student a worksheet or put Sts in pairs and give each pair a worksheet. Tell Sts to write the words in the crossword. Set a time limit, e.g. five minutes.
- If Sts worked individually, get them to compare with a partner, and then check answers. Model and drill the pronunciation of any words your Sts find difficult to pronounce.

> **ACROSS**
> **8** scruffy **9** sleeveless **10** loose **13** classic **15** go with
> **16** denim **17** get changed **18** fit

> **DOWN**
> **1** old fashioned **2** checked **3** spotted **5** hooded
> **6** dress up **7** casual **11** suede **12** plain **14** smart

- Now focus on **Activation** and put Sts in pairs, **A** and **B**. Sts **A** read a clue from the worksheet and Sts **B** (not looking at the worksheet) guess the word. Make sure they swap roles.

3A Air travel

An alphabet race

Sts race to complete sentences with the correct word. Copy one worksheet per student or one worksheet per pair.

LANGUAGE
air travel

- Put Sts in pairs and give out the worksheets to individual Sts or pairs. Focus on the instructions and tell Sts that they have to complete as many answers as they can in five minutes. Highlight that each word begins with a different letter of the alphabet. Point out that not all letters of the alphabet are used here. You may want to give Sts a bit longer than five minutes, or stop the activity when one pair has finished.
- Check answers. Model and drill the pronunciation of any words your Sts find difficult to pronounce. The first pair to complete all the answers correctly wins, or the pair with the most correct answers at the end of the time limit wins.

> **B** boarding pass **C** check-in desk **D** domestic **E** excess
> **F** fill in **G** gate **H** hand **I** illegal **J** jet lag **L** long-haul
> **M** metal **N** noisy / naughty **O** online **P** pick up
> **Q** queue **R** runway **S** Security **T** turbulence **U** unpack
> **V** visa **W** wait

- Now focus on **Activation**. Put Sts in pairs and tell them to turn the worksheet over. Sts test themselves by trying to go through the alphabet in order and remembering the words. They should add extra ones for as many letters as they can, e.g. *B boarding pass, Baggage reclaim*, etc.

3B Adverbs and adverbial phrases

A vocabulary completion and discrimination activity

Sts complete the sentences with the correct adverb / adverbial phrase. Copy one worksheet per student or one worksheet per pair.

LANGUAGE
adverbs and adverbial phrases

- Put Sts in pairs and give out the worksheets to individual Sts or pairs. Tell Sts to circle the correct adverbs / adverbial phrases. Set Sts a time limit, e.g. five minutes.
- If Sts worked individually, get them to compare with a partner, and then check answers. Model and drill the pronunciation of any words your Sts find difficult to pronounce.

> **2** at the moment **3** late **4** hardly **5** in the end
> **6** specially **7** even **8** still **9** nearly **10** lately **11** Ideally
> **12** at the end **13** ever **14** near **15** hard **16** in fact
> **17** yet **18** actually **19** apparently **20** obviously
> **21** basically **22** eventually **23** gradually **24** certainly

214

- Now focus on **Activation**. Put Sts in pairs and get them to discuss each topic, giving as much information as possible.
- Get some feedback.

4A Weather

An information gap activity

Sts define words / phrases to help their partner complete a crossword. Copy one worksheet per pair and cut into **A** and **B**.

LANGUAGE

weather

- Put Sts in pairs, **A** and **B**, ideally face to face, and give out the crosswords. Make sure that Sts can't see each other's worksheets. Explain that **A** and **B** have the same crossword, but with different words missing. They have to describe / define words to each other to complete their crosswords.
- Give Sts a minute to read their instructions. If they don't know what a word means, they can refer to **Vocabulary Bank** Weather p.156.
- Sts take turns to ask each other for their missing words (e.g. *What's 1 down? What's 3 across?*). Their partner must define / describe the word until the other student is able to write it in his / her crossword. Sts should help each other with other clues if necessary.
- Monitor and make sure Sts are pronouncing the words and phrases correctly.
- When Sts have finished, get them to compare their crosswords to make sure they have the same words and have spelled them correctly.

5A Feelings

A vocabulary discrimination activity

Sts read sentences and guess the correct feeling adjective. Copy one worksheet per pair and cut into **A** and **B**.

LANGUAGE

adjectives of feeling

- Put Sts in pairs, **A** and **B**, ideally face to face, and give out the worksheets.
- Focus on the instructions in **a** and **b**, and give Sts time to read the sentences to each other and complete the words.
- Check answers. Model and drill the pronunciation of any adjectives your Sts find difficult to pronounce.

Student A
1 miserable   2 bewildered   3 stunned   4 devastated
5 fed up   6 gutted   7 desperate   8 offended   9 thrilled
10 homesick
Student B
1 down   2 upset   3 delighted   4 shattered   5 lonely
6 scared stiff   7 overwhelmed   8 terrified   9 proud
10 relieved

- Now focus on **Activation** and put Sts in pairs. Get them to test each other by acting out the feelings that they completed.

EXTRA IDEA If you think your Sts won't enjoy the miming / acting activity, you could tell them to do the activity again, but this time Sts **A** read the sentences in random order, Sts **B** should cover their worksheet and try to complete the adjectives from memory. Sts then swap roles.

7A Verbs often confused

A vocabulary discrimination activity

Sts circle the correct verb. Copy one worksheet per student or one worksheet per pair.

LANGUAGE

verbs which are often confused

- Either give each student a worksheet or put Sts in pairs and give each pair a worksheet. Give Sts time to circle the verbs.
- If Sts did the activity individually, get them to compare with a partner, and then check answers. Model and drill the pronunciation of any verbs your Sts find difficult to pronounce.

2 advise   3 refuses   4 discuss   5 warned   6 wait
7 denied   8 lying   9 reminded   10 preventing
11 robbed   12 lent   13 avoid   14 realizes   15 laid
16 beat   17 matter   18 notice   19 mind   20 stole
21 win   22 rises   23 remember   24 arguing   25 expect
26 raising   27 hope   28 borrow

7B The body

A pairwork vocabulary race

Sts race to read a series of clues and write the words. Copy one worksheet per pair.

LANGUAGE

the body

- Put Sts in pairs and give out the worksheet pairs. Focus on the instructions and tell Sts that they have to complete as many answers as they can in five minutes. Highlight that each word begins with a different letter of the alphabet. You may want to give Sts a bit longer than five minutes, or stop the activity when one pair has finished.
- Check answers. Model and drill the pronunciation of any words your Sts find difficult to pronounce. The first pair to complete all the answers correctly wins, or the pair with the most correct answers at the end of the time limit wins.

2 brush your teeth   3 thigh   4 touch your toes   5 lungs
6 waist   7 heel   8 bite your nails   9 wink
10 blow your nose   11 raise your eyebrows   12 yawn
13 hug   14 wave   15 shake hands   16 nod your head
17 elbow   18 stare   19 stretch   20 frown

- Now focus on **Activation** and put Sts in pairs, **A** and **B**. Sts **A** read clues 1–10 from the worksheet and Sts **B** (not looking at the worksheet) guess the words. Then they swap roles and Sts **B** read clues 11–20 for Sts A to guess.

215

8A Crime and punishment

An alphabet quiz

Sts read the sentences and complete them with the correct word. Copy one worksheet per student or one worksheet per pair.

LANGUAGE

crime and punishment

- Put Sts in pairs and give out the worksheets to individual Sts or pairs. Focus on the instructions and tell Sts that they have to complete as many answers as they can in five minutes. Highlight that each word begins with a different letter of the alphabet. You may want to give Sts a bit longer than five minutes, or stop the activity when one pair has finished.
- If Sts did the activity individually, get them to compare with a partner, and then check answers. Model and drill the pronunciation of any words your Sts find difficult to pronounce.

B burglar **C** committed **D** dealer **E** evidence **F** fraud
G guilty **H** hacker **I** innocent **J** judge **K** kidnapped
M mugger **P** proof **Q** question **R** robberies **S** stalker
T theft **V** verdict **W** witnesses

- Now focus on Activation and put Sts in pairs, **A** and **B**. Sts **A** read clues A–J from the worksheet and Sts **B** (not looking at the worksheet) guess the words. Then they swap roles and Sts **B** read clues K–W for Sts **A** to guess.

8B The media

A pairwork vocabulary race

Sts race to read definitions and write the answers into the spaces. Copy one worksheet per pair.

LANGUAGE

the media

- Put Sts in pairs and give out the worksheets.
- Focus on the instructions and point out that the missing letters are all consonants. Set a time limit for Sts to complete as many words as they can in the time limit.
- Check answers. Model and drill the pronunciation of any words your Sts find difficult to pronounce. The first pair to complete all the answers correctly wins, or the pair with the most correct answers at the end of the time limit wins.

2 headline **3** objective **4** journalist **5** paparazzi
6 sensational **7** freelance **8** censored **9** agony aunt
10 accurate **11** row **12** clash **13** critic **14** commentator
15 presenter **16** editor

- Now focus on **Activation** and put Sts in pairs, **A** and **B**. Sts **A** read clues 1–8 from the worksheet and Sts **B** (not looking at the worksheet) guess the words. Then they swap roles and Sts **B** read clues 9–16 for Sts A to guess.

9A Business

An information gap activity

Sts define words / phrases to help their partner complete a crossword. Copy one worksheet per pair and cut into **A** and **B**.

LANGUAGE

business

- Put Sts in pairs, **A** and **B**, ideally face to face, and give out the crosswords. Make sure that Sts can't see each other's worksheets. Explain that **A** and **B** have the same crossword, but with different words missing. They have to describe / define words to each other to complete their crosswords.
- Give Sts a minute to read their instructions. If they don't know what a word means, they can look it up in **Vocabulary Bank** Business p.162.
- Sts take turns to ask each other for their missing words (e.g. *What's 1 down? What's 3 across?*). Their partner must define / describe the word until the other student is able to write it in his / her crossword. Sts should help each other with other clues if necessary.
- Monitor and make sure Sts are pronouncing the words and phrases correctly.
- When Sts have finished, get them to compare their crosswords to make sure they have the same words and have spelled them correctly.

9B Word-building

A gap-fill activity

Sts complete sentences by adding suffixes / prefixes to a given word or writing new nouns. Copy one worksheet per student.

LANGUAGE

prefixes, suffixes, irregular nouns

- Give out the worksheets. Focus on the instructions and on the three sections. Set a time limit. Tell Sts that they have to complete the sentences with the correct form of the words in brackets. They must write as many words as they can in the column on the right in the time limit.
- Check answers. Model and drill the pronunciation of any words your Sts find difficult to pronounce.

Prefix:
2 underpaid **3** multimillionaire **4** subtitled
5 monolingual **6** autobiographies **7** antivirus
8 misread **9** post-war **10** megabyte
Suffix:
1 comfortable **2** sleepless **3** cheerful **4** recognizable
5 terrorism **6** improvement **7** inflation **8** weakness
9 elegance **10** childproof
Irregular:
1 heat **2** loss **3** height **4** death **5** Hunger **6** success
7 strength **8** width **9** thought **10** belief

- Now focus on **Activation**. Put Sts in pairs and get them to cover the column on the right. Sts test themselves or each other by trying to complete the sentences.

216

Revision

A pairwork card game

Sts define words / phrases for their partner to guess. Copy and cut up one set of cards per pair.

LANGUAGE
revision from Files 1–10

- Put Sts in pairs and give them a set of cards face down, or in an envelope.
- Demonstrate the activity. Take a card, tell Sts what the word group is, and define the first word for the class to guess.
- Sts continue in pairs, picking a card, saying the topic, and describing the words and expressions on it for their partner to guess. Remind Sts that they mustn't use the word itself in the definition. They should try to take no longer than two minutes per card.

EXTRA IDEA Put Sts in pairs. Copy one worksheet per pair and cut it down the middle. Give each student half the worksheet, and continue as above.

2A VOCABULARY Illnesses and injuries

● Work with a partner. Complete the words as quickly as you can.

1 Three parts of the body that we use with 'ache'.
e_ar_rache, **s**_tomach_ ache, **t**_ooth_ache

2 Something that can be high, often because of stress or bad diet.
bl_____ **pr**_____

3 Something you could get on the beach if you're not careful.
s_____

4 What you should take if you have a headache, e.g. aspirin or paracetamol.
p_____**s**

5 A phrasal verb that means to recover from an illness.
g_____ **o**_____ an illness

6 When you have a cold you
sn_____ and **c**_____.

7 A condition when something you eat can make you feel ill. You should take antihistamine tablets. an **a**_____ **r**_____

8 You should do this when you feel unwell or tired.
l_____ **d**_____ (on a sofa)

9 A verb and a phrasal verb that mean to become unconscious, and a phrasal verb that means to become conscious again.
f_____ , **p**_____ **o**_____ , **c**_____ **r**_____

10 An infectious illness like a very bad cold that causes fever, pain, and weakness. **fl**_____

11 If you cut your finger with a sharp object, it will **bl**_____.

12 An injury to your leg which means you can't walk.
a **spr**_____ ankle

13 This can happen if you drop very hot liquid on yourself.
b_____ yourself

14 Something you should put on a small cut.
a **pl**_____

15 You might get this if you eat food which is past its sell-by date.
f_____ **p**_____

16 This can happen to you if a piece of food gets stuck in your throat. You might **ch**_____

17 Adjective to describe a part of your body that has got bigger because of an injury. (a) **sw**_____ (finger)

18 Two verbs that mean to be sick.
v_____ , **thr**_____ **u**_____

ACTIVATION

Work with a partner. Have you had any of the following illnesses or injuries recently? How long were you unwell for? Did you have any treatment?

- a temperature
- a rash
- sunburn
- a sore throat
- a blister on your foot
- an allergic reaction

218

English File fourth edition Teacher's Guide Upper-intermediate   Photocopiable © Oxford University Press 2020

2B VOCABULARY Clothes and fashion

● Look at the clues and fill in the crossword.

Across →

4 the material that comes from a sheep or goat
8 a word to describe a person whose hair / clothes / appearance is untidy or dirty
9 an adjective which describes a top without arms
10 an adjective which is the opposite of tight
13 simple and traditional in style or design
15 a phrasal verb which means to combine well with something
16 a type of material that is usually blue and often used for making jeans
17 a verb which means to take off one set of clothes and put on another
18 a verb which means to be the right shape and size for somebody

Down ↓

1 an adjective which means not modern
2 a pattern of squares, usually in two colours
3 an adjective that describes a regular pattern of round dots
5 an adjective describing e.g. a jacket or sweatshirt which has a part which covers the head
6 a phrasal verb that means to put on clothes which are more formal and elegant than those you usually wear
7 an adjective which means not formal
11 a type of soft leather with a surface like velvet on one side
12 no pattern, simple
14 an adjective which means well dressed in fashionable and/or formal clothes

ACTIVATION

Cover the crossword. In pairs, take turns reading out a clue. Try to remember the answers.

3A VOCABULARY Air travel

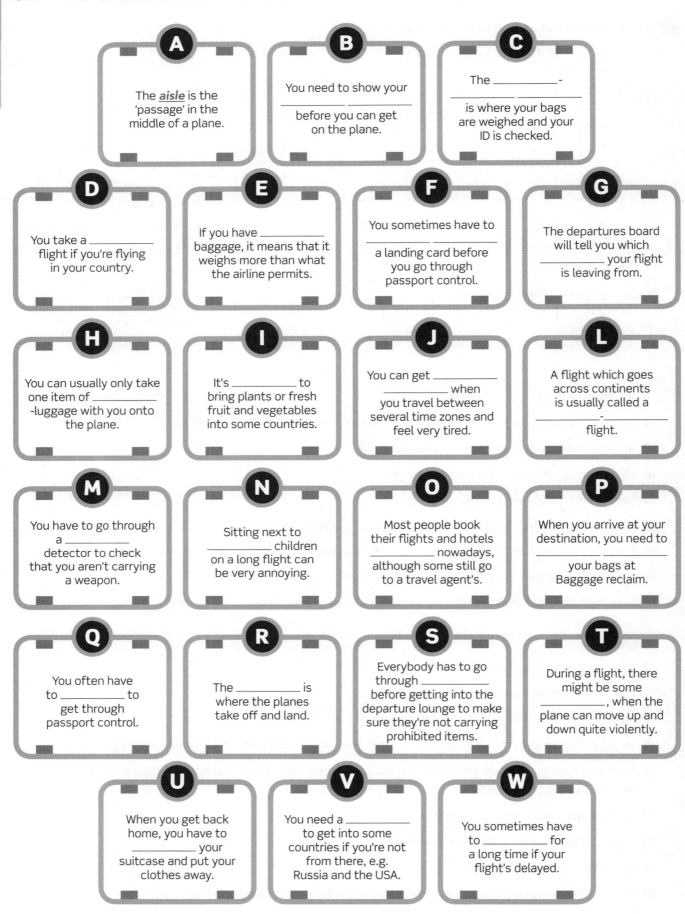

A The *aisle* is the 'passage' in the middle of a plane.

B You need to show your _____ before you can get on the plane.

C The _____ is where your bags are weighed and your ID is checked.

D You take a _____ flight if you're flying in your country.

E If you have _____ baggage, it means that it weighs more than what the airline permits.

F You sometimes have to _____ a landing card before you go through passport control.

G The departures board will tell you which _____ your flight is leaving from.

H You can usually only take one item of _____-luggage with you onto the plane.

I It's _____ to bring plants or fresh fruit and vegetables into some countries.

J You can get _____ when you travel between several time zones and feel very tired.

L A flight which goes across continents is usually called a _____-flight.

M You have to go through a _____ detector to check that you aren't carrying a weapon.

N Sitting next to _____ children on a long flight can be very annoying.

O Most people book their flights and hotels _____ nowadays, although some still go to a travel agent's.

P When you arrive at your destination, you need to _____ your bags at Baggage reclaim.

Q You often have to _____ to get through passport control.

R The _____ is where the planes take off and land.

S Everybody has to go through _____ before getting into the departure lounge to make sure they're not carrying prohibited items.

T During a flight, there might be some _____, when the plane can move up and down quite violently.

U When you get back home, you have to _____ your suitcase and put your clothes away.

V You need a _____ to get into some countries if you're not from there, e.g. Russia and the USA.

W You sometimes have to _____ for a long time if your flight's delayed.

ACTIVATION

In pairs, go through the alphabet and remember the words about air travel.

3B VOCABULARY Adverbs and adverbial phrases

● Circle the correct adverb or adverbial phrase.

1 I love chocolate, **especially** / **specially** dark chocolate.
2 I'm working part-time **at the moment** / **actually**, but I think they'll offer me a full-time job soon.
3 I stayed up **late** / **lately** last night, so I'm really tired today.
4 Ben is really busy, so we **hard** / **hardly** see him now.
5 It was raining on the day of the picnic, so we didn't go **in the end** / **at the end**.
6 This dress has been **especially** / **specially** designed for her, so no one else will have one like it.
7 I love unusual foods. I've **even** / **ever** tried fried insects!
8 We **yet** / **still** haven't decided where to go on holiday this summer. We've been talking about it for weeks!
9 I can't believe that I've been a teacher for **nearly** / **near** 25 years now!
10 Sally hasn't been feeling very well **lately** / **late**, so she's going to make an appointment to see her doctor.
11 **Ideally** / **Gradually**, you should wash wool by hand, as that way there's less chance it will shrink.
12 I'll pay you back **in the end** / **at the end** of the month.
13 Have you **even** / **ever** been camping in the mountains?
14 They're building a motorway **nearly** / **near** my house. The noise is terrible.
15 Sara works really **hard** / **hardly**, but her boss won't give her a promotion.
16 Rosie's looking absolutely fantastic, but **ideally** / **in fact**, she's been ill for the last three months.
17 Oh, don't go **yet** / **still**! Stay for a bit longer.
18 Her dress looks really expensive, but **at the moment** / **actually**, it was quite cheap.
19 I thought my boss was retiring next year, but **apparently** / **eventually**, she wants to carry on working until she's 70!
20 Mark's unemployed, so **gradually** / **obviously**, he doesn't have much money to spend on going out.
21 I won't give you the details now, but **ideally** / **basically**, the plan's very simple.
22 After looking for his mobile all morning, my son **eventually** / **obviously** found it under the sofa!
23 I've been learning French for ages, and **ideally** / **gradually**, I'm starting to feel more confident.
24 It's a pity you couldn't come to the concert with us. You would have **certainly** / **eventually** enjoyed it.

ACTIVATION

In pairs, say something you…

- find really hard to do.
- you'll probably do tonight.
- would ideally never do again.
- you've started doing lately.
- you nearly bought (but didn't).
- you're excited about at the moment.

4A VOCABULARY Weather

Student A

a. Look at your crossword and make sure you know the meaning of all the words you have.

b. Ask **B** to define a word for you. Ask, for example, *What's 3 down? What's 5 across?* Write the word in.

c. Now **B** will ask you to define a word.

Across/Down visible entries: DAMP, SCORCHING, BLIZZARD, BELOW ZERO, BRIGHT, ICY, THICK, FLOOD, DRIZZLING, HEATWAVE

Student B

a. Look at your crossword and make sure you know the meaning of all the words you have.

b. **A** will ask you to define a word.

c. Now ask **A** to define a word for you. Ask, for example, *What's 1 down? What's 8 across?* Write the word in.

Visible entries: CHILLY, MONSOON, BREEZE, LIGHTNING, CHANGEABLE, ICY, COOL, DROUGHT, BLIZZARD, HURRICANE, CLEAR

222 English File fourth edition Teacher's Guide Upper-intermediate   Photocopiable © Oxford University Press 2020

5A VOCABULARY Feelings

Student A

a Read the sentences to your partner. Do **not** say the words in brackets.

1 Is everything OK? You look a bit ▓▓▓. (**down**)
2 Marta's lied to me, several times. I just found out. I'm really ▓▓▓. (**upset**)
3 This is such good news! I can't stop smiling. I'm ▓▓▓. (**delighted**)
4 It's been a really long day and I haven't had any time to sit down. I'm absolutely ▓▓▓! (**shattered**)
5 I haven't seen anyone all week. I'm feeling quite ▓▓▓! (**lonely**)
6 Oh, I think can hear something downstairs! No, don't leave me, I'm ▓▓▓ ▓▓▓! (**scared stiff**)
7 Thanks so much for coming, everyone. It means such a lot to me, I'm a bit ▓▓▓. (**overwhelmed**)
8 There's a s-s-spider? I can't go in. They scare me! I'm ▓▓▓! (**terrified**)
9 My wife just got a promotion! She's brilliant and I'm really ▓▓▓! (**proud**)
10 We thought we would never see our cat again, but we found him! We're so ▓▓▓. (**relieved**)

b Now listen to your partner. Complete the words.

1 m_____ 2 b_____ 3 st_____ 4 d_____ 5 f_____ u_____
6 g_____ 7 d_____ 8 o_____ 9 th_____ 10 h_____

ACTIVATION

Test your partner. Choose one of the adjectives or expressions that you completed in **b**. Act it out for your partner to guess.

- -

Student B

a Listen to your partner and complete the words.

1 d_____ 2 u_____ 3 d_____ 4 sh_____ 5 l_____
6 sc_____ st_____ 7 o_____ 8 t_____ 9 pr_____ 10 r_____

b Now read your sentences to your partner. Do **not** say the words in brackets.

1 The holiday was awful. It rained every day. I was so ▓▓▓! (**miserable**)
2 I just…I can't understand this! What does it mean? I'm ▓▓▓. (**bewildered**)
3 It's such a surprise. I don't know what to say! I'm ▓▓▓. (**stunned**)
4 She's the love of my life and now she's gone. I'm just ▓▓▓. (**devastated**)
5 Matt has been complaining for hours! I can't listen to it anymore, I'm ▓▓▓ ▓▓▓. (**fed up**)
6 It's a shame I couldn't go to Helen's party. I heard it was amazing. I'm ▓▓▓. (**gutted**)
7 I've been trying to find a job for months. I need the money for rent. I'm getting ▓▓▓. (**desperate**)
8 Well! It's really late. He accepted the invitation and he clearly isn't coming. I'm quite ▓▓▓! (**offended**)
9 We won the cup! We won! Yes! We need to celebrate! I'm so happy. I'm really ▓▓▓! (**thrilled**)
10 I've been living in India for six months now. I really miss my country; I feel ▓▓▓ (**homesick**)

ACTIVATION

Test your partner. Choose one of the adjectives or expressions that you completed in **a**. Act it out for your partner to guess.

English File fourth edition Teacher's Guide Upper-intermediate   Photocopiable © Oxford University Press 2020

7A VOCABULARY Verbs often confused

● (Circle) the correct word.

1 I **hope** / **wish** I knew the answer to this question.

2 The chemist can **warn** / **advise** you which is the best medicine to take.

3 When I ask my son what the problem is, he just **denies** / **refuses** to talk about it.

4 Don't you think we need to **argue** / **discuss** this before we make a decision?

5 Emily's boss **warned** / **advised** her that if she was late for work again, she'd lose her job.

6 Hurry up! I can't **expect** / **wait** forever.

7 When the police accused Jim of the crime, he **denied** / **refused** being there that night.

8 I love **laying** / **lying** on the beach with a good book in summer.

9 I **remembered** / **reminded** him that the meeting was at 2 p.m.

10 What's **preventing** / **avoiding** you from applying for the job? You've got all the right qualifications.

11 I was **robbed** / **stolen** when I took the train home last night.

12 Has she returned the jacket you **borrowed** / **lent** her?

13 If we leave at about 6.30 p.m., we'll be able to **prevent** / **avoid** the rush hour.

14 I don't think Marcus **notices** / **realizes** how important it is for me to have my own income.

15 The vet picked up the dog carefully and **lay** / **laid** it on the bed.

15 Miriam is really good at table tennis. I don't think you will be able to **win** / **beat** her.

17 It doesn't **mind** / **matter** if you can't pay me back until next week. I don't need the money right now.

18 Did you **notice** / **realize** how many times Ella checked her phone over dinner?

19 Does Catherine **mind** / **matter** that you can't go to her wedding?

20 Somebody **robbed** / **stole** my wallet when I was taking a photo of Big Ben in London.

21 Who do you think is going to **win** / **beat** the Champion's League this year?

22 When it rains heavily, the river level **rises** / **raises** by several centimetres.

23 Did you **remember** / **remind** to set the alarm?

24 My two sisters don't get on. They're always **arguing** / **discussing**.

25 You can't **expect** / **wait** me to believe you.

26 Have you heard? The government is **rising** / **raising** taxes by 2% next month.

27 Do you think it will snow tonight? I **hope** / **wish** not.

28 I had to **borrow** / **lend** some money from my parents to pay the bills.

English File fourth edition Teacher's Guide Upper-intermediate Photocopiable © Oxford University Press 2020

7B VOCABULARY The body

1 When you do a lot of exercise, you can feel this organ beating very fast.

h `e` `a` `r` `t`

2 If you don't do this, you might have to go to the dentist's.

br ☐☐☐ y ☐☐☐ t ☐☐☐☐

3 The top part of your leg.

th ☐☐☐

4 If you do yoga or you're very flexible, you can probably do this easily.

t ☐☐☐☐ y ☐☐☐ t ☐☐☐

5 Without them, you can't breathe.

l ☐☐☐☐

6 A belt usually goes around this.

w ☐☐☐

7 It's the back part of your foot, below the ankle.

h ☐☐☐

8 If someone looks at your fingers, they can tell if you have this nervous habit.

b ☐☐☐ y ☐☐☐ n ☐☐☐☐

9 You can do this with one eye to show you're not being serious.

w ☐☐☐

10 You do this with a tissue when you have a cold.

bl ☐☐ y ☐☐☐ n ☐☐☐

11 A way of showing surprise using the top part of your face.

r ☐☐☐☐ y ☐☐ e ☐☐☐☐☐☐

12 When you're bored or tired, you open your mouth and do this.

y ☐☐☐

13 Put your arms around someone to show that you like them.

h ☐☐

14 Say goodbye using your hand.

w ☐☐☐

15 What two people often do when they meet for the first time.

sh ☐☐☐ h ☐☐☐☐

16 You can do this instead of saying yes.

n ☐☐ y ☐☐☐ h ☐☐☐

17 The part of your body between your upper and lower arm.

e ☐☐☐☐

18 When you look at something for a long time.

st ☐☐☐

19 You should do this after doing exercise.

str ☐☐☐

20 Move your forehead and eyebrows to show you aren't pleased.

fr ☐☐☐

ACTIVATION

Test your partner. Student **A** read clues 1–10 and Student **B** (page face down) try to remember the words. Then change roles for 11–20.

English File fourth edition Teacher's Guide Upper-intermediate   Photocopiable © Oxford University Press 2020

8A VOCABULARY Crime and punishment

A The police stopped me and a c c u s e d me of dangerous driving.

B When we got home last night, we discovered that a b☐☐☐☐☐☐ had broken into our house and stolen our laptops.

C The police still don't know who c☐☐☐☐☐☐☐☐ the crime.

D The name for a person who sells illegal drugs is a drug d☐☐☐☐☐.

E There wasn't enough e☐☐☐☐☐☐☐ to prove that he was guilty.

F The banker tried to commit f☐☐☐☐ by changing real notes for fake ones.

G The jury found the accused not g☐☐☐☐☐ of the crime.

H I was furious when a h☐☐☐☐☐ used my identity on Twitter.

I He's i☐☐☐☐☐☐☐! On the day of the crime, he was with me all day!

J The j☐☐☐☐ sentenced him to 12 years in prison.

K The gang k☐☐☐☐☐☐☐☐ the businessman and then demanded money for his return.

M A m☐☐☐☐☐ is somebody who attacks or threatens you in the street and tries to steal something from you.

P There wasn't any p☐☐☐☐ that the gun belonged to him.

Q The police wanted to q☐☐☐☐☐☐☐ the suspect about his alibi.

R There have been several r☐☐☐☐☐☐☐☐ at this bank. They've taken thousands of pounds and the police haven't caught them yet!

S A s☐☐☐☐☐☐ is somebody who watches and follows another person in a frightening way.

T A common crime on the internet is identity t☐☐☐☐.

V Depending on the v☐☐☐☐☐☐, the accused will either be sentenced or be released.

W Neither of the two w☐☐☐☐☐☐☐☐ were particularly reliable. They both told completely different stories!

ACTIVATION

Test your partner. Student **A** read clues A–J and Student **B** (page face down) guess the words. Then change roles for K–W.

English File fourth edition Teacher's Guide Upper-intermediate Photocopiable © Oxford University Press 2020

8B VOCABULARY The media

● Read the definitions. Complete the column on the right.

1 A word which means when, e.g. a newspaper shows favour towards a certain group or opinion.

`B I A S E D`

2 The title of a newspaper article, usually printed in big letters.

`□ E A □ □ I □ E`

3 Not influenced by personal opinions or feeling.

`O □ □ E □ □ I □ E`

4 Somebody who writes for a newspaper or magazine.

`□ O U □ □ A □ I □ □`

5 Photographers who follow celebrities and sell the photos they've taken of them.

`□ A □ A □ A □ □ I`

6 An adjective used to describe an article that tries to get your interest by presenting facts or events as worse or more shocking than they really are.

`S □ □ S □ □ □ □ □ □ □`

7 A type of journalist who sells work to different newspapers, but doesn't work for any particular one.

`□ □ E E □ A □ □ E`

8 If a newspaper article is considered offensive or immoral it might get ▬▬.

`□ E □ □ O □ E □`

9 This kind of journalist can help you with your problems if you write to her.

`A □ O □ □ A U □ □`

10 An adjective used to describe a story which has the facts right.

`A □ □ U □ A □ E`

11 A word used in headlines which means the same as an argument.

`□ O □`

12 A word used in headlines which means the same as disagree.

`c □ □ □ □`

13 A journalist who expresses opinions about music, books, films, etc.

`□ □ I □ I □`

14 A person who works on the radio and describes, e.g. a sporting event while it's happening.

`□ O □ □ E □ A □ O □`

15 A person who works on TV and introduces a programme.

`□ □ E □ E □ □ E □`

16 This person decides what goes into a newspaper and what shouldn't.

`E □ I □ O □`

ACTIVATION

Test your partner. Student **A** read clues 1–8 and Student **B** (page face down) guess the words. Then change roles for 9–16.

English File fourth edition Teacher's Guide Upper-intermediate Photocopiable © Oxford University Press 2020

9A VOCABULARY Business

Student A

a Look at your crossword and make sure you know the meaning of all the words you have.

b Ask **B** to define a word for you. Ask for example, *What's 3 across?* Write the word in.

c Now **B** will ask you to define a word.

9B VOCABULARY Word-building

● Complete the column on the right with the correct form of the word in brackets.

Add a prefix

1 The bill should have been less than this. I think the waiter has ▇ us. (**charged**) — *overcharged*

2 Teachers don't earn enough. They're definitely ▇. (**paid**) — _____

3 My cousin won a fortune on the lottery. She's a ▇ now! (**millionaire**) — _____

4 Do you prefer watching a dubbed film or one which is ▇? (**titled**) — _____

5 Is that dictionary ▇ or is it French–English? (**lingual**) — _____

6 Famous people often write their ▇ when they are still quite young. (**biographies**) — _____

7 You should always install good ▇ software to protect your computer. (**virus**) — _____

8 Sorry, I must have ▇ the number. I thought it was a '3' and not an '8'. (**read**) — _____

9 Much of London was rebuilt in the ▇ era. (**war**) — _____

10 My first computer only had half a ▇ of memory. (**byte**) — _____

Add a suffix

1 I like to wear ▇ clothes when I'm at home. (**comfort**) — _____

2 We had a ▇ night last night. The baby just wouldn't stop crying! (**sleep**) — _____

3 My mum's one of the most ▇ people I know. She's always happy! (**cheer**) — _____

4 One of the most easily ▇ symptoms of an allergic reaction is a rash. (**recognize**) — _____

5 One of the main problems facing governments today is ▇. (**terror**) — _____

6 Since Jane's been going to the gym, she's noticed a definite ▇ in the way she looks and feels. (**improve**) — _____

7 The rate of ▇ has been very low in my country this year. (**inflate**) — _____

8 Martin's biggest ▇ is that he can't concentrate for very long. (**weak**) — _____

9 Kathy always dresses with such ▇. (**elegant**) — _____

10 Medicine bottles have to be ▇ so that young children can't open them. (**child**) — _____

Irregular nouns

1 Although there's a sauna at my gym, I never use it because I can't stand extreme ▇. (**hot**) — _____

2 There are hundreds of weight ▇ books on the market at the moment. Do you think any of them actually work? (**lose**) — _____

3 Did you know that the average ▇ of a European male is 1.77 metres? (**high**) — _____

4 My mother inherited a lot of money after my grandmother's ▇. (**die**) — _____

5 ▇ is still a big problem in several African countries. (**hungry**) — _____

6 The band's recent tour was a great ▇. (**succeed**) — _____

7 Could you tell me what your greatest ▇ is? (**strong**) — _____

8 It's about 5 metres in ▇. (**wide**) — _____

9 The ▇ of going to the dentist makes me feel ill. (**think**) — _____

10 Contrary to popular ▇, drinking coffee can be good for your health. (**believe**) — _____

> **ACTIVATION**

Cover the column on the right. In pairs, read the sentences and try to remember the words.

English File fourth edition Teacher's Guide Upper-intermediate   Photocopiable © Oxford University Press 2020

VOCABULARY Revision

Illness and injuries	Clothes and fashion
swollen	scruffy
food poisoning	silk
to bleed	loose
a blister	patterned
flu	go with
an allergic reaction	to dress up

Air travel	Weather
customs	a drought
to take off	changeable
long-haul flight	a heatwave
jet lag	smog
runway	damp
gate	to pour

Feelings	Verbs often confused
devastated	to expect
relieved	to discuss
thrilled	to deny
shocked	to warn
shattered	to beat
scared stiff	to remind

The body	Crime and punishment
an ankle	to burgle
hips	a witness
to wave	to bribe
to shake hands	jury
to stare	blackmail
to scratch	hacking

The media	Word-building
a newsreader	overcrowded
biased	homeless
censored	multicultural
a presenter	bulletproof
paparazzi	neighbourhood
a critic	bilingual

Business	Sleep
a recession	to yawn
a profit	to snore
a branch	to oversleep
to do market research	insomnia
to set up a company	pillow
to go out of business	blanket

English File fourth edition Teacher's Guide Upper-intermediate Photocopiable © Oxford University Press 2020